Financial Adviser Series

Women and Money
Matters of Trust

Mary Quist-Newins

FA204.02.1

This publication is designed to provide accurate and authoritative information about the subject covered. While every precaution has been taken in the preparation of this material, the authors, and The American College assume no liability for damages resulting from the use of the information contained in this publication. The American College is not engaged in rendering legal, accounting, or other professional advice. If legal or other expert advice is required, the services of an appropriate professional should be sought.

© 2009 The American College
270 S. Bryn Mawr Avenue
Bryn Mawr, PA 19010
(888) AMERCOL (263-7265)
theamericancollege.edu
All rights reserved
Library of Congress Control Number 2009925584
ISBN 10: 1-932819-83-5
ISBN 13: 978-1-932819-83-0
Printed in the United States of America

Financial Advisor Series

Sales Skills Techniques

Techniques for Exploring Personal Markets
Techniques for Meeting Client Needs
Techniques for Prospecting: Prospect or Perish
Women and Money—Matters of Trust

Product Essentials

Essentials of Annuities
Essentials of Business Insurance
Essentials of Disability Income Insurance
Essentials of Life Insurance Products
Essentials of Long–Term Care Insurance
Essentials of Multiline Insurance Products

Planning Foundations

Foundations of Estate Planning
Foundations of Retirement Planning
Foundations of Financial Planning: An Overview
Foundations of Financial Planning: The Process
Foundations of Investment Planning

The American College

The American College® is an independent, nonprofit, accredited institution founded in 1927 that offers professional certification and graduate-degree distance education to men and women seeking career growth in financial services.

The Center for Financial Advisor Education at The American College offers both the LUTCF and the Financial Services Specialist (FSS) professional designations to introduce students in a classroom environment to the technical side of financial services, while at the same time providing them with the requisite sales-training skills.

The Solomon S. Huebner School® of The American College administers the Chartered Life Underwriter (CLU®); the Chartered Financial Consultant (ChFC®); the Chartered Advisor for Senior Living (CASL®); the Registered Health Underwriter (RHU®); the Registered Employee Benefits Consultant (REBC®); and the Chartered Leadership Fellow® (CLF®) professional designation programs. In addition, the Huebner School also administers The College's CFP Board—registered education program for those individuals interested in pursuing CFP® certification, the CFP® Certification Curriculum.[1]

The Richard D. Irwin Graduate School® of The American College offers the master of science in financial services (MSFS) degree, the Graduate Financial Planning Track (another CFP Board-registered education program), and several graduate-level certificates that concentrate on specific subject areas. It also offers the Chartered Advisor in Philanthropy (CAP®) and the master of science in management (MSM), a one-year program with an emphasis in leadership. The National Association of Estate Planners & Councils has named The College as the provider of the education required to earn its prestigious AEP designation.

The American College is accredited by:

> The Middle States Commission on Higher Education
> 3624 Market Street
> Philadelphia, PA 19104
> 267.284.5000

The Middle States Commission on Higher Education is a regional accrediting agency recognized by the U.S. Secretary of Education and the Commission on Recognition of Postsecondary Accreditation. Middle States accreditation is an expression of confidence in an institution's mission and goals, performance, and resources. It attests that in the judgment of the Commission on Higher Education,

---

1. Certified Financial Planner Board of Standards, Inc., owns the certification marks CFP®, CERTIFIED FINANCIAL PLANNER™, and CFP (with flame logo)®, which it awards to individuals who successfully complete initial and ongoing certification requirements.

based on the results of an internal institutional self-study and an evaluation by a team of outside peer observers assigned by the Commission, an institution is guided by well-defined and appropriate goals; that it has established conditions and procedures under which its goals can be realized; that it is accomplishing them substantially; that it is so organized, staffed, and supported that it can be expected to continue to do so; and that it meets the standards of the Middle States Association. The American College has been accredited since 1978.

The American College does not discriminate on the basis of race, religion, sex, handicap, or national and ethnic origin in its admissions policies, educational programs and activities, or employment policies.

The American College is located at 270 S. Bryn Mawr Avenue, Bryn Mawr, PA 19010. The toll-free number of the Office of Professional Education is (888) AMERCOL (263-7265); the fax number is (610) 526-1465; and the home page address is theamericancollege.edu.

TheAmericanCollege.edu

Through The American College's website, theamericancollege.edu, students can access information on a variety of topics including:

- **General Information on Courses:** Course descriptions, chapter or assignment topics, and required study materials for all Solomon S. Huebner School, Richard D. Irwin Graduate School, and the Center for Financial Advisor Education courses are listed.

- **The American College Online:** The College provides online study materials for this course, including an interactive version of the sample exam, designed to be used in conjunction with the printed study materials to enhance the learning experience. This material is provided only through password access to students registered for this course. To obtain a password, students should complete the e-mail address section of the course registration form; The College will send the student a password and instructions on how to access these materials.

- **Course Pages/Updates:** New developments in the subject area, important study points, links to other useful governmental and organizational websites, and errata in course materials are included. All information is accessible with a password at blackboard.theamericancollege.edu.

- **Course Registration Procedures:** Secure online registration plus registration forms that can be printed and faxed/mailed to The College are available.

- **Examinations on Demand (EOD) Testing Procedures:** The policies and requirements for EOD testing, as well as links to lists of our more than 3,000 test centers, are provided.

- **Educational Policies and Procedures:** The education, experience, ethics, continuing education, and transfer of credit requirements for The College's designation and graduate programs are explained.

Contents

Financial Advisor Series iii

The American College iv

TheAmericanCollege.edu vi

Table of Contents vii

Preface xiii

Acknowledgements xv

About the Author xvii

Special Notes to Financial Consultants xviii

About the Financial Advisor Series xx

Overview of the Book xxi

1 Women and Money — Matters of Trust: Why it Matters to You 1.1

Introduction—The Women's Market Paradox 1.1
Women and Money—The Opportunities 1.2
Drivers of Her Wealth—Education, Employment and
    Earnings 1.4
Her Ethnicity 1.13
The Future 1.15
Women and Money—The Challenges 1.15
Singlehood 1.16
Financial Literacy 1.18
Financial Unpreparedness 1.20
Poverty 1.20
The Second Paradox 1.21

Matters of Trust	1.22
Schemes, Scandals and Greed in the Marketplace	1.22
What She Is Looking For	1.23
Building Trust as Her Financial Consultant	1.24
The Consultative Planning Process	1.29
Chapter Summary	1.33
Chapter 1 Resources	1.34

2 The "Women's Market" and Your Marketing "MAP" 2.1

Introduction	2.1
What Does "Marketing" Mean?	2.2
Marketing Products versus Marketing Services	2.2
Marketing for Financial Service Firms versus Practitioners	2.4
From Market Segments to Market Niches	2.6
Life-Stage Segments in the Women's Market	2.6
Carving Niches In The Women's Market	2.12
Creating a Marketing Plan	2.25
The Communications Strategy—Message and Media	2.26
The Marketing Activity Plan	2.31
Chapter Summary	2.36
Chapter 2 Tools and Resources	2.37

3 Earning Her Trust and Her Business: The Consultative Planning Process 3.1

Introduction	3.1
Communications and Trust	3.2
Communications Barriers	3.3
Communications Builders	3.4
The Art of Discovery	3.13
Listening and Asking versus Telling and Selling	3.13
The Art of Asking Questions	3.14
Addressing Objections	3.18
Building Trust through the Consultative Planning Process	3.19
Women—Predisposed to Planning?	3.20
Planning for Her Success	3.20
The Benefits of Consultative Planning to Financial Consultants	3.22
Consultative Planning Scope	3.23
Chapter Summary	3.33
Chapter 3 Tools and Resources	3.34

4 Protecting Her Financial Position and Security 4.1

Introduction	4.1
Managing Risks	4.3
Types of Pure Risk	4.3
Alternative Approaches to Managing Pure Risk	4.4
Risk Management and Her Financial Position	4.6
Helping Her Manage Cash Flow	4.9
Helping Her Build Cash Reserves	4.12
Where Women Save Money	4.13
Increasing Cash Reserve Yields	4.16
Helping Her Manage Debt	4.19
Risk Management and Transference	4.22
Identifying Risks	4.22
Risk Measurement and Analysis	4.24
Property Risks	4.25
Women and Property Insurance	4.26
Women, Cars and Driving Risks	4.26
Women and Auto Insurance	4.26
Saving Money on Auto Insurance	4.27
Women and Their Homes	4.28
Women and Homeowners Insurance	4.30
Saving Money on Homeowners Insurance	4.31
Liability Risks and Insurance	4.31
Types of Liability Losses	4.32
Women and Medical Risks	4.33
What Health Issues Affect Women More Than Men?	4.33
Chapter Summary	4.36
Chapter 4 Tools and Resources	4.37

5 Addressing Her Personal Risks—Disability, Long-Term Care and Survivor Needs 5.1

Introduction	5.1
Disability Risks—Underestimated and Underinsured	5.2
Women and Their Disability Risks	5.3
Identifying Women's Disability Risks	5.4
Women, Disability and Financial Literacy	5.6
Her Disability Income Plan	5.6
Identifying Her Disability Awareness and Concerns	5.7
Disability Risk Analysis	5.8
Disability Plan Considerations	5.9
Disability Product Considerations	5.13
Disability Summary	5.14
Long Term Care—A Crisis in the Making?	5.14
Women and Long-Term Care: Double Jeopardy	5.15
Her Long-Term Care Plan	5.20

Identifying Her Long-Term Care Awareness and Concerns 5.20
Long-Term Care Risk Analysis 5.22
Long-Term Care Plan Considerations 5.24
Long-Term Care Summary..5.30
Her Survivor Needs and Life Insurance...................................5.30
Women and THEIR Survivors...5.30
Women as THE Survivor 5.31
Planning for Survivor Needs 5.32
Identifying Survivor Needs 5.33
Survivor Risk Analysis and Planning......................................5.33
Plan Considerations..5.35
Planning for Women Who Are Survivors 5.41
Life Insurance Considerations 5.43
Survivor Needs Summary 5.43
Chapter Summary 5.44
Chapter 5 Tools and Resources..5.44

6 Managing Her Legislative and Speculative Risks—Taxes and Investments 6.1

Introduction 6.1
Income Taxes and Legislative Risk...6.3
Income Tax Basics 6.3
Managing Her Taxes..6.7
Her Tax Facts...6.7
Reviewing Her Tax Situation 6.9
Managing Her Taxes..6.11
Women and Investing 6.14
Women and Investing—An Abundance of Caution................6.14
The Role of Trusted Financial Consultants and Investment Decisions...6.18
Providing Objectivity and Managing Emotions 6.18
Her Investment Plan 6.19
Identifying Her Investment Risks 6.19
Major Forms of Speculative Risk 6.20
Discovering Her Investment Objectives 6.25
Determining Her Risk Tolerance 6.26
Developing Investment Recommendations.............................6.26
Her Investment Plan—The Math and The Homework.............6.27
Doing the Math 6.27
Doing the Homework 6.29
Managing Investment Risks 6.30
Developing Her Investment Strategies 6.32
Product Considerations 6.33
Chapter Summary 6.38

    Chapter 6 Tools and Resources 6.39

7 Reinventing Retirement and Planning Her Legacy 7.1

    Introduction 7.1
    The New Retirement Realities 7.2
    The Need for a New Retirement Paradigm 7.3
    Picturing a New Future–The Third Age 7.4
    Women and Retirement—Her Five Big Risk Factors 7.5
    Her Longevity 7.6
    Her Retirement Resources 7.7
    Singlehood, Widowhood and Divorce 7.7
    Health Challenges and Older Women's Insurability 7.8
    Financial and Retirement Literacy 7.8
    Her Retirement Plan 7.9
    Dreams versus Goals 7.10
    Special Planning Considerations for Women 7.14
    Social Security and Women 7.14
    Employer-Sponsored Qualified Plans and Women 7.19
    Individual Retirement Plans 7.22
    Investing In Retirement 7.23
    Estate Planning and Women 7.24
    Women and Their Health—Durable Powers of Attorney and
        Living Wills 7.24
    Women and Their Wealth—Transfers of Her Property 7.27
    Goals of Estate Planning 7.29
    Estate Planning and Property Ownership 7.30
    What Is Included In Her Estate? 7.31
    Taxes Assessed on Transfers of Her Wealth 7.32
    Intergenerational Wealth Transfer Strategies 7.35
    Transferring Property at Her Death 7.37
    Chapter Summary 7.41
    Chapter 7 Tools and Resources 7.41

8 Exceeding Her Expectations Through Client Service 8.1

    Introduction 8.1
    Why is Client Service So Important? 8.2
    The Objectives of Client Service 8.4
    How Do Financial Consultants Develop Loyal Female
        Clients? 8.6
    Promises Kept and Expectations Set 8.7
    Service Focus: Customers and Products versus Clients and
        Plans 8.8
    Servicing the Plan 8.9
    Delivering Exceptional Service – The Service Plan 8.12

Segmenting the Client/Customer Base 8.13
Why Segment The Client/Customer Base? 8.14
How Segmenting Works 8.15
Systematizing the Service Plan..8.18
Sample Service Plan and Investment....................................8.19
Service Activities and Ideas 8.21
Measuring Client Satisfaction 8.25
Client Satisfaction Survey—What to Learn? 8.26
How to Implement a Client Satisfaction Survey....................8.26
The Rewards of Excellent Service—Repeat Business and
   Referrals 8.27
Repeat Business 8.27
Referrals..8.29
Chapter and Book Summary 8.36
Chapter 8 Tools and Resources 8.38

Appendix A   Informational Interview..**A.1**

Appendix B   Initial Interview Cover Letter **B.1**

**Appendix C   30-Minute Financial Position Checkup
Worksheet**...**C.1**

Appendix D   Document Checklist **D.1**

Appendix E   Prospect Phone Approach Model and Script **E.1**

Appendix F   Solution Presentation Summary Letter............................**F.1**

Appendix G   Review/Financial Check-Up Cover Letter......................**G.1**

Appendix H   Financial Check-Up Checklist...**H.1**

Appendix I   Client Satisfaction Survey Cover E-Mail or Letter **I.1**

Appendix J   Client Satisfaction Survey **J.1**

Index..**I.1**

Preface

How is it that American women own more than half the nation's wealth, and yet are at increased risk of poverty when compared to American men? Why don't women trust financial professionals more despite the significant benefits most realize when they work with them? What can professionals do to improve the lives of female clients while growing their business in the process? These are the fundamental questions addressed in this book.

Just about twenty years ago, I started out as a fledgling financial consultant after a stint in packaged-goods marketing with the E & J Gallo Winery and Chesebrough-Ponds. A career in financial services had appeal as a chance to make a positive difference in the lives of others, enhance work/life balance and generate an attractive income. I have not been disappointed. For the better part of these last two decades, I developed successful financial planning practices in California and Maryland. The remaining years were spent in corporate leadership positions at American Express (now Ameriprise) and ING.

Over time, two passions emerged: (1) helping women increase both their financial security and empowerment; and (2) helping financial professionals become more successful. Having worked with and developed plans for hundreds of female clients, I have become acutely aware of the financial challenges and attitudes that many have. Along with this, my esteem and affection for competent, trustworthy financial professionals have grown deep. As such, it is a privilege to have the opportunity to serve both communities through this book and in my position as State Farm Chair in Women and Financial Services at The American College.

Throughout this text, I have sought to integrate professional and personal experience together with significant research on the subject of women and money. I have drawn upon my career in financial services working with clients, field leaders and professionals to bring together best practices in marketing and consulting. Findings from an extensive array of industry, academic and government studies have also been incorporated. Last, I have tapped into the massive expertise of The American College faculty to support and amplify key areas of technical competency that benefit women most. My hope is that by connecting these dots, the reader will have a better grasp of the issues and opportunities in the women's market. In the end, the goal is to support the financial success of both American women and the financial professionals who serve them.

Finally, all of the individuals noted on the acknowledgments page made this a far better book. There are also many other individuals, working behind the scenes, to whom I owe my thanks. For the gifts of all their time, intellect, feedback and encouragement, I am truly grateful. In spite of the help of all these capable individuals, however, some errors have undoubtedly eluded the reviewers, editors and me. For these I am solely responsible. At the same time, "I accept full credit for giving those of you who find these errors the exhilarating intellectual experience produced by such discovery." (C. Bruce Worsham)

Mary Quist-Newins

Acknowledgements

This book was written with the collaborative assistance of many talented individuals. Without their expertise, encouragement and support, the successful completion of this project would not have been possible. I am especially grateful for the contributions of the following past and present faculty members of The American College:

- Larry Barton, president and CEO, for his leadership, advocacy and great enthusiasm for this project.

- Patricia Cheers, appropriately named seeker of source permissions.

- Constance J. Fontaine, associate professor of taxation, for her technical expertise and contributions to chapter 7.

- David A. Littell, professor of taxation, for his technical expertise and contributions to chapter 7.

- Alison Pettine, my indispensible assistant, for her great diligence and production assistance.

- Glenn E. Stevick, assistant professor of insurance, for his invaluable feedback, and writing the companion workbook and moderator guide to this text.

- Walt J. Woerheide, executive vice president and dean of academic affairs, for his guidance and ongoing encouragement.

- C. Bruce Worsham, former faculty member of The American College, for his contributions to chapters 4, 5 and 6.

- Eileen McDonnell, former faculty member and current executive vice president and chief marketing officer, The Penn Mutual Life Insurance Company, for her contributions to women's market research.

I also wish to acknowledge these industry experts who provided wise counsel and input on content:

- Karen Eilers Lahey, professor of finance, University of Akron, for her critical eye and scholarly advice.

- Donald Swanson, senior financial consultant at Thrivent Financial, for helping keep it real.

- Susan D. Waring, executive vice president, chief administrative officer, State Farm Life, for her pragmatism and passion for improving the financial security of American women.

My acknowledgements would be incomplete without recognizing the valued contributions of Marlene England, Jane Hassinger, Evelyn Rice, Emily Shu, and Virginia Webb who have helped make this a better book.

Last, I give thanks to my dear husband Dean, and our children, Scott and Sarah, for their limitless love, patience and support.

Mary Quist-Newins
Assistant Professor of Women's Studies
State Farm Chair in Women and Financial Services
The American College

About the Author

Mary Quist-Newins, CFP®, ChFC®, CLU®, has the distinction of holding the State Farm Chair in Women & Financial Services at The American College—the first and only endowed academic chair in the country devoted exclusively to the study of women and financial services issues. In this role, she works to increase The College's understanding of women's financially related expectations, attitudes, and actions.

During her nineteen year career in financial services, Ms. Quist-Newins achieved success as both a field producer and a corporate leader. *Treasury & Risk* recognized her significant contributions to the financial services industry by naming her to the magazine's elite list of "25 Outstanding Leaders in Finance Who Happen to be Women" in November 2008.

Prior to joining The College, Professor Quist-Newins was a Senior Financial Consultant and Regional Management Associate with Thrivent Financial. In this role, she was responsible for recruiting and training new associates, as well as a client base of over 2,400 households and more than $75 million in assets under management. While at Thrivent, she consistently performed among the top ranks of producers and qualified for the Million Dollar Round Table every year.

Professor Quist-Newins' industry background also includes positions as a Region Vice President with the ING Advisors Network and Director of Field and Distribution Channel Marketing at American Express. At both ING and American Express, she counseled field leaders and financial associates in representative recruiting, client acquisition and retention, and operational best practices.

In addition to holding a master's in Business Administration from the Garvin School of International Management, she has earned the Certified Financial Planner®, Chartered Life Underwriter®, and Chartered Financial Consultant® advanced designations. Ms. Quist-Newins received her BA from the University of Washington.

Ms. Quist-Newins lives in Frederick, MD, with her husband and two children.

Special Notes to Financial Consultants

Text Materials Disclaimer

This publication is designed to provide accurate and authoritative information about the subject covered. While every precaution has been taken in the preparation of this material to ensure that it is both accurate and up-to-date, it is still possible that some errors escaped detection. Moreover, some material may become inaccurate and/or outdated either because it is time sensitive or because new legislation will make it so. Still other material may be viewed as inaccurate because a company's products and procedures are different from those described in the book. Therefore, the author, contributors and The American College assume no liability for damages resulting from the use of the information contained in this book. The American College is not engaged in rendering legal, accounting, or other professional advice. If legal or other expert advice is required, the services of an appropriate professional should be sought.

Caution Regarding Use of Illustrations

Any illustrations, fact finders, sales ideas, techniques and/or approaches contained in this book are not to be used with the public unless the financial consultant has first obtained approval from his/her company. A company's general support of The American College's programs for training and educational purposes does not constitute blanket approval of any illustrations, fact finders, sales ideas, techniques, and/or approaches presented in this book unless so communicated in writing by the financial consultant's company

Financial Consultant, Consultant, Financial Professional or Professional

Use of the terms "Financial Consultant, Consultant, Financial Professional or Professional" in this book are specifically intended to reference those who hold themselves to the high standards of ethical, competent and professionalism as outlined in Chapter One. The terms are meant to be used interchangeably to avoid unnecessary redundancy. In addition, the terms were chosen for their descriptive qualities—"consultant" connotes expertise; "professional" conveys both competence and ethical behavior. In light of these criteria, the four terms apply to the following roles in the financial services industry:

Special Notes to Financial Consultants   **xix**

- Account Executive
- Advisor
- Agent
- Associate
- Broker (Stock or Insurance)
- Employee Benefit Specialist
- Estate Planner
- Financial Advisor
- Financial Consultant
- Financial Planner
- Financial Planning Professional
- Financial Representative
- Financial Services Professional
- Health Underwriter
- Independent Agent
- Independent Financial Planner
- Investment Advisory Representative
- Insurance Professional
- Life Insurance Agent
- Life Underwriter
- Producer
- Planner
- Practitioner
- Property & Casualty Agent
- Registered Investment Advisor
- Registered Representative
- Retirement Planner
- Senior Advisor
- Tax Advisor

About the Financial Advisor Series

The mission of The American College is to raise the level of professionalism of its students and, by extension, the financial services industry as a whole. As an educational product of The College, the Financial Advisor Series shares in this mission. Because knowledge is the key to professionalism, a thorough and comprehensive reading of each book in the Series will help the financial consultant better serve his or her clients. This task is difficult as the typical client is becoming more sophisticated each passing day and demands that her financial professional be knowledgeable about the latest products and planning methodologies. By providing financial consultants with up-to-date, authoritative information about various marketing and sales techniques, product knowledge, and planning considerations, the books of the Financial Advisor Series will enable many financial consultants to continue their studies in order to develop and maintain a high level of professional competence.

When all books in the Financial Advisor Series are completed, the Series will encompass 16 titles spread across three separate subseries, each with a special focus. The first subseries, Sales Skills Techniques, will focus on enhancing the financial consultant's marketing and sales skills but will also cover some product knowledge and planning considerations. The second subseries, Product Essentials, will focus on product knowledge but will also delve into marketing and sales skills, as well as planning considerations in many of its books. The third subseries, Planning Foundations, will focus on various planning considerations and processes that form the foundation for a successful career as a financial services professional. When appropriate, many of its books will also touch upon product knowledge and sales and marketing skills. Current and planned titles are listed earlier in this book.

Overview of the Book

"Women and Money—Matters of Trust" is designed to increase the financial professional's readiness and effectiveness in marketing to, working with and serving female clients. It incorporates:

- the latest research on women and money;

- best practices in marketing, relationship building and consultative financial planning; along with

- the six content areas of financial planning and their special implications for American females.

Since trust is essential for success in the "women's market" and it is often absent in how women view financial professionals, we start our discussion there. Chapter 1 examines why financial consultants should care about developing a trust relationship with female prospects and clients, along with the barriers and builders of trust. Foremost among trust builders are integrity, professionalism, competence and a planning approach when addressing financial goals and risks. The chapter introduces the "how-to's" of gaining trust and working effectively with female clients through the eight-step marketing/consulting process.

Chapter 2 discusses the first two steps of the marketing/consulting process—how to successfully market to female target audiences, generate leads and convert leads to clients. The examination includes how to identify niche markets, develop a compelling value proposition, implement an efficient media plan and focus marketing activities.

Chapter 3 continues with the six steps of the consultative planning process and how it aligns with financial planning and risk management approaches. The underlying premise is that women are both receptive to and benefitted by a planning, versus transactional, or product focused sales approach. Planning not only strengthens relationships and trust with female clients, but also increases the financial professional's case size and cross sell in the process.

The mid-section of the book, Chapters 4–7, focuses on the six content areas of planning: financial position, protection needs, investments, taxes, retirement and estate planning. Attention is paid to research on the financial risks that women often face disproportionately to men, along with how they can be effectively managed. Relevant areas of technical expertise and product considerations are also discussed. It is assumed that the reader has at least a basic understanding of products. As such, orientation on product mechanics and sales techniques are not addressed in detail.

The concluding chapter examines how to develop and implement a service plan that exceeds client expectations, creates loyalty and increases repeat business and referrals.

The book includes the following features designed to improve awareness of the issues and opportunities present in the women's market; along with increased proficiencies in marketing, relationship building, financial planning and client service. Among the features found in this book are:

- learning objectives

- tables, graphs and examples

- key terms and concepts

- appendix of selected best practice tools

- index

Although much of the information presented may be new, some will, no doubt, refresh knowledge one has acquired in the past. In either case, all material is intended to lead to increased skill, competency and understanding for those seeking to build a more profitable and professionally fulfilling practice with female prospects and clients.

1

Women and Money — Matters of Trust: Why it Matters to You

Learning Objectives
An understanding of the material in this chapter should enable the student to
1-1. Describe the women's market paradox.
1-2. Explain the three primary drivers of women's wealth.
1-3. Define the opportunities of multicultural marketing and the growth of three emerging ethnic majorities.
1-4. Detail the major financial challenges that many women face.
1-5. Describe the second paradox dealing with financial professionals and trust.
1-6. Explain how trust is built and reinforced by the financial consultant's ethics, professionalism and behavior.
1-7. Identify the eight steps of the marketing/planning process.

INTRODUCTION—THE WOMEN'S MARKET PARADOX

Why should financial professionals be interested in working with women prospects and clients? Why is earning their trust today more important than ever? What do professionals need to do to become and remain the trusted and indispensible financial consultant for their female clients? We explore these fundamental questions in this chapter and in this book, beginning with the women's market paradox.

When examining the women's market, a paradox, or seemingly self-contradictory statement, emerges that is as striking as it is telling. Understanding the paradox sets an important context, as it gives perspective on both the market's scope and complexity.

women's market paradox

The women's market paradox is this: *American women are more educated and affluent than ever, yet are also at increased risk of poverty.* How can this be? One underlying reason is that there really is no such thing as a monolithic, homogeneous women's market. Another reason is that among American women, there is an extremely broad distribution of wealth. Because of these underlying issues associated with the women's market, it is important for financial consultants to be mindful of not only the opportunities that working with women present them; but also the challenges their female clients may disproportionately, or even uniquely face.

In this chapter, we explore the women's market paradox further, including the growing economic opportunities for women and their potential financial consultants. Our discussion covers the important drivers of wealth creation for women; how these drivers have evolved over the past half century; and what the future might bring. We will also look at the formidable challenges many women face that threaten their financial security and increase their risks of poverty. Both aspects of the paradox are relevant to the work that financial professionals do.

The conclusion one might reasonably draw by studying the women's market, is that women have an unprecedented and virtually unlimited need for trusted, trustworthy financial consultants. This conclusion brings us to a second paradox dealing with women and financial services providers. That is, while studies show *many women benefit substantially from working with a financial professional, most do not trust the financial services industry or its representatives.* As such, we also examine the dimensions of trust and the qualities women seek in a trusted financial consultant. Last, we turn our attention to how financial consultants can better earn the trust of their female prospects and clients, while significantly growing their own business in the process.

WOMEN AND MONEY—THE OPPORTUNITIES

To say that American women today have more financial clout than their predecessors would be an understatement. Representing more than half of the U.S. population, contemporary American women are better educated, earn more, and live longer than ever before in history. As a result, they have become one of the world's most powerful economic forces, not only in terms of their spending power but also in their share of wealth ownership. Consider these facts:

- Women control more than half of the investment wealth in the United States.[2]

- Women represent more than 40 percent of all Americans with gross investable assets above $600,000.[3]

- Sixty percent of high net worth women have earned their own fortunes.[4]

---

2. Elayne Clift. "USA:Women Moving Millions". *News Blaze*, September 16, 2008, http://newsblaze.com/story/20080916135110tsop.nb/topstory.html.
3. Capital Reflections, Inc., "Women: The Largest Consumer Market," February 1999.
4. Marie Swift, "Beyond Mars and Venus," *Financial Planning,* July 2007, 66–69.

- Forty-five percent of American millionaires are women.[5]

- Forty-eight percent of estates worth more than $5 million are controlled by women, compared with 35 percent controlled by men.[6]

- In the next 40 years, American women are expected to receive a "double-dip" inheritance. The first installment will come from their parents and the second from their husbands. It is also possible they may inherit wealth from their husbands' parents. Estimates for this transfer of assets range from $14 to $25 trillion.[7]

These compelling statistics are certainly not lost on the financial services industry. For roughly the past 20 years, women have been increasingly "targeted" as an attractive and growing market by the leading manufacturers of financial products and services. Among financial professionals, however, only a minority intentionally market to female audiences. According to the Life Insurance Marketing and Research Association (LIMRA), just 16 percent of male representatives, versus almost half of all female representatives, plan to target this market.[8] In addition, LIMRA points out that female representatives are three times more likely to contact women prospects than are their male counter parts.[9]

Here we have an underserved, yet increasingly wealthy market that presents significant revenue and growth opportunities for financial professionals. In light of the opportunities, it may seem strange that so few financial professionals express interest in marketing to female prospects and clients. One reason for this may be that the ranks of those in field distribution remain largely male dominated. Industry studies consistently reveal that men outnumber women across all industry models (i.e., insurance agents, registered representatives, investment advisors, financial planners, and so on) by a margin of at least three to one. As such, many consultants may have a lower comfort level in working with clients of the opposite sex. Or, there may be a low appreciation of the significant opportunities that women may represent for their financial services practice. Whatever the reasons, astute financial professionals who make it a priority to more effectively market to and work with women will stand to benefit both now and well into the foreseeable future.

---

5. Barry W. Johnson and Brian G. Raub, "Personal Wealth, 2001," *Statistics of Income Bulletin* 25, no. 3 (Winter 2005–2006): 120–146. http://www.irs.ustreas.gov/pub/irs-soi/06winbul.pdf.
6. Fara Warner, *The Power of the Purse: How Smart Businesses are Adapting to the World's Most Important Consumer Women* (New Jersey: Pearson/Prentice Hall: 2006).
7. Paul Hodge, "Living Younger Longer: Baby Boomer Challenges," (testimony presented at the 2005 White House Conference on Aging on October 1, 2004); Paul Schervish, "Great Expectations," *American Demographics* (May 1, 2003).
8. *Women's Market, Market Awareness Series 2007*. DVD. Hartford, CT: LIMRA, 2008.
9. Ibid.

Drivers of Her Wealth—Education, Employment and Earnings

By understanding where women have been, are today and are headed tomorrow, financial professionals will be better positioned for success with female prospects and clients. As Ben Franklin said, "Today is yesterday's pupil." By extension, tomorrow will be today's student. To fully recognize the opportunities the future holds in the women's market, it is useful to understand important trends.

Over the past six decades, American women made tremendous gains in *education, employment, and earnings*. There can be little doubt that the advancements realized in this relatively short window of time have changed not only where women are today, but also our society as a whole.

If financial consultants find themselves wondering what the point of all this history and context might be, it is this: the most affluent and potentially lucrative segments of the women's market are now in their second half of life. They either witnessed or took part in the transformation of women's roles in the economy and at home. Many of these women may become the consultant's very best clients in the decades to follow. Understanding their life experiences and perspectives through both their collective and individual histories provides an important competitive advantage. Evaluating influential trends also sheds light on the market potential and direction, along with what the future might hold.

Education

education

When analyzing the three drivers of wealth, American women in the U.S. have made the most dramatic strides in education. While the number of male college graduates in America more than doubled from the middle to the end of the 20th century, the number of female college graduates almost tripled. Among those earning a college degree in 2000, women outnumbered men, representing 57 percent of graduates—quite a shift from 1950, when females comprised less than one of four (23 percent) graduates.[10] For nearly three decades, women have earned more bachelor and master degrees each and every year than men.[11] The chart below shows the percentages of degrees granted recently by gender, according to the U.S. Census Bureau.

As women have become better educated, so too has the way in which society perceives them and their capabilities been transformed. In addition, women have grown more affluent as a result of their gains in higher education. According to CEG Worldwide, one-third (33.1 percent) of wealthy women in the United States have a graduate degree, and just short of two-thirds

---

10. "High School and College Graduates," *InfoPlease® Database*, (2007). http://www.infoplease.com/ ipa/A0112596.html.
11. "Professional Women: Vital Statistics Fact Sheet 2009,"Department for Professional Employees, June 2009.

(61 percent) have undergraduate degrees.[12] Attendant with their educational achievements, it logically follows that American females have made substantial gains in the workplace as well.

Percentage of Degrees Granted to Women In 2005–2006 School Year	
Undergraduate	59%
Graduate	60%
PhD	47%
JD	52%
MD	46%
Source: Newsroom Facts, 2005–2006 School Year, U.S. Census Bureau, February 22, 2006	

Employment

employment

In 1950, just about one in three women worked full-time outside the home. The rest worked full-time inside the home—cooking, cleaning, taking care of families and husbands. Back then, the "feminine ideal" portrayed in advertising and the media was the woman as homemaker.

Just one to two decades later, the ways that women were portrayed in the public eye began to shift dramatically. Many credit this transformation to Betty Freidan, author of the *Feminine Mystique*.[13] A homemaker and mother herself, Friedan challenged the role of the full-time housewife, as one in which women lose their identities and sense of self-worth. Controversial feminist literature, such as that written by Friedan, as well as the changing depiction of females in the American media, served to influence an entire generation of women. As a result, in the latter half of the twentieth century, successful women were portrayed as those who could "have it all"—family, career and financial freedom. As one memorable fragrance commercial put it: "I can bring home the bacon, fry it up in a pan and never let you forget you're a man…[be]cause I'm a *woman*."

By 2000, 60 percent of women—nearly twice as many as in 1950—were working full-time outside the home. For most families today, having one spouse working exclusively in the home is no longer economically feasible. Indeed, the costs of housing, health care, funding retirement and raising/educating children have increased dramatically in the last 50 to 60 years. Along with increases in basic living expenses, the American appetite for goods and services has also grown. Many couples now see the need for both spouses to generate income just to make ends meet, let alone get ahead. Beyond financial need is also the desire that many women have to work outside the home for both personal satisfaction and financial gain.

---

12. John Bowen Jr., "Women of Wealth: Many Affluent Women Have Earned–Not Inherited Their Wealth," *Financial Planning* (November 1, 2006):1.
13. Betty Friedan, *The Feminine Mystique*. (New York: W.W. Norton & Company, Ltd, 2001).

work

Work Outside the Home, Its Impact and Implications. Without question, the achievements women have made in employment have altered the face of the American family and the woman's role within it. Today, most contemporary females in the U.S. are both homemaker and moneymaker in their households. Consider these facts:

- It is estimated that two-thirds of families today depend on two incomes.[14]

- Only 25 percent of U.S. households today represent the "traditional" nuclear family.[15]

- Increasingly, mothers—even those with younger children—are entering the workforce. More than two out of three mothers with children under age six now work outside the home. This telling chart reveals just how dramatic the shift has been for working mothers over the past 50 years:

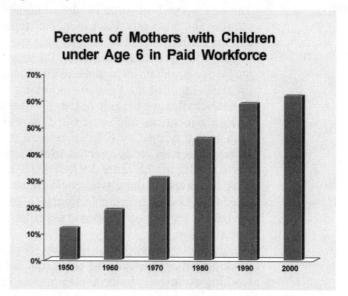

Source: Edward J. McCaffery, "Women and Taxes," National Center for Policy Analysis, February 28, 2002.

Not only are more women at work than ever before, but their financial contributions to the family income are growing as well. According to the U.S. Census Bureau in 2003, at least half of all wives earned as much or more than their husbands, with at least one-third earning more.[16]

---

14. Ed McCarthy, "Smarter Selling to Women," *Senior Market Advisor* (December 1, 2008).
15. "American Fact Finder," U.S. Census Bureau, 2005.
16. U.S. Census Bureau of Labor Statistics, 2003.

As a result of the Great Recession of 2008/2009, it is likely that even more women now out-earn their husbands. Evidence for this emerging trend can be found in a range of studies, including recent surveys reported by PayPal and Money Magazine. In a 2008 study by PayPal, one in 10 American families had seen the primary breadwinner change, due to ongoing financial difficulties.[17] According to Money Magazine in June 2009, the jobless rate for American men was 10 percent versus 7.6 percent for women.[18]

Despite her changing role as an income generator, today's working woman also continues to fulfill the primary responsibilities of family care giving and housekeeping. In households where both spouses work, women tend to take on more duties. According to Salary.com, working dads reported an average of 38.7 hours of "at home work" compared to 49.0 hours for working moms.[19] In addition, the average woman takes 12 years out of her working life to care for children or parents.[20] As a result, a common experience shared by many working mothers is sometimes referred to as "time poverty."

Since the demands on their capacity are both significant and unrelenting, many women do not take the time needed to plan for their financial future, or meet with a financial professional. Further compounding the difficulties of reaching and scheduling appointments with employed women and their spouses are their respective work schedules. Four in 10 working women work evenings, nights, or weekends on a regular basis, and 33 percent work shifts different than their spouses or partners.[21]

professions

Professions. Where do women work? While by no means a comprehensive listing, the industries in Table 1-1 represent those with the greatest majority of female workers as perspective.

For those interested in marketing to women by their occupational choices, the U.S. Census Bureau provides a wealth of information by geography and gender at www.census.gov.

In addition to the industries they dominate, women are also succeeding in positions of leadership. More than half of all persons employed in management, professional, and related occupations are female.[22] According to Susan Sweetser, J.D., MBA, CLU®, and ChFC®, and expert on American women in leadership positions, there are more than 1.3 million female executives in the United States

---

17. Jennifer Openshaw, "The 15-Minute Tip: Recession-Proof Relationships," *The Wall Street Journal: Market Watch*, (February 18 2009).
18. George Mannes, "Is the Economy Ruining Your Marriage?" *Money*, (August 21 2009), http://money.cnn.com/2009/08/10/news/economy/economy_marriage.moneymag/index.htm.
19. www.salary.com/sitesearch/layoutscripts/sisl_display.asp?filename== destinationsearch/par662_body.
20. "Facts and Figures," Social Security Administration, January 2005.
21. "Working Women Speak Out," Business and Professional Women's Foundation, 2004.
22. "Women in the Labor Force: A Databook," U.S. Department of Labor, September, 2006.

earning more than $100,000 per year. One third of this group are in managerial or professional specialty positions, including doctors, lawyers and CPAs.[23]

Table 1-1
Female Dominated Occupations

Occupation	Percent of workers who are women
Dental hygienists	99
Speech-language pathologists	98
Preschool teachers	97
Kindergarten teachers	97
Secretaries and administrative assistants	97
Dental assistants	96
Child care workers	95
Licensed practical and vocational nurses	93
Receptionists and informational clerks	93
Medical and health information technicians	93
Registered nurses	92
Teachers assistants	92
Medical assistants	91

Source: "Current Population Survey," U.S. Bureau of Labor Statistics, 2007.

Despite their progress among the ranks of leaders in organizations and professions, the glass ceiling remains a frustrating reality for some: in 2009, just 16 percent of Fortune 500 corporate officers were female. Further, women represented less than 3 percent of Fortune 500 Company CEOs.[24] On the whole however, the gains women have made in leadership over less than half a century are really quite remarkable.

business owners

Business Owners. Beyond improving their employment status, women are also creating their own opportunities; launching new businesses at twice the rate of men.[25] Today, three out of four new businesses are owned by women.[26] To illustrate the size, growth and composition of this group, consider these facts:

---

23. Susan Sweetser, "Mining Gems: The Secrets of Creating Successful Client Relationships with Women," *LIMRA MarketFacts Quarterly*, Fall 2006.
24. Barbara Frankel, "Why are Women CEOs Still So Rare?", Diversity Inc., April 13, 2009.
25. Marti Barletta, *Marketing to Women* (Chicago, IL: Dearborn Trade Publishing, 2006).
26. "Key Facts about Women-Owned Businesses," Center for Women's Business Research, 2009.

- More than 10 million firms in the United States are majority or equally owned by women.[27]

- In 2004, nearly half of all privately held firms were at least 50 percent owned by women.[28]

- Between 1997 and 2004, the number of ethnically diverse women-owned firms increased six times faster than all firms during the same period (55 percent versus 9 percent).[29]

- About one in five (21 percent) of women-owned businesses are owned by a woman of color.[30]

As additional perspective, the biggest growth industries for female business owners from 1997 to 2006 were:

- wholesale trade firms (283.4 percent growth)[31]

- professional, scientific, and technical services (88.1 percent increase in annual sales)[32]

- health care and social assistance companies (84.2 percent expansion)[33]

- administrative and support services (79.9 percent increase in revenues)[34]

One of the most appealing aspects of marketing to women business owners is the dual opportunities it presents. Qualified financial consultants who specialize in business markets can address both the needs of the female business owner, and her employees as well. Here are two statistics that demonstrate some of the upside that this market segment offers:

1. As business owners, just one in four women (26 percent) have put a formal succession plan in place for their business.[35]

---

27. "Women Business Owners and Their Enterprises," National Women's Business Council, July 2007.
28. "Fact Sheet," National Women's Business Council, March 2005.
29. Center for Women's Business Research, 2005.
30. "Women Business Owners and Their Enterprises," National Women's Business Council, July 2007.
31. "Women-Owned Businesses in the United States (Fact Sheet)," Center for Women's Business Research, 2006.
32. Ibid.
33. Ibid.
34. Ibid.
35. "Small Business Owners Report," LIMRA International, 2005.

2. Only one-fifth of women owners say they are satisfied with their firm's current benefits package.[36]

Taking care of employees retained by women business owners represents potential for big business. According to the National Association of Women Business Owners and the Small Business Administration, female business owners employed approximately 27 million Americans in 2007.[37] These business owners and their employees have need for financial services and products, of course. In 2004, the Center for Women's Business Research found that women-owned businesses spent an estimated a total of $546 billion in 2004 with $492 billion allocated to salaries/wages, and the remainder ($54 billion) on employee benefits. The center also determined that health insurance comprised the largest share of benefit expenditures, estimated at $38 billion.[38]

The growth and development of women-owned businesses are significant trends for discerning financial professionals to both observe and build their expertise around. Equally important are the opportunities to market to more narrowly defined niches within the business owner segment, as we shall see in Chapter 2.

Earnings

earnings

The success that women have realized in education and employment have led to significant gains in income as well. One of the more notable outcomes has been the narrowing of the much publicized and frequently debated pay or earnings gap—the discrepancy in average incomes earned by men and women.

In 1963, Congress passed, and President John F. Kennedy signed, the Equal Pay Act, requiring that men and women be given equal pay for equal work in the same establishment. Despite this legislation, the earnings gap stubbornly persisted through the end of the century—and still exists today, though to a much lesser extent. In fact, the pay gap actually increased after the Equal Pay Act was signed. Back in the early 1960s, women's average earnings were 60 cents on the dollar compared to men, or about 40 percent less.[39] By the advent of the 21st century, the gap had narrowed to a 26 percent disparity, with American women earning roughly 74 cents compared to men.[40] Over the 40-year period between 1960 and 2000, women realized a 23 percent overall increase in pay parity (but just half a percent when compounded annually).

---

36. "Women-Owned Small Business: Results from the 2005 U.S. Small Business Study," LIMRA International, 2005.
37. "Women in the Workplace, Marketplace and Society," National Association of Women Business Owners & Small Business Administration, 2008.
38. Center for Women's Business Research, 2005
39. The Prism, *The Path of the Women's Rights Movement*, http://www.ibiblio.org/prism/mar98/path.html.
40. "Woman's Earnings as a Percentage of Men's Earnings by Race and Hispanic Origin: 1960 to 2007"U.S. Census Bureau.

Some attribute at least part of the pay gap to lower-paying career choices, family demands that often dictate women's decisions to work part-time versus full-time, and the fact that women often leave the workforce to care for family members.

According to the U.S. Census Bureau, in 2008, the gap was narrowest between younger women and men, and expanded among older age groups.[41] This suggests generational differences in pay disparity and that younger women may have benefitted from the gains made by their older peers. The chart below reflects differences in male/female average earnings by three age groups.

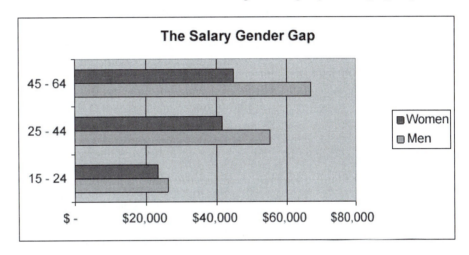

Source: U.S. Census Bureau data found in Lyric Winik and Meg Massey, "Intelligence Report,"*Parade* (January 18, 2009).

With continued gains in education and employment, it is reasonable to expect that the earnings gap will continue to narrow even further. The smaller differences between younger males and females give partial support to this expectation. Recently enacted and proposed legislation will likely have an impact as well. In 2009, Congress passed, and President Obama signed into law, the Lilly Ledbetter Fair Pay Act[42] which extends the time that a worker can sue a former employer for pay discrimination. Another piece of related legislation, the Fair Pay Act, is currently under review.

---

41. U.S. Census Bureau, 2008
42. National Women's Law Center, *Lilly Ledbetter Fair Pay Act.*, http://www.nwlc.org/fairpay/ledbetterfairpayact.html.

Women and Money

wealth drivers

Summary of Wealth Drivers—The "Big Three E's"—Education, Earnings and Employment

The chart below depicts the dramatic gains women have made in the three drivers of wealth—education, employment and earnings—in a relatively short span of just decades. It represents the following trends at the inception of each decade between 1940 and 2000:

1. the ratio of females to males earning a bachelors degree

2. the growth in full-time employment among women aged 16 and over

3. the earnings ratio (or pay gap) reflecting the percent of dollars earned by women on average, compared to the average for men

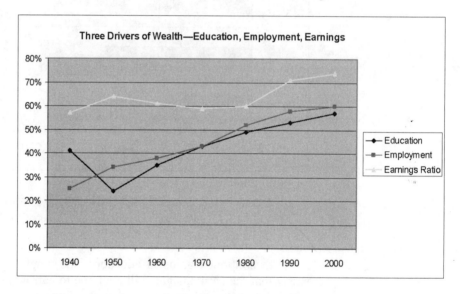

Education Source: "High School and College Graduates," *InfoPlease® Database*, (2007). http://www.infoplease.com/ ipa/A0112596.html.
Employment Source: "Women in the Labor Force," *InfoPlease® Database*, (2007). http://www.infoplease.com/ ipa/A0104673.html.
Earnings Source: The Gender Wage Gap: 2008, Institute for Women's Policy Research, http://www.iwpr.org/ pdf/C350.pdf.

Since the middle 1980s, progress in women's education, earnings, and employment have all been on positive trajectories of accelerated growth. Females now coming into their formative earning years have seen nothing but gaining momentum on all three fronts. What does this mean to financial professionals? These increasingly empowered women are now in their prime earning phases of life. This means significant opportunity for well-positioned

Her Ethnicity

ethnicity

Beyond the three main drivers of wealth are also important societal shifts, including the emergence of three influential ethnic segments of the women's market. Together, Hispanics, Blacks, and Asians are among the fastest-growing ethnic segments of the U.S. population.[43] Contemporary marketers categorize these three primary ethnic markets as *emerging majorities*, acknowledging their combined economic influence.[44] As evidence of this, 90 percent of high-net-worth households in 1990 were Caucasian, falling to 78 percent in 2007.[45] The following is a discussion of noteworthy aspects and the potential of each emerging segment within the women's market.

Hispanic Women

Hispanic Women

There are several reasons why Hispanic women are an attractive market. The Hispanic community is the largest ethnic minority in the United States, constituting 15 percent of the nation's total population in 2009.[46] By 2050, Hispanics are projected to make up 24 percent of the U.S. population.[47]

> Sixty-four percent of Hispanic-origin people are in households of Mexican background. Another approximately 10 percent are of Puerto Rican background, with about 3 percent each of Cuban, Salvadoran, and Dominican origins. The remainder are of Central American, South American, or other Hispanic or Latino origins.

In addition to their burgeoning numbers, is the growing wealth of Hispanics. There are more than 3.7 million affluent Hispanics in the United States, and over half of all Hispanic households make over $50,000 per year.[48] The affluent segment of the Hispanic market alone is thought to have a buying power in

---

43. U.S. Census, 2000
44. Jeffrey M. Humphreys, "The Multicultural Economy 2003: America's Minority-Buying Power," GBEC 63, no. 2, 2003.
45. "2007 Phoenix Wealth Survey Executive Summary," Phoenix Equity Planning Corporation, 2007.
46. "Facts for Features," U.S. Census Bureau, July 15, 2009, http://www.census.gov/Press-Release/www/releases/archives/facts_for_features_special_editions/013984.html
47. U.S. Census Bureau, 2000.
48. Carlos Ulibarri, *Marketing to Affluent Hispanics*, http://www.brandchannel.com/papers_review.asp?sp_id=332

excess of $300 billion.[49] Yet, despite their numbers and wealth, less than 5 percent of advertising targets affluent Hispanics.[50]

Asian Women

Asian Women

Asian-Americans have the highest average household income of all emerging minority groups, and together represent more than $400 billion in purchasing power.[51] According to 2000 U.S. Census numbers, their median income is 32 percent higher than the median income of the general population.[52] Images of success and aspiration resound with Asian women in general, and with younger Asian women in particular. The Asian population places a high emphasis on education and is three times more likely to get a college degree than Americans as a whole. In addition, Asian women own more than 359,000 businesses, representing one of the fastest-growing segments of women-owned businesses.[53]

Black Women

Black Women

The growing socioeconomic status of Black women presents additional opportunities for financial consultants. Increased education—35 percent of Black women attend college—has resulted in higher earnings. Single, never married Black women also represent a strong market opportunity. According to the US Census Bureau, in 2001, almost half (49.5 percent) of Black women aged 30 to 34 have never been married, compared with 17.1 percent of white women in the same age group.[54]

Black women, more so than the general population, manage the family household budget. Research by Fannie Mae in 2001 found that 68 percent of Black women, compared with 55 percent of all women, said they solely managed their household's budget.[55] The growing education, affluence, and independence of Black women will make them increasingly important as a target market for financial services.

---

49. Ibid.
50. Ibid.
51. Karen Krebsbach, "Affluent Asian Americans Elusive for Some Banks," US Banker 117, no. 2, 2007, 12.
52. U.S. Census Bureau, 2000
53. Center for Women's Business Research, "Asian Women Business Owners in the U.S.," (funded by Wells Fargo Bank), 2003.
54. National Healthy Marriage Resource Center, *Trends in Percent Ever Married by Age and Race/Ethnicity*, http://www.healthymarriageinfo.org/docs/marriedbyrace.pdf.
55. "2002 Fannie Mae National Housing Survey," Fannie Mae, 2002

The Future

What might the future hold for financial professionals choosing to work more effectively with female prospects and clients? The women's market and their demand for financial services will continue to evolve. Forward thinking professionals must be prepared. Interpreting key trends and projecting them towards the future reveals new opportunities, issues and implications for financial consultants. Females who earned their bachelor's degrees in the 1970s, and master's in the 1980s, are amassing larger sums of wealth as they prepare for retirement. Women who graduated in the 1990s and the 2000s are building their careers and families. In addition to their earned wealth, many will be in line to manage inherited family fortunes as well. By some estimates, in 2030, American women will control as much as two-thirds of the nation's wealth.[56]

Trends in education, employment and earnings point to a bright future for many women and their financial professionals. Emerging ethnic groups hold promise of greater prosperity for their members; as well as those who serve them. As female clients learn and earn more, they will become more financially sophisticated. This means they will also demand more competence and expertise from their financial consultants.

Paradoxically, there is a flip side to the bright prospects ahead for many American women and their professional advisors. Focusing only on the brightest aspects of the market potential would not alert financial professionals to the challenges many women will face.

WOMEN AND MONEY—THE CHALLENGES

Despite the extraordinary achievements that many females have realized in the past few decades, there are four major financial challenges that most share. While there is a broad range of additional risks among the six areas of financial planning that we will discuss later, these four particular challenges are common for many women:

1. singlehood
2. low financial literacy
3. low financial preparedness
4. increased risk of poverty

These challenges further heighten the need for women to have capable, trustworthy financial consultants to advise them—even if they cannot afford to pay for services. At times, the consultant may find him- or herself in the role of non-profit counselor, working with a woman who might be what some call a "charity case." Stepping into the role of unpaid counselor versus paid

---

56. "New Investment Strategy Recognizes Women's Unique Financial Concerns." *PRLog,* July 10, 2009. http://www.prlog.org/10278786-new-investment-strategy-recognizes-womens-unique-financial-concerns.

product/service provider can truly make a difference in the lives of those living close to the margins. Here is a brief overview of each of these significant challenges that many women experience.

Singlehood

The rapid expansion of single women has created a substantial, if not seismic, shift in American society. The ratio of married to unmarried people, particularly among younger demographics, has been declining steadily for decades. As a result of increased economic independence, greater longevity, life circumstance, or some combination, more women are single than ever before in history.

Today, *more than half* (51 percent) of the female adult population in America is single. A recent New York Times article captured a telling quote from Dr. William H. Frey, demographer with the Brookings Institution: "Since women continue to outlive men, they have reached the non-marital tipping-point—more non-married than married. This reflects the culmination of post-1960 trends with greater independence and more flexible lifestyles for women."[57]

It is believed that the vast majority (90 percent) of American women will become single during their adult lifetimes.[58] Among all U.S. households, more than one in four (approximately 31 million), are currently headed by a woman only. Over 9 million of those households are headed by a woman who never married, 12 million by divorced or separated women, and 9 million by widows.[59] In addition to the personal trauma that divorce and widowhood often create, there are heightened financial risks. Households headed only by a woman survive on about half (52 percent) of the income generated by all other American households.[60]

Divorce

divorce

Divorce is a life circumstance that can hit a woman especially hard. According to Morningstar Investment research, one year after a divorce, a woman's standard of living falls about 30 percent on average, while a man's rises 10 percent.[61] This difference may be due in part to the judicial process and enforcement, since only 15 percent of divorcing women are awarded any form

---

57. Sam Roberts, "51 percent of Women Are Now Living Without Spouse," *The New York Times* (January 16, 2007).
58. Kerry Hannon, *Suddenly Single*, (New York: John Wiley & Sons, Inc., 1998).
59. Ruth Mantell, "Women survive on 52% of typical household income," MarketWatch, December 2, 2008.
60. Ibid.
61. "The Woman's Guide to Money Matters," MorningStar Investment Research Center, 2008.

of court ordered spousal support; and fewer than half of all women with court ordered child support ever get the full amount.[62]

Widowhood

widowhood

Becoming a widow in the second half of life is a common reality for many American women. In 1999, there were more than four times as many widows (8.4 million) as widowers (1.9 million).[63] By 2007, 42.2 percent of women past the age of 65 were widowed.[64] The chart below reflects the population of widows, by age group, according to the 2008 U.S. Census.

Population of Widows in the United States	
Age Group	**Widow Population**
15-17 years	6,000
18-19 years	3,000
20-24 years	29,000
25-29 years	62,000
30-34 years	74,000
35-39 years	118,000
40-44 years	219,000
45-49 years	355,000
50-54 years	618,000
55-64 years	1,862,000
65-74 years	3,281,000
75-84 years	4,988,000
85+ years	2,698,000
Total Widows in US	14,313,000
Source: U. S. Census Bureau Current Population Survey, 2008 Annual Social and Economic Supplement, Table A1. Marital Status of People 15 Years and Over, by Age, Sex, 2008.	

The "double-whammy" of widowhood is that it not only creates deep emotional loss, but also financial losses on a scale that may lead to poverty, as evidenced by these sad statistics:

---

62. Kerry Hannon, *Suddenly Single*, (New York: John Wiley & Sons, Inc., 1998).
63. AARP, 2008
64. U.S. Census Bureau, "Current Population Survey, Annual Social and Economic Supplement, 2007.

- When a woman outlives her husband, her income decreases by 50 percent on average, yet expenses only decrease by 20 percent.[65]

- One in four of women are broke within 2 months of being widowed.[66]

- Roughly 80 percent of widows living in poverty were not poor when their husbands were alive.[67]

By contrast, the highest percentage of single high-net-worth females (37 percent) are in fact widowed, compared to affluent single males of which only 15 percent are widowers.[68] This represents another example of the women's market paradox—the broad economic disparities and distributions of wealth among American females. Further magnifying risks associated with singlehood are the relatively low rates of financial literacy that many women share.

Financial Literacy

financial literacy

It should come as no surprise to most financial professionals that much of the American public is either misinformed, or more likely uninformed, about their personal finances. In a 2007 survey by the Jump$tart Coalition for Personal Financial Literacy, one out of four adults failed a quiz with questions covering money basics (e.g., inflation, interest rates, debt, savings vehicles).[69] The same research revealed that women were almost three times more likely to fail the quiz than men; 42 percent scored an F, compared with 15 percent for men.[70]

Disturbing gaps in financial literacy are also evident in the generally low familiarity that many women have with common financial products. The chart below, derived from a recent study by Prudential Financial, reveals that, even on core products like annuities, mutual funds, and long-term care insurance, large percentages of women did not display high rates of financial literacy. Nearly half of respondents in the study said they did not understand these products well, or at all. It is worth noting that two of these three (annuities and long-term care insurance) are products with particular relevance and importance to women, as we shall see in coming chapters.

Some academics speculate that part of the reason for low financial literacy rates among females may be attributed to gender stereotyping. For centuries, American women were neither engaged nor empowered financially. Common law, which developed in England and migrated to the United States, greatly

---

65. *LIMRA Market Facts Quarterly*, Fall 2006
66. Federal Interagency Forum on Aging Related Statistics, "Older Americans 2008: Key Indicators of Well-Being," March 2008.
67. Kerry Hannon, Suddenly Single, 1998.
68. "When Marketing, Life Insurers Must Also Target the Ever-growing 'Suddenly Singles,'" Best Wire, Real-Time Insurance Newsletter, 2007.
69. Liz Weston, "9 Money Rules to Live By," MSN Money, January 16, 2008.
70. Ibid.

influenced the economic status of women up until the latter part of the 20th century. For example, under common law, an unmarried woman could own property, make a contract, sue or be sued. However, a married women, gave up her name, and virtually all her property came under her husband's control. During the early history of the United States, a man essentially owned his wife and children, as he did his material possessions.[71]

Product Literacy Rates Among Women		
Financial Product	% Understanding Somewhat/Very Well	% Understanding Not Too Well/Not At All
Annuities	41%	59%
Mutual Funds	53%	47%
Long-Term Care Insurance	54%	46%
Estate Planning, Trusts and Wills	54%	46%
Individual Stocks and Bonds	56%	44%
401k, 403b and 457 Plans	70%	30%
Life Insurance	84%	16%
Savings Accounts	98%	2%
Source: Financial Experience and Behaviors Among Women, Prudential Financial, 2006		

In light of both the historical context and the gender stereotyping that went along with it, most women were not educated or expected to take up financial responsibilities. Today, many women remain significantly behind in their financial education. Despite the strides made by women in their earnings, education and employment, they have not progressed as successfully in the area of financial literacy.

According to a survey conducted by Allianz in 2007, 57 percent of female respondents said they wish they had learned more in school about money and finance.[72] Industry and academic studies also reveal that boys have typically received more encouragement to earn and save, as well as to excel in math, than girls. Findings of the landmark Gender Investment Comparison Study by the Dreyfus Corporation, and the National Center for Women and Retirement Research support these conclusions.[73] The survey found that sons were more likely to be encouraged by parents to earn money at a much earlier age (13) versus daughters (16–18). In addition, boys were twice as likely to be encouraged by their parents to save money. The study also determined that

---

71. The Women's International Center, "Women's History in America," www.wic.org
72. Allianz Life Insurance Company, Harris International, Age Wave, "Women, Money & Power Study," 2008.
73. Dreyfus Corporation and the National Center for Women and Retirement Research, "Gender Investment Comparison Study," 1997.

women who were well supported in math achievement by parents or teachers early in life were more confident with math during school and later more confident in their financial management abilities. Conversely, women who were uncomfortable with math during high school were more prone to financial worry in adulthood and likely to be more conservative in their investment choices.[74]

Regardless of the causes of low financial literacy, the unfortunate consequences are often inaction and poverty. The likelihood of an individual being on welfare is inversely proportionate to financial literacy levels.[75] In other words, the lower the literacy rate, the higher the risk of poverty. Further, 43 percent of adults with the lowest level of financial literacy live in poverty, compared to only four percent of those at the highest level.[76]

Financial Unpreparedness

Limited understanding of financial issues and instruments can also create inertia, or being "stuck," when it comes to financial planning and decision making. It is not uncommon for people to say that the seemingly endless barrage of financial information is often difficult to absorb. This sentiment was captured in a 2007 study by Allianz, in which 44 percent of women surveyed said they found financial information overwhelming or too hard to sort through.[77] One of the outcomes of being overwhelmed may be that women feel ill-equipped to make prudent financial decisions. Research by Prudential Financial found that less than one in four women said she was "very well" prepared for financial decision making.[78]

How can prospects and clients of either gender chart a deliberate course of financial action, when the details are not well analyzed or understood? A striking example of financial unpreparedness is the fact that approximately 25 percent of women have no savings at all for retirement.[79]

Poverty

Financial risks increase significantly as a result of singlehood, low financial literacy and lack of preparation. Far too many women find themselves in financial jeopardy, especially later in life. Nearly three out of every four Americans over 65 living in poverty are women, and older women living alone

---

74. Ibid.
75. Virginia Credit Union League, "Financial Literacy Statistics," 1997–2005. http://vacul.com/fin_lit/stats.htm
76. Ibid.
77. Allianz Life Insurance Company of North America, "Allianz: Women Keen on Finance," June 24, 2008.
78. Prudential Financial, "Financial Experience & Behaviors Among Women," 2008.
79. Employee Benefit Research Institute and Investment Company Institute Survey.

are more than twice as likely to be impoverished than are men.[80] Even more disheartening is that the United States has the highest poverty rate for elderly women of all post-industrial nations.[81]

For some women, particularly those of the Baby Boom generation, the future holds higher risks of poverty after decades of inadequate preparation for retirement and the significant loss of wealth in the aftermath of the 2008 market meltdown. Supporting this prognostication are results from a recent survey by the Employee Benefit Research Institute and market research company Mathew Greenwald & Associates. Their study reveals that in 2008, only 13 percent of Americans were very confident about having enough money to retire, down from 27 percent in 2007.[82] Since Baby Boomer females, in general, earned less and therefore saved less than their male peers; the lack of financial education, preparation and singlehood may put many of these women in financial peril.

> "I believe every right implies a responsibility; every opportunity, an obligation; every possession, a duty."
>
> John D. Rockefeller, Jr.

THE SECOND PARADOX

The women's market paradox presents financial consultants and the financial services industry both tremendous opportunity and obligation—the opportunity to manage and protect growing wealth, and an obligation to help women at risk. In light of this paradox, one could readily come to the conclusion that there is an enormous and even urgent need for qualified, trustworthy financial consultants to advise American women. There is. Consider these findings from recent research:

- One in three women is eager to strengthen her financial planning skills but does not know where to begin.[83]

- One half of women prefer to learn about financial products through financial consultants.[84]

- More than two in three women (64 percent) feel more knowledgeable about money because they are working with a financial professional.[85]

---

80. Social Security Bulletin, "Life-Cycle Aspects of Poverty among Older Women," 1997.
81. Business and Professional Women's Foundation, "101 Facts on the Status of Working Women," October 2004.
82. Employee Benefit Research Institute, "2009 Retirement Confidence Survey."
83. Allianz, "Allianz: Women, Money & Power Study," 2008.
84. Ibid.
85. Oppenheimer Funds, "Women & Investing," 2006.

If only women had more faith, confidence, and trust in financial professionals. Research shows that the majority of American women simply do not trust financial advisors and insurance agents. In State Farm's 2008 "Musts of Trust" survey,[86] less than half (44 percent) of the women surveyed said they trusted insurance agents. For financial advisors and stock brokers, the results were even worse, with only one in three (36 percent) women indicating trust in these professionals.[87] These findings are all the more unsettling when compared to trust levels for medical doctors, in which 79 percent of women said they trusted physicians.[88] In the same research, three in four women (75 percent) admitted to being skeptical and distrustful when first meeting with a financial consultant.[89]

Thus, the *second paradox* is the great need many women have for the assistance of a qualified, capable financial professional, and also the unfortunate suspicion of them that many share. Without a foundation of trust, how effective can financial consultants be when seeking to succeed in the women's market?

MATTERS OF TRUST

Industry and academic studies consistently affirm that the most desired quality in a financial consultant is his or her integrity. Being both trusted and trustworthy is the nexus of guiding principles for the best financial professionals. While this book is intended to help build the financial consultant's understanding, skills, and expertise for working more effectively with female prospects and clients, bear in mind that all people deserve nothing less than the utmost in trustworthy advice and service.

> "Trust is the highest form of human motivation. It brings out the very best in people. But it takes time and patience, and it doesn't preclude the necessity to train and develop people so that their competency can rise to the level of that trust."
>
> Stephen Covey

Schemes, Scandals and Greed in the Marketplace

The environment that financial professionals operate in today is a demanding one to say the least, when it comes to establishing trust with prospects—female or male. Within the financial services industry and in various media, there has been a great deal of buzz lately about the trustworthiness of financial professionals. Almost daily, there is increasing scrutiny by regulators,

---

86. State Farm "The Musts of Trust" Women Consumer Survey, Kelton Research, Golan-Harris, Newsworthy Analysis published May 2008
87. Ibid.
88. Ibid.
89. Ibid.

as the media exposes the unsavory and abusive business practices of the industry's "bad apples." Breaches of trust, caused by astonishing greed and lack of scruples, paint the financial services industry—and every industry professional—with a broad brush stroke of public disdain.

Since the beginning of the global economic crisis, approximately 40 percent of the public said their trust in the financial services industry had weakened.[90] In the same research study, respondents described financial institutions as greedy (32 percent), impersonal (26 percent) and opportunistic. Only slightly more than 10 percent said that these institutions were honest and trustworthy. Two-thirds said they did not believe the financial services industry would help them regain the wealth they lost during the economic downturn.

Equally, if not more concerning, are the findings from a 2008/2009 CNN opinion poll, in which 74 percent of Americans said they believed that the behavior of Bernard Madoff, arguably the biggest swindler of all time, is common among financial consultants and institutions.[91]

As a result of the highly visible and egregious breaches of public trust, increased regulation imposed on financial services companies and their affiliates is virtually guaranteed. There is movement towards significant regulatory overhaul, including controversial new regulations and broader application of fiduciary standards. While details have yet to unfold, it is likely that sweeping regulatory changes will deeply affect both financial consultants and their clients for years to come.

> "In the middle of difficulty lies opportunity."
>
> Albert Einstein

What She Is Looking For

In light of these troubling circumstances, what are contemporary American women looking for in a trustworthy financial consultant? How can professionals position themselves better to overcome trust barriers and inspire increased confidence among female prospects and clients? In the discussion that follows, we look at builders of trust. More important, we examine specific qualities and behavior that women seek in their financial consultants, as well as the ethical and professional standards to which financial consultants should adhere.

The 2008 State Farm "Musts of Trust" research looked at trust relationships across five service industries (lawyers, real estate agents, doctors, financial advisors and insurance agents). The following chart outlines the top five qualities the survey found to be the most sought after in service providers from three professions: (1) medical doctors, (2) financial advisors and (3) insurance agents by rank order (most important is number one).

---

90. "Consumers Have Little Trust in Financial Services Companies," Insurance Insider News, January 28, 2009.
91. Journal of Financial Planning, March 2009.

Women and Money

Women's "Musts of Trust" for Service Providers		
Medical Doctors	**Financial Advisors**	**Insurance Agents**
1 Friendly and Warm	Comes Recommended	Composed and Confident
2 Impressive Qualifications	Honesty	Honesty
3 Honesty	Highly Knowledgeable	Clear Explanations
4 Clear Explanations	Customized Approach	Solve Problems Quickly
5 Takes Responsibility	Knows My Name	Comes Recommended

Source: State Farm "The Musts of Trust" Survey, Kelton Research, May 2008

The survey results support the hypothesis that the building blocks of trust differ greatly depending on the service provided. These research findings also reveal that a trusting relationship is the sum of many parts, and that not all parts are created equal.[92] We explore the key components of building trust in the section below.

Building Trust as Her Financial Consultant

It is important for financial consultants to recognize that while the reputation of the company, or the products they represent, reinforce prospect/client confidence, the actions and capabilities of the individual financial professional take center stage when it comes to earning trust. Approximately 80 percent of Americans say that the behavior of their consultant is more important than the company he or she represents.[93]

What behaviors can financial consultants adopt to inspire the increased confidence and faith placed in them by female prospects and clients? Trusted financial professionals must:

- comply with state and federal regulations on the sale of insurance and investment products, as well as fee-based advisory services if applicable

- adhere to principles of professionalism along with codes/canons of ethical conduct

- demonstrate behavior consistent with expectations of integrity, competence and commitment to the client's best interests

- apply ethical and professional behaviors throughout the client-consultant relationship and the process of delivering high quality financial advice

---

92. State Farm "The Musts of Trust" Women Consumer Survey, Kelton Research, Golan-Harris, Newsworthy Analysis published May 2008.
93. State Farm "Musts of Trust" Survey, Kelton Research, August 2008.

Compliance

compliance

Compliance means following the laws, regulations and company policies that apply to the placement of all financial products and services. Meeting compliance requirements is a *bare minimum standard* and a necessary first step in professional conduct. Beyond fulfilling the responsibilities required by regulators, legislation or compliance officers/departments, financial consultants must also act ethically and professionally.

Ethics and Professionalism

ethics
professionalism

Generally, laws and regulations are encoded ethics. Ethical conduct and professionalism demand more than mere compliance with company policies, laws and regulations for the sake of avoiding punishment. Being ethical and being professional go hand-in-hand; both are about doing the right thing.

There are many codes of ethics in the financial services industry, some are relatively simple, and others are far more complex. Almost every major industry organization has its own standards. For those who hold advanced designations, there are yet more principles to which professionals must adhere. For the most part, these codes bear striking resemblance to each other. As perspective, The American College Code of Ethics, including the Professional Pledge and Canons follows.

The American College Code of Ethics
The Professional Pledge and the Canons

The Pledge to which all Huebner School designees subscribe is as follows:
In all my professional relationships, I pledge myself to the following rule of ethical conduct: I shall, in light of all conditions surrounding those I serve, which I shall make every conscientious effort to ascertain and understand, render that service, which, in the same circumstances, I would apply to myself.
 	
The eight Canons are:
   I. Conduct yourself at all times with honor and dignity.
  II. Avoid practices that would bring dishonor upon your profession or The American College.
 III. Publicize your achievement in ways that enhance the integrity of your profession.
 IV. Continue your studies throughout your working life so as to maintain a high level of professional competence.
  V. Do your utmost to attain a distinguished record of professional service.
 VI. Support the established institutions and organizations concerned with the integrity of your profession.
VII. Participate in building your profession by encouraging and providing appropriate assistance to qualified persons pursuing professional studies.
VIII. Comply with all laws and regulations, particularly as they relate to professional and business activities.

Professionalism also encompasses specific behavior, including demonstrating respect for all clients and prospects, protecting client confidentiality, providing transparency and disclosure, building competencies, and following a specific process in meeting client needs.

Behavior

In addition to behaving with fairness, objectivity, honesty, and integrity, financial consultants must also treat male and female clients with equal respect. It is an unfortunate reality, documented by industry research, that many women feel disrespected, misunderstood, and overlooked by some financial service and product providers. These disconnects may be partly responsible for why many women hold the financial services industry in such low regard. According to a 2008 survey of over 12,000 females, the Boston Consulting Group found that, out of 34 industries, financial services was ranked as the industry least in tune with how women want to be treated.[94] In a recent article in the Harvard Business Review, survey authors, Michael Silverstein and Kate Sayre, describe scathing comments by women about providers of financial goods and services including "lack of respect and poor advice."[95] Among the verbatim quotes from respondents: "Financial service reps talk down to women as if we cannot understand more than just the basics." Clearly, demonstrating respect for female prospects and clients is a critical element to inspiring their trust.

Key elements of respectful behavior that women seek can be inferred from recent research:

- seventy percent of affluent women focus on the financial consultant's ability to listen well[96]

- having a financial advisor who "knows my name" is ranked among the top five trust building attributes sought out by women[97]

- ninety two percent of wealthy women say that if personal and professional chemistry is not there with a prospective financial consultant, "it's a true deal breaker"[98]

Since one's behavior is so critical to building a high trust relationship with female clients, in Chapter 3 we examine how to develop more effective skills in greater detail.

---

94. Michael J. Silverstein and Kate Sayre, The Female Economy, Harvard Business Review, September 2009.
95. Ibid.
96. John J. Bowen, Jr., Women of Wealth: Many Affluent Women Have Earned—Not Inherited Their Wealth, Financial Planning Magazine, New York, November 1, 2006.
97. State Farm "Musts of Trust" Survey, Kelton Research, August 2008.
98. John J. Bowen, Jr., Women of Wealth: Many Affluent Women Have Earned—Not Inherited Their Wealth, Financial Planning Magazine, New York, November 1, 2006.

Confidentiality

confidentiality

All prospects and clients are entitled to a high level of confidentiality regarding the personal information they give to their consultants. Financial professionals are not only expected, but also required by laws and regulations to keep information private and not share it with others without advance approval from the prospect or client. In the initial interview, it can be helpful to say something like: *"Protecting your privacy is of the utmost importance to me. Our discussions and your sensitive information are always confidential."* (Note: The author has used, and prospects seem to enjoy, the phrase: *"While you can talk about me as much as you want, I'll never talk about you."*)

Transparency and Disclosure

disclosure

Financial professionals must also present enough information to enable the client to make an informed decision. Disclosure should include how one is paid (commissions and/or fees), along with all expenses and costs of products and services. Some consultants are squeamish about revealing this information. However, being up front with prospects and clients from the very start frequently removes one of the biggest sources of distrust. Here is a best practice approach to disclosing how one is paid:

Disclosure—How You Are Paid

"Many people are curious about how I'm paid. This should never be a secret, so I'd like to tell you right up front.

(Company) does not pay me a salary and does not pay for my overhead. I am paid and I pay my staff/office expenses through commission(s) on insurance/investment products placed through (Company) and our affiliates. (My staff and) I work very hard to earn and continue to deserve your trust.

(If appropriate) I am also compensated through fees for some financial planning and wealth management services you might choose.

At all times, we will discuss any expenses associated with a product or service before we do anything together. Nothing should ever come as a surprise to you.

Any costs, along with product and service benefits, must be clear to you so that you can make informed financial decisions.

The last and perhaps best way that I'm paid is through referrals or recommendations to others when you are satisfied with my services and the value I provide. Your recommendations affirm that I am worth every penny you pay me.

Are you comfortable with this approach to doing business together?"

The great majority of prospects and clients both recognize the need for and want to pay for valuable services rendered by professionals. Disclosing compensation practices at the onset of a relationship not only builds trust, but also helps consultants avoid misspent time and resources. It is far better to find out early that a prospect does not value the professional's expertise before committing to work for which there may be no compensation.

Competency

competency

Professionalism also means building and maintaining high levels of expertise, skills, and competence. The rigorous education that medical doctors undertake in order to practice is well understood by patients. Compare the relative uniformity of medical education to the financial industry's bewildering array. Financial consultants must choose, and the public, media and consumers must discern, from among a multitude of credentials. The American College recently identified more than 267 different financial service designations. Some require just a few hours of training; others take hundreds of hours of rigorous study and examinations. This "alphabet soup" of designations is not only confusing, but it also seriously compromises public faith and confidence in the competence of financial professionals.

Regardless of which credentials a financial consultant pursues, he or she must be fully aware of the legal and tax ramifications of recommendations made to the client. In addition, one must be able to outline the positive and negative implications of the various investment and insurance options available so that prospects and clients can make informed financial decisions. This means having a thorough understanding of legislative and economic environments, products and services represented; as well as the unique situations/challenges of the client.

The depth and breadth of expertise required can challenge even the most seasoned financial professional. That said, women expect their consultant to be highly knowledgeable and to educate them on financial concepts. The more affluent the client is, the more expertise she will expect. To illustrate, according to research by Oppenheimer Funds, 90 percent of wealthy female investors have the expectation that their consultant will fully explain financial concepts, as well as advise them on financial decision making.[99]

For those who take up the challenge of continually increasing their competencies, the rewards are well worth the effort: more business, more referrals, less client turnover, and more personal fulfillment. The promise of quality advice is important to women, and they will refer a knowledgeable, trustworthy financial services professional twice as often as men will.[100] Further, industry studies have consistently shown that income and revenue generation increase substantially as the consultant progresses his or her advanced education. Taken together, these factors can yield a more important

---

99. Oppenheimer Funds Survey, 2006.
100. Susan Sweetser, Real Opportunity, MDRT, 2007. May/June.

dividend—improved quality of life for the financial consultant and his or her family.

> "Far and away the best prize that life offers is the chance to work hard at work worth doing."
>
> Theodore Roosevelt

How do financial consultants apply their ethics, professionalism and competencies in a series of behaviors that continually earn the client's trust and make her a client for life? Beyond professionalism and ethics, the *process* followed when working with female clients is key.

The Consultative Planning Process

Consultative Planning Process

Perhaps it is no accident that women place highest trust in their medical doctors. Almost eight in ten women trust physicians, more than twice the rate for financial consultants and insurance agents.[101] Beyond the Hippocratic Oath (which essentially begins with "First, do no harm"), and well acknowledged educational requirements, what else can the medical profession teach us about creating and maintaining trust with our female prospects and clients?

Diagnosing Before Prescribing

In order to prescribe a course of action, physicians must first diagnose or assess the patient's physical condition. This standard practice may seem overly obvious; however, since ours is an industry with more than its fair share of malpractice, regulatory oversight, and slanted media, perhaps a simple standard that has worked in the medical profession for thousands of years is worth considering.

A doctor's assessment includes a thorough fact-finding of medical and family histories, along with an exploration of the client's health issues and symptoms. The diagnostic process begins with careful inquiry and should result in an understanding of the patient's ailments. By contrast, many women feel this deliberate process of discovery is often overlooked or incomplete when they are working with financial professionals. How else could nearly nine in ten (84 percent) women investors surveyed by Yankelovich, say that their financial advisor did not understand their investment objectives?[102] These diagnostic and relationship-building gaps seriously compromise a trust relationship from the very start.

The consultative planning process is also about putting the identification and achievement of her objectives before the placement of product and services. It includes a deliberate and well-thought-out examination of her

---

101. State Farm "Musts of Trust" Survey, Kelton Research, August 2008.
102. Yankelovich Monitor.

financial opportunities and challenges prior to coming to conclusions about the appropriate financial vehicle to address them. Explaining the process one has for helping the client achieve her goals and address financial risks demonstrates diligence and professionalism. Further, it is a key element to winning trust and business. As evidence of this, 75 percent of affluent female prospects say they want to know what the prospective consultant's approach is to planning before hiring that individual.[103]

> "The amateur salesperson sells products; the professional sells solutions to needs and problems."
>
> Stephen Covey

The Benefits of Consultative Planning Process to Financial Consultants

As we explore the objectives and steps of the consultative planning process, it is helpful to keep in mind its substantial benefits to financial consultants. Industry research has consistently demonstrated that when financial professionals adopt a planning approach, they generate more revenue per client. For example, this chart from a recent LIMRA study illustrates significantly higher product ownership across virtually all product groups when a written plan is in place.

Product Ownership and Having a Formal Written Plan			
	Ownership Without Plan	Ownership With Plan	Ownership Increase With Plan
IRAs	60%	69%	15%
Individual Life Insurance	55%	63%	15%
Mutual Funds	52%	69%	33%
Stocks	47%	59%	26%
Money Market Mutual Funds	42%	57%	36%
Deferred Annuities	24%	34%	42%
Medicare Supplement	25%	33%	32%
Long Term Care Insurance	19%	29%	53%
Immediate Annuities	5%	12%	140%

Source: LIMRA, Advisor Impact on Retirement: Opportunity Is Knocking, 2007, (2006 survey of 3,393 pre-retirees and retirees with >$50k investable assets.)

---

103. John J. Bowen, Jr., Women Have Earned—Not Inherited Their Wealth, Financial Planning Magazine, November 1, 2006.

This classic "win-win" situation means much higher rates of implementation and cross sell, translating to greater security for female clients and higher income for the financial professional. By implementing a well thought out consultative planning approach, along with a deep understanding of the issues, financial consultants align professionalism, ethics and competencies with behavior. The process encourages confidence and inspires trust on behalf of female clients, and in doing so, increases the consultant's earnings.

What Is the Consultative Planning Process?

The consultative planning process described in this book is a broadly used approach. As we shall see in Chapter 3, while there are minor variations between financial planning, risk management planning and consultative planning, all possess essentially the same process steps:

- identify the goal (or in some cases, risk exposure)
- gather information on current state
- analyze gap between current and desired state
- develop strategies and tactics to address gap
- implement strategies and tactics
- monitor strategic and tactical effectiveness

When processes are both consistent with client expectations and operate smoothly, both client satisfaction and profitability increase. Many financial consultants are pulled in so many different directions that they may not pay attention to how process efficiencies also improve their net profitability.

Having an appreciation for and grasp of process can enormously benefit financial professionals, in consultative planning and in how they run their businesses. Here is a useful definition of process and its role in driving client satisfaction:

What Is a Process?

Almost everything companies do involves a process. A process is any activity or group of activities that takes an input, adds value to it, and provides an output to an internal or external customer.

Companies, regardless of their size, utilize thousands of processes every day to create their products and services.

The profitability of banks, insurance companies, brokerage firms, and the like [e.g., financial professionals] depends primarily on the quality of their process...companies profit only when the quality of their process meets or exceeds their customers' expectations.[104]

It is important to recognize that consultative planning is a "process within a process." The bigger process picture relates to the total prospect/client experience, beginning with marketing. Clients start out as prospects. Steps one and two, depicted below, represent marketing activities that generate prospects and move them toward a consultative, client-focused relationship. Steps three through eight are the consultive planning elements of the process. Here is a high level diagram of the fully integrated marketing/planning process:

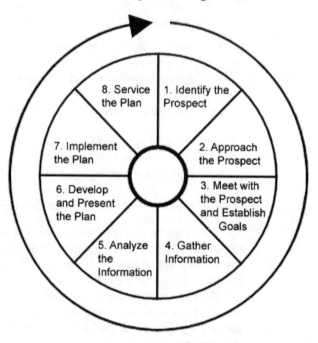

The diagram illustrates the integrated marketing/planning process as a continuous circle, reflective of the continuous working relationship with prospects and clients to help them achieve goals and manage risks.

Since it can be helpful to not only visualize what the steps are, but also what one hopes to accomplish along the way, the following chart depicts a "rolled out" illustration of the marketing/planning process, along with the specific objectives associated with each step.

---

104. Mikel Harr, PhD and Richard Schoeder, *The Breakthrough Management Strategy*, New York, NY: Doubleday, 2005, 12.

The Marketing/Planning Process							
Identify the Prospect	**Approach the Prospect**	**Meet with the Prospect and Establish Goals**	**Gather Information**	**Analyze the Information**	**Develop and Present the Plan**	**Implement the Plan**	**Service the Plan**
• Build awareness among female niche market members. • Generate high potential leads.	• Begin the trust relationship. • Prospect sees the benefit of meeting you.	• Reinforce trust. • Transform the relationship from prospect to client. • Disclose compensation, referrals and mutual expectations. • Client sees benefit of working with you.	• Fulfill ethical and suitability requirements. • Begin thinking through possible options, pros/cons to meet clients' best interest.	• Determine and quantify magnitudes of risk, goal funding gaps. • Identify strategic and tactical alternatives for risk and investment management.	• Reinforce trust. • Review and educate client on both strategic and tactical options. • Gain commitment to action and mutual accountabilities.	• Reinforce trust. • Take action to manage risks and achieve goals.	• Reinforce trust. • Adjust plan/actions as indicated. • Increase client satisfaction, commitment, and loyalty. • Build cross-sell opportunities.

(Objective)

In coming chapters, we explore the details of the marketing/planning process and how financial consultants can improve their effectiveness in each step when working with female prospects and clients.

CHAPTER SUMMARY

The women's market is a paradox, presenting both opportunities and challenges for female clients and their trusted financial consultants. The future is bright, but also fraught with risk for many women. As such, there is an unprecedented need for trustworthy financial professionals.

For financial consultants, there is limitless marketing and business potential for those who demonstrate integrity and competent behavior through a consistent client-focused approach. In the chapters that follow, we examine how to create and implement successful marketing plans that generate high quality female prospects. Our exploration also covers how to improve consulting skills that enable more effective working relationships with female clients; which, in turn, generates more revenue for the consultant. Last, we explore the importance of extraordinary client service along with industry best practices for financial consultants to implement.

In Chapter 2, we extend our discussion of the marketing aspect of the client experience, including how to:

- identify female prospects aligned with the consultant's skills, interests, and expertise

- build a value proposition and messages that appeal to a chosen target audience

- create and implement a media plan to build awareness among a chosen target audience

- generate prospect leads among individuals who are most likely to become clients

- build and sustain an effective marketing activity plan

Chapter 3 explores in detail the consultative planning process and its benefits for female clients in particular. We also study the key elements of effective communication and behavior when working with female prospects and clients. In other words, treating them the way they want to be treated in order to build strong and effective relationships. We conclude our discussion of the marketing/planning process in Chapter 8, which addresses how to monitor their progress toward meeting goals protection needs, while providing excellent service.

In the middle sections of the book, we look at women, their risks, challenges and opportunities associated with the six areas of financial planning:

- financial position

- taxes

- protection planning

- investing

- retirement

- estates and legacy

An Ant's Life
"Proverbs 6:6-8 talks about the ant, "which having no chief, overseer, or ruler, provides her food in the summer and gathers her supplies in the harvest." You need to be like the ant. You need to be a person who is self-motivated and self-disciplined; who does what is right because it is right, not because someone may be looking or because someone is making you do it."
Source: Meyer, Joyce, *Ending Your Day Right*, Copyright © 2004 by Joyce Meyer, Time Warner Book Group

CHAPTER 1 RESOURCES

- Courses from The American College
    - CE 126 Ethics for Certified Financial Planner Designees
    - FA 290 Ethics for the Financial Service Professional
    - GS 831 Ethics and Human Values
    - FA 262 Foundations of Financial Planning—An Overview

- HS 300 Financial Planning—Process and Environment

2

The "Women's Market" and Your Marketing "MAP"

Learning Objectives
An understanding of the material in this chapter should enable the student to

2-1. Define the term "marketing" and how it is different from "sales."

2-2. Explain how marketing for financial consultants differs from marketing for financial companies.

2-3. Characterize the five common life stage segments of the women's market.

2-4. Describe niche marketing—what it is, how it benefits financial consultants, and how they can identify niches to target in the women's market.

2-5. Describe the elements of a niche communications strategy, including message and media.

2-6. Outline the elements of a marketing activity plan in terms of new client acquisition and lead generation.

INTRODUCTION

As we begin our discussion on marketing financial services to women, we first consider:

1. What exactly is the "women's market"?

2. How is the "women's market" different than the "men's market?"

These questions challenge the thinking of those who seek to "specialize" in the women's market. For practical marketing purposes, there is no such thing as a monolithic "women's market," or "men's market," for that matter. While most women, just as most men, share some broadly common characteristics; as a group, they possess a vast range of diversity in life stages, lifestyles, culture, ethnicity, interests, and occupations. As such, marketing to the "market" is simply too broad a net to cast to be effective.

This recognition, of course, complicates things. What might be appealing to some is offensive and off-putting to others. To successfully market to any group of people, financial consultants must first understand it's unique qualities and needs. Once that is achieved, the effective professional is able to address those needs through a distinctive and compelling value proposition. The more narrowly the target is defined, the more efficient and successful marketing efforts can become.

Throughout this chapter, we explore various aspects of marketing, along with key concepts to help financial consultants become more effective in delivering value to their selected female target audiences. We also examine how to create marketing plans that drive purposeful activities.

WHAT DOES "MARKETING" MEAN?

marketing

Now that we understand what the women's market is (or perhaps more appropriately, is not), what exactly does "marketing" mean? Marketing is an often misused and misunderstood term that is sometimes confused with sales. While the two overlap in the process of distributing goods and services, for the most part, they represent separate yet complimentary disciplines. Generally speaking, marketing encompasses the following steps:

- filtering, studying and selecting target markets

- creating products and services to meet target market needs

- developing and implementing media and promotional campaigns to build awareness and entice trial (of product and/or service)

- growing competitive market share from the distribution of products and services

In some companies, especially those that manufacture and distribute consumer-packaged goods (like toothpaste and laundry detergent) marketers may also be responsible for aspects of sales performance, sometimes called "sell-through."

Marketing Products versus Marketing Services

In financial services, both marketing and selling are far more complex than with consumer-packaged goods. This greater complexity is due to both the enormous range and intangibility of financial solutions, along with their more complicated sets of benefits.

For financial professionals seeking to make a big impact in any given market segment or niche, being able to distinguish between marketing and sales is important. Further, it is essential for consultants to understand the difference between product and service marketing. Here is one marketing expert's take on the distinction between the two:

The "Women's Market" and Your Marketing "MAP" 2.3

What Makes a Service Unique?

Pop Quiz. Question: What's the First Law of Marketing?

Answer: People don't buy products, they buy solutions to problems. Looking at it this way, there is no difference between a product and a service. Both are simply vehicles for delivering solutions.

But anybody can tell you a service is not the same as a product. When you buy a service, you don't get to take something home in a box. And that fact of life brings with it a host of issues for marketers.

Services have characteristics that set them apart from products:

- **Products are tangible, services are intangible**. Buyers can't see, feel, smell, hear or taste services before they agree to buy it. When they purchase services they have to purchase a "promise" of satisfaction, and that requires a leap of faith that purchasing a product does not.

- **Services can't be separated from their providers**. To buy a service, you must come in contact with the one who provides it…The degree to which inseparability matters varies from offering to offering. But the fact that we see services as inseparable from their providers affects you in a fundamental way.

- **Services are perishable**. Services provided by people can't be stored. Suppose you're a dentist, and you're expecting a patient at 10 o'clock. When the patient blows you off, it's too late to sell 10 o'clock to someone else. Your service is not like a product that will sit on the shelf, waiting for a buyer.

Source: "What Makes a Service Unique?" from *The Complete Idiot's Guide To Marketing*, 2/E by Sarah White, copyright (c) 1997, 2003 by CWL Publishing. Used by permission of Alpha Books, an imprint of Penguin Group (USA) Inc.

For our purposes, marketing covers everything up to that point in time when the prospect first meets with the financial consultant and agrees to take the next step (i.e., pursue a business relationship). This agreement implies that the prospective client values the consultant's expertise and advice. After securing her consent to move forward, the relationship then shifts from marketing to consultative planning. As such, marketing has to do the first two steps of the consolidated process we discussed in Chapter 1: identifying and approaching the prospect. The table below provides perspective of both process steps and their corresponding objectives.

Women and Money

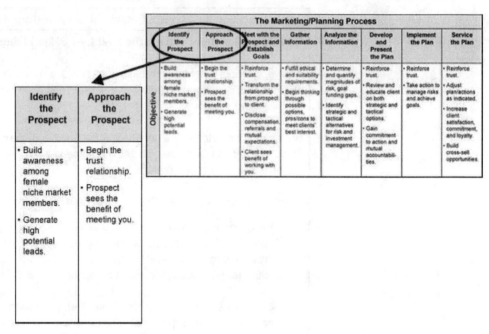

The objectives of these two initial phases in the marketing process are to build awareness, generate high quality prospect leads, meet with prospects to establish trust and ultimately, convert those prospects to clients. The steps for financial consultants (and their team) who support these phases are to

- understand the "big picture" of the market and its primary segments

- evaluate the current and desired business model of the financial consultant, relative to competitive position, environment and points of leverage

- research and identify possible niches and target audiences

- create messages and media plans that resonate with chosen target audiences

- implement media plans and marketing activities to generate awareness and leads

- monitor success and adjust as needed

Marketing for Financial Service Firms versus Practitioners

As we discuss the steps and range of activities required for marketing effectiveness, it will be helpful to draw important distinctions between how financial services companies and financial professionals approach marketing. Though related, they are distinctively different.

Companies in the financial services industry typically market at the life-stage segment level. Their marketing activities not only include life-stage research, product design, development and delivery, but also advertising and promotional campaigns. The goal is to appeal to the specific needs and aspirations of the targeted segment.

Manufacturers and marketers of financial products depend on the size and success of their distribution network to generate revenue. While there are some boutique product developers and distributors in the financial services industry, they are the exception. Financial products are generally designed for mass appeal and volume potential so that they generate adequate return on investment and earnings. Product revenue and profitability of mass marketers hinge on volume; the higher the better.

Most financial services companies have resources to fund at least some mass media presence (e.g., printed newspapers, magazines) in order to generate brand awareness. In addition, companies often have sophisticated websites with robust client inquiry, client service, and representative interface. As such, product revenues and product margins must be adequate to support marketing activities on a large scale.

product specialists

people generalists

To achieve sufficient product volume, marketing departments continually research important segment trends in order to align their current and future offerings. These marketers seek to distinguish themselves at the product level, which translates to competitive features and price differentiators. The more broadly products can be distributed through the sales organization/channels, the greater the scale (volume) of customers that can be reached. Product and service offerings can then be geared toward relatively broad needs, as well as groups of people with minimal customization. In other words, most financial services companies are *product specialists* and *people generalists*.

product generalists

people specialists

By contrast, financial consultants are *product generalists* and *people specialists*. Individuals, or even teams of financial professionals, do not have the same marketing resources as their affiliate companies. Competitive product features of quality and price are "like good hygiene," according to financial services marketing expert, Matt Oeschli.[105] Potential consumers view these product features as bare minimum standards, what some call a "cost of entry." Put another way, the public expects nothing less than good quality products with competitive features and pricing from financial service providers.

That said, how does the trusted financial professional set him- or herself apart from the competition? Moreover, how can consultants create high impact marketing plans, increase efficiencies, lower costs, and raise client satisfaction and profitability, all at the same time? The marketing advantage that financial consultants have is the ability to know, understand and appeal to the needs of

---

105. Matt Oescheli, The Oeschli Institute, Selling the Affluent, Thrivent Presentation, October 2007.

their chosen target audience better than anyone else. They do this by breaking the market down from segments to niches.

FROM MARKET SEGMENTS TO MARKET NICHES

Unlike a mass or even segment marketing approach, financial consultants must focus their marketing efforts more finitely in order to maximize their value proposition, competitiveness, and return on resources invested. As a practical matter, paying for sufficient levels of advertising, promotional and public relations efforts directed at mass or even segment audiences is far beyond the reach for most.

Beyond pure marketing economics, breaking target markets down to more manageable levels enables greater specialization and ultimately, satisfaction for the financial consultant. It takes research and self-examination to find the right fit among potential target audiences. It may even take courage to specialize in the needs that a chosen audience might have, possibly forsaking business opportunities elsewhere.

Narrowing one's focus leads to more effective marketing efforts and increased sales; as well as improved client service and back-office operations. Greater clarity and purpose in targeting markets yields greater alignment of competencies, skills and business practices. These enhancements position the financial consultant to better meet, and ideally exceed, client expectations. When expectations are consistently exceeded, clients are happy, loyal and eager to refer. Since industry research has found that women refer their financial professional more often than men do, consultants gain even greater marketing leverage.

To help zero in on possible target audiences, it is instructive to first look at the bigger picture—segments in the women's market—then consider what it means to niche market and how it is done.

Life-Stage Segments in the Women's Market

Segments

Generally speaking, while risks vary between genders across major life-stage segments, many broad financial goals and needs are alike. Industry organizations, companies and marketing experts frequently characterize life-stage segment needs in categories similar to these:

- young adults
- family and/or asset builders
- pre-retired
- early retired
- late retired

The discussion that follows provides a brief description of these five segments. The commonly shared financial needs and wants, as well as select

Starters

financial products that are frequently marketed to each segment are summarized at the conclusion of this section.

Young Adults (Starters)

This group consists of young adults (21–34) who are starting out—formulating their identities, careers, and future. For younger women, the historical norm has been to move from singlehood to wife, then mother. While this norm is unquestionably changing, many common needs, wants, and goals are still shared by this life-stage group.

Marketers refer to the majority of today's generation of starters as "Millenials," or part of "GenY." The balance of the starter group straddles over to the younger members of "GenX."[106] This stage has been referred to by some as the "quarter-life crisis." The crisis aspect refers to a period of anxiety, uncertainty, and the inner turmoil that often accompanies transition to adulthood. It is increasingly common for this generation of "20-somethings" to move back in with mom and dad, particularly in light of sour economic times and employment prospects. In addition to dealing with an adverse economic climate, there are personal growth issues and challenges to experience as well:

- The average young American changes jobs eight times before the age of 21.[107]

- The average college graduate accrues over $20,000 in education loan debt.[108]

- The average age of getting married is now 27, which is older than in previous generations.[109]

As a result of either environmentally imposed or self-generated financial challenges, sixty percent of 20-somethings feel they are facing tougher money pressures than young people did in previous generations.[110]

Not surprisingly, about 80 percent of women in this age group rate themselves as needing help in at least some areas of financial decision making. One-third indicate they need "help in many areas" or are "beginners." In addition, these younger women also are the most worried about a secure

---

106. In their 1991 book *Generations*, William Strauss and Neil Howe defined "Generation X" members as those being born between 1961 and 1981. "Millenials" or those among the "Generation Y" population are those born after 1982, according to Howe and Strauss. (Source: Wikipedia, Generation X, Generation Y, accessed 10/8/2009)
107. Alexandra Robbins and Abby Winner, *The Quarter-Life Crisis* (Bloomsbury Publishing, 2001).
108. Ibid.
109. Ibid.
110. Mindy Fetterman and Barbara Hansen, "Young People Struggle to Deal with the Kiss of Debt, NEFE Poll," *USA Today*, 2006.

financial future versus other generations. Where do female starters turn for financial information? Friends/family and the internet are their top two preferred resources, with financial advisors ranked third.[111]

Family and/or Asset (Builders)

Builders

Family and/or asset builders (35–49) are moving into their prime earning years. Many have established at least base (and frequently inadequate) levels of cash reserves, insurance protection and retirement funding. For those with children, establishing education plans and/or funds often come into play. With dual careers and income, taxes may also become a growing concern. Due to expanding economic contributions and responsibilities to their families, many Americans, especially women, are significantly under planned, under insured and under saved at this life-stage, as we shall see in coming chapters.

Builders often find themselves juggling the multiple priorities of family, professional and personal responsibilities. Time can be a precious and rare commodity. As noted in Chapter 1, most women in this stage are at work, both outside and inside the home. For many—married, partnered, or single—there may be tween or teen children in the picture. As such, financial planning by women in this phase of life is often relegated to a lower priority.

In "marketing speak," the majority of today's builder segment are the more seasoned members of GenX. According to research by Prudential, GenX women are somewhat more concerned than other age groups about survivor needs. Three in four (76 percent) female GenXers rated "being financially secure if I outlived my spouse" as "very important." (As perspective, the same response was shared among 66 percent of GenY/Millenials, 72 percent of Boomers, and 68 percent of Matures).[112]

Women in this stage of life are also comfortable using technology to research their financial options. In fact, the most preferred source for GenX females is the internet (67 percent), followed by friends/family (61 percent), and a financial advisor (58 percent.)[113]

Preretired (Maximizers)

Maximizers

As is the case with women in the builder age group, pre-retireds (50–64) may also be pressed for time. However, by now their concerns may shift to maximizing asset building with a heightened focus on retirement. In addition, education funding at this life stage usually has to do with actually paying for versus saving for college. Preretireds in general, and women in this group in particular, may be part of the "sandwich generation," squeezed between attending to the needs of both their child/ren and aging parent(s).

---

111. 2008–2009 Prudential Study on the Financial Experience and Behaviors Among Women.
112. Ibid.
113. Ibid.

Financial issues, planning, strategies and solutions typically become both more lucrative and complex when working with clients in this segment. Preretirement years are among the highest earning years for both men and women. In addition, intergenerational wealth preservation and transfer issues are often dealt with at this stage, as parents' declining health and death are common events. These conditions increase the likelihood that income tax, transfer taxes (e.g., capital gains, estate), retirement and (possibly) education funding may all need to be simultaneously addressed by the client and the consultant. Last, it is during this phase of life that long-term care planning can be its most effective and proactive.

Those representing the largest proportion of this group are known as Baby Boomers. More than any other stage of life, these women prefer to get their financial information from an advisor (62 percent for Boomers versus 58 percent for GenX; 55 percent for Mature; and 46 percent for Millenial).[114]

As the fallout from the worldwide economic crisis continues, and even after its end, many Boomer women will find their financial situation has become increasingly complex, particularly when preparing to secure lifelong income in a just few short years. In light of these circumstances it is reasonable to expect that even more of these women will turn to knowledgeable and trusted financial consultants than ever before.

Early Retired (Preservers)

Preservers

Adverse economic conditions have also affected a large percentage of women in their early retirement years, known as preservers or Matures (ages 64–79). On average, retirement portfolios diminished between 30-40 percent in 2008 and early 2009. Since individuals in this stage tend to be the most concerned about preserving their assets and income for the remainder of their lives, many may need to reevaluate both their circumstances and lifestyles. Lifestyle adjustments may also be necessary due to increasing health problems and long-term care needs.

While these women are less reliant on financial professionals than maximizers; as a group, they are still receptive to financial advice. Slightly more than half of preservers (or Matures) seek out financial information from a professional advisor. In addition, compared to younger groups, preservers respond more favorably to receiving financial information via marketing materials (40 percent) and seminars (32 percent).[115] These preferences can yield more favorable response rates and return on investment for direct mail and seminar marketing efforts than for younger age groups.

---

114. Ibid.
115. Ibid.

Elders

Later Retired (Elders)

The elder life stage (80+) has rarely been a targeted market segment for financial services. Until recently, there was not much of a segment to speak of. It was not so long ago that reaching the age of 80 was heralded as a remarkable achievement. A great deal has changed since them. Advancements in longevity have significantly influenced not only the growth, but also the quality of life for this age group. Elders today are living both longer and better. We see more "youthful" and active elders than ever before.

There are more than nine million individuals in the United States who are 80 years of age or older. With advancements in medical research and treatments, ongoing increases in longevity are expected to further grow the ranks of octogenarians. According to the United Nations report on populations around the globe, the 80-plus age group is the fastest growing in the United States and the world.[116] Since women tend to outlive men, they represent the significant majority of this expanding segment.

Women over 80 may also be concerned about adequate income for the rest of their lives. For some elders and members of their families, an increasing need for help with the activities of daily living often emerges. Creating a plan for passing on not only assets, but also values to family members becomes a high priority to many.

Since financial planning for elders may entail difficult choices about one's legacy, income and asset distribution, as well as health and long term care issues; significant expertise is often required. For consultants seeking to specialize in advising elders, working towards an advanced designation (e.g., Chartered Advisor in Senior Living or CASL®) is worth considering. Financial professionals are encouraged to carefully research senior speciality designations, seeking out those that originate from accredited colleges and institutions and require significant study/testing. It is important to note that Congress has raised significant concern over the preponderance and abuses of designations that are easily obtained. In particular, the greatest area of concern and scrutiny relates to those designations/designees dealing with seniors.

Life-Stage Segmentation Summary

The chart that follows provides an overview of life-stage segments and the financial needs/goals that women frequently share. While by no means a complete listing, this chart provides a snapshot of commonly held needs, wants, and goals, along with possible financial solutions often targeted at respective life-stage groups.

---

116. Population Division, DESA, United Nations, "World Population Aging 1950–2050," www.un.org/esa/population/publications/worldageing19502050/pdf/90chateriv.pdf

Stage	Age Group	Common Life Needs, Wants, and Goals	Common Products and Services*
Young adulthood (Starters)	21–34	• Stabilizing cash flow, reserves, and debt • Paying off college loans • Protecting decades-long income and survivor needs • Protecting investment value • Growing assets for special purpose/s (e.g., home, education) • Establishing retirement funds with employer • Smooth asset transfer	• Banking, credit, budgeting software • Disability income, level term life, property/casualty • Mutual funds, bank products • Employer-sponsored qualified plans • Basic asset titling, wills/trusts
Family and/or Asset (Builders)	35–49	• Improving/maintaining financial position • Protecting income and expanding asset pool • Reducing tax bite • Expanding/managing retirement funds • Figuring out how to pay for college • Smooth asset transfer and care for dependents	• Banking, credit management • Disability income, cash value life insurance products (e.g., universal, variable universal, whole life), liability protection • Employer-sponsored qualified plans, annuities, IRAs • 529 plans, Education IRA, Coverdells, Roth IRAs
Pre-Retired (Maximizers)	50–64	• Maximizing income and retirement plan contributions • Reducing tax bite • Dependent parents • Some concern about long-term health care • Dependent children • Smooth asset transfer and contingencies for parent and/or children wealth management	• Employer-sponsored qualified plans, annuities, IRAs • Municipal bonds, tax credit passive investments, inside build-up of life insurance cash value, Roth IRAs, liability protection • Financial aid for children's college education • Care-giving (home health aide) • Long-term care insurance
Early Retired (Preservers)	65–79	• Wanting to enjoy life • Wanting to enjoy grandchildren • Minimizing expenses and taxes • Staying healthy • Living and leaving a legacy • Smooth transfer of assets to family	• Retirement income distribution, annuities, wealth management, modified endowment contract (MEC) life insurance • Tax management • Health and wellness programs, Medicare supplements • Estate planning
Late Retired (Elders)	80+	• Quality of life, lived with dignity • Independence, if possible • Health care needs and costs • Passing values and wisdom • Smooth transfer of assets to family	• Life income annuities • Elder care law • Independent, assisted, nursing care • Estate planning • Philanthropy

*Note: "Common" reflects a marketing approach, which by its nature, is relatively general at the life-stage segmentation level. Since client needs are unique, a more tailored, needs-driven approach is warranted.

Carving Niches In The Women's Market

Having journeyed through the life-stage segments, we are now ready to examine the *what*, *why* and *how* associated with niche marketing. By far, the most common and costly marketing mistake made by financial professionals is trying to be *all things to all people*. Successful consultants find that it is far better to ultimately become *all things (financial) to some people*.

This becoming *all things* carries with it the responsibilities and privileges of being indispensable, or essential, central, vital, necessary, requisite and key. The indispensable financial consultant is the very first person that a client will think of when it comes to money management, financial planning, investing, and protecting wealth. Being necessary, however, does not mean being the exclusive provider of financial solutions. Rather, it means acting as a resource broker—organizing and integrating the breadth of financial solutions that the client might need. To borrow a medical analogy, indispensability is comparable to being the patient's primary care provider.

In their landmark and controversial white paper, The Future of the Financial Advisory Business, Part II, the money management firm, Undiscovered Managers, presented an intriguing dissertation about this concept of being indispensable. They liken it to being a gatekeeper.[117] As background, the purpose of the white paper was to provide financial professionals with insight and strategies in order to become successful niche competitors. Their hypothesis was that, out of both opportunity and necessity, financial professionals needed to more quickly and effectively increase their competitive edge because of growing pressures in the marketplace. They predicted that two types of financial service professionals would emerge as the most viable and profitable competitors in the future: *vendors* and *gatekeepers*.

Before identifying one or more female target audiences, the consultant must first analyze his or her current business and make an important and fundamental choice: vendor or gatekeeper? Either is a completely valid and viable approach to business. However, the implications of that choice are profoundly important, as they affect how consultants build their competencies, go to market and run their business operations.

Vendors

In essence, vendors seek to be *some things to many people* by focusing more narrowly on a limited set of products, expertise, and/or services. Their marketing plans frequently target broad market segments, versus smaller niche groups. When targeting a segment or mass audience, building awareness is both more challenging and expensive. Generating enough impressions (i.e., number of times a message is delivered to a target audience) and cutting through the media clutter to create awareness within a large group of people can be very

---

117. "The Future of the Financial Advisory Business Part II: Strategies for Small Businesses, Research Report, Undiscovered Managers", September 2000.

costly. Measuring the success (or failure) of resources spent marketing to a broader audience is also more difficult.

An important characteristic of the vendor's business model is *scale*, or *volume*. Operations need to be "scale-able" to be efficient, meaning operational systems and processes must be able to handle large and growing volumes of business. Their business practices also need to be highly streamlined, repeatable, and error-free in order to sustain client satisfaction and profitability.

Vendors work with *customers*. To succeed in the long term, vendors must create the infrastructure necessary to deliver superior customer service at lower cost than their competition. In other words, vendors are product specialists and people generalists. Undiscovered Managers portrayed vendors this way:

> "The role of the vendor can be profitable, but it is very different from a [niche competitor]. Vendors have no control of their pricing and hence, they must be a low cost producer of their service or product to survive. They also function largely like a utility—simply providing a service and having no sustainable relationships with clients. Their profitability is tied to volume and their services are focused on *one specialty*. Should another specialty organization be able to deliver the same service at a lower price, the vendor's survival would be imperiled."[118]

Gatekeepers

gatekeepers

clients

By contrast, gatekeepers endeavor to be all things to some (select) people through a value-added, problem solving approach. This direction enables the professional to purposefully and methodically move toward becoming the indispensible provider of financial solutions. According to Undiscovered Managers, "taking a *holistic approach* to advice, addressing all of the client's problems, will make the [consultant] a critical gatekeeper."[119]

Gatekeepers work with *clients* versus customers. They focus on *rate* versus *volume* of business, often by working with fewer clients. This means they typically generate significantly more business per client than vendors. In addition, gatekeepers are highly effective niche marketers. Finding niche positions enables financial consultants to channel their expertise and passions, as well as to continuously improve their value proposition.

Gatekeepers not only achieve tremendous marketing efficiencies, but they also strive to become indispensible to their preferred clients. Perhaps one of the greatest benefits of becoming a gatekeeper is the satisfaction it brings when one works with clients who might be called "ideal" clients. What are some characteristics of ideal clients, regardless of gender, earnings or net worth?

---

118. "The Future of the Financial Advisory Business Part II: Strategies for Small Businesses, Undiscovered Managers, Research Report", September 2000.
119. Ibid.

- First, there is mutual trust. It is important to remember that trust is a two-way street. The client not only trusts the financial consultant, but the financial consultant also trusts the client. In this litigious age, some clients create not only liability exposures, but also risks to one's reputation and standing in the community.

- They respect the financial consultant as a professional. They recognize the right of the financial professional to receive adequate compensation for the value of competent, trustworthy advice and time spent on their case.

- They value the consultant's expertise and financial planning capabilities.

- They gladly refer family, friends and colleagues.

- They increasingly place more trust in the consultant's abilities, and conduct more business with the consultant as a result.

While all gatekeepers are niche marketers; vendors can also benefit from understanding and incorporating some of the same marketing techniques we discuss in the following sections.

Why Niche Market?

In the "Information Age," most Americans are confronted with a relentless barrage of excessive and often conflicting information, choices, decisions and tasks. Information overload is acutely felt by many women, especially those who must work outside the home, and also care for their spouses, children, and/or parents. As a result, many women feel stymied, unable or unwilling to take action to improve their financial situation.

Niche marketing can help consultants break through information overload and inertia to become the financial professional of choice for a specific community of individuals. Carving a niche yield these specific benefits as well:

- It creates competitive advantage as a result of becoming the unrivaled financial expert in the niche members' needs and concerns.

- It allows for greater message awareness and impact, stemming from communications tailored to meet the needs of the niche.

- It enables more efficient use of marketing dollars and efforts, thus adding more to the bottom line.

- It builds a firmer foundation of trust, and therefore, a referral base created within a niche community.

Becoming a successful niche marketer means dominating the environment in which one competes. As marketing experts Jack Trout and Al Ries put it: "…find something to be first in. It's better to be a big fish in a small pond (and increase the size of the pond) than to be a small fish in a big pond."[120]

What Is Niche Marketing?

niche marketing

It takes knowledge, time, energy, vision and commitment to narrowly define and successfully pursue a niche market. However, the rewards—both short term and especially long term—are well worth the effort.

How do successful gatekeepers and niche marketers get that way? Undiscovered Managers found there were six traits commonly held among successful niche competitors.[121] Understanding these traits and their application to the financial consultant's own business practices can be both instructive and illuminating. Here is an overview:

Six Traits Common to Successful Niche Competitors

1. **Perception That Their Products Are Essential:** Clients perceive successful niche companies' goods and services as essential. Generic alternatives will not suffice.
2. **Continual Improvement of Quality and Perception of Products:** The basis of all niche strategies is that clients will pay premium prices for niche competitors' products and services that they perceive as superior.
3. **Ability to Anticipate Clients' Future Needs:** As situations inevitably change over time, anticipating the future needs of clients can be particularly challenging because financial consultants must identify their clients' most complex future problems and develop the capability to solve them.
4. **Operate Efficiently:** Although niche companies target a select group of clients, they still may face strong competition. Successful niche companies are very efficient; with strong cost controls. They continually improve their operating efficiency to lower operating costs and, in turn, boost margins.
5. **Possess Adequate Scale:** Although relatively small, niche companies possess the necessary scale to be profitable. In order to make money, they must spread fixed operating costs across a sufficient base of revenues. Consequently, there are minimum scale requirements for niche competitors to prosper.
6. **Dominant Market Share Within the Niche:** Market share is also an important factor to long-term profitability of niche competitors. Organizations that are able to capture and maintain a large part of a niche market for a specific product or service will have a significant and potentially sustainable competitive advantage.

Source: The Future of the Financial Advisory Business Part II: Strategies for Small Businesses, Undiscovered Managers, Research Report, September 2000 (www.jpmorganfunds.com).

---

120. Al Ries and Jack Trout, *Positioning: The Battle for Your Mind.* New York, NY: McGraw-Hill, 2001.
121. "The Future of the Financial Advisory Business Part II: Strategies for Small Businesses, Undiscovered Managers, Research Report," September 2000.

Identifying Niche Markets

When determining a niche in the women's market, it is necessary to identify groups with shared interests that might also translate to common financial needs. In order to maximize marketing effectiveness, selecting a niche market that has a built-in communications network, is perhaps even more important.

Shared Interests. Ideally, the chosen niche will share some of the same interests, concerns and passions that the financial consultant has. It is both more authentic and enjoyable to target an audience with whom one has a natural affinity. In addition, selected niche financial needs should align with skills and competencies already possessed by the financial consultant, as well as those he or she seeks to develop.

Most often, niche groups combine several segmentation variables, such as lifestyle, life-stage, culture and/or interests. Lifestyle choices or circumstances generally fall along marital status and occupational lines. There are niche organizations that cater to single, divorced and widowed individuals, as well as a large number of professional interests. Since careers and work outside the home generally consume more than one-third of an individual's waking hours each year, a significant aspect of self-identification is tied to one's work life. As such, it is common for individuals who share similar occupations to participate in professional affiliations, as well as have similar financial attitudes, sophistication and wherewithal. The example that follows reflects a niche that combines a life-stage variable (i.e., motherhood) with occupational interest.

Example

Adam is interested in working with professional women. His wife, Lisa is a marketing director for a large local company. Adam has actively supported her career, including putting her through graduate school.

Adam has found that among his best clients are several female executives. Through their feedback, he has learned that these clients have enjoyed working with him, and appreciated his help in putting together a plan to achieve their goals and address protection needs. His organized approach saved them time in pulling together information, researching alternative product solutions and taking action on their plan.

At this stage in his financial services career, Adam has developed the expertise, skills, and product array to appeal to families with children. This combination of interests and expertise leads him to consider targeting professional women who are also mothers.

Through his research, Adam discovers an organization called Executive Moms in Touch (fictitious name) with a local chapter/presence whose members match his ideal profile. He also learns that there are no major competitors working with this group and that they have a built-in communications network of regular meetings and a newsletter.

To get things started, Adam contacts the chapter president, describes his background and objectives, and sets up a meeting to explore the possibilities of working with the local Executive Moms in Touch organization.

Shared Communications Networks. Why is having a shared communications network a key, if not primary, criterion in selecting a niche? It is simply that a shared communications network provides an efficient platform for the financial consultant to build awareness through systematically promoting her or his message.

It may be helpful to think of a communications network as a system of different media. Large marketers strategically develop media plans and purchase media (e.g., television, print, radio, website, direct mail) to improve consumer familiarity with and appreciation for their products. Niche marketers do the same thing, but on a smaller and far more cost-effective scale.

Shared communications networks enable the development and implementation of a niche media plan directed towards a desired audience. Examples of niche media include an organization's website, newsletters and meetings. As with any effort, marketing or otherwise, the financial consultant must first seek permission from decision maker(s) within the organization before taking action.

Creating Niches through Social Networking

social networking

Today, it is entirely conceivable that financial consultants could create their own shared networks and niche markets. We are witnessing a revolution in community building take place right before our eyes. The popularity and broad expansion of sites like Twitter, Facebook, MySpace, and LinkedIn create new opportunities through social networking. These new tools make it possible for individuals and groups to form their own networks or "tribes," as marketing guru Seth Godin, author of *Permission Marketing*, calls them.[122]

Within the life insurance producer community, a recent article in the "Million Dollar Round Table" (MDRT) magazine summarized these best practice opportunities for social networking:

---

122. Seth Godin, Tribes: We Need You to Lead Us, Penguin Group, New York, NY, 2008.

More than Socializing
Social networking builds connections with prospective clients and referral sources.
Social networking isn't just for kids. Fifty-eight million Baby Boomers are joining social networks like MySpace, Twitter, Facebook, and LinkedIn to connect and learn more about their friends and business associates. What many might not realize, however, is that with the right approach, these networking sites can be a great resource to interact with current and prospective clients. Adding clients, referral sources, and colleagues to your online social network is the first step. You can use these sites to see who they associate with, and if they are connected to anyone you are seeking to do business with. David E. Appel, CLU®, ChFC®, a 13-year MDRT member from Newton, Massachusetts, told Round the Table magazine that he uses LinkedIn as a means to gain the trust of potential new clients. "If I get a referral from someone, I use LinkedIn to see if we have anything in common," Appel said. "I also use it to back up referrals that I've already been given by mentioning the names of the connections when I call. If I can help potential new clients realize there are more connections with whom to check on me, I think it builds a level of trust." **Connect through groups:** Facebook, MySpace, and LinkedIn enable you to join groups based on your professional interests, which can assist you in making online connections. Joining online groups related to professional organizations can offer benefits, as well. **Promote your business:** Social networking sites increase the ability to share information. As a financial advisor, you can use these sites to offer yourself as a resource and promote your business, but each site requires a different approach. Twitter is especially useful for displaying your knowledge through expertise. Although the posts are limited to 140 characters, some people use this space to write about a specific interest and link to articles about the subject. The most professional of social networking sites, LinkedIn, offers the opportunity to post discussion topics and answer other people's questions. By answering a question, you can display your expertise and possibly connect with a new client. LinkedIn users can also seek recommendations from people with whom they've done business. These recommendations are displayed on the LinkedIn profile. Having a large number of recommendations helps other users to perceive you as a trustworthy professional. MySpace pages include an embedded blog. You can use this blog to write about different financial trends you see in the industry and just give general advice. Broadcasting your knowledge makes it more likely that a prospect will consider doing business with you in the future. Appel lists his company location and specialties on his Facebook profile. He also uploads photographs from conferences he attends and his speaking engagements. Connecting with the people you already know on Twitter, MySpace, Facebook, and LinkedIn is easy. If you take the right approach, these connections could easily lead to new business prospects.
Source: April Samuelson, "More than Socializing," MDRT Magazine, May/June 2009.

Caveat: Social networking has created new challenges for many a compliance officer. Since use of these sites may create regulatory and compliance issues (i.e., consideration as advertising), financial consultants are advised to check with their affiliate company to determine guidelines/permission for use.

Selecting and Targeting Niches

Identifying and selecting a female target audience requires both self-assessment and market research. As with any business-related planning process, financial consultants and their teams need to reflect first on the current state of their business, and the environment in which they operate. The focus then shifts to researching market opportunities (for our purposes, possible niches) that may represent a good fit.

S.W.O.T. Analysis

Conducting a S.W.O.T. Analysis. Throughout the self-assessment phase, it is essential to look with a critical eye at the consultant's and/or team's strengths and weaknesses. It is also important to identify competitive and environmental threats or opportunities that may derail or enhance marketing efforts. To facilitate the process of self-assessment, marketers often use a "S.W.O.T." analysis. This simple, but useful, tool helps identify the Strengths, Weaknesses, Opportunities, and Threats of an individual's or team's business. Essentially, a S.W.O.T. analysis represents an environmental scan for the financial consultant, looking at both internal (strengths and weaknesses) and external environments (opportunities and threats). The following steps are followed when performing a S.W.O.T. assessment:

1. **Evaluate the team's or consultant's practice, including individual interests, skills and expertise**. Identify positives, along with areas needing improvement. Add identified qualities in the strengths/weaknesses boxes. Throughout this task, it is helpful to create a complete inventory of personal passions, interests, hobbies, belief systems, talent, societal concerns and affinity organizations for all individuals. The inventory can be helpful in identifying possible niche interests and/or organizations to investigate further.

2. **Add environmental factors that present market opportunities or threats**. Opportunities might include identified organizations, institutions or affiliations where the consultant or team could leverage strengths. They might also be present in favorable marketing conditions (e.g., lack of competition in a select market, special needs of a niche market which are largely unmet). Conversely, the consultant (and team) will also want to determine what elements, or threats, have the potential to sabotage or slow down marketing effectiveness (e.g., successful competitor present, adverse regulatory environment and/or tax legislation).

3. **After completing the S.W.O.T. analysis, identify conclusions and their implications for the business**. What are the distinctive interests and competencies that the consultant and/or team possesses? What weaknesses need to be addressed? Where are there opportunities to leverage skills, expertise and marketing efforts? What possible niche

markets have already been identified? What threats need to be guarded against or minimized?

Example

Below is a sample S.W.O.T. analysis for a three-person team of financial professionals; Adam, Maya, and Scott. After completion of the analysis, which also included assessing niche market opportunities, the team decides to focus part of their energies on targeting professional working mothers. Through their research of related niche organizations, they agree to start this initiative through building a strong working relationship with the local leadership and chapter of Executive Moms in Touch.

Completing a S.W.O.T analysis can take anywhere from a few minutes to several hours. Regardless of the amount of time one spends completing it, a S.W.O.T. helps crystallize the environmental framework for the financial consultant's practice. This important step also sets the stage for a more grounded and purposeful marketing strategy.

Internal Environment—Our Team	
Strengths	**Weaknesses**

• three professionals, one administrative assistant
• one CLU®, one ChFC®, one CPCU
• combined years of experience: 14
• community involvement:
    – Adam – Sunrise Rotary
    – Maya – Executive Moms in Touch
    – Scott – Habitat for Humanity
• existing core competencies
    – risk management, education and retirement planning for young families
    – property and casualty insurance
    – life and disability insurances
    – annuities
• We have organized planning processes, which generate positive client feedback and repeat business.
	• We are relatively young and still growing in experience.
	• We have insufficient cash flow to do all we could and should.
	• Our business model may not apply well to some clients/customers.
	• Our operational processes are not as efficient as we'd like.
	• While keeping our core clients happy, we must aggressively grow the business to achieve our goals.
	• We are not wealth management/investment, tax or legal experts.

External Environment – Economy, Competition, Regulators, Markets	
Opportunities	**Threats**
• Growth of markets (e.g., women's market) and segments (e.g., starters and builders) present both short- and long-term opportunities. • Attractive niche markets (e.g., local, working professional moms) are aligned with our vision, uniqueness, and areas of specialization. • Legislative environment (rising taxes) will likely add complexity to clients' lives and we will be there to help them.	• Misdeeds and mismanagement by others in the financial services, challenging our reputations. • Ongoing adverse market conditions, distract our focus and reduce our productive capacity. • Regulatory environment is likely to change dramatically, requiring education and adaptation.

Finding a Niche

How does one go about finding a niche that has high potential to align business practices, skills and competencies with? By completing the environmental scan (i.e., S.W.O.T. analysis), the consultant may identify specific niche markets to research further. If that is not the case, then one can look to his or her client base, or natural market, for possible niche organizations.

For those financial professionals with a few years of experience in the business and a reasonably well-developed client base (e.g., over 200 households), a useful starting point can be identifying female clients who fit into their vision of ideal. What stage of life are they in? What is their lifestyle? What kind of work do they do? What interests do they have? What organizations do they belong to? Who do they know? Are they willing to help? Are there commonalities they share that might point to an affinity group?

If the financial consultant is new to the business and has fewer clients, he or she may ask the same questions of natural market members—those female acquaintances, colleagues, family and friends that represent what the consultant considers to be an ideal client.

Finding the right niche can be a process of trial and error. There are two basic research phases in this process: (1) identifying and investigating women's organizations in the community or within marketing/service reach; and (2) conducting informational interviews with key members of possible target groups.

women's organizations

Researching Women's Organizations. By going through the client and/or natural market lists, the financial consultant may find possible niche groups; or, one may be starting with a blank slate. Either way, the consultant and/or a team member will likely need to spend time researching those women's organizations that hold out promise as possible niche audiences. The goal is to identify three to five possibilities that one will want to explore further through informational interviews.

An enormous range of women's organizations exist, representing communities who share similar interests and offer excellent niche marketing opportunities for financial consultants. As perspective, here are categories of women's organizations classified by the Gale Directory, a global leader in cataloguing companies and associations:

- athletic and sports
- chambers of commerce trade, and tourism
- cultural interests
- educational pursuits
- engineering, technological, natural and social sciences
- environment and agricultural
- fraternal, nationality and ethnic
- greek and non-greek letter societies, associations, and federations
- health and medical organizations
- hobbies and avocations
- labor unions, associations and federations
- legal, governmental, public administration, military
- public affairs
- religious
- social welfare
- trade, business, and commercial
- veterans, hereditary and patriotic

Source: Gale Directory Library, Cengage Learning.

In 2004, the directory listed 583 women's organizations across an amazingly diverse set of 17 categories. While it is possible to obtain organization lists from services similar to the Gale Directory, there generally are subscription costs involved. In addition to the Gale Directory, here are several free lists of organizations available online:

- Yahoo directory—lists business and women's organizations (dir.yahoo.com)

- Open directory project—lists women's organizations (www.dmoz.org)

- Job hunt directory—lists women's occupational organizations (www.job-hunt.org)

If the organization is well established, an internet search may provide significant information about its mission, members and activities. The consultant might also learn about how the organization communicates and what network(s) may be in place. Even in the best of circumstances, however, it is important to recognize that the extent of secondary research is limited. By simply looking up a group online, it may be difficult or impossible to determine if there are any competitors present; what local events, communications networks and activities the group engages in; who the key leaders are; and possible shared financial needs, issues and goals. To determine these variables, successful niche marketers conduct primary (i.e., first hand) research of their own, through informational interviews.

informational interviews

Conducting Informational Interviews. Once secondary research is complete, and the consultant has created a short list of three to five possible female audiences, he or she is ready to begin informational interviews. These discussions with influential members of niche communities may be among the most important steps in the entire process of becoming a successful niche marketer.

Meetings are generally easy to schedule and pleasant, assuming one's interest in the group's mission and its members is genuine. Offering to conduct the interview over breakfast or lunch at the consultant's expense, can also help set the appointment.

Informational interviews are especially productive if one already has a supportive acquaintance (e.g., client, family, friend, colleague) who will introduce the financial consultant to the local leadership of the organization. Some call these significant contacts Centers of Influence (COI). A COI is an individual in a niche or occupation (e.g., attorneys, CPAs and allied financial professionals) who will help connect the consultant with others or their organization and/or field.

If one is new to the area, it may take longer to establish and build relationships among key influential people in the niche. However, the process is the same, starting with an introductory call(s) to one or more of those prominent individuals. The goal is to determine if there is potential to convert them to advocates and COIs.

Example

All it takes to get things started is a simple phone call to the COI, saying something like this:

I am looking to specialize in helping women in (group/organization/field) achieve greater financial security and freedom. Could I buy you breakfast or lunch in the next couple of weeks? During that time, I would like to ask you a few questions about (niche group/organization) to learn what's important to its members, areas of financial need and how they might view people like me.

I'd also like to get your thinking about how I might best serve the members of (niche group/organization) and who else you would talk to if you were in my shoes.

Does that sound reasonable?

After setting the appointment with a COI, the financial consultant or his/her team will send a letter thanking the COI, and confirming the appointment date/time/location. Once the informational interview is conducted, a follow-up note of thanks is also warranted.

(An informational interview template can be found in the Appendix.)

Prioritizing and Selecting Female Niche Markets. Of course, some niches make better target markets than others. After conducting preliminary research and an informational interview; it can be helpful to prioritize marketing efforts, based on those niches in the women's market that hold the most promise. The tool below is designed to assist in the evaluation phase of the process by ranking up to five different niches based on the primary criteria of a shared communications network and shared interests. In addition, there are criteria for revenue potential and competition within the respective niches.

Once the "homework" of assessing the environment, as well as researching and identifying possible female niche markets is complete, the next step is to shape a marketing plan and activities that build prospect awareness, generate leads and create ideal women clients.

> "The vital task rarely must be done today, or even this week. The urgent task calls for instant action. The momentary appeal of these tasks seems irresistible and they devour our energy. But, in the light of time's perspective, their deceptive prominence fades. With a sense of loss, we recall the vital task we pushed aside. We realize we've become slaves to the tyranny of the urgent."
>
> Charles E. Hummell

Evaluating Niches—Selection Criteria					
	Possible Women's Market Niches				
Criteria	1	2	3	4	5
Shared communications network					
Publications/newsletters (online and/or print)					
Regular local meetings and events					
Robust website with member information and outreach potential					
Member contact potential (e.g., direct mail, e-mail, blogging)					
Subtotal					
Shared interests/needs and their fit with consultant's interests/expertise					
Financial needs aligned with expertise					
Personal traits, interests, values					
Subtotal					
Niche revenue and referral potential					
Member earnings/assets					
Referral potential					
Size of niche within financial consultant's reach					
Subtotal					
Level of competitiveness					
The number of competitors is few					
The competition is not firmly established					
Subtotal					
Total					

Notes: Based on researching niche market/s and characteristics, enter in up to five different groups under consideration. Score low to high—0 to 5

CREATING A MARKETING PLAN

marketing plan

The best marketing plans are never truly done. People, markets, and economies change—and financial consultants change, too. Marketing goal identification (i.e., what results marketing will generate) is usually done once a year, as part of the business planning cycle. However, building and refining marketing strategies and tactics are continuous tasks for the most effective marketers and financial professionals.

Marketing plans can be both elaborate and exhaustive. For our purposes, we keep things relatively simple by focusing on the communications and activity aspects that successful financial consultants find most meaningful and productive.

The Communications Strategy—Message and Media

A critically important element of the marketing plan and effective niche marketing is the development of a communications strategy. It is through the creation and implementation of a winning communications strategy that awareness among targeted prospects is built. The two essential components of a communications strategy are the message and the media. Understanding what makes a memorable and compelling message; along with how to put those messages together, is essential for niche marketers. Examining the fundamentals of a well-developed and executed media strategy is also instructive. In other words, not only *what* is communicated, but also *how* and *where* the message is delivered are key considerations. The section that follows discusses how to develop a communications strategy with high impact.

The Message

Communications plans that have the greatest impact and appeal begin with explicitly defined benefits. Customers and clients, whether male or female, do not acquire products or pay for services unless they perceive them to be beneficial. As basic as this seems, it is sometimes lost on well-meaning financial professionals and corporate marketers. Rather than communicate how products or services will improve the target consumer's circumstance, these providers focus instead on the features and attributes of their offering(s). Simply put, a feature is a fact-based statement that relates to the product or services being promoted.

features

Common features among financial professionals across virtually all business models (e.g., insurance agents, registered representatives, registered investment advisors, financial planners) include:

- length of time/tenure in business

- specific areas of high competency and expertise

- reputation among target audiences and/or community

- scope of financial solutions (i.e., breadth of services and products)

- affiliated firm/s (i.e., home office) public image and brand strength/recognition

- competitive quality and pricing

- administrative and operational efficiencies

- client service practices and systems

benefits By contrast, a benefit statement answers the question: "What's in it for me?" (A good acronym to remember for this helpful inquiry is "WIFM.") Through preparation of well-conceived answers to WIFM, financial professionals are better able to differentiate themselves with a compelling message.

It is sometimes helpful to bridge a feature and a benefit with the phrase "What this means to you is..." For example: "I work with a team of professionals that has 37 years of experience in (this industry, with this company, dealing with this topic). What this means to you is that we are able to offer you a wide range of education, options, and solutions that are tailored to meet your specific needs." The more one is able to align his or her message with the features and benefits that appeal to a chosen female niche market, the more compelling the message will be.

The culmination of analyzing the financial consultant's features and benefits, along with what may appeal to the targeted niche, should result in two written statements: a *value proposition* and *positioning statement*. If one is targeting two or more markets that have very different needs (for example, women with young children and senior women), one may have to create separate positioning statements and value propositions for each.

positioning ***Positioning.*** The positioning statement consists of one short paragraph. It is a private declaration of how one wishes to be perceived by the target audience. The statement should guide everything the financial consultant does—from prospecting methods, advertisements, and planning approaches to client service. It is the basis of the value proposition that one communicates to targeted female prospects. The positioning statement consists of the features that the financial consultant offers and should answer the following questions:[123]

- Who are you?

- What business are you in?

- What do you do?

- With whom do you compete?

- What will differentiate you from your competitors?

---

123. Harry Beckwith, *Selling the Invisible* (New York: Warner Books, 1997):113–114 (an adaptation of questions Beckwith recommends).

> ***Example***
>
> Adam is a financial consultant who helps working mothers who are executives accumulate assets for their retirement and children's education, as well as protect their families' financial futures. Unlike other life insurance and mutual fund providers, Adam offers information and access to resources that will help parents manage their children's educational progress and plan the logistics related to applications to schools, for financial aid, and for scholarships.

value proposition

The Value Proposition. Using the positioning statement as a starting point, one can then create a value proposition. Unlike the positioning statement, the value proposition is for external communication to prospects and other interested parties.

While it may sound simple in principle, crystallizing benefits, especially when describing one's unique qualities, is not always easy. It can be challenging to both spend the time taking an inventory of strengths, and distilling them into benefits that are compelling to the target audience. Marketing guru and author of *Permission Marketing*, Seth Godin says it this way: "Many of us are taught to do our best and then let the world decide how to judge us. I think it's better to do your best and decide how you want to be judged." Godin implies that there is work to do in deciding how one wants to be perceived, requiring both forethought and planning.[124]

Simply stated, a value proposition states the compelling reason(s) why prospective clients should do business with the financial consultant. The value proposition conveys the benefit of services/expertise delivered and how they are distinctive from the competition. Some call this "shaping the perception of value."

While communicating the value of expertise and benefits to prospective female clients are both essential, it may also be worth incorporating personal passions or interests in a value proposition, especially when niche marketing. Marketing experts and authors of *The Brand Called You*, Peter Montoya and Tim Vandehey contend that one should not only communicate benefits, but also highlight "a set of characteristics—your military experience, your travels, your family's local history, your previous career racing cars, whatever—that makes you stand out from the crowd, and then hammer those characteristics home over a period of time through consistent marketing efforts."[125] Obviously, how much one should use personal interests to position oneself depends on the targeted

---

124. Seth Godin, Tribes: We Need You to Lead Us, Penguin Group New York, NY, 2008
125. Peter Montoya and Tim Vandehey, *The Brand Called You: Personal Marketing for Financial Advisors* (Costa Mesa, CA: Millennium Advertising, 1999), p. 30

niche market. Some target audiences will not respond to such an approach, but others will find personalization of their financial consultant quite appealing.

An effective value proposition is both conversational and repeatable. It conveys core messages quickly and succinctly. Some marketing experts call the value proposition an "elevator speech." The point is, the speech can be delivered in just a short amount of time and in a few sentences that communicate one's unique and compelling value to an intended audience. Here are two examples:

- *"I specialize in helping executive women build financial independence, reduce their risks and save time researching financial options."*

- *"We are experts in working with women business owners to increase their own financial security, while also lowering employee benefit costs."*

Once the consultant has developed his or her value proposition or "elevator speech," committing it to memory so that it sounds fluid and natural every time is essential. It can also be helpful to share both the positioning statements and value propositions with niche market COIs for feedback and improvement.

The Media

media

Having determined what one wishes to communicate, next comes how and where to build awareness among the target niche audience. As far as the how of media planning goes, a basic media formula that large marketers use when building awareness may provide helpful perspective. When large multinational marketing firms commit mega-millions to advertising campaigns, they think in terms of generating "impressions." Impressions among a specified target audience are a direct result of two basic elements: (1) *frequency,* and (2) *reach*.

According to marketing consultants, Susan Ives and Bill McGaw, "Reach is the number of different people who are exposed to an advertising message at least once. Frequency is the number of times they are exposed to the message."[126] Others refer to the concept of frequency in a related and familiar phrase: *"Tell them seven times in seven ways."* Of course, communicating a message seven times in seven ways can be both expensive and time consuming. This fact brings us back to one of the most attractive benefits of niche marketing: media efficiency. When financial professionals access the shared communications network of a niche market, there is little media waste (meaning the message is delivered to the intended audience versus those outside of the target). Further, shared communications networks offer relatively inexpensive media opportunities versus purchasing space/time on more broadly distributed vehicles (e.g., billboards, television or radio commercials, print and online advertising). This means niche media can be both efficient and effective.

---

126. Internet Odyssey, Market Your Business on the Internet, Part I, Marketing Basics, Reach & Frequency, www.texas.net

media plan

The Media Plan. Here are several examples of communications vehicles that a niche organization may have in place that could be included in a media plan:

- website with local presence/representation

- website links to affiliate organizations that may also become part of the niche marketing strategy

- webcasts (i.e., simultaneously broadcast speaking or training opportunities)

- webinars (i.e., pre-recorded, on-demand speaking or training opportunities)

- newsletters; virtual or printed

- sponsorship opportunities

- face-to-face events, for example:
    - chapter/local meetings and seminars
    - regional and national conferences, forums and webinars

- direct (snail) mail campaign(s)

- member directory (with advance permission to use by a decision maker in the organization and where use conforms to compliance and privacy requirements)

When putting together a media plan, advertising agencies, media planners, and large company marketers use calendars to lay out the frequency of message exposure toward a specified target market. This enables proactive versus reactive messaging against a selected target audience. Financial consultants can easily do the same thing by creating a niche media/event plan and reviewing it throughout the year.

The table below is an example of a simple media plan for Adam, a financial consultant who specializes in working with members of the local chapter of Executive Moms in Touch. By implementing the media and event plan, Adam hopes to generate as many as 19 potential impressions to niche members over a 12-month period.

Media and Event Calendar for Executive Moms in Touch												
	Jan	Feb	Mar	Apr	May	June	July	Aug	Sept	Oct	Nov	Dec
Newsletter Column	X			X			X			X		
Events		Tax Clinic w/ CPA			Mom's Day Brunch Sponsor				Seminar on College Funding			Holiday Party Sponsor
Chapter Meetings	Attend	Speak	Attend	Attend					Attend	Attend	Attend	
Direct Mail	Mailing on Tax Clinic			Mailing on Mom's Day Brunch				Mailing on College Funding		Holiday Card and Mailing on Party		

Laying out a media and event calendar helps the consultant "get out in front" of the communications plan, rather than haphazardly promoting key messages. It enables the consultant to plan for administrative needs and/or partnering with others for high visibility activities throughout the year. Equally important, a media and event calendar can also support the determination and budgeting of resources (both financial and people) that are needed to successfully implement the plan.

The Marketing Activity Plan

marketing activity plan

Along with creating a sound communications strategy, the financial consultant must plan for the marketing activities that will be the driving force of revenue generation for his or her business. Given all the distractions and demands on their time, financial consultants greatly benefit from translating their goals into manageable activities. It has been said that "All great plans ultimately devolve to work." Nowhere could this be more true than in the case of financial services professionals as they seek to take on their ideal clients, both female and male.

Focusing Marketing Activities

A marketing activity plan starts with identifying how much revenue the financial consultant wishes to generate, and then looks at quantifying how many new clients are required to support the revenue goal. Revenue comes from two sources: (1) current clients, and (2) newly generated clients. To get started, one needs to examine sources of revenue, beginning with ongoing streams of income (e.g., trailers, renewals, retainers).

According to research conducted by The American College in 2009, among its students and graduates, the greatest amount (over 89 percent) of producer revenue is generated from one of three sources:

- *commissions* on new product placement

- *fees* generated from new services (e.g., financial planning, wealth management and advisory services)

- *recurring revenue* from trailers, residuals and retainers from existing clients

To gain a sense of what weekly marketing activities must be, one starts by first estimating the recurring revenue expected from existing clients for the year. That amount is then subtracted from annual gross income/revenue requirements. If there are cases and/or business pending from existing clients, their estimated revenues are also deducted. Any remaining revenue required will need to come from new clients. Dividing total revenue by average case size per new client equals the number of new clients one needs to generate. Dividing total new clients required by weeks worked per year determines how many new clients need to be acquired each week.

Example

Assume Adam needs to gross $150,000 per year to accomplish his net (after expenses and taxes) income requirement. As a consultant in his third year of business, he has estimated that his trailer-based compensation is $20,000 per year. He needs to generate the remaining $130,000 in new business.

Adam has also identified a number of cases among existing clients that will be implemented with additional investment and/or insurance business. His most conservative (i.e., worst-case) estimates are that new business from existing clients will add another $25,000 in income. As such, new business from new clients will have to make up the balance of $105,000.

Upon further inspection of his business, Adam determines that his average case size (i.e., revenue generated) per new client is $2,188 in new business commissions. As a result, his targeted annual number of new clients is 48 ($105,000 divided by $2,188/client revenue.) (Note: The higher revenue rate per client, the lower volume of new clients needed, and vice versa.)

Last, Adam would like to break his marketing activity down to a weekly level so that it will be both meaningful and easily measured. Assuming he plans to work 48 weeks (net of vacations and holidays), Adam needs to take on one new client per week worked.

After identifying how many new clients are needed every week to achieve desired annual revenue, the question becomes: How many new prospects (a.k.a. leads) need to be generated every week to gain one new client?

Generating Prospect Leads—Rate x Volume

When determining the number of weekly leads required, the same principles of rate and volume discussed in the niche marketing section also apply here. However, the volume and rate variables are different when it comes to the financial consultant's marketing activity. In this context, marketing activities have to do with the number of new clients as the desired outcome. As such, client acquisition is a result of generating sufficient prospects and effectively implementing tasks associated with converting those prospects to clients.

Volume is the number of prospects, and rate has to do with percentage of prospects who become clients due to the effectiveness of the consultant's conversion activities. Increasing either variable—number of prospects or their rate of conversion—will yield incrementally more clients. This concept is illustrated in the simple equation below:

Volume	X	Rate	=	Outcome
Number of Prospects	X	Conversion Activities	=	Clients

Activities that support the generation of prospect leads include:

- approaching natural market members—friends, family, acquaintances, and colleagues

- conducting seminars—events that one promotes, holds, and pay for

- speaking engagements—events where the financial consultant is asked to speak

- asking for referrals—from clients, natural and niche markets, and centers of influence

- lead programs or lists approved by the financial professional's affiliate company and compliance department

Higher value leads are those that have a higher likelihood of becoming clients. In other words, they have the highest rate of conversion. Most often, the best leads are sourced from individuals or groups with whom one already has an affinity relationship. Prospects generated from these sources are often called "warm" leads. Industry studies have consistently revealed that rates of conversion are significantly higher (sometimes as much as four to ten times higher) on these warm sources than cold leads. Sources for warm leads include those generated from niche and natural markets, as well as referrals. The warmer the lead source and the higher rate of conversion, the lower volume of leads required. The opposite is also true; colder lead quality translates into a higher volume of prospects that the financial consultant must generate.

While the lead quality can certainly influence conversion rates, it is by no means the only contributing factor. Building effectiveness in conversion processes, tasks and skills are also important contributors to increasing the rate. Specifically, these other factors include how the prospect is contacted, how frequently contact is made, and the quality of communications between the prospect and financial consultant and/or support staff.

Activity Management Systems

activity management systems

The best known activity management systems focus on numbers of phone dials and number of times the consultant asked for an appointment, along with initial appointments set, seen and sold. The key ratios, (or "magic numbers" as some call them), that many of these systems apply are fairly standard in the industry. The most commonly used benchmark is 10 initial appointments seen per week for newer producers.

Unless financial professionals first identify and generate enough leads to support appointment activity, they may find themselves without enough prospects to contact. The lead pipeline will be dry. If one is using an activity management system that does not include the marketing component of lead generation, it is helpful to add it. Understanding how many leads are needed every week depends on where they come from and the consultant's effectiveness in converting those prospects into clients. Adding this information to the system one is already using will help create a database to determine which leads from which source ultimately become clients. That said, a rule of thumb sometimes used in the financial services industry calls for 30 leads, from any source, generated every week. Here is a sample of weekly marketing activity goals for new financial professionals used by one market leading company:

The "Women's Market" and Your Marketing "MAP" 2.35

Prospect Generation and Client Conversion Activities	Weekly Numbers
Leads (from all sources)	30
Dials	300
Asks for initial interview appointment	60
Initial interviews set	12
Initial interviews seen	4
Clients generated (i.e., prospect commits to doing business with you, at least in principle)	1

This basic model assumes a rate of 50 new clients per year. While an individual consultant's numbers will vary, based on case size per client, revenue goals, lead types (i.e., cold or warm), and conversion rates, these benchmarks provide helpful perspective.

It is important to track weekly activity to determine what actual versus planned activity results are. With several months of tracking data, the financial consultant will easily be able to pinpoint both areas of strength and needed improvement. For example, which lead sources have higher rates of conversion and/or case sizes that should receive more attention and resources? Which types of leads convert at lower rates?

> "If you don't have daily objectives, you qualify as a dreamer."
>
> Zig Ziglar

Improving Rates of Conversion from Prospects to Clients

conversion

Once one has successfully identified a female prospect (generated a lead), then the goal is to raise the likelihood of her meeting with the consultant and embarking on the consultative planning process. Financial consultants may want to implement industry best practices to increase conversion by following these steps and using support tools.

1. **Send out a letter of introduction** (also known as a pre-approach letter) to the prospect, along with a biography. The letter should include the name of the referring individual (if applicable), and the value proposition statement. It should also mention that the consultant will call within the next two weeks. This is the first promise to the female prospect and it is imperative that one delivers on it (i.e., calls within two weeks or sooner).

2. **Call the prospect as promised in the letter.** There are three objectives of the call: (1) start the relationship building process, (2) determine if she is a good fit for the consultant's practice, and (3) identify how the consultant might add value. In this call, it is important to uncover at

least one of her primary financial concerns. It is essential that she sees the benefit of meeting with the consultant. If not, then the potential for a "no show" is high. *(A sample phone script is included in the Appendix.)*

3. ***Follow the phone call with a letter*** There are two types of follow-up correspondence: (1) if she did not set up an appointment due to legitimate scheduling reasons, the consultant should send a letter to let her know he or she will call her at an agreed upon later date; or (2) if she scheduled the initial interview, the consultant should send a letter of confirmation. Along with the letter of confirmation, it is helpful to include a homework assignment.

   An industry best practice is to send the prospect 30 minutes of homework to prepare in advance of the appointment. The homework assignment asks her to capture high-level financial information and key documents to bring to the appointment. Some financial consultants, particularly those newer to the business, have reservations about asking for what they might consider sensitive financial information so early on in the relationship. It is important to recognize this concern and overcome it. As a trustworthy financial consultant, one acts and should be perceived as a professional. Having her prepare and bring in financial information demonstrates professionalism, increases her commitment to the meeting, and puts the consultant in a better position to add value at the very beginning of the relationship. *(An initial interview cover letter, 30-minute checkup worksheet and checklist are included in the Appendix.)*

Before implementing these steps and support tools, the financial consultant is advised to check with his/her compliance and marketing departments. They may have variations of these tools for use and/or specific guidelines that must be followed.

> "The greatest thing in this world is not so much where we are, but in which direction we are moving."
>
> Oliver Wendell Holmes

CHAPTER SUMMARY

This chapter discussed the definition of marketing and how approaches differ for larger organizations versus at the financial consultant level. Since most financial consultants do not have unlimited marketing resources, we examined the why, what and how associated with being an effective niche marketer. We then covered important life-stage, lifestyle and special interest considerations to take into account when selecting a niche within the "women's market." Our exploration also included how to build awareness among targeted prospects, generate leads and convert those prospects to clients.

We emphasized that client service is also a vital aspect of marketing. In the end, it can be more cost effective, as well as professionally and personally fulfilling, to keep those ideal clients than to generate new ones. Delivering outstanding service that exceeds client expectations yields higher client satisfaction and loyalty, which, in turn, generates repeat business and referrals. These two benefits of client service—repeat business and referrals—can significantly increase the consultant's return on marketing investment. Because of its importance, we will focus our entire attention on delivering outstanding client service in Chapter 8.

In the next chapter, we look at how to work successfully with female clients, including:

- the barriers and builders of productive working relationships

- possible gender-based communications preferences

- the impact of social styles on communications

- the art of asking the right question at the right time

- how to apply communications skills throughout the consultative planning process

Effective comunications when displayed throughout the stages of consultative planning, builds higher trust and higher revenue per client.

CHAPTER 2 TOOLS AND RESOURCES

- Tools
    - Informational Interview Template
    - Appointment Setting Phone Script
    - 30-Minute Checkup: Worksheet and Document Checklist

- Courses from The American College
    - FA 200 Techniques for Prospecting
    - FA 201 Techniques for Exploring Personal Markets

- Recommended Reading
    - *Positioning: The Battle for Your Mind*, Al Ries and Jack Trout, McGraw-Hill, 2001

    - *Effortless Marketing for Financial Advisors*, Steve Moeller, American Business Visions, 1999

    - *The Future of the Financial Advisor Business, Part II: Strategies for Small Business*, Research Report, Undiscovered Managers, September 2000

- *Tribes: We Need You to Lead Us*, Seth Godin, Penguin Group, 2008

- *The Complete Idiot's Guide to Marketing*, 2nd Edition, Sarah White, CWL Publishing, 2003

- *The Brand Called You: Personal Marketing for Financial Advisors*, Peter Montoya and Tim Vandehey, Millennium Advertising, 1999

3
Earning Her Trust and Her Business: The Consultative Planning Process

Learning Objectives
An understanding of the material in this chapter should enable the student to
3-1. Describe the barriers and builders to effective communications and relationship building.
3-2. Explain communications preferences that may be gender based.
3-3. Illustrate the difference between open and closed questioning techniques.
3-4. Describe how both the consultative planning process (six steps) and scope (six areas) benefit women.

INTRODUCTION

How can financial consultants build stronger, more productive and trusting relationships with their female clients? This is the fundamental question we examine in this chapter. Our discussion of the consultative planning process begins where Chapter 2 left off—converting female prospects into clients. We now turn our attention to the barriers/builders of relationships and effective communication, including gender and stylistic preferences. Our exploration covers consultative planning in depth; what it is, why it is particularly effective in helping women take necessary action and how it can be readily integrated in the financial consultant's practice.

The table below illustrates the specific steps (3 through 8) of the process and their respective objectives on which we will focus our discussion.

		The Marketing/Planning Process					
Identify the Prospect	Approach the Prospect	Meet with the Prospect and Establish Goals	Gather Information	Analyze the Information	Develop and Present the Plan	Implement the Plan	Service the Plan
Build awareness among	• Begin the trust relationship.	• Reinforce trust. • Transform the	• Fulfill ethical and suitability requirements.	• Determine and quantify magnitudes of	• Reinforce trust. • Review and	• Reinforce trust. • Take action to manage risks and achieve goals.	• Reinforce trust. • Adjust plan/actions as indicated. • Increase client satisfaction, commitment, and loyalty. • Build cross-sell opportunities.

Meet with the Prospect and Establish Goals	Gather Information	Analyze the Information	Develop and Present the Plan	Implement the Plan	Service the Plan
• Reinforce trust. • Transform the relationship from prospect to client. • Disclose compensation, referrals and mutual expectations. • Client sees benefit of working with you.	• Fulfill ethical and suitability requirements. • Begin thinking through possible options, pros/cons to meet clients' best interest.	• Determine and quantify magnitudes of risk, goal funding gaps. • Identify strategic and tactical alternatives for risk and investment management.	• Reinforce trust. • Review and educate client on both strategic and tactical options. • Gain commitment to action and mutual accountabilities.	• Reinforce trust. • Take action to manage risks and achieve goals.	• Reinforce trust. • Adjust plan/actions as indicated. • Increase client satisfaction, commitment, and loyalty. • Build cross-sell opportunities.

COMMUNICATIONS AND TRUST

communications

When it comes to transforming the relationship from prospect to client, both words and actions must demonstrate trustworthiness. Communications and ethical behavior are inextricably linked. Being able to communicate effectively is an essential skill that needs continual attention and refinement for financial consultants seeking to earn the ongoing confidence of their clients—female or male. There is no escaping the need for this skill. Communication permeates everything one does; from developing a compelling value proposition, to establishing and maintaining mutually beneficial client relationships, to effectively leading or participating in a team.

In his book *The Speed of Trust*, Stephen Covey writes that certain types of consistent behavior and communications are the underpinnings of an effective relationship. Through his study of leaders who had high trust relationships with their followers, Dr. Covey identified 13 common behaviors and found that two of the most important were demonstrating respect and being a good listener. Although these behaviors are universally desired, he found that how women and men perceive they are respected and heard is different.[127] In the sections that follow, we will discuss male/female communication preferences and their affect on behavior.

---

127. Stephen M.R. Covey, *The Speed of Trust* (New York, NY: Free Press, 2006).

What does it take to improve communications and rapport building skills, particularly with regard to female clients? Since it is helpful to establish a common understanding of key communications barriers and preferences by gender and/or social style, we will start there. Then, we examine how communications and the consultative planning process not only strengthen relationships, but also add more value to female clients and their consultants as well.

Communications Barriers

As discussed in Chapter 1, there is an unfortunate reality that many women do not feel they are well understood or respected by some producers in financial services. These perceptions largely stem from a breakdown in communications, and lead to unsettling implications for the financial services industry and its professionals. The consequences to the industry are damaging and include client turnover; degraded reputations; loss of premiums; and fees/assets under management, as illustrated in these research findings:

- A nearly universal, 99 percent of affluent women have switched advisors at some point.[128]

- Almost three out of four widows change advisors within three years of their husband's death.[129]

As regrettable as it is for the financial services industry and its representatives to suffer the fallout associated with unhappy clients; it is even more devastating to women who may not get the financial planning help they need. The lack of adequate planning support may put them at greater financial risk when confronted with life crises and challenges. According to a 2009 study by the AARP, women are more likely to experience life crises than men are because they live longer. AARP found that almost two out of three women, (65 percent) aged 40 to 79, had experienced a major life crisis, such as divorce, widowhood, serious illness or disability of a family member and job loss. Most of these women felt unprepared to deal with the economic consequences and the vast majority said they experienced significant financial challenges as a result.[130]

---

128. Russ Alan Prince and Hannah Shaw Grove, *Women of Wealth* (CITY: The National Underwriter Company, April 2004).
129. Marti Barletta, *Marketing to Women* (New York: Kaplan Publishing, January 2006).
130. AARP Financial Inc., Boston Research Group, PR Newswire, "AARP Financial Inc. Survey Finds: Women More likely Than Men to Experience a Life Crisis- and Struggle With Its Financial Impact," August 11, 2009.

Yet, just the opposite occurs when women find trustworthy and capable financial consultants with whom they can work. Women receive the professional assistance they need and gain improved financial security and peace of mind. This is evidenced in findings from a recent study by Oppenheimer Funds, where nearly two out of three women said they were more knowledgeable as a result of working with a financial professional. The same research revealed that almost three in four (73 percent) were more comfortable with investing and nearly two in three (63 percent) said they were more confident about having money for the future.[131]

Many women today are looking to build relationships with financial professionals who understand, value, and respect them. They gravitate toward those financial professionals with whom they have an affinity or bond. Research points to an overwhelming majority of affluent women saying that a personal and professional chemistry was critical, and that the way in which the financial professional asked about their personal goals was of high importance to them.[132]

Communications Builders

So, how do women prospects and clients wish to be treated? What if any, are the preferences between the genders? Are communications preferences and styles merely gender based? In the section that follows, we discuss key distinctions between men and women, based on recent research and how those differences may affect social interactions and financial attitudes. Since not all women and not all men think or communicate alike according to their respective sex, we also explore social style preferences along with how to adapt one's approach to create more favorable communication exchanges and rapport.

Working effectively with clients, both male and female, requires skill—not only in understanding and addressing their financial goals and concerns, but also in adapting one's style to match their unique needs and preferences. The financial consultant must first have an in-depth appreciation for the client's needs, opportunities and issues in order to develop well-conceived recommendations. As Stephen Covey famously coined in *The 7 Habits of Highly Effective People®*, "seek first to understand, then to be understood."[133]

Communications and Gender

It is essential to recognize that how information and perceptions are processed are frequently influenced by gender. Despite the fact that men

---

131. Women & Investing, Oppenheimer Funds, 2006
132. Russ Alan Prince and Hannah Shaw Grove, *Women of Wealth* (CITY: The National Underwriter Company, 2004).
133. Stephen Covey, *The 7 Habits of Highly Effective People®*, (New York: Simon & Schuster, Inc., 2004).

and women share nearly 99 percent of the human genetic code,[134] there are seemingly small nuances in body chemistry and brain biology that account for big differences between men and women. Beyond chemical and biological variations between genders, family history and society can play important roles in how we think, act and feel. Some call this the "nature versus nurture" debate.

> "We see things not as they are, but as we are."
>
> Henry Major Tomlinson

nature or nuture

Nature or Nurture. Are the differences between the sexes a result of heredity or environment—and does it really matter? The nature versus nurture debate will likely never be won, but 40 years of advances in science and technology have certainly moved the debate forward. New discoveries about the human brain have added new dimensions to our understanding of how women and men relate to the world differently; what shapes their reality; and what influences their priorities, attitudes and preferences, behavior, and communication styles.

While not all women (or men) are alike, most females possess strong connections to home and family; which, in turn, play important roles in how they communicate and make decisions. For example, women generally view talking in a relationship as a way to reinforce intimacy, while men typically view it as a way to reinforce their independence.

Recent advancements in scientific and sociological study have yielded fascinating insights. Almost every area of inquiry in human behavior—from anthropology and linguistics to neurology and biology—has produced exciting new discoveries about the human brain. Research findings have contributed to driving fresh perspectives about marketing, communications and marketing techniques to reach women consumers. These insights can be beneficial to consultants when considering how best to market to and communicate with female consumers. Understanding where women are "coming from" will help financial professionals communicate more effectively and develop stronger connections with their female clients.

female brain

The Female Brain. While men and women have the same number of brain cells, the female brain develops differently than the male brain, growing more connections in the communications, observation and emotional centers that are located in both lobes of the brain. Scientists believe the female brain architecture supports contextual thinking and relationship building. According to psychologists, women regularly think in context, placing common elements together and integrating them into a bigger picture.[135]

---

134. Louann Brizendine, *The Female Brain* (New York, NY: Morgan Road Books/Random House, 2006).
135. Ibid.

A woman is biologically hardwired to reinforce the importance of the intimacy of relationships. Her world view and her behavior are shaped by a biological and evolutionary imperative for connection, relationships, and social harmony. Females possess a larger hippocampus—that part of the brain dedicated to emotion and memory—than men. In addition, females have 11 percent more neurons dedicated to language and hearing.[136] As a result, social scientists have learned that women are significantly more verbal than men, using more words than men do to express their thoughts and feelings.

From birth, girls are keenly observant. Newborn girls will sustain eye contact more than twice as long as baby boys.[137] What are they observing? Baby girls are learning to read emotions in faces, body language, and through the tone of a person's voice. As girls grow up, they develop these attributes into social talents, like empathy and communication skills, that help them connect with a larger community. Girls develop social skills to maintain smooth relationships that ensure their place in the community. What about women's intuition? It may not be just a myth. Women's intuition may be a function of their finely-tuned senses and ability to absorb and process more subtle information.[138]

By contrast, men seem to be biologically hardwired to compete and protect their domain. Early males competed in their communities to maintain their independence.[139] Men have larger brain areas associated with aggression and libido.[140] In addition, the neurological structure of male brains is also more localized than women's, with clearly specialized functions. The emotional center of a male brain is located on the right side only, and probably accounts for a man's more singular focus. Men feel emotions as strongly as women, but fewer connections between emotional and verbal centers may explain why men generally articulate their feelings less often than women.

How might brain biology influence the way in which men and women communicate? The following chart summarizes some of the key differences and preferences common to members of both genders, based on research findings.

---

136. Ibid.

137. Deborah Tannen, *You Just Don't Understand* (New York: Quill/Harper Collins, 1990): 24–26.

138. Louann Brizendine, *The Female Brain* (New York: Morgan Road Books/Random House, 2006).

139. Deborah Tannen, *You Just Don't Understand* (New York: Quill/Harper Collins, 1990): 24–26.

140. James Geary, "Women and Money I: What's Biology Got to Do With It?" *CFP Board Report*, February 7, 2007, http://www.cfp.net/certificants/boardreport_2_2007.asp#2.

Communications and Interpersonal Preferences	
Female	**Male**
• *Build intimacy and relationships.*[141] Women relate to others as individuals in a network of connections.	• *Maintain independence.*[142] Men relate to others as individuals in a hierarchical social order.
• *Connect through affinity.* Women are more highly programmed to promote relationships. They seek sharing, collaboration and cooperation in a group.	• *Bond through competition.* Men compete to preserve their independence.
• *Build social harmony.* Women achieve social status by fostering and preserving harmonious relationships.	• *Improve social status.* Men use their physical and negotiating skills to improve their status in their group.
• *Solicit input.* Women are more likely to brainstorm, seek advice and counsel from a range of sources.	• *Make their point.* Men are predisposed to interrupt others in conversation and make more direct statements when communicating ideas.

Financial Worry and Inaction. There is another important attitudinal distinction between women and men. That is, women are considerably less confident and more likely to worry about finances. Since women often face greater financial risks than men do, some concerns are well founded. As a result, they place high priority on their ability to achieve financial independence. In a recent study, Allianz found that women ranked financial security and freedom 15 to 20 times more important to them than money-related status or respect.[143]

At its best, worrying can be positive and productive, especially when it motivates action (e.g., when mom's warnings are heeded, children's lives are spared). On the other hand, Wikipedia says that worry refers to "negative self-talk that often distracts the mind from focusing on the problem at hand."[144] At its worst, worrying can be debilitating and, ultimately, self-defeating—which is frequently the case when it comes to women and money. Despite the anxiety many women share about money, there are often disturbing and wide-ranging gaps between their concern and action. Industry studies have consistently pointed to this disconnect. Consider these findings:

- Concern

---

141. Deborah Tannen, *You Just Don't Understand* (New York: Quill/Harper Collins, 1990): 24–26.
142. Ibid.
143. Allianz Life Insurance Company, Harris International, Age Wave, "Women, Money and Power Study," 2008
144. "Worry." *Wikipedia.* http://en.wikipedia.org/wiki/Worry.

- Women worry more about money than men do. Thirty two percent of women describe themselves as worriers versus 18 percent of men.[145]

- About half (46 percent) of women have the fear of becoming destitute or homeless. Even those who are relatively high income earners share this concern, with almost half (48 percent) of women with $100,000+ incomes feeling this way.[146]

- Of women polled in a 2008 Prudential Financial survey, 73 percent said they worried about their financial future. Nearly one-third of respondents indicated they worried "all the time or often." Yet, in the same study, 72 percent of survey participants admitted to procrastination.[147]

• Inaction

- Oppenheimer Funds' research revealed that while the near universal majority (93 percent) of Baby Boomer women indicated that saving for retirement was their primary investment goal, almost half (47 percent) were not contributing to a retirement plan.[148]

- In a 2006 study conducted by Prudential Financial, 53 percent of women surveyed said they anticipated saving and investing more in the next 12 months. In follow-up research conducted two years later, just 11 percent of this same group had invested in stocks or mutual funds for the first time and only 14 percent had opened some kind of IRA or retirement account.[149]

So, why the inertia? If women are so worried about money, why are they not taking the action necessary to address their concerns? One possible reason might be how we are wired as human beings, regardless of gender. Neuro-imaging research from David Laibson, professor of economics at Harvard University, suggests a strong bias toward immediate versus delayed gratification: "Brain biology and human tendency is to delay taking actions

---

145. James Geary, "Women and Money I: What's Biology Got to Do With It?" *CFP Board Report*, February 7, 2007, http://www.cfp.net/certificants/boardreport_2_2007.asp#2.
146. Allianz Life Insurance Company, Harris International, Age Wave, "Women, Money and Power Study," 2006
147. 2008–2009 Prudential Financial Study, "Financial Experience & Behaviors Among Women."
148. OppenheimerFunds, "Women and Investing Survey," 2005.
149. 2006 Prudential Study, "Financial Experience & Behaviors Among Women."

that require effort, including actions about financial issues . . . to procrastinate, instead of taking action for a healthier financial future.[150]

Beyond the common urge among both genders to seek instant gratification, women frequently describe other roadblocks to financial action. As previously discussed, many women may be stymied as a result of information overload, or skepticism when considering professional advice. In addition, a 2008 Prudential Financial study points out these other commonly cited reasons:

- Of married women, 36 percent indicated, that "The immediate needs of my family/my children take priority."

- Almost four in ten (38 percent) of single women agreed with the statement: "I just don't want to spend the effort." (Considering a single woman's higher risk of poverty, this statistic is more than a little troubling!)

- For those nearing (within five years of) retirement, 34 percent said "I'm afraid I'll make the wrong decision, so I tend to avoid thinking about it."[151]

Another reason some women procrastinate in seeking help and taking action is that they may be afraid to confront the realities of their current financial situation and its implications on their future. In other words, they may not want to know how bad it really is or could be. (Note: The author has witnessed this on a number of occasions with both female prospects and clients.)

Understanding the very human tendency to procrastinate and its potentially negative and severe consequences for women, creates a clarion call for financial consultants. That call is to build the awareness among their female prospects, family and friends about their financial risks and the impact of those risks. When working directly with women clients, communicating effectively and helping them act on decisions throughout the consultative planning process are essential elements in overcoming both worry and inaction.

> "Let our advance worrying become advance thinking and planning."
>
> Winston Churchill

Communications and Social Styles

Of course, no two women (or men) act, feel, or think the same. In addition to differences between the genders, each individual has a dominant social style that influences behavior. A social style is the behavior one exhibits when interacting

---

150. "Frozen in the Headlights: The Dynamics of Women and Money," A Women & Money Program Incubator Sponsored by the National Endowment for Financial Education and AARP, Washington, D.C., February 15-17, 2000.
151. 2008–2009 Prudential Financial Study, "Financial Experience & Behaviors Among Women."

with others. People are like thermostats; they are constantly seeking a state of equilibrium or comfort. As soon as another person enters the picture, tension results, and each person must reestablish his or her balance and comfort zone. Knowledge of social styles and adapting to the female prospect's or client's preference helps shape the communication exchange and maximize her comfort level.

There are a number of social style models, such as Myers Briggs, DISC, and The Platinum Rule. The Four Social Styles, the model most frequently used in financial services, was developed in the 1960s by Dr. David W. Merrill, Dr. James W. Taylor, and Roger Reid.[152] Here is how they explain social styles:

> "We all say and do things as a result of certain habit patterns, and people make predictions about us because they come to expect us to behave in a particular way–the fact is that even though each of us is unique, we tend to act in fairly consistent, describable ways. All of us use habits that have worked well for us, habits that make us comfortable, and these habits become the social style that others can observe."[153]

drivers
amiables
expressives
analytics

Merrill, Taylor and Reid created their model based on extensive research that found most individuals could be reliably categorized into four basic social styles: *analytic, driver, amiable* and *expressive*. While most people are a blend of social styles that can change by situation, one style is usually dominant or preferred.

The visual below illustrates the four social styles, along with their respective communications preferences and behaviors.

Analytics and drivers tend to be lower in relationship orientation and more focused on tasks/facts than amiables and expressives. A woman with an analytic style is logical and may be guarded about developing relationships. She makes fact-based decisions, preferring to focus on the depth and quality of information presented. Her primary need is to be right. This means she may avoid risks in order to digest facts that are presented before taking action. (Some refer to this phenomenon as: analysis paralysis).

Drivers are also fact-based decision makers but typically come to conclusions more quickly than analytics since drivers are strongly results-oriented and willing to take risks. A woman with a driver style wants information presented as a summary or "bottom line." Drivers have a strong need for control.

---

152. " Social Style." *Wikipedia.*http://en.wikipedia.org/wiki/Social_style.
153. David W. Merrill and Roger H. Reid, *Personal Styles and Effective Performance* (Boca Raton, FL: CRC Press LLC, 1999).

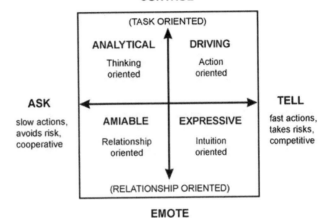

The Four Social Styles

An expressive is often motivated by a need for recognition. A female client's expressive style can be recognized in her enthusiastic and outgoing demeanor, along with an inclination to rely on intuition. She is relatively comfortable with risk taking.

Similar to expressives, amiables are also highly relationship oriented. An amiable woman has a high need for security, both financial and interpersonal. This means she will often be risk avoidant. In addition, she will tend to rely more strongly on her feelings and emotions than the other social styles.

The table below summarizes the characteristics of each social style and indicates how one might best establish rapport with female clients, based on their dominant style.

As financial consultants build relationships with women, it is important to remember that communication and preferences are both gender and social style based. Recognizing that there are differences and responding appropriately are the first steps toward relationship building and converting female prospects to clients through the consultative planning process. The most trusted financial consultants know what to say, how to say it, when to speak, and when to listen.

> "Only those who respect the personality of others can be of real use to them."
>
> Albert Schweitzer

Responding to Social Styles		
Social Style	**Style Characteristics**	**How to Respond**
Analytic *Need: To be right*	• Logical, quiet • Is uncomfortable with small talk • Wants respect • Is systematic	• Be accurate • Stick to an agenda • Support her principles and thinking • To encourage decisions, provide evidence and service
Driver *Need: To be in control*	• Forceful, direct • Will not waste time on small talk • Wants power • Is controlling	• Be efficient • Move right along • Support her conclusions and actions • To encourage decisions, provide options and probabilities
Expressive *Need: To be recognized*	• Outgoing, enthusiastic • Enjoys discussing personal projects and dreams • Wants recognition • Is energizing	• Be interesting • Take time to listen • Support her visions and intuitions • To encourage decisions, provide testimony
Amiable *Need: To be secure*	• Easygoing, dependent • Enjoys discussing personal relationships • Wants approval • Is supportive	• Be cooperative • Find areas of common involvement • Support her relationships and feelings • To encourage decisions, provide assurances

Note: The Social Style Model is now owned by TRACOM, a workplace performance company. Information presented here is by permission.

THE ART OF DISCOVERY

listening

Listening and Asking versus Telling and Selling

Everyone wants to be respected, listened to and heard. Fortunately, human beings are engineered for listening. According to industry veteran, expert and author Alan Parisse, scientists have learned that while we can speak about 120 words per minute, we not only hear but also understand more than three times that amount during the same increment of time.[154]

In their book, *Questions Great Financial Advisors Ask*, Alan Parisse and his co-author, David Richman, state that the extra listening capacity we are equipped with can sometimes backfire. For example, financial consultants often "tune out" in the initial stages of a meeting. Instead of listening, there is a common tendency to drift and begin thinking about other things. "Be careful," Parisse and Richman warn, "If you go too far afield you'll lose your place and not be able to reconnect with what the client is saying. Be on the lookout for ways you might drift from your meeting, including:

- *Trying to rush the process*. "When is she going to stop talking so I can move the meeting along?" "I know exactly what she needs." "My product does that." "I know what she's trying to say."

- *Searching for the answer too soon*. Concerned that we may not know the answer, many of us start hunting through our mental files for an answer before the client has finished asking the questions. We sometimes then end up answering the wrong question."[155]

active listening

How does one overcome these familiar tendencies and habits? By being an *active listener*. Active listening has to do with not only paying attention, but also resisting thoughts that distract from what is being said. It is also important to demonstrate that one is, in fact, listening. Here are several effective techniques to do just that:

- *Using reflective statements*. These include phrases such as: "If I understand you correctly..." "What you're saying is..." and connecting these phrases with a summary of her concern/goal. To confirm the validity of a reflective statement, one might ask, "Did I get that right?"

- *Sustaining eye contact*. Men are sometimes uncomfortable with prolonged eye contact. Females, however, typically connect through maintaining eye contact. Being able to "look her in the eye" while both listening and talking fosters mutual trust with many women.

---

154. Alan Parisse and David Richman, Questions Great Financial Advisors Ask, (Chicago: Kaplan Publishing, 2006).
155. Ibid.

- **Watching body language.** It is important to project that one is listening to the other party and is receptive to his or her message. Non-verbal cues such as leaning forward, taking notes and nodding one's head demonstrates engagement and can be effective techniques.

> "It seems rather incongruous that in a society of super-sophisticated communication, we often suffer from a shortage of listeners."
>
> Erma Bombeck

The Art of Asking Questions

questions

Very rarely do prospects come to financial consultants with all of the personal and financial information that is required for them to benefit from the professional's advice. Moreover, most do not have clarity on what their financial goals and needs really are. In other words, "they don't know what they don't know." While this is certainly the case for most men and women, it can be particularly true for females, since they generally lag behind men in financial literacy.

A lack of knowledge and/or preparation puts the onus on the financial consultant to uncover important facts and feelings in order to develop a well conceived plan of action. Knowing what questions to ask and when to ask them is an essential skill for relationship building and problem solving. Foundational to that skill is understanding the distinction between open and closed questions (also known as open and closed probes).

Closed Questions

Closed questions are inquiries that can be answered with a short phrase or single word (e.g., yes or no). They are useful when one is looking for a fact-based response or a quick and easy answer. They also keep the individual posing the question in control of the conversation.

Closed questions begin with words like: if, would, do, did, are, were and will. One can also turn a statement into a closed probe by ending it with a question such as "isn't it?", "right?", "don't you?" Here are some examples of closed questions that a financial consultant might ask, along with their intended purpose:

Closed Questions	
Purpose	**Examples**
To open a conversation in a non-intrusive, casual way.	• It's a beautiful day, isn't it? • Did you have any problems finding our office?
To demonstrate that you are listening and that you understand her.	• If I heard you correctly, you would like to put your kids through four years of college at the University of Washington. Is that right? • Let me make sure I understand. You want to retire at age 67 with at least $50,000 per year in income, correct?
To move her to action.	• Do you think you will have enough funds to put your kids through four years at the University of Washington? • Do you think you're doing everything you can to fund your retirement goal?
To gain her commitment in principle to proceed.	• Would you like to know if you're on track to achieve your goal of putting the kids through college? • If I can show you ways to achieve your goal of retiring at 67, would you be interested in working with me? • I suggest we meet to discuss your education and retirement goals in the next two weeks. Does that sound reasonable? • I don't see any reason why we shouldn't proceed, do you? • Are you comfortable with the approach that I've described for working together?

On the other hand, open questions generally require a longer, more fully contemplated response. The overall purpose of open probes is to elicit more detailed information from the prospect or client. Open questions invite the prospect or client to think about her response, as well as to share opinions and feelings (versus facts). When open probes are used, the control of the conversation is turned over to the respondent.

Open questions begin with words or phrases like: what, why, how, tell me, describe. Here are examples of open probes often asked by financial professionals:

Open Questions	
Purpose	**Examples**
To follow-up on a closed question.	• What concerns you most about retirement?
To demonstrate genuine interest or concern.	• Tell me, how did you get involved with the Executive Moms in Touch organization? • How are you feeling about your finances these days?
To discover her specific financial needs, goals and concerns.	• Many of the women I work with are concerned about saving enough for retirement and protecting their family if they should become ill or die prematurely. Which of these matters to you the most? • What money concerns keep you up at night? • What is going well for you financially? What could go better? • What have been your experiences with people like me?
To help realize the extent of a problem, risk or need.	• Who in your family might you be called upon to provide care for? • What have you done so far to save for your children's education? • What do you know about what the government will and will not pay for should you or a family member need long-term care? • How has your situation changed since you purchased this policy (investment or financial plan?)

Questions and Social Styles

One can also use questions in a way that acknowledges the needs (for control, to be right, to be recognized, to be secure) of each of the four basic social styles. Here are key words to use and sample questions by style type:

- ***Drivers–Need to control:***
    - *Key words*: direct, control, command, manage, strategy, take charge, organize, command
    - *Sample questions:*
        ♦ What aspects of your financial situation would you like to gain better control over?
        ♦ What strategies have you put in place to achieve financial freedom?

- ♦ Do you see how this approach can improve the ability to direct your investment strategy?

- *Analytics–Need to be right:*
  - *Key words*: precise, exact, accurate, specific, careful, meticulous, logic, methodical, rational, systematic
  - *Sample questions:*
    - ♦ What analysis have you done so far to determine your approach?
    - ♦ What exactly are you trying to achieve?
    - ♦ Do you see the logic of this approach?

- *Expressives–Need to be recognized:*
  - *Key words*: compared, qualified, accepted, professional, praised, acclaimed, renowned
  - *Sample questions*:
    - ♦ How well would you say you are doing financially compared with where you want to be?
    - ♦ What benefits do you see in working with a well-known and respected company?
    - ♦ Do you see how working with a qualified financial professional can help you?

- **Amiables–Need to be secure:**
  - *Key words*: confident, assured, protected, dependable, steady, reliable, stable, sheltered, security
  - *Sample questions*:
    - ♦ How confident are you that you will be able to retire?
    - ♦ How dependable has your current financial advisor been?
    - ♦ If I can show you a way to improve your financial security, would you be interested in working with me?

Regardless of social style, striking a balance between open and closed questions is the basis for creating an exchange that is fluid, informative and leads to action. To summarize, open probes are used to get the prospect or client thinking and talking about what she believes is (or is not) important to her; while closed questions are helpful to get conversation on a topic started, demonstrate that you are listening, and gain commitment to proceed.

"What we think of as the moment of discovery is really the discovery of the right question."

Jonas Salk

Addressing Objections

objections

Objections are inevitable, and how they are addressed can either enhance or detract from a trust relationship. Traditional salespeople think in terms of overcoming objections, meaning they seek to counter them by reasserting how the prospect will benefit from their product or service. This approach is frequently a one-way, "telling and selling" exchange. Financial consultants, on the other hand, deal with objections by getting to the root of the issue and then working with the client toward a mutually acceptable outcome.

Questions or objections women raise are not usually a challenge to their financial consultant's expertise or integrity. Most women are voracious information seekers, and their questions present consultants with the opportunity to demonstrate professionalism and competence, as well as affirm that their concerns are important. Even when well intentioned, there can be a dangerous tendency to rush the process. The financial consultant may believe he or she is helping the client by keeping questions to a minimum and staying focused on the subject. However, she may perceive this as both disrespectful and manipulative, even if the intention is to be considerate of her time. Worse yet, her impression may be that the consultant is trying to control the situation by overcoming or shortchanging her need for information.

What is the most effective way to address objections? Here are four suggested steps:

1. **Identify the objection**. Probe to clarify concerns in a nonconfrontational way, using statements such as, "Help me understand your concerns about this approach." or "Tell me more." As she gives her response, be sure to actively listen for the underlying questions or issues.

2. **Acknowledge the issues or concerns**. Use a reflective statement/probe to confirm that you understand her: "If I hear you correctly, you are concerned about how much this might cost you, is that right?"

3. **Express empathy**. Demonstrate genuine concern and a spirit of partnership, "I understand how you might feel that way." or "I appreciate your concerns about cost. I share those with you."

4. **Offer alternatives and opportunities for compromise**. While the financial consultant's recommended solution might be the best approach; offering alternatives and their respective pros/cons reflects professionalism. Whether or not she implements the suggested approach or some sort of compromise, she is aware of her options and is taking at least some action to improve her financial security. It may be that additional steps are required in the future to realize the full benefits of the initial recommendation.

BUILDING TRUST THROUGH THE CONSULTATIVE PLANNING PROCESS

consultative planning

consultative selling

Throughout this book, the terms "consultant" and "consultative planning" are intentionally used to describe effective financial professionals and how they work with female clients. A consultant is defined by Webster as an individual who gives professional advice and services.[156] As such, consultants are viewed by others as experts in their field, meaning that the consultant must go beyond simply acting as a product vendor to being a highly knowledgeable and proficient solution provider.

The concept of consultative planning is derived from the "consultative selling" approach that first became practice in the 1970s. Consultative selling was coined by New York Times best-selling author Linda Richardson as an alternative to a transactional sales model. As perspective, here is a useful definition of consultative selling that is relevant to the financial services industry:

> Today, *consultative selling* is almost a household word. It is an approach to selling in which customer needs are used as the basis for a sales dialogue. When the word "consultative" was applied to sales in the 1970s, it was revolutionary. It marked a major transition from the salesperson as a purveyor of information and the customer as the recipient, to a much more collaborative interaction – one in which the customer's needs, not the product—was the focal point of the sale.
>
> By the early 1980s, the term began to be misunderstood as a long, arduous sales process that focused on needs at the expense of closing business. In fact, effective consultative selling, because the needs are clear and the recommendations made therefore are more likely to be on target, actually accelerates the sales cycle.
>
> There are three primary differentiators that mark a so-called consultative salesperson:
>
> 1. They ask more questions
> 2. They provide customized versus generic solutions
> 3. Their relationships with customers are interactive

Consultative selling is all about the dialogue between the salesperson and the customer. The word dialogue comes from the Greek and

---

156. "Consultant." *Webster Online Dictionary.* http://www.merriam-webster.com/dictionary/consultant.

means "to learn." In consultative selling, the salesperson learns about customer needs before talking product.

Product knowledge is transformed into tailored solutions when the solution is delivered and positioned based on the customer's needs and language. Needs are identified through a combination of preparation and effective probing.[157]

Women—Predisposed to Planning?

The consultative planning approach—with its focus on interactive, meaningful exchanges—can be powerfully effective in helping women achieve and protect their financial security. This hypothesis is supported not only by industry studies but also by research on women's decision-making tendencies and brain biology. As stated earlier, while men are more highly adapted to narrower focus and acuity, women prefer to understand issues in context with each other and then integrate them into a bigger picture. Due to higher levels of apprehension and lower financial literacy, the consultative process is one that both educates and increases confidence in taking needed action.

For financial consultants, these tendencies suggest that comprehensive planning versus a single product, transactional approach might be more effective when working with most women. Identifying the connections and tradeoffs across a range of financial issues can be both enormously helpful for women and absolutely crucial in planning for a secure future. By examining a range of financial issues, the comprehensive approach often makes dollars work more efficiently and stretch further. This means "connecting the dots" between her financial goals, needs, family, and life by addressing more than just one aspect of her financial plan. Further, the fact that women prefer to process and synthesize information more gradually than men do also supports the wisdom of delivering financial advice and services through a process versus a single- or even two-step transactional approach.

> "Long-range planning does not deal with future decisions, but with the future of present decisions."
>
> Peter Drucker

Planning for Her Success

Women who work with a professional to develop a financial plan report significantly higher confidence in their financial security, knowledge, decision making, and ability to meet emergencies. Many women want to plan, but need guidance in getting their plan together. According to research by Allianz, one in three women are eager to strengthen their financial planning skills but do

---

157. "Consultative Selling." *Wikipedia*, http://en.wikipedia.org/wiki/Consultative_selling.

not know where to begin.[158] Similarly, a study of women investors conducted by Merrill Lynch, found that female clients were significantly more likely to have a formal financial plan in place than were male clients (77 percent versus 62 percent).[159]

Further, in a 2008 survey by the Financial Planning Association and Ameriprise, women with a professionally prepared plan, were three times as likely to feel "very" or "extremely" prepared for retirement, versus women with no professional support (42 percent versus 14 percent).[160] The same study found that both women and men benefitted significantly more when their financial professional developed a comprehensive plan versus limiting advice to just one or two financial issues.[161] In addition, women with a comprehensive plan—compared to those who were either self-directed or worked with a professional on just one or two financial issues—were significantly more likely to say they:

- felt more in control of their financial futures

- were on track to meet goals of retirement planning, college funding and adequate protection/insurance

- had an optimistic outlook about their future, even during market downturns

- were better prepared for unexpected events because they had made cash reserves/emergency funds a priority

- had a greater depth of understanding of financial issues and their own financial activities[162]

In a nutshell, consultative planning works. In 2005, The University of Michigan Retirement Research Center conducted a study that surveyed more than 1,200 individuals, about 60 percent of whom were women older than age 50 (average age 66). Key findings revealed:

- Only about 30 percent of respondents had tried to understand how much money they would need for retirement.

- Of those who tried to calculate how much they needed, nearly two-thirds had developed a plan.

---

158. Allianz Life Insurance Company, Harris Interactive, Age Wave, "Women, Money and Power Study", 2008.
159. "When It Comes to Investing, Gender a Strong Influence on Behavior," Merrill Lynch Investment Managers (MLIM), 2005.
160. "The Value of Financial Planning," Harris Interactive study commissioned by Ameriprise and the Financial Planning Association, 2008.
161. Ibid.
162. Ibid.

- Of those who developed a plan, more than 85 percent said they almost or mostly stuck to the plan.

The best news for financial consultants is that nearly two-thirds (59.8 percent) of women who had done planning and were committed to action cited that they had consulted with a financial professional.[163]

In light of these benefits, why is it that just slightly more than one in four (28 percent) women have a financial plan in place?[164] Beyond procrastination, another big impediment is the perception of high cost that many have about working with a financial professional to develop a plan. Almost three in four women say they do not have enough assets, income, or cannot afford a plan or consultant.[165] This is an unfortunate misperception indeed, when one considers both the financial opportunities and risks that many women have.

> "Planning is bringing the future into the present so that you can do something about it now."
>
> Alan Lakein

The Benefits of Consultative Planning to Financial Consultants

Industry research also reveals that planning strengthens the client-consultant relationship, as well as financial professional's income. In a 2009 study by the Partnership for Retirement Education (PREP), professionals who identified themselves as planning experts reported that their typical client had twice the total assets invested with them, as compared to professionals focused on individual product sales. In addition, those who took a long-term planning approach had three times the assets under management and 40 percent higher annual revenue than the non-planners. It is important to note that PREP found that there was no significant difference between planners and non-planners in years of experience, size of firm, job function or types of products they offer. In other words, one does not have to be called a "financial planner" to take a planning approach.

The bottom line is that planning is mutually beneficial. Women prefer working in a consultative planning relationship and benefit from taking action to increase their financial security. Consultants benefit by acquiring more business and referrals. The overall reputation of the financial services industry is enhanced when clients are informed, have taken prudent action and are satisfied with their consultant.

---

163. Annamaria Lusardi, "Planning and Financial Literacy: How Do Women Fare?" (Dartmouth College, University of Michigan, Retirement Research Center and NBER, 2006).
164. "The Value of Financial Planning," Harris Interactive study commissioned by Ameriprise and the Financial Planning Association, 2008.
165. Ibid.

Consultative Planning Scope

six areas

Six key areas are addressed in the most comprehensive financial plans. While the financial consultant may not be the sole provider of solutions within each of these areas, understanding their scope establishes a valuable framework. The point here is not to turn the consultant into a comprehensive financial planner who addresses each of the six areas. His/her company, business model, and professional goals may not support the comprehensive planning approach. However, the more one is able to identify financial issues and risks needing attention, even when they fall outside of the consultant's specialty, the more value is brought to the client. While the financial consultant may not personally be engaged in addressing all areas, as the client's indispensible advisor, he or she will help hold the client and other advisors accountable for necessary and agreed upon action. While there are slight variations across the industry in terms of the scope of financial planning, these are most commonly included areas:

1. **Current Financial Position**
    - managing cash flow (income and expense) efficiencies
    - improving balance sheet (assets and liabilities) and structure (e.g., debt management)
    - building cash reserves for emergencies and/or opportunities

2. **Protection Planning**
    - managing personal, business, property, and liability risks
    - incorporating employee insurance benefits (e.g., health, disability, life, key person and long-term care)
    - working with risk management professionals where indicated

3. **Tax Planning**
    - incorporating earned, investment and business income, as well as asset transfer (estate, capital gains) tax liabilities
    - integrating tax management with the other five areas of the plan
    - working with accounting professionals, where indicated

4. **Investment Planning**
    - building, managing, and distributing investments for a specified purpose (e.g., children's education, retirement, asset purchase)
    - determining client risk tolerance and portfolio risk/return balance
    - incorporating employee investment benefits (e.g., stock options, grants)
    - working with investment professionals where indicated

5. **Retirement Planning**

- identifying pre-retirement capital and income requirements to meet client goals
- developing post-retirement sources of income, including distribution of assets
- incorporating employee retirement benefits (e.g., defined contribution and defined benefit plans)

6. **Estate Planning**

   - planning for the preservation of assets and their orderly, efficient passing at the end of life
   - integrating charitable giving, where desired
   - working with estate planning professionals, where indicated

Since there is high overlap across these six areas, the more holistically they are integrated, the more efficient that plan will be. In chapters 4 through 7, we will examine the six areas of planning in greater detail, along with the issues or risks many women face related to each of them.

> "Particulars are not to be examined till the whole has been surveyed."
>
> Emanuel Celler

Prioritization of Needs and Goals Across The Six Areas

Obviously, not all financial goals and needs are equal in priority or weight. Most clients, whether male or female, single or married/partnered, do not possess sufficient resources to address all of their goals and risk management priorities. How do financial consultants help clients prioritize action across these six areas? It may be helpful to start with the most commonly articulated financial priorities according to gender as identified in research conducted by the Financial Planning Association and Ameriprise Financial in 2008. Here is a summary of some of their key findings:

What are your primary financial goals?	Male	Female
Saving/planning for the future	89%	92%
Planning for retirement	61%	64%
Saving money/accumulation of wealth	60%	53%
Insurance or financial protection	14%	19%
Reducing taxes	17%	14%
Estate planning	16%	15%
Saving for education	12%	18%
Used with permission. *The Financial Planning Association (FPA) and Ameriprise Value of Financial Planning Study Consumer Attitudes and Behaviors in a Changing Economy*, was conducted online within the United States by Harris Interactive on behalf of the Financial Planning Association and Ameriprise Financial Services, Inc., between June 27 and July 18, 2008.		

While the rank order of goals is consistent between the genders, there are interesting and telling differences between men and women regarding their priorities, as revealed in the chart. Specifically, more women than men said that saving for the future, retirement, insurance and education planning were important. The inference that can be drawn here is consistent with findings from other industry research, indicating that women are more concerned than men about financial security and taking care of family needs.

However, goals are not the only consideration when helping clients prioritize financial strategies and action. For example, only one out of five women and one out of six men in the study said that insurance protection was a primary goal. Yet, having adequate protection is a foundational element of a well-developed and balanced plan. Without it, a client's financial security, let alone the achievement of longer-term goals, can be seriously compromised by unaddressed financial risk.

financial planning pyramid

Increasing the client's recognition of risk and helping her align priorities accordingly can be aided by educating her on the basics of the *financial planning pyramid*. While there are variations of the pyramid across the industry, the core principles are consistent: financial balance begins with establishing a solid foundation of economic security and the ability to meet emergencies. In other words, adequate protection and cash reserves come first.

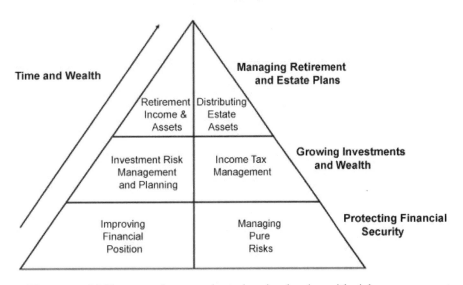

The pyramid illustrates how prudent planning begins with risk management and proceeds in a systematic way to build and ultimately distribute wealth. The base level represents protecting against life's uncertainties and possibilities of significant financial loss. Once that foundation is laid, then one can transition to the second level, which represents the wealth accumulation component of the plan. As the client moves up the pyramid (that is, as her financial security and well being improves), the focus of the plan shifts from protection to building capital, which typically involves systematically growing investments for goals such as retirement, education, and special purposes (e.g., downpayment on a house, buying a business, vacation or investment property). The top of the pyramid becomes important as wealth grows and accumulation goals are achieved. This last component addresses the management and distribution of retirement assets, as well as the preservation and distribution of her estate.

Comparing Planning Processes

planning processes

Besides its scope, financial planning is also defined by process. Over the past few years, there has been heated debate about what financial planning is and is not. It seems that there are as many definitions of financial planning as there are people who believe they are engaged in it. Regardless of all the controversy about what financial planning is, there is little debate about the process of planning. Consultative, insurance, investment, and financial planning (and for that matter, ANY type of planning) all use the same basic steps. Planning is planning is planning.

This chart illustrates the consistencies between the processes of consultative, risk management, and financial planning (as defined by the Certified Financial Planner Board):

Step	Consultative Planning	Risk Management Planning	Financial Planning
1	Meet the prospect and establish goals	Determine objectives	Establish and define the advisor–client relationship
2	Gather information	Identify risk	Determine goals and gather data
3	Analyze information	Analyze/measure risk	Analyze and evaluate the data
4	Develop and present the plan	Consider alternative risk treatment devices and select the device(s) that best address the risk	Develop and present a plan
5	Implement the plan	Implement the plan	Implement the plan
6	Service the plan	Monitor the plan	Monitor the plan

It is important to recognize that the process of planning does not have to be exhaustive, time consuming or labor intensive. Not all situations and not all clients warrant rigorous analysis or extensive examination of their goals and/or protection needs. Further, not all consultants wish to be viewed as a financial planner. That said, the point here goes back to the process of "diagnosing before prescribing" discussed in Chapter 1. In other words, one takes a needs-based versus product-based approach, even if the process itself is collapsed into just one meeting with the client.

For the purposes of our discussion, detailed consultative planning incorporates the following steps and objectives:

1. **Meet the Prospect and Establish Goals.** In this step, one seeks to establish rapport, explain his or her business purpose, ask thought provoking questions and *listen, listen, listen*. Most often, this step is completed during the initial interview.

    The financial consultant's objectives at this stage of the process are to:

    - reinforce trust

    - establish mutual expectations

    - help her see the benefit of working together

    - transform the relationship from prospect to client

    Throughout the initial interview, the consultant needs to earn the client's faith and confidence in order to move to the analysis phase. This includes these tasks:

    - explaining the financial consultant's role and approach, including disclosure on compensation

    - asking questions to identify her needs, goals, problems, priorities and attitudes

    - reviewing, at least preliminarily, the financial worksheet and/or checklist if she brought them with her, within the context of her goals and concerns

    - demonstrating, in general terms, how the financial consultant can help her, including describing the planning process he/she uses

    - motivating her to take action to meet those needs, achieve her goals and address risk areas

    - obtaining agreement to proceed to the information-gathering step

    At the conclusion of these tasks, if she has not yet made a commitment to work with the financial consultant, she is evaluating whether or not to proceed. Likewise, the consultant may need to follow-up and gather more information to assess whether or not to do business together. In other words, does she qualify as a potential, and preferably, ideal client? Does she have a need for the financial consultant's products and services? Can she afford them? What are her expectations? Is she motivated to achieve her goals and manage her risks? Perhaps most importantly, is she the type of person with whom the consultant wishes to work?

> "Clarifying expectations sometimes takes a great deal of courage. It seems easier to act as though differences don't exist and to hope things will work out than it is to face the differences and work together to arrive at a mutually agreeable set of expectations."
>
> Stephen Covey

2. **Gather Information.** At this point, both client and consultant have determined to move on to the next phase of the working/planning relationship. The consultant has already achieved a certain level of trust and gained permission to do additional work on the client's behalf. The objectives for the consultant at this point are to:

    - fulfill ethical and suitability requirements (e.g., gather enough information to complete a thorough analysis and to meet regulatory requirements to "know your customer").

    - begin thinking through possible options, including their pros and cons to meet the client's best interest

    It is imperative that the consultant learns as much as possible about the client to support analysis, conclusions and recommendations. One must determine not only the facts, but also her feelings about her personal and financial situation. An effective and compliant fact finder can be a helpful tool to uncover much of the quantitative information required for analysis.

    Before completing this step, it is helpful to confirm the consultant's understanding of the client's goals and priorities. In addition, it is a best practice to ask her how much money (in capital and/or cash flow) she is willing to dedicate to implementing her plan. Recommendations must be based on both her willingness and ability to fund goals/needs or they will not be implemented.

3. **Analyze the Information.** Once the required information has been assembled and the financial goals—along with planning assumptions—have been identified, then the consultant will develop an analysis of her situation and risks relative to her financial objectives. The purposes of the information analysis phase are to:

    - identify and measure risks and goal funding shortfalls

- determine strategic and tactical alternatives for risk and investment management

A detailed analysis includes the following considerations:

- analyzing appropriate financial statements and documents

- projecting the outcomes of the current plan (if she does nothing differently than what she is doing now)

- analyzing her current and desired situations as they relate to the major planning areas: insurance planning and risk management, employee benefits, investment planning, income tax planning, retirement planning, and estate planning

- identifying obstacles to achieving the desired outcomes

- determining viable alternatives including analysis of options which may produce results that are inferior to the consultant's ultimate recommendation (e.g., higher tax rates, lower rates of return, costs and so on)

- quantifying the opportunity costs and trade-offs of each viable alternative

- comparing the costs of implementing solutions with her willingness/ability to fund them

(Note: The scope and level of detail of the analysis will depend on the extent of client needs, as well as consultant's ability to address them.)

planning software In light of the complexities associated with most aspects of financial planning, the consultant will need to turn to planning software to support analysis. There is simply no way to adequately plan for financial decisions that often impact decades of financial security without the help of analysis software. The days of "yellow pad" planning, in which one uses paper and pencil to craft a high level solution, are long gone.

An extensive array of planning tools is available to the public and financial professionals, and these tools often yield a correspondingly wide range of results. Generally speaking, the more input required to complete the analysis, the higher the quality of analysis output.

goal-based A key distinction between analysis tools is whether they are based on goals or cash flow. While both usually incorporate inflation and rate of return assumptions, goal-based software programs take a "top down" approach. That is, they take a high level number (e.g., total current income or expenses) and apply that figure, or a percentage of that figure, in a projection. The most common example of the top down method is where retirement calculators require plugging in a percentage of current income (e.g., 80 percent) as the amount desired in retirement. This is sometimes referred to as the "replacement ratio." Cash-flow based software, on the other hand, uses a "bottom up" approach. Through a bottom up method, one works with his/her client to build assumptions at the line item level for both income (e.g., earned, investment, pension, social security) and expenses (e.g., mortgage, rent, food, auto, clothing, discretionary items, and so on.)

cash-flow driven

Cash-flow planning software provides the consultant with a high degree of control over data through the ability to turn income and expense streams on and off, as well as apply inflation assumptions specific to a line item. Since inflation rates can vary significantly by expense category, it can be important to reflect those that increase disproportionately. For example, medical expenses have outpaced general inflation by almost three times in the last 10 years. Without the ability to specifically call out medical expenses and apply an inflation rate unique to that line item, there is a high risk of understating amounts needed for long range retirement and survivor needs.

Regardless of the planning tool used, it is important to recognize limitations so that one can accommodate them in "workarounds," if necessary. Even if one uses a fairly simple calculator to quantify an investment or insurance need, the focus remains on the diagnosis (analysis) before moving to the prescription (products).

4. **Develop and Present the Plan.** After analyzing the client's situation and possible options, the consultant is ready to finalize the plan and recommendations. The objectives at this stage are to:

- reinforce trust

- review and educate client on both strategic and tactical options

- gain commitment to action and mutual accountabilities

In this step, education is an essential ingredient, if not a requirement, to her willingness to take action. It is important that the consultant or his/her team spend time reviewing options and preparing recommendations. When providing alternative solutions, one should include a synopsis of their relevant advantages and disadvantages, as well as a discussion of costs and outcomes.

strategy call

A best practice is to conduct a "strategy call" with the client. This call occurs after one has completed the analysis and identified possible alternatives, but before the solution presentation. During this call, the consultant reviews analysis findings with the client and describes options, including their respective benefits, costs, and risks. The strategy call helps both the client and consultant determine what she likes or does not like about the recommendation(s), and if there are alternatives needing further exploration. The primary benefit of this step is that both client and consultant act as partners in developing financial solutions that make sense and are fully disclosed. This reinforces trust and helps surface objections or the need for additional information/education prior to her being able to take action. Finally, by agreeing to strategies in advance, there is little to no tension or anxiety on either the client's or the consultant's part during the solutions presentation.

When presenting the plan and recommendations, the following steps are effective:

- recapping her financial needs, wants, and desires
- restating her situation
- reviewing the analysis findings and conclusions
- describing the alternatives and their pros/cons
- presenting recommendations and rationale.
- gaining commitment in principle to move forward

> "The effective execution of a plan is what counts, not mere planning on paper."
>
> J.R.D. Tata

5. **Implement the Plan.** When one has communicated well, conducted thorough fact finding, developed a well-thought-out analysis and partnered on developing strategic solutions, then implementing the plan is simply a matter of logic. The objectives of this stage are to:

   - reinforce trust
   - take action to manage risks and achieve goals

   Once the prospect has agreed to action, the financial consultant's role is to help her implement the plan by acquiring the products and/or services agreed to. Implementation can include such activities as completing all of the required forms and applications in good order and delivering an insurance policy.

   Of course, not every client will implement every recommendation. Even the best financial consultant may need to make several attempts to gain agreement and move to action. Sometimes, the client may postpone action, and the consultant is then forced to make several appointments and compensate for a lapse of time between the presentation and implementation.

It is important to document all recommendations. This means identifying the action to take (what), along with the rationale (why), responsibilities (who) and timing (when). Capturing action items does not have to be an arduous, time-consuming task. Rather, this step can often be accomplished through a straightforward one-page summary letter that identifies what needs to be done next, by when and by whom. The letter might include a simple action table like this one:

Recommendation	Rationale	Timing	Responsible
Purchase $378,000 of 20 year level term life insurance on Janice.	The analysis reveals a $378,000 gap in Bob's survivor income until his retirement when he is then eligible for his pension.	Today (March 1st)	Janice and (insert your name)
For Jason's college education, contribute to a 529 plan in a growth oriented mutual fund.	The analysis shows a monthly funding shortfall of $450 invested at 8% for Jason's college fund. You are only able to commit $350/mo at the present time.	Today (March 1st)	Bob and (insert your name)
Increase contributions to Jason's college fund by $100 per month when Janice gets her raise.	Increase to full funding when cash flow becomes available.	October 1st	Bob and (insert your name)

Beyond demonstrating professionalism, this step sets one apart from the competition, and according to research by LIMRA, increases product ownership (as much as 40 percent higher than undocumented recommendations.)[166] Documenting next steps also establishes the expectation that more business will be implemented in the future, along with the timeframe for when that may occur. Few clients are able to implement a broad course of action in just one sitting.

Last, drafting and delivering written recommendations can be an important means of documenting agreements and protecting oneself in a regulatory and sometimes litigious environment. *(A sample summary letter of recommendations is included in the Appendix.)*

6. **Service the Plan.** In this final step, the financial consultant works to create a client for life. Service cements the relationship, yielding important dividends in incremental revenue and referrals. When monitoring and servicing a plan, the consultant's objectives are to:

---

166. LIMRA, "Advisor Impact on Retirement: Opportunity is Knocking," 2007. (2006 survey of 3,393 pre-retirees with >$50k investable assets.)

- reinforce trust
- adjust plan/actions as indicated
- increase client satisfaction, commitment and loyalty
- build cross-sell opportunities

Some service is reactive—initiated by clients requesting a needed change, such as an increase in coverage or change in beneficiary. In these situations, the client should reasonably expect to receive good service. However, what often differentiates good from great financial professionals is the proactive nature of his or her service strategy. Many people buy a product and never hear from a salesperson again. Proactive servicing strategies, such as monitoring the plan through periodic reviews and relationship-building activities, enable the consultant to stay in touch with clients. It is high-contact and proactive service that builds clientele. The consultant should set expectations about his or her service promise and make those promises reality.

CHAPTER SUMMARY

This chapter has explored the aspects of building strong working relationships with women clients, in order to earn their trust and their business. Fundamental to these outcomes is the understanding of her needs and preferences, which may be influenced by her gender and social style. The development of exceptional communications skills is also essential to the creation and maintenance of a productive and mutually beneficial association. These skills are heavily relied upon throughout the consultative planning process and the scope of areas examined.

The coming chapters will delve more deeply into the six areas of planning, with particular emphasis on those aspects of special importance or concern to women, specifically:

1. Improving and protecting her financial position. Since risk management and financial soundness are vitally important to women, in Chapter 4, we examine:

    - the two categories of risk—pure risk and speculative risk

    - the alternative approaches to risk management

    - how to help the client manage cash flow, emergency reserves and debt

    - the basics of women and property/casualty, liability and health

2. Protecting her income, assets, and family (Chapter 5)

3. Managing taxes (Chapter 6)

4. Investing with purpose and intent (Chapter 6)

5. Increasing retirement security (Chapter 7)

6. Maximizing her legacy (Chapter 7)

Chapter 8 will focus extensively on the final phase of the consultative selling process: servicing the plan.

> "The future belongs to those who believe in the beauty of their dreams."
>
> Eleanor Roosevelt

CHAPTER 3 TOOLS AND RESOURCES

- Courses from The American College
    - FA 262 Foundations of Financial Planning – An Overview
    - FA 263 Foundations of Financial Planning – The Process
    - FA 290 Ethics for the Financial Services Professional
    - HS 300 Financial Planning: Process and Environment
    - HS 332: Financial Planning Applications

- Tools
    - Financial worksheet and checklist
    - Recommendations summary letter

- Recommended Reading
    - *Questions Great Financial Advisors Ask...And Investors Need to Know*, Alan Parisse and David Richman, Kaplan Publishing, 2006

    - *Values-Based Selling, The Art of Building High-Trust Client Relationships*, Bill Bachrach, Aim High Publishing, 2003

    - *The Female Brain*, Louann Brizendine, Morgan Road Books/Random House, 2006

4

Protecting Her Financial Position and Security

Learning Objectives
An understanding of the material in this chapter should enable the student to

4-1. Describe the two categories of risk—pure risk and speculative risk—and their differences. 2, 3,

4-2. Define the three types of pure risk.

4-3. Explain the alternative approaches to managing pure risk.

4-4. Describe why it is important to gather information on her cash flow and financial position when helping her manage risks.

4-5. Detail three possible strategies to improve yield on cash reserve assets.

4-6. Explain why it is important to be aware of risks that women may be exposed to even if financial consultants are not personally involved in placing insurance coverage to address those risks.

4-7. Outline the basic elements of property/casualty, liability and health insurances.

INTRODUCTION

In Chapters 1 through 3, we discussed how financial consultants can set themselves apart from the competition by marketing effectively to and building high trust relationships with female prospects and clients. This is achieved through strong relationship-building skills and following the steps of the complete marketing/planning process.

Now, we turn our attention to the scope, or six areas, of financial planning. By increasing one's awareness of issues that women face in these six areas, along with acquiring greater technical competence and expertise, female clients receive more valuable information and advice. More value delivered means more revenue generated. Our examination of the scope of planning follows the hierarchy of the Financial Planning Pyramid, reflected below.

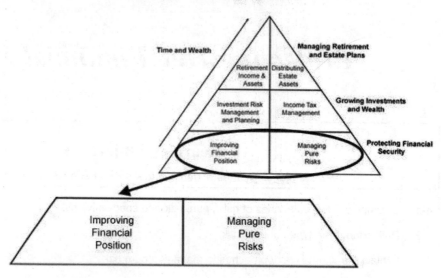

Financial Planning Pyramid

The underlying concept of the pyramid is that one must first must lay a firm foundation of financial security upon which wealth is then built. Establishing a solid base through risk identification, measurement and planning is fundamental to the client's well-being. Although the media and consumers often direct their attention towards the middle and upper tiers of the Financial Planning Pyramid—the more sensational aspects of building investments and wealth—wise financial consultants know that wealth can be wiped out in an instant, without a sound foundation of cash reserves and adequate protection. Helping a female client establish and protect her current financial position, represented as the base of the pyramid, is an essential first step.

In Chapters 4 and 5, we explore those issues and obstacles that threaten financial well-being, including the disproportionate risks that women face. Two categories of risk are covered in Chapter 4—*pure risk* and *speculative risk*—along with an overview of the three types of *pure risk*: *property*, *liability* and *personal*. Since financial position is critical to the client's ability to meet those risks, one must always know how to help her make the most of cash flow, emergency cash reserves and debt management. The examination of risks in Chapter 4 also evaluates financial losses that are frequently difficult to measure and quantify—specifically property, liability and health risks. Chapter 5 focuses exclusively on helping women plan for personal risks associated with disability, long-term care and survivor needs, which they are more prone to experience.

After establishing the basic framework for strengthening and protecting the client's financial position, in Chapters 6 and 7, we turn our attention to the top two layers of the pyramid—wealth management and distribution.

MANAGING RISKS

The financial consultant's ability to clearly and objectively explain risks to clients, both male and female, can help them better prepare to meet them. The prospect of financial loss is often an emotionally charged issue for clients of any gender. Thinking about and evaluating the magnitude and consequences of economic demise are tasks that many people prefer to avoid. That is why the role of trusted financial professional is so important. Consultants are uniquely positioned to help clients understand what risks they may be exposed to, so that they can be managed effectively through the use of insurance and/or other risk handling techniques.

For financial planning and insurance purposes, the term *risk* equates to the possibility of financial loss. In applying this definition, the client must recognize there are two ways that financial loss can occur. The most common concept of loss relates to a reduction in value of something that is possessed. For example, the value of the client's home can be reduced by fire, the value of her income-earning ability can be reduced by disability, or the value of her bond portfolio can be reduced by an increase in interest rates. However, a loss can also arise from a reduction in value of something she does not already possess, but expects to receive in the future, such as experiencing a 2 percent loss on an investment that was expected to generate a 10 percent return, or receiving a smaller inheritance because the executor of the estate had done a poor job in its administration. Since loss can arise from a reduction in either the value of something she already possesses, or something she expects to receive in the future, risk can be said to involve the possibility of financial loss. Defined this way, risk can be divided into two categories:

pure risk

1. *pure risk*—involves only the possibility of financial loss

speculative risk

2. *speculative risk*—involves not only the possibility of financial loss, but also the possibility of financial gain

Both pure and speculative risks involve the potential for financial loss. However, with pure risk the possibility of gain is essentially absent and all that remains is either loss or no loss.

Types of Pure Risk

Pure risks can be categorized as *property risks*, *liability risks* and *personal risks*:

property risks
liability risks
personal risks

- *property risks*—involve the possibility of
  - direct losses associated with the need to replace or repair damaged or missing property
  - indirect (consequential) losses, such as additional living expenses that are caused by direct loss

- *liability risks*–involve the possibility of
  - loss from damaging or destroying the property of others
  - loss causing the physical or financial injury to others
- *personal risks*–involve the possibility of
  - loss of income earning ability due to
    - premature death
    - disability
    - unemployment
    - retirement
  - extra expenses associated with illness, accidental injuries, or the inability to perform some activities of daily living (ADLs)—bathing, dressing, toileting, eating, transferring from bed to chair and maintaining continence

With these definitions in mind, the consultant needs to understand specific risk exposures female clients may have and how those risks may be managed.

Alternative Approaches to Managing Pure Risk

Financial professionals have a two-fold responsibility to provide clients with education and options. The more the consultant is able to provide both, the more female clients are empowered to make well-informed financial decisions. In the best of circumstances, a client's decision about whether or not to insure a risk should emerge after a full exploration of alternatives.

loss control
loss financing

The techniques typically available to individuals and families for handling pure risks are grouped in two categories: *loss control* and *loss financing*. Loss control (sometimes referred to as risk control) deals with either reducing the probability that events resulting in financial loss will occur or minimizing the impact if those losses do occur. Since some losses occur whether or not any control activities are taken, loss financing deals with how to fund those losses.

Both loss control and financing include methods for handling pure risk. Approaches to loss control include *risk avoidance*, *prevention* and *reduction*. The two most commonly used techniques for pure loss financing are *risk retention* and *transference* (through insurance).

Loss Control

risk avoidance
risk prevention
risk reduction

1. **Risk Avoidance** eliminates the activity or condition that gives rise to a particular risk, so that the possibility of loss becomes nonexistent. For example, Sally used to live in an area prone to flooding. Last year, she moved to higher ground, removing herself from flood risk. By doing so, Sally eliminated her possibility of property loss due to flooding. While risk avoidance is potentially the most powerful risk management action; in most cases, it is difficult to accomplish. To

illustrate, if the client is concerned about liability risk associated with driving her car, to eliminate the risk, she would need to seek other forms of transportation. In most areas of the country, public transportation is inadequate to replace the use of a car. Since it is neither possible nor practical to avoid all risks, it is therefore necessary to consider techniques that prevent, reduce or finance losses.

2. ***Risk Prevention*** involves attempting to reduce the impact or frequency of a loss by preventing its occurrence. Risk prevention actions tend to be directed at hazards or conditions that increase the likelihood of the loss occurring. For example, losing weight and exercising regularly can mitigate certain health risks. These prevention measures lower the probability of the client's potential for certain chronic illnesses. However, they do not totally eliminate her health risks. While the goal of risk prevention is to eliminate the occurrence of the event; not all exposures can be totally prevented. Therefore, some effort should also be made to prepare for and minimize the magnitude of the losses if/when they occur.

3. ***Risk Reduction*** aims to reduce the severity of losses that might happen. Risk reduction can be used before, during or after one has experienced financial loss. Two examples of loss reduction action relative to the possibility of fire are maintaining fire extinguishers and installing smoke detectors in the home.

Loss Financing

risk retention

1. ***Risk Retention*** is the process of financing or paying for one's own losses. Individuals frequently purchase insurance for pure risks and fail to consider other loss financing techniques. Yet, in many cases, voluntary and deliberate risk retention can be a useful tool for handling pure risks. However, involuntary or unintentional risk retention due to failure to identify exposures can be a serious problem.

   Women are frequently unaware of some of their most financially devastating risks and, as a result, inadvertently retain those risks. For example, long-term care is a risk that is all too often retained with frequently dire financial consequences. (This risk is explored in detail in Chapter 5.)

   In cases where the client consciously practices risk retention, she may set aside funds specifically earmarked for a particular risk. Building up cash reserves to pay several months of expenses if she becomes unemployed or temporarily disabled is an example of conscious risk retention.

   Retention is a cost-effective approach for handling pure risk when the maximum possible loss is too small to cause financial hardship. On the other hand, retaining risks where the probability of loss is small, but the potential amount of loss is severe, is a dangerous practice. For example, Samantha is a young parent with dependent children who decides not to purchase life insurance because of the small probability of death at her age. However, Samantha's retention of this risk could have very serious consequences for her family, and her children especially, if she met an untimely end.

Retaining some risk is often practiced even when insurance is placed. For example, a deductible or waiting period may apply before the insurance coverage pays a benefit, or the loss exposure may be excluded under an insurance contract.

risk transference

2. ***Risk Transference*** is a risk-financing technique that transfers the financial burden of risk from one party (the insured) to another party (the insurer) for a price (premium). In addition, insurance involves the insurer pooling together a large number of similar risks to make losses more predictable and, thus, to reduce risk. A technique for handling pure risk must have both of these features—risk transfer and risk pooling—in order to be insurance.

Translating and communicating these alternative approaches to the client's personal situation can be highly effective in helping her understand and "own" her plan of action. Which risks of financial loss might she be able to withstand by having adequate reserves to finance them? Are there opportunities for her to evade some risks and/or prevent others from happening?

transfer all, some or none

For those risks that cannot be avoided, reduced or prevented, there are three basic options: (1) transfer all, (2) transfer none, or (3) transfer some of the risk. The risk management aspect of the consultative planning process helps the financial professional explain what risks she may be exposed to, how much she can retain and how much she could or should transfer.

RISK MANAGEMENT AND HER FINANCIAL POSITION

Risk management is the discipline of determining the client's risk exposure and how her risk might be dealt with; whether it is avoided, prevented, reduced, retained and/or transferred. The initial step in the process is to identify her potential to reduce or eliminate a given risk. If neither is possible, then the consultant needs to determine her capacity to retain or absorb risks before investigating transference (i.e., insurance) alternatives. Her capacity to absorb risk can only be understood by thoroughly examining her financial position to meet them.

financial position

It is not unusual for those solely focused on selling financial products, versus the consultative planning process, to overlook the details of a prospect's or client's financial situation. Some producers, particularly those newer to the business, may be concerned about asking questions they fear are intrusive. Others may believe that details about finances are not required in order to make product recommendations. Regardless of the consultant's intent, ignoring the client's financial position seriously compromises the quality of advice given and, worse yet, can lead to inappropriate product placement. It is helpful therefore, to ask thought filled questions about her goals to improve her financial security. Here are useful questions to ask when uncovering facts and attitudes about her financial position:

The Art of Discovery—Her Financial Position
• What do you feel is standing in the way of improving your cash flow?
• What is preventing you from saving on a regular basis?
• How would you cope with a sudden financial emergency (like a job loss), or if you needed to help a family member?
• If you could change just one thing about your current financial position, what would it be? Why is that important to you?
• If things don't improve, what do you think might happen?
• If I could help you improve your financial position, would that be worth meeting for an hour?

Of course not every client will want to share specifics about her finances. However, it is the consultant's obligation to inform her of the importance of having all the facts and to attempt to collect relevant data. After all, patients do not expect their doctors to diagnose illnesses, let alone prescribe treatment, without providing symptoms and possibly undergoing testing first. The same principles apply to financial professionals when determining an individual's readiness to achieve goals and mitigate risks.

To help communicate the importance of collecting and inspecting financial data, one should be candid with clients: *"I believe a prescription without a diagnosis is malpractice. For me to best help you, I need to understand your current financial health in order to arrive at appropriate recommendations that meet your situation. Does that make sense?"*

A close examination of her financial position may also strengthen the trust bond between client and consultant and by doing so, may have higher appeal to women. As we have seen, a woman's heightened interest in achieving financial security not only reflects a frequently low confidence in money management, but also inherent fears about her risks of becoming destitute. These findings from recent studies underscore just how common these worries are:

- According to a study by LLuminari, nearly three out of four women place a high importance on financial security, compared to less than one in three men.[167]

---

167. "Study Reveals Women Who Proactively Manage Their Finances Are Healthier and Happier," *Business Wire,* June 25, 2008.

- Even before the global economic downturn, 90 percent of women said they were worried about their financial security,[168] and almost half (46.9 percent) said they were not at all satisfied with their current financial situation, versus just one third of men (36.3 percent).[169]

Since these research studies were conducted before the so-called Great Recession of 2008/2009, one can only imagine how fears most likely have grown since then. Of course, women are not alone in their concerns about financial well-being and readiness to handle risk. The spending and savings behaviors of Americans over the last decade or so have been reckless, to say the least. Prior to the economic crisis, it is estimated that half of all Americans were living paycheck to paycheck.[170] Further, the U.S. savings rate had been the lowest of any major industrial nation,[171] averaging about 2 percent since 2000. The rate even briefly dipped into the negative in 2005, meaning Americans were spending more than they earned.[172] For perspective, the chart below reflects savings patterns by quarter from 2000–2008:

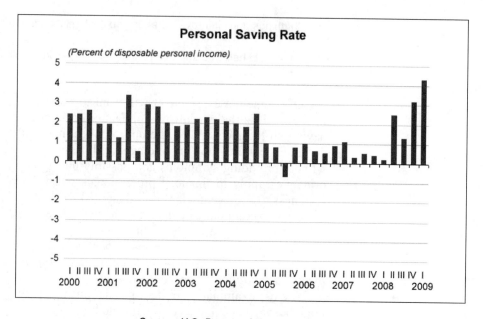

Source: U.S. Bureau of Economic Analysis

---

168. "Allianz Women Money and Power Study," 2006.
169. Myvesta.org, "Myvesta.org Survey Finds Debt Equals Depression for Many," November, 2001.
170. Virginia Credit Union League, "Financial Literacy Statistics," http://vacul.com/fin_lit/stats.htm
171. Ibid.
172. U.S. Department of Commerce.

One ray of light among the anguish from the economic downturn is that frugality is once again fashionable, at least for the time being. Many Americans once again are studying their habits and seeing what expenses might be eliminated and reduced. Most, however, lack a plan that helps create necessary financial discipline and motivation to stick with a long-term pattern of saving and investing.

Helping Her Manage Cash Flow

cash flow

Managing cash flow is not just about where money is being spent. It is also about the achievement (or lack of achievement) of goals. Uncovering financial objectives through consultative planning is a powerful step in improving both cash flow and risk management, as it establishes a necessary sense of purpose. Strong, unwavering purpose and resolve is often required in order for clients to make necessary sacrifices for the sake of greater financial security and their long-term goals.

Unless the client is committed to meaningful financial objectives, how successful can any savings and/or protection plan be? Evaluating cash flow must not only consider where the money goes, but also where it is not going. This is important for women, since they earn less than men on average, take time out of work for caregiving, and as a result, have less saved. It is not surprising that more than half (53 percent) of women want to know how to start saving or investing on limited income.[173]

The financial consultant can begin assessing cash flow issues and opportunities as early as the initial interview, if the prospect/client has brought an income and expense statement with her (*see the 30 minute financial checkup tool referenced in Chapter 2 and in the Appendix*). If she has not yet completed this exercise, then the consultant will need to go through a more detailed fact-finding process. When working on a cash flow plan, it is important to create a line item level of expense identification, determine excess income, and categorize committed versus discretionary expenses.

Committed expenses are those necessary to maintain a basic standard of living, such as housing, utilities, medical care, insurance, and transportation. If one is not able to reduce committed expenses (the "needs"), at least in the short term, there usually is some (often a good amount of) room in those expenses that are discretionary (the "wants"). When evaluating cash flow, a good place to start is determining if there already is excess unallocated income that can be diverted to fund financial objectives or fill a void in risk protection. This is done before analyzing committed versus discretionary spending. In other words, is there more money left over at the end of the month, or more month left than money? If there is excess income, ask the client how much she is willing to dedicate to savings and/or risk management as a starting point.

Identifying discretionary dollars that can be reallocated, along with savings she may achieve by improving cost efficiencies, can be important sources of

---

173. "Allianz Women Money and Power Study," 2008.

incremental funds for financial security and goal achievement. The power of the consultant's objectivity in this regard is demonstrated to the client in three ways by: (1) helping her determine possible sources of cash that can be redirected; (2) quantifying the impact and opportunity costs to her goal achievement and financial security if no changes are made; and by doing both, (3) partnering on a plan of action and accountability.

Some liken the process of identifying additional funding sources to playing "dollar detective." In this role, the consultant looks for expenses that can be reduced or eliminated, incremental income (i.e., in excess of regular earnings), as well as sources of capital that may be earmarked for goal achievement and/or risk transference. Many female clients find great value in an objective, trustworthy appraisal of their cash flow, especially in the context of their current and future financial security. The chart, "Funding Sources," itemizes cash-flow areas where there might be excessive discretionary spending; or unallocated income/capital, that could be redirected for goal or risk management funding.

Uncovering sources of funds can at times be a tedious practice. Because of this, the client needs to "own" the work and must be motivated to do the work necessary to achieve her goals. It is important that the client is committed to her own responsibilities of financial management. The consultant's responsibility is to encourage and ultimately hold her accountable for actions that are inconsistent with her goal achievement. While one is not paid for this process, the rewards are worth it, in terms of gaining her commitment upfront and removing doubts about her abilities to fund goals and/or protection. Unless one is a fee-based financial planner that clients compensate for financial management services, many financial consultants will have to make a conscious decision early on about how much of their time and effort is invested in her case. The acid test: is she both willing and able to do what is necessary to improve her current and future financial security?

The objective is not to develop a punitive or overly confining budget that will be difficult to adhere to in the long run. Rather, it is to build her awareness of the financial trade-offs between current spending patterns and those things that matter the most to her. One of the most powerful dynamics of the consultative planning process is that it quantifies the price tag of the client's dreams, aspirations and security concerns. In other words, it makes the vague, distant and intangible, increasingly real and present.

Protecting Her Financial Position and Security

Funding Sources		
Reductions in Discretionary Expenses		**Increases in Capital and Income**
Discretionary Expense Sources		Capital
Home Improvements, Cleaning	Hobbies, Gym, Subscriptions	Sale of Property, Business, Assets
Dining Out	Vacations	CD, Bonds and Notes Maturing
Babysitter (while not at work)	Clothing	Bonuses
Children's Allowance	Personal Care	Stock Options
Children's Extra-Curricular	Family Gifts	Restricted Stock
Cable TV, DVDs, Music Downloads	Charitable Gifts/Donations	Inheritances/Gifts
Movies, Theater, Concerts	Pet Food, Care and Boarding	Income Tax Refund
Reductions in Other Expenses		Increases in Other-Controlled Income
Loans Maturing or Paid Off		Pay Raises
Restructuring Debt to Lower Rate	FICA Paid Off for Year	401k, 403b Employer Match
Childcare No Longer Needed	Over-Withheld Income Tax	Spouse Goes/Returns to Work
Premium Savings (e.g., increasing deductibles, replacing with lower cost/equal quality coverage, reducing excess coverage).	Income Tax Saved (e.g,. pre-tax contributions to retirement, repositioning assets to tax exempt or deferred).	Trust Income

Example   Assume that Kate, a 45-year-old single professional, has unallocated excess cash flow of $300 per month. In addition, Kate spends about $300 per month dining out. She hopes to retire in 15 years with a lifestyle she has discussed in detail with her financial consultant, Craig. Together, they have looked at Kate's current cash flow and determined how expenses and income will change in the future to support her retirement goals. Kate already has a substantial amount of assets earmarked for retirement and is contributing regularly to her 401k. However, her retirement analysis reveals that she needs to save an additional $450 per month for retirement. Now Kate has conscious choices to make. Which does she value more—having $300 of unallocated excess cash flow and the freedom to spend $300 each month on dining out, or fully funding her retirement goals—leaving her with fewer dinners out each month? Whichever decision she makes, Craig has already provided a valuable service. From this point on, she is *intentionally* spending or saving, and is aware of the consequences of both.

Beyond increasing the financial consultant's ability to identify misspent or misused funding sources, examining her cash flow also forms the basis of important assumptions used when managing risks and achieving goals. It is a required step when performing cash-flow driven (i.e., bottom up) analysis and planning.

Helping Her Build Cash Reserves

cash reserves

Helping the client build emergency cash reserves and manage debt are vitally important areas to address in her financial position. Cash reserves are funds available to meet emergencies and absorb financial loss. The more reserves she has in place, the less risk needs to be transferred to insurance, thereby lowering premium costs. Conversely, the higher her debt, the greater her risk exposure, protection need and expense.

Since women, in general tend to have both a lower risk threshold and tolerance than men do, many are predisposed to cash reserves. In a study by Mathew Greenwald & Associates, more than two out of three (67 percent) women said that having a cash reserve was important, versus less than half (47 percent) of men feeling the same way.[174]

General guidelines indicate that three to six months of expenses should be set aside in a cash reserve. If the client is single and/or in an occupation subject to downsizing or uneven income (e.g., commissions), then more than six months may be prudent. In the event she has other stable sources of income (e.g., spouse/partner earnings, investments, trust, pension), a lower reserve may suffice. Beyond these guidelines and considerations are her attitudes towards cash reserves.

---

174. Pat Regnier and Amanda Gengler, "Men, Women + Money, *Money Magazine,* New York 35, no. 4, April 2006, 90.

Older women, in particular, frequently have substantial assets in cash equivalents. It is fairly common to see an entire life's savings in CDs, up to the FDIC insurance limit, scattered across a number of local banks. For women with a significant portion of their wealth invested in CDs, it is helpful to devise a plan that creates separate reserves for health care, emergency needs and short-term capital expenditures (e.g., buying a new car, repairs on her home). Funds not required for these capital outlays may then be available for retirement investment/income, insurance and/or estate planning purposes. Many seasoned financial professionals and their elderly female clients like to hold at least 12 months of expenses in reserve for peace of mind.

Regardless of the amount that might be appropriate for her situation, creating and maintaining cash reserves should be viewed differently than investing. While both usually require setting aside income or assets, a higher priority should be placed on establishing an emergency cash reserve, since it is foundational to her financial security. This does not mean that she cannot save for both reserves and longer term goals simultaneously, but a significantly greater weight should be placed on reserve building. In addition, since the explicit purpose of cash reserves is to meet emergency needs, they should be "liquid;" that is, principal is readily accessible without significant cost or market risk. For example, it would be inappropriate to suggest that she put her cash reserves into an annuity with surrender charges or a stock mutual fund subject to market volatility. Rather, cash reserves should be put into high quality, fixed income instruments with little to no risk of principal loss due to market fluctuation or issuer default (e.g., FDIC-insured savings and CDs, money markets, short/intermediate term treasuries, accessible cash value in a life insurance contract with a highly rated insurer, and high quality municipal obligations).

Cash reserves are not only to buffer against life's uncertainties. They also enable the client to avail herself of opportunities. For example, being in a position to purchase a favorably price investment asset.

Where Women Save Money

savings

Most American women place their cash reserves in banks, savings and loan associations, credit unions, and money market funds. These accounts offer a high degree of liquidity, along with relative safety of principal. The following table from the most recent U.S. Census study on Asset Ownership of Households shows the percentages of households (married, male, female) that own common financial instruments.

Percentage of Households Owning Savings Instruments			
	Married Couples	**Male Heads of Households**	**Female Heads of Households**
Any type of savings	72.80%	55.40%	55.00%
Passbook savings	60.90%	43.20%	43.70%
Money market deposit accounts	14.50%	8.20%	8.70%
Certificates of deposit (CDs)	14.60%	9.30%	13.90%
Interest-earning checking	41.40%	28.80%	27.70%
U.S. government bonds	2.00%	1.10%	1.40%
Municipal or corporate bonds	3.60%	1.90%	2.60%
Source: Asset Ownership of Households. U.S. Census, 1998			

Not surprisingly, the study revealed that married couples tend to have more reserves built up than single people (male or female). Although women earn somewhat less money than men on average, single women are just as likely as single men to save money in almost all types of instruments. However, women are more likely than men to own CDs and bonds.

The table below shows that women's interest in CDs increases with age. Single women of all ages are more likely to own CDs than single men. Anecdotal evidence also suggests that in married couples, CD purchase decisions often are driven by women.[175]

Percentage of Households Owning CDs			
Age Range	**Married Couples**	**Male Heads of Households**	**Female Heads of Households**
Under 35	5.10%	3.20%	3.30%
35 to 54	10.80%	5.80%	6.60%
55 to 64	20.10%	11.10%	12.90%
65 and older	33.20%	26.30%	29.00%
Source: Asset Ownership of Households. U.S. Census, 1998			

---

175. U.S. Census, "Asset Ownership of Households," 1998.

Protecting Her Financial Position and Security **4.15**

CDs

Why Do Women Like CDs?

Women find CDs attractive savings options for these reasons:

- CDs generally offer the security of FDIC insurance.

- CDs usually pay higher rates of interest than other bank deposits (for example, passbook savings or money market deposit accounts).

- Women have traditionally been more trusting of banks versus other financial services institutions.

- They are predictable, with a level interest rate and a fixed maturity.

Financial professionals who help women obtain CDs should be able to explain CDs in general, and FDIC insurance specifically. In addition, they should suggest how women can shop for CDs that pay attractive current interest rates.

FDIC Insurance

Key Points about FDIC Insurance

FDIC insurance is provided by the Federal Deposit Insurance Corporation, an independent agency of the federal government. The FDIC was created in 1933 to instill confidence in U.S. banks and savings and loans after many such institutions failed during the Great Depression.

FDIC deposit accounts are currently insured up to $250,000 per depositor, per insured institution. Retirement plan accounts held in deposit instruments, including IRAs and Keoghs, are insured up to $250,000. FDIC insurance covers deposits only, including checking, Negotiable Order of Withdrawal (NOW) and savings accounts, money market deposit accounts, and CDs. The FDIC does not insure investment products, money markets that are not deposit accounts, life insurance products, or annuities sold through banks. FDIC insurance covers depositors only in the event of a bank failure. In the event that funds are lost in a robbery, flood, hurricane or act of war, FDIC insurance does not cover losses, although most banks have fidelity bonds that do cover these events.

How to Help Women Shop for High-Yield CDs

Because FDIC insurance coverage is identical for all banks and thrift institutions that participate in it, there is little difference between a given deposit product offered by one bank and another (except for the interest rate). Banks tend to compete most aggressively for one-year CD business.

The internet has created a quiet revolution in savings deposit products that can be very attractive to women savers. Each week, internet sites scan thousands of FDIC-insured products nationwide and post lists of those offering the highest yields. One of the most comprehensive and frequently updated lists can be found at http://www.money-rates.com/cdrates.htm. In addition to current rates for various maturities of FDIC-insured CDs, this site has links to banks that specialize in online applications and services. All of FDIC-insured banking services can be accessed online. For example, the money-rates.com site provides the national average rate for bank CDs and money market funds. The highest rates listed online for specific banks often are well above the averages.

Increasing Cash Reserve Yields

Working with the client to increase yield on cash reserves while maintaining principal accessibility and security can be an excellent way for financial consultants to add value. Three best practice strategies are to build a *cash reserve pyramid*, *ladder CDs* and use *tax exempt* vehicles. These are described below.

Cash Reserve Pyramid

cash reserve pyramid

Some successful financial professionals use a "cash reserve pyramid" to balance liqiuidity, capital preservation and yield. The pyramid starts with a foundational base of low yield, short-term instruments such as savings and money market accounts, and gradually layers on those instruments with higher yields. In this approach, approximately 50 percent should be in the base level, 30 percent in the second tier and 20 percent in the third.

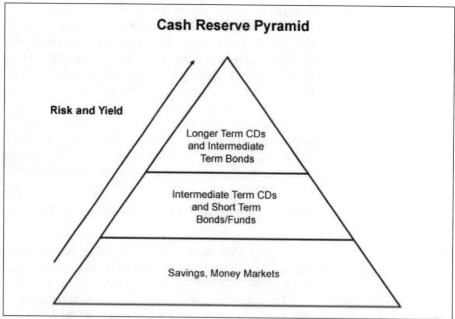

The underlying objectives of this technique are to raise cash reserve yields without putting principal at significant risk. While there may be some interest rate risk when one extends maturity dates on fixed income instruments, the greater proportion of lowest risk savings allocated to the base balances this. This strategy is best used when the yield curve is normal (sloping upwards); that is, when shorter term fixed income instruments pay lower interest rates than those with longer maturities.

CD Laddering

CD Laddering

Another effective practice to increase cash reserve yields and manage interest rate risk is laddering CDs, or staggering maturity dates. When implementing this technique, the consultant will want to verify there are sufficient accessible funds in savings and/or money market accounts. The premise of a ladder is that as CDs mature, they are then renewed at a lower or higher interest rate depending on market conditions. The continued "rolling over" of CDs as they mature can generate higher yield, and reduce interest rate risk (discussed in Chapter 6).

Example

Assume that (70 years old) Margaret, has annual expenses of $70,000 per year and $150,000 in savings, earning 2.25% at the Bank of the Southwest. Her financial consultant Karen, has discussed Margaret's foreseeable needs for cash with her and learned that later this year, Margaret will travel to Asia and replace the roof on her house. She estimates that she will need $30,000 to fund both. Margaret has also shared that she would be comfortable with $70,000 in reserves. The remaining $50,000 can be invested for retirement income once she sees the analysis and recommendations that Karen develops. In the meantime, she is looking to Karen for suggestions on her cash reserves. Karen recommends a base amount in savings and laddering the balance in CDs, as shown in the table below.

Sample CD Ladder	
50 percent in savings earning 2.25%	$35,000
50 percent in five CDs:	
One year CD earning 3.0%	$7,000
Two year CD earning 3.5%	$7,000
Three year CD earning 4.0%	$7,000
Four year CD earning 4.5%	$7,000
Five year CD earning 5.0%	$7,000

The overall effect? Margaret's weighted yield is increased from 2.25% to 3.12%, or just over $600 more in annual interest earnings, without compromising safety of principal. In addition, if interest rates drop, she has locked in higher yields through the CD ladder. On the other hand, if interest rates increase, her CDs renewing each year enable her to capture some of that new upside.

Tax Exempt Cash Reserve Strategy

municipal bonds

If the client (and her spouse, if married) falls into the upper federal income tax brackets (e.g., 28 percent and over), the financial professional may want to construct a reserve pyramid with money markets and high-quality, intermediate term bond funds invested in municipal obligations. Municipal bonds are issued by a city or other local government agency. Interest income from municipal obligations is generally exempt from federal income taxes and income tax in their state of origination. (Note: Since there are certain municipal bonds subject to federal income taxation, the consultant is advised to check the prospectus prior to recommending.)

For some clients, the taxable equivalent yield—defined as the return that a fully taxable investment needs to generate to equal the return on a tax exempt investment—may be significantly higher than in fully taxable investments. The formula used to calculate taxable equivalent yield is:

$R(ey) = R(te)/(1 - t)$ where:

$R(ey)$ = taxable equivalent yield for the investor
$R(te)$ = return on tax-exempt yield
t = her marginal tax rate

Example

For example, assume that Rachel and her husband Scott are in the 28% federal tax bracket. Their financial professional, Adam, is evaluating whether to recommend a high quality municipal bond fund as part of their reserve strategy. The fund pays an average 4 percent (federal tax exempt) yield annually. Using the formula above, Adam calculates that for Sarah and Scott, the taxable equivalent yield of the fund is:

$R(ey) = 0.04 / (1 - 0.28)$
$R(t) = 0.05556 = 5.556\%$

If Rachel and Scott are not able to achieve a 5.556% yield on a taxable bond or CD with comparable maturity and quality (e.g., comparable ratings/risk of default), then it may be wise to recommend the municipal bond fund.

Helping the client build and manage her cash reserves in suitable savings vehicles, provides a vital service that many competitors ignore. Some financial professionals ground their entire practice in helping clients manage their emergency reserves. By focusing on this foundational aspect of planning, they crowd out the competition and significantly increase the value they add, along with the trust and additional business that clients place in their hands.

Helping Her Manage Debt

Consultants can also improve the client's well-being by looking at her debts, as well. For the past quarter century, the debts of U.S. households have increased at a faster rate than their income. Since the 1970s, the U.S. has gradually become a poorer country at the household level because of declining personal savings and rising personal borrowing.

Credit

credit

How can Americans persistently spend more than they earn? The short answer: by borrowing it. In the early 1980s, at just about the same historic moment that Americans began to save less, they began to borrow more. The Federal Reserve measures the amount of borrowing on credit cards and consumer loans (e.g., automobiles, college education, and so forth) but not home mortgages. In 1980, total U.S. consumer credit was about $350 billion, or roughly $3,000 per household. By 2007, consumer credit had grown to $2.4 trillion, or about $23,000 per household[176]

According to the Federal Reserve, the total "U.S. house credit market debt outstanding"—a measure of consumer credit plus home mortgages, increased from $1.3 trillion in 1980 to $12.8 trillion in 2007. Home mortgages remain the biggest source of household debt, and those increased substantially as well. Not counting home mortgages, American households were spending nearly 15 percent of their incomes just to repay debts, prior to the economic crisis in 2009.[177] The following table summarizes the vast increase in U.S. household credit that took place between 1980 and 2008.

---

176. Total Consumer Credit Outstanding, Board of Governors of the Federal Reserve System.
177. Total U.S. Credit Market Debt Outstanding, Board of Governors of the Federal Reserve System.

Increase in U.S. Household Credit			
	1980	2008	Compound Annual Growth
Total consumer credit outstanding	$352 billion	$2.6 trillion	7.40%
Household credit market debt outstanding	$1.3 trillion	$12.8 trillion	8.80%
Disposable personal income	$1.9 trillion	$9.9 trillion	6.30%
Household debt service payments as percentage of disposable personal income	11.10%	14.50%	0.96%
Source: Board of Governors of the Federal Reserve System			

Reducing or Restructuring Her Debt

debt

Direct involvement in restructuring debt is generally outside the scope of what most consultants offer. However, the client's liabilities are critically important to take into account since they increase her financial jeopardy and interfere with, or detract, from even the smallest recommendations made. Before the 2008/2009 Great Recession, about four in ten American women perceived their level of debt to be excessive[178] and nearly half had a primary financial goal of paying off a loan or credit card debt.[179] Women also tend to internalize their worry about debt more than men do. A study by Myvesta.org found that 58 percent of women reported signs of depression as a result of debt, versus 36 percent of men.[180] The point is, that while debt may not be a priority for the financial consultant, it may very likely be so for the female client.

It is important then, to understand both facts and feelings about how her liabilities are structured. What percent of her overall income is consumed by debt payments? What are the terms—secured/unsecured, maturities, interest rates, payment frequencies? What concerns her most about her debt? What has debt been used for (e.g., committed or discretionary expenses)? How will additional debt be avoided in the future? What is her credit score? Once this information has been determined, the financial professional is in a better position to guide her toward resources for better debt management.

---

178. Myvesta.org, "Myvesta.org Survey Finds Debt Equals Depression for Many," November, 2001.
179. Prudential Financial, "Financial Experience and Behaviors Among Women," 2006.
180. Myvesta.org, "Myvesta.org Survey Finds Debt Equals Depression for Many," November, 2001.

When Debt is Deep

bankruptcy

On occasion, prospects and even some clients may be so deeply in arrears that there is nothing that the financial consultant can do to help. While more women file for bankruptcy each year than men, there is a commonly held misconception that a woman's severe debt is brought about by frivolous and irresponsible spending. The unfortunate realities are usually quite different. It is estimated that approximately 90 percent of women who file for bankruptcy do so because they have lost their jobs, had medical emergencies, or experienced divorce, separation, or the death of a spouse.[181] Further, according to recent findings by the Federal Reserve, the median credit card debt of single women was $1,900, compared to an average debt of $2,000 for single men.[182] Other data suggest that although single women may spend more on credit cards than men, they do a better job managing credit and paying off balances before they balloon.

While financial professionals may not be able to help a prospect or client with severe credit problems, they can suggest how she seek help from a reputable agency that can negotiate with creditors and provide budget counseling. Since there are unscrupulous and suspect debt-settlement companies (including nonprofits) to be aware of, Consumer Reports suggests the following guidelines:

- Research possible debt-settlement providers through the National Foundation for Credit Counseling (www.nfcc.org) and the Association of Independent Consumer Credit Counseling Services (www.aiccca.org).

- Investigate records of the organization's services and complaint history with a consumer protection agency (e.g., the Better Business Bureau).

- Look for high fees to set up and maintain payment services.

- Watch for misleading claims about how much debt the organization says they might be able to reduce.

- Ask for written details about services, beware of hidden charges, and review any contracts before signing.

- Ensure the service also helps with budgeting and credit management.[183]

---

181. Sandra Guy, "Bankruptcy Law Pushes Women Closer to Edge," *Women's e-News,* October 27, 2005, www.womensenews.org.
182. Time Magazine,"Lay Off, Suze Orman!", Anita Hamilton, April 5, 2007.
183. Consumer Reports, "Money Advisor," March 2009.

In the most extreme debt cases, the consultant may want to provide a list of attorneys who can assist with bankruptcy filing and protection.

RISK MANAGEMENT AND TRANSFERENCE

Incorporating plans to deal with the client's pure risks are sometimes described in the insurance industry as *risk management* or *needs analysis*. Regardless of terminology used, the methodology used is essentially the same as the consultative planning process described in Chapter 3.

	Consultative Planning	Risk Management Planning
1	Meet the prospect and establish goals	Determine objectives
2	Gather information	Identify risk
3	Analyze information	Analyze/measure risk
4	Develop and present the plan	Consider alternative risk treatment devices and select the device(s) that best address the risk
5	Implement the plan	Implement the plan
6	Service the plan	Monitor the plan

While the same basic steps are taken in virtually any planning process, several key words from the table above are worth noting as they relate to specifically risk management: *identify risk*, *analyze/measure risk* and *consider alternative(s)*.

Identifying Risks

The typical female client leads a life that is both complex and financially matrixed—that is, almost everything she does and certainly those things she possesses have the potential for risk and loss. Identifying and addressing all the risks that she and her family are exposed to can be near impossible in just one meeting, let alone analyzing and measuring their impact. To illustrate the complexity of risk identification, consider this sample case:

> **Risk Identification Sample Case – Janet and Bill Wolfe**
>
> Janet is 45 and married to Bill, also 45. Together, they have a son, Eric (17), and a daughter, Jessica (22). Janet is a nurse with average earnings of $72,000 per year. Bill is a sole proprietor (Schedule C) electrician with an average annual before tax-income of about $72,000. He has two full-time employees. Bill also owns two trucks and the building his business is in.
>
> The Wolfe's purchased a home five years ago for $225,000. They also own a vacation home at the lake that Bill and Janet bought before they had children. While they only paid $65,000 for the property and made some minor repairs to the existing cabin, they estimate the total vacation place is now worth over $450,000. Since they have been careful with their debt, they have no debt on the place at the lake. Their only mortgage is $100,000 remaining on their residence, with 10 years left in payments at 5% interest. In addition to their residences, Janet has a 403b invested exclusively in an S&P 500 index fund currently valued at about $238,000. Bill has a SEP/IRA at the bank in CDs earning between 3.5 and 5 percent. Bill also inherited an assortment of blue chip stocks from his parents worth $77,000 total.
>
> Janet's parents, Jim, a retired military physician, aged 84, and homemaker, Ruth (79), live two blocks away. Janet's father is in failing health and unable to perform three Activities of Daily Living (ADL). A lung cancer patient, he is at home mostly through support from Ruth, but also a home-health-care aide who works 40 hours per week. In addition, Janet and her sister, Carole, help on alternating weekends.

Here is a partial listing of the pure risks that the Wolfe family faces:

- property risks
    - direct losses
        - residence, vacation home and business property
        - furniture, clothing, personal items, collectibles, and so on.
        - personal automobiles
        - business trucks
    - indirect losses
        - additional living expenses, if residence is damaged
        - rental car insurance, if automobiles are out of commission
- liability risks
    - residence, vacation home and business property
    - automobiles; personal and business
    - professional, through Janet's work as a nurse

- professional, through Bill's work as electrician
- Bill's employee worker's compensation

• personal risks
- loss of health due to accident or injury
- disability or premature death of Janet or Bill
    ♦ income for family and spouse's lifetime
    ♦ health care expenses
    ♦ value of Bill's business

On the surface, the risk identification process often appears to be relatively simple, but there are frequently more risks than meet the eye. In addition to the partial list above, what are other issues that can be identified? How about Janet's parents and their need for long-term care? What if Eric wants to go to university? Has this goal been factored into survivor needs and disability income planning? What else?

Some consultants and their clients feel that it is a waste of time to formalize the risk-identification process. However, the consequences of neglecting to adequately identify and measure risk can lead to financial ruin. Financial professionals needs to manage their own risk exposures, as well. In an increasingly litigious environment, there have been cases of legal action taken by family members against producers who failed to adequately identify areas of risk exposure.

Risk Measurement and Analysis

Data analysis requires at least two important activities when dealing with pure risk:

1. measuring possible losses associated with identified pure risks

2. evaluating these risks relative to their potential financial impact on the client and her family

Theoretically, risk measurement should include information on both the frequency (probability of occurrence) and severity of loss. In order for risk to be measurable, there must be a considerable number of similar exposures to which a probability can be applied in order to estimate the outcome. In most cases, pure risk situations faced by a particular individual or family involve only one or a few exposures to loss. Therefore, probabilities of loss do not help measure pure risks faced by such clients. The major emphasis in risk measurement must be on the severity of the loss. When dealing with pure risks faced by individuals and families, it is safest to assume *total loss* and identify this as the maximum possible loss.

In Chapter 5, we explore how to identify and analyze personal risks, specifically disability, long-term care and survivor needs. These forms of risk often require significant analysis and measurement to determine their impact on the client's current and future security. We will also more fully address alternative approaches to dealing with those risks. Since property loss risks are relatively easily measured and conversely, liability and medical risks are very difficult to measure, they require less analysis and planning than personal risks. As such, we will address property, liability and medical risks in the section that follows.

PROPERTY RISKS

While the financial consultant may not directly place property/casualty and liability insurances, one should be aware of some basic considerations as they may help reduce the client's risk and increase the consultant's value proposition. According to a recent survey by the Chubb Group of insurance companies, just one out of two financial professionals surveyed said they review their clients' property/casualty insurances.[184] This means that almost half do not review these coverages. Failure to carry appropriate property/casualty and liability insurances can result in a severe uninsured loss that can undermine the client's otherwise sound plan for capital accumulation and preservation.

Focus on Ethics
When financial consultants address a client's financial security, they often emphasize future income production and protection. The goals are to produce a level of wealth that will generate a sufficient stream of income for retirement, or to ensure a chosen lifestyle, should there be an interruption in income protection.
Many financial professionals are not licensed to place property and liability insurance, and frequently overlook the threat posed by property destruction or major liability claims. An underinsured home destroyed by fire or natural disaster can destroy even the best wealth accumulation and/or protection afforded by personal insurance. The same consequence can occur if the client is underinsured and loses a major liability suit resulting from an accident, professional negligence, or other reason.
Financial consultants, whether or not they place property and liability insurance, must sensitize the client to those needs, as well. Insurance can minimize losses associated with these risks. Protecting her assets is an essential part of planning. Just because a consultant is less knowledgeable in these areas does not reduce the need or the responsibility.
Source: C. Bruce Worsham, *Foundations of Financial Planning: An Overview*, The American College Press, Bryn Mawr, Pennsylvania, 2009

---

184. "Chubb Insurance Companies Press Release: Financial Planners Pay More attention to P/C Insurance and Risk Management," March 21, 2006, Warren, NJ, (http://www.chubb/com/corporate/chubb4930html

Women and Property Insurance

The majority of property insurance contracts owned by Americans cover their residences and automobiles. For the most part, women need the same types of property and liability insurance as men. However, as illustrated in the table below, women tend to be less confident than are men that their house, car and possessions are adequately insured.

Confidence That House, Car and Possessions Are Adequately Insured	Male	Female
Very confident	58.60%	46.70%
Somewhat confident	26.90%	35.30%
Not very confident	8.60%	11.40%
Not at all confident	4.80%	4.30%
Not sure	1.10%	2.40%
Source: Country Insurance and Financial Services, http://www.countryfinancialsecurityindex.com/demographic.php?id=0 =gender accessed 3/29/07.		

Women, Cars and Driving Risks

Despite some misperceptions about female drivers, women tend to have fewer accidents than men. Recent statistics from the U.S. Department of Transportation reflect that males were involved in

- 1.4 times as many total crashes
- 1.5 times as many property damage-only crashes
- 1.3 times as many injury crashes
- 2.9 times as many fatal crashes[185]

Women and Auto Insurance

A woman's basic need for auto insurance is the same—whether she is a college student with little money and purchasing insurance on her first car, a married woman purchasing insurance for the family fleet, or a newly single retiree. Regardless of life-stage, segment or niche, the client's minimum need is to obtain insurance that complies with compulsory insurance laws and the requirements of any loss payee providing an auto loan or lease. Beyond these

---

185. Calculated from U.S. Department of Transportation, National Highway Safety Administration 2005 data on accident rates per 100,000 licensed drivers. http://www.iii.org/media/facts/statsbyissue/highway/

basics, many options are available with specifics varying by state (e.g., no fault and uninsured/underinsured options) and the underwriting company's rules. Endorsements for special needs may also be available. Here is a summary of the most common variable elements and related considerations:

- **Liability Limits:** Explore what assets and future income potential the client has to protect. Determine the same for her husband, if married. Many basic policies have liability limits of $300,000 to $500,000. Many clients, male and female, have assets exceeding that amount, along with valuable streams of future earning potential that could be garnished if successfully sued. It is essential for financial professionals to inspect auto liability limits (in addition to other exposures to liability) and add additional coverage in the basic policy or an umbrella as net worth and income grows.

- **Physical Damage:** Understand current deductibles, age of car and what, if any collision or other physical property damage coverage the client might have, need or could reduce. In choosing deductibles, ask about her cash reserves and suggest ways she can build a financial cushion. As warranted, increase physical damage deductibles, with a commensurate decrease in premium, reflecting her ability to tap an emergency fund if her car is seriously damaged in an auto accident. If the vehicle is leased, mention gap insurance, which closes the gap between what the auto insurance company pays if the car is totaled or stolen, and what is still owed to the lease finance company.

- **Medical Payments:** Compare the auto coverage to the client's current medical expense coverage and consider any possible gaps in that coverage, especially if she is currently or temporarily uninsured.

Saving Money on Auto Insurance

Helping the client save money on any type of insurance, without sacrificing essential protection or carrier quality, demonstrates that the financial professional puts her interests first. Remember, more than half of all women want to save more money using limited resources. Some possible ways she might save money on her auto insurance are listed below.

Saving money on one type of insurance can free up money that can then be put into emergency reserves, or redirected toward another risk management need or financial goal.

Women and Money

Dollar Detective
Saving Money on Auto Insurance
• Qualify—or become qualified—for available premium discounts for a safe driving record, safety devices, driver training, student-away, and other somewhat controllable factors. • Compare insurance costs before buying a car. • Purchase the lowest auto liability limits that meet the underlying insurance requirements of her personal umbrella policy. • Consider higher physical damage deductibles. • Eliminate physical damage coverage on older cars. • Buy homeowners and auto coverage from the same insurer. • Take advantage of low-mileage discounts. Sometimes car pooling or using public transportation can significantly reduce insurance costs. • Maintain good credit.

Women and Their Homes

homes

The other basic form of risk associated with loss of property concerns the client's home and its contents. More than ever, women play a significant role in the purchase of a home. It is estimated that women directly purchase or influence the purchase of 91 percent of all new homes.[186] According to the National Association of Realtors, married home buyers are still in the majority, but the picture is changing. In 2006, married couples were 60 percent of home buyers. Just twelve years ago, however, married home buyers represented 70 percent of the market.[187]

Increasingly, single women are purchasing homes. The table below, titled "Percentage of Home Buyers" illustrates this trend. As this table shows, the percentage of home buyers who are single women has shown a dramatic increase since 1981, while the percentage of single male home buyers has stayed about the same.

---

186. U.S. Women's Chamber of Commerce, "How the American Economy is Leaving Women Behind," 2006.
187. Jim Wasserman, "Single Women Head for Homes," *The Sacramento Bee*, February 18, 2007, (Citing statistics from the National Association of Realtors, http:///www.sacbee.com/103/v-print/story/124852.html)

Percentage of Home Buyers		
Year	Single Women	Single Men
1981	11%	10%
1985	10%	6%
1987	10%	7%
1989	14%	10%
1991	14%	10%
1993	16%	10%
1995	14%	9%
1997	14%	11%
1999	18%	9%
2001	15%	7%
2003*	21%	11%
2004	18%	8%
2005	21%	9%
Source: National Association of Realtors * Survey based only on partial year's data.		

What demographic forces are responsible for this trend? Important factors include the following:[188]

- Women—and men—are marrying later.

- As many as half of new marriages end in divorce.

- Women tend to live longer than men.

- Unmarried women have more money than ever.

- Amendments to the Fair Housing Act in 1974 made it easier for single women to get a mortgage in their own names.

Single women who buy homes tend to have a lower income than their male counterparts, and they tend to purchase less costly homes that require a higher percentage of their income. In light of these statistics, it is especially important

---

188. Ibid

for financial consultants to ensure adequate cash reserves and protection against both personal and property risks, when advising single female homeowners.

Women and Homeowners Insurance

homeowner insurance

A client's gender may affect the premium rate for auto insurance, but is not a homeowner's rating factor. Generally, the need and rates for homeowners insurance is independent of the insured's gender or marital status. However, standard insurance policy language is designed for either single individuals or a traditional nuclear family, which represents an increasingly smaller proportion of families. Unmarried couples, partners or roommates may present special considerations, whether they live together, or jointly own a home. Eligibility rules may preclude homeowners coverage in some cases. Property loss adjustment can become complicated, because it is often difficult to determine which personal property is owned by whom. Challenges associated with liability may also be involved when determining the responsible party. The resolution of these and other issues may depend on insurance company rules and state regulations. These issues are beyond the scope of this book, but it is important for the financial professional to be aware that there may be complicating factors.

Although mortgage holders generally require only enough insurance to pay off the mortgage, homeowners also need to protect their own property and liability interests. Basic homeowners insurance generally offers options of the following types:

- choice of an appropriate coverage form for single-family homes, condominium units, mobile homes, or dwellings that do not meet homeowners eligibility requirements

- flood insurance

- property limits that reflect the replacement cost value of the building

- additional limits on other structures, if needed

- property limits that reflect the actual cash value of the client's personal property (or replacement cost value if the replacement cost endorsement is added)

- liability limits, preferably beyond basic limits and, if applicable, that meet the underlying insurance requirements of an umbrella policy

There is no requirement for renters who live in a single-family home, an apartment building, or a condominium unit to purchase homeowners insurance or flood insurance. Even the name "homeowners insurance" wrongly implies that the coverage is available only for clients who own homes. Many renters never consider it, and they do not even realize that coverage may be available at a relatively low cost. This can be a serious mistake for many younger clients who often have valuable possessions to protect, like a car, furnishings, computers, plasma/panel televisions, phones and stereos. Homeowners insurance covers both property and liability claims, and liability claims can result in very serious financial loss. In a sense, a tenant's liability exposure is likely to be greater than that of a single-family homeowner because the tenant's negligence might cause a fire that destroys an entire apartment complex.

Saving Money on Homeowners Insurance

Here are some ways a client might be able to reduce her homeowners insurance costs:

Dollar Detective
Saving Money on Home Insurance
• Take advantage of premium discounts for security systems and fire protection devices, if applicable. • *Before* buying a home, get a Claims Experience Report on the home's loss history. • *Before* buying a home, consider the factors that affect insurance costs. • Do not confuse the home's market value with its insurable value (e.g., replacement cost). • Purchase the lowest personal liability limits that meet the underlying insurance requirements of the client's personal umbrella policy. • Make the home disaster resistant. • Avoid filing small claims for water damage and other losses that might concern an underwriter. • Consider higher deductibles, especially since it is unwise to file small homeowners claims. • Buy auto and homeowners coverage from the same insurer. • Maintain a good credit record. • Stay with the same insurer. • Review limits and values at least once a year.

LIABILITY RISKS AND INSURANCE

Over the past few decades there has been a surge of liability litigation, directed both toward individuals and businesses/business owners. At the same time, women-owned wealth and businesses have also been on the upswing. Having a basic understanding of liability risks can help consultants direct their clients toward the appropriate professionals if they do not place this coverage themselves. Further, if one specializes in working with a niche market of women business owners, a firm grasp of their potential liability risks, types of policies available, approximate premiums and affiliated professionals who offer coverage will add significant value. As such, one should become familiar with the need to protect her against possible lawsuits or claims arising out of products and services rendered.

Types of Liability Losses

Liability claims involve an alleged responsibility to pay damages. Damages can be categorized as compensatory or punitive:

- **compensatory damages**

- **punitive damages**

- *Compensatory damages* are meant to financially compensate or reimburse a claimant who has suffered a loss.

- *Punitive damages* are intended to punish a wrongdoer, whose outrageous conduct has caused another party to suffer a loss.

Liability insurance policies are designed primarily to cover compensatory damages. Some policies exclude punitive damages and some state laws prohibit insurers from paying punitive damages. The rationale is that a wrongdoer is not really punished when the "punishment" is absorbed by his or her insurance.

The types of liability losses typically covered by property and liability insurances fall into the following categories:

- *Bodily injury* occurs when a person suffers bodily harm, sickness or disease; and medical care, loss of services and death happen as a result. The injured party may also incur tangible losses such as medical bills and lost income. Damages can be awarded for pain and suffering, medical expenses, wrongful death and loss of companionship.

- *Property damage* is destruction or harm to someone else's real or personal property and can consist of actual damage. It can also include lost income or extra expenses as a result of an inability to use the property.

- *Personal injury* refers to a group of offenses that generally include libel, slander, invasion of privacy, defamation of character and other similar behaviors.

- *Contractual liability* arises when a person or business fails to meet contractual obligations. Breach of contract may result in responsibility for property damages or failure to fulfill warranties explicit or implied.

- *Wrongful acts* are defined broadly to include a wide range of acts or omissions, (e.g., errors, misrepresentations, neglects, omissions, and so on).

Personal property and casualty insurances typically provide some liability protection against bodily injury and property damages. Umbrella policies can be purchased to extend the amounts of coverage available. How much insurance against these risk areas should the client carry? The total upside potential of these risks is often difficult to measure. Since damages are often court awarded and can be substantial, there are no hard and fast answers. A general guideline is coverage of at least 2.5 times the individual's total net worth. However, the client's future earnings capability must also be considered.

Women who own a business may also be exposed to liabilities associated with contractual obligations and wrongful acts. Common liability insurances for businesses protect the enterprise and its assets from mishaps that occur on its premises, or as a result of others using the products sold. In addition, if the client is a service professional, she may require professional liability coverage (e.g., errors and omissions, malpractice).

In light of the significance of risks associated with property/casualty and liability insurances, financial professionals should, at minimum, be able to identify areas of exposure and have a working relationship with qualified agents who provide the appropriate coverage.

WOMEN AND MEDICAL RISKS

medical risks

This section deals with health care costs associated with medical bills that arise from an accident or illness. (Chapter 5 covers health care costs associated with lost income or expenses rising out of disability or long-term care needs.)

While Congress, as of this writing, is considering alternatives to makng health insurance more broadly affordable and available, it is improbable that "universal health care" will become a reality, at least not in the very near future. Therefore, it is important for financial consultants, when advising female prospects and clients, to understand the health challenges and risks that many women disproportionately face. This knowledge helps consultants ask better questions, consider possible issues to analyze and shape recommendations in order to address the client's risks more effectively.

What Health Issues Affect Women More Than Men?

Health statistics show a pervasive difference in disease and illness between women and men, revealing that a much higher proportion of women suffer from certain conditions that may not directly cause death. The fact that women live on average, five to seven years longer than men tends to increase their health care needs, as they are more prone to suffer from chronic conditions as they age. This chart reflects medical challenges that affect females more than males:

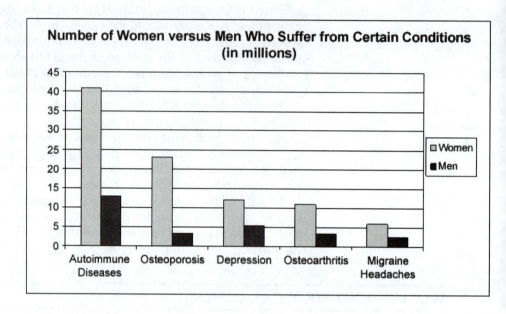

Source: http://www.womenshealthresearch.org/site/PageServer?pagename=hs_sbb_suffer

When reviewing this chart, it is worth noting that:

- There are more than 80 known autoimmune diseases, including systemic lupus erythematosus (SLE), multiple sclerosis, rheumatoid arthritis, juvenile onset diabetes, scleroderma, and Grave's disease. Autoimmune diseases can attack the heart, kidneys, liver, lungs, blood and/or brain and can therefore become life threatening.

- Women comprise 80 percent of the population suffering from osteoporosis. Hip fractures in people with osteoporosis increase the risk of death by 24 percent. Nearly 50 percent of those who do survive an osteoporotic hip fracture lose their independence.

- Females are two to three times more likely to experience depression due in part to the fact that women's brains make less of the hormone serotonin. Major depression increases the risk of heart attacks.

- Virtually everyone over age 75 is affected in at least one joint by osteoarthritis.

- Migraine sufferers experience on average, one or more attacks each month, incapacitating them for hours to days.

In addition to these chronic health concerns, heart disease kills on average 500,000 American females each year—over 50,000 more females than males. Women tend to experience heart attacks 10 years later than men, and are more likely to have a second attack within a year of the first one.[189]

Women and Medical Insurance

medical insurance

Far too many women fall through the cracks in the health insurance system. They are either not working full-time and have no coverage through an employer; or they are working in a low-paying job that does not offer medical insurance coverage; or they are married, not working, and have no dependent coverage through spouses. Many women who need insurance are not poor enough to qualify for Medicaid, and not wealthy enough to acquire health insurance on their own. Consider these statistics about women and health insurance:

- Nearly two out of three (61.5 percent) of Americans without health insurance are female.[190]

- Almost two-thirds of uninsured women are in families with at least one full-time adult worker.[191]

- Just 21 percent of uninsured women are in families with no working adult.[192]

Since almost one in ten women is a business owner, securing medical insurance through her business may be an important strategy to include in discussions with her. Almost all employers with 200 or more employees offer some type of medical expense plan. However, only about 60 percent of all employers offer such coverage, and the percentage continues to decrease, particularly for employers with fewer than 10 employees.[193]

If the consultant is working with a woman who does not have health insurance, the reality may be that she has limited means and is unable to afford private medical insurance coverage. For a discussion of options for women who are uninsured and unable to afford private insurance, see www.womenshealth.gov/faq/health-insurance-women.cfm.

---

189. The Society for Women's Health Research, "Exploring the Biological Contribution to Human Health: Does Sex Matter?" Institute of Medicine report, 2001.
190. eeHealth Insurance survey, "Who is the Average Uninsured American Searching for Health Insurance?" *Market Wire,* August 12, 2009.
191. The Henry J. Kaiser Family Foundation, "Fact Sheet, Women's Health Policy Facts," February 2007.
192. Ibid
193. The Henry J. Kaiser foundation and Health Research & Educational Trust, Employer Health Benefits, 2008, p. 35

Some women may feel they do not need health insurance at the moment because they are young and strong and healthy. They may feel ready to risk their financial health on a bet that they will not become ill or have an accident. Still others may overlook the coverage because they are overwhelmed and dealing with a recent loss such as divorce or the death of a spouse. They may forget that their medical insurance was tied to the spouse. Financial consultants should be alert to the possibility that medical insurance may be missing. Since a medical problem with the attendant costs of care is the leading reason for personal bankruptcy; health insurance must be considered as the most basic and essential part of a well-balanced insurance portfolio. [194]

CHAPTER SUMMARY

In this chapter, we have examined the importance of laying a sound foundation of risk management and a balanced financial position to a female client's overall security. Since many clients tend to overlook these essential basics in favor of the more sensational aspects of investment and retirement planning, indispensible financial consultants can add significantly unique value by addressing them.

Establishing the relationship of the client's financial position to her current and future security and helping her improve cash flow, build emergency reserves and manage debt can go a long way to creating an ideal client for life. In addition, by addressing these issues and helping her maximize efficiencies in her current financial position, the financial consultant is better positioned to her needs, to add value and to capture assets/premiums.

This chapter provided a discussion of the difference between *pure* and *speculative* risks, along with how the alternative approaches to managing risk:

- risk avoidance
- risk reduction
- risk prevention
- risk retention
- risk transference

Finally, we identified risks that women may be exposed to with regard to her property, possible liabilities and her medical needs. We continue our discussion of risk management in Chapter 5. There we examine these risks that women frequently are more prone to—specifically, disability, long-term care and survivor needs. We will look at:

- the process of identifying, analyzing, of developing sound strategies to manage their disability, long-term care and survivor risks

---

194. Study published by the journal *Health Affairs* from research carried out jointly by researchers at Harvard Law School and Harvard Medical School on bankruptcy filings in five federal districts in 2001; Dr. David Himmelstein, lead author.

- special considerations for women by their life-stage and/or lifestyle.

CHAPTER 4 TOOLS AND RESOURCES

- Courses from The American College
    - FA 251 Essentials of Business Insurance
    - FA 222 Essentials of Multiline Insurance Products
    - HS 311 Fundamentals of Insurance Planning
    - HS 313 Individual Health Insurance
    - HS 325 Group Benefits
- Tools
    - Financial position worksheet
- Websites
    - www.moneyrates.com/cdrates.htm
    - www.womenshealth.gov/faq/

5

Addressing Her Personal Risks—Disability, Long-Term Care and Survivor Needs

Learning Objectives
An understanding of the material in this chapter should enable the student to

5-1. Identify key health risks that increase a woman's likelihood of becoming disabled.

5-2. Describe the disability risk management process.

5-3. Explain disability planning considerations, including life-stage, life style and product.

5-4. Define what is meant by the term "double jeopardy," as it relates to women and long-term care.

5-5. Describe the long-term care risk management process.

5-6. Explain long-term care planning considerations including life stage, life style and product.

5-7. Identify gaps in planning and life insurance for women clients as both the insured and as the survivor.

5-8. Describe the survivor needs planning process.

5-9. Explain planning considerations for survivor needs by life stage and life style product.

INTRODUCTION

The personal risks associated with disability, long-term care and survivor needs are generally more challenging for women than for men. This is due to the combination of higher health and widowhood risks, along with lower product familiarity and preparation. These risks are underestimated by the American public at large, and by women in particular, in terms of their severity, probability and economic consequences. To help female clients more effectively recognize and address the risks of a disabling accident, illness, widowhood and premature death, financial professionals need a solid understanding of best practices planning techniques and strategies. There are also special considerations for select segments in the women's market that consultants should take into account when working with specific target audiences.

As with securing a sound financial position, ensuring adequate protection against personal risks is essential to the client's financial plan. Disability, long-term care and survivor needs should ideally be addressed prior to turning one's attention to building or distributing wealth. Addressing these risks is part of establishing a firm financial foundation as discussed in Chapter 4.

The underlying premise of this chapter is a focus on planning versus product. Disability, the need for long-term care and survivor risks are perils that can generally be analyzed or measured. By doing so, one becomes far more precise in developing recommendations and rationale of what adequate protection might be. While the end result usually culminates in product placement, the process of planning builds both client trust and confidence in the financial consultant. Taking a planning approach with the client demonstrates that one is willing to take the time necessary to fully understand her needs, analyze her situation, assess and present alternatives, and create a recommendation that will ultimately work for her.

As we have seen, planning not only builds client trust, but also improves the likelihood of product placement. For example, LIMRA found that product ownership of life insurance and long-term care increased by 15 to 53 percent when a written plan was in place.[195] The benefits to the financial consultant are larger case sizes and higher rates of implementation, meaning that less volume of marketing activities and their associated expense are required.

> "Failure to plan is expensive. Choosing to anticipate is the way to head off the big financial blows, because you are buying a commodity more precious than money: time."
>
> Mary Hunt

DISABILITY RISKS—UNDERESTIMATED AND UNDERINSURED

disability

The risk of losing earned income because of a disability is far more common than most people realize. An accident or an illness will keep one of five Americans out of work for at least a year during their careers.[196] One in seven workers may become disabled for five years or more before retirement,[197] and nearly one quarter (22 percent) of retirees report having to retire earlier than they had planned due to poor health.[198] Worse yet, the chances of becoming disabled are growing. According to the Social Security Administration, the number of disabled workers has increased by more than 35 percent since 2000.[199]

---

195. LIMRA, "Advisor Impact on Retirement: Opportunity Is Knocking," 2007. (2006 survey of 3,393 pre-retirees and retirees with >$50k investable assets.)
196. U.S. Census Bureau, December 1997.
197. Health Insurance Association of America, "Commissioners Disability Table, 1998," *The New York Times,* February 2000.
198. Anna M. Rappaport, "Improving the Financial Status of Elderly Women: Issues in Savings, Pension Plans, and Social Security," *Benefits Quarterly* 23, no. 1, (first quarter), 34–45.
199. Social Security Administration.

Along with the high probabilities of disability is the major financial hit it can create, such as facing poverty as a result of a premature and therefore unprepared retirement. Disability can also lead to the loss of property. According to the National Safety Council reported in 2004, almost half (48 percent) of all home foreclosures were due to disability.[200] While the Great Recession of 2008/2009 has likely changed the percentage of foreclosures due to disability, it likely remains a significant contributing factor.

Despite both great odds and negative financial impact of a disabling accident or illness, few are aware of their risks, and ready to meet them. A survey by the Council for Disability Awareness found that more than 80 percent of workers believe their chances of becoming disabled are far lower than actual statistics report.[201] Perhaps a result of either low awareness, complacency, or both, just four percent of U.S. workers have individual disability insurance[202] and less than one third (30 percent) have employer-sponsored coverage.[203] Many mistakenly believe that Social Security provides the disability coverage they need. The reality is that Social Security benefits are awarded to only 39 percent of those who apply and petition for them.[204]

Women and Their Disability Risks

As significant as the odds of disability are for the American public, they are even greater for its women. Over the past decade, the rate of disability among working females has accelerated almost twice as fast as that for males.[205] The Social Security Administration reports that from 1999 to 2009, disability rates for women increased by about 72 percent, versus 42 percent for men.[206] Recent government statistics also show that women are three times more likely than men to miss work due to a disabling injury or illness.[207]

While women have increasing disability risks, most are uninsured or at least, underinsured. Women are more likely to be employed by businesses that do not offer disability insurance (DI) coverage. On a related note, the Social

---

200. National Safety Council Injury Facts, 2004.
201. Council for Disability Awareness, "2007 Disability Awareness Survey," 2007.
202. "LIFE: Workers Overestimate Income Protection," National Health and Underwriter, May 12, 2008. http://www.lifeandhealthinsurancenews.com/News/2008/5/Pages/LIFE–Workers-Overestimate-Income-Protection.
203. Ibid.
204. Allsup.com, "More Women Turning to Social Security Disability Benefits; Mothers Should Know Their Options," April 5, 2009, http://www.allsup.com/about-us/news-room/current-news/women-and-ssdi.aspx
205. MohaveDailyNews.com, "Working Women Less Prepared for Income-limiting Disability," July 30, 2007.
206. Allsup.com, "More Women Turning to Social Security Disability Benefits; Mothers Should Know Their Options," April 5, 2009, http://www.allsup.com/about-us/news-room/current-news/women-and-ssdi.aspx
207. Health Insurance Association of America (HIAA) 2000.

Security Administration reports that women generally receive lower benefits than men, since they are likely to earn less during their careers. The average Social Security disability insurance (SSDI) benefit distributed to women is about 22 percent less than for men ($920.47 per month versus $1,188.57).[208] This lower amount is attributed in part to lower-paying careers, and also to cycling in/out of the workforce to care for children and family members.

What is the primary health condition that disables both women and men? It may come as a surprise that arthritis is the leading cause of disability among working-age people, according to the Center for Disease Control.[209] However, women have higher rates of arthritis-related disability than men, even at younger ages. By some estimates, American females are more than twice as likely to be disabled by arthritis as are males.[210]

As a result of their greater risks, women may not be approached by some producers for disability coverage, because females can be harder to underwrite and their declinations or ratings are more common. In addition, some have concern for their female clients about the higher premium rates women often have to pay for coverage, versus men, because of higher incidence of disability. That said, these factors should not dissuade consultants from working to help women put a disability risk management plan in place.

Identifying Women's Disability Risks

Risks are further magnified when they are not fully understood, grasped and appreciated. Low awareness often leads to unintentional risk retention, as discussed in Chapter 4. Even today, some women (and some financial professionals, as well) think of their husbands as the main household provider, and therefore, do not consider their income to be as important to their families. Only 32 percent of purchasers of disability income insurance were women, according to a 2004 LIMRA study.[211] Yet, the Department of Labor reported that in that same year, 46 percent of the workforce was female.[212]

Perhaps low awareness is why fewer women have disability income insurance coverage than men, despite the fact that they head 13 percent of all family households and contribute significantly in dual-income families. While the collective awareness of the risks that women face is generally low, the

---

208. Allsup.com, "More Women Turning to Social Security Disability Benefits; Mothers Should Know Their Options," April 5, 2009, http://www.allsup.com/about-us/news-room/current-news/women-and-ssdi.aspx.

209. L. Jans and S. Stoddard, "Chartbook on Women and Disability in the United States, an InfoUse Report," (Washington, DC: National Institute on Disability and Rehabilitation Research, 1999), www.infouse.com/disabilitydata/womendisability/1_3.php.

210. Ibid.

211. Kenneth Isenberg, Karen Terry, Linda Rowland, The Disability Income Buyer Study: United States, LIMRA, 2004.

212. U.S. Department of Labor, Bureau of Labor Statistics, 2004.

intent to address these risks is even lower. In some cases, women may well be aware and concerned, but have not taken any action. Consider these findings:

- According to the Council for Disability Awareness, nearly half of working women expressed concern that they might suffer a disability lasting three months or longer – but only 38 percent of women surveyed had discussed with their spouse how they would manage the onset of such an event.[213]

- In a 2006 study by Prudential Financial, while 67 percent of women felt it was important to protect investments and retirement savings in the event of a disability, only 15 percent said they were confident in their ability to achieve that goal.[214]

As more women are working outside the home than ever, the income they generate can no longer be considered incidental or trivial. Whether the client is a young single woman with no dependents, a working mother who is the head of household and sole breadwinner, or a married woman with a working spouse, her disabling illness or accident can put an abrupt end to a much-needed income stream. For most working women, their ability to earn an income and their future stream of earnings is their most valuable asset—by far. This holds true even for those with relatively lower incomes. Consider the table below, which quantifies the present value of annual earnings at 20, 30 and 40 year intervals, assuming three percent annual cost-of-living increases.

Present Value of Future Earnings Potential			
Annual Income	20 Years	30 Years	40 Years
$25,000	$383,095	$504,711	$595,205
$50,000	$766,190	$1,009,423	$1,190,410
$75,000	$1,149,285	$1,514,134	$1,785,616
$100,000	$1,532,380	$2,018,845	$2,380,821
$125,000	$1,915,475	$2,523,557	$2,976,027

How many clients—female or male—are in a financial position to replace hundreds of thousands (or even millions) of dollars in the event of a disability? Yet, this is exactly what is at stake for many, if not most.

---

213. Council for Disability Awareness, "Disability Awareness Survey," 2007.
214. Prudential Financial, "Financial Experience and Behaviors Among Women," 2006.

Women, Disability and Financial Literacy

Women may be reluctant to purchase disability insurance due to a low familiarity with the product, relative to other forms of coverage. A 2009 study on disability awareness and attitudes by The Guardian Life Insurance Company underscores this point. The survey found that just over half (58 percent) of disability policy owners (male and female combined) understand disability insurance extremely or very well, versus 73 percent for life and 77 percent for auto insurances.[215] The study also revealed that women lag behind men in disability product literacy:

- Sixty three percent of male respondents compared to 57 percent of women said they understood disability insurance "extremely well" or "very well."[216]

- Forty one percent of women who have disability insurance know the amount of DI they have, versus 52 percent of men.[217]

According to LIMRA however, the "silver lining" may be that while fewer women feel they know enough about disability insurance, more women want to learn about this subject than men.[218]

The bottom line is that most women do not realize just how catastrophic the sudden cessation of their earnings could be. This underserved market presents opportunity for financial professionals. Women care about protecting themselves and their loved ones, and they want to know the risks they face. Many need both education on their disability risks, and a plan to address them.

HER DISABILITY INCOME PLAN

When developing a disability risk management plan, one must identify and acknowledge her desires to have financial security and protect her family. Helping her determine exactly what is at risk is therefore extremely important. Without her continual stream of earned income, the following may well be in jeopardy:

- her home

- her ability to meet basic, committed expenses (e.g., housing, utilities, food, medical costs, transportation, child care, and so on)

- her funding and preparations for retirement

---

215. The Guardian Life Insurance Company of America, "Spotlight on Individual Disability Insurance," 2009.
216. Ibid.
217. Ibid.
218. LIMRA Study, "How to Market Financial Services to Women."

*Addressing Her Personal Risks—Disability, Long-Term Care and
Survivor Needs*

- her ability to fund the children's college costs

- the security and support of her children, including extra-curricular activities (e.g., tutoring, sports, camp, music lessons)

Identifying Her Disability Awareness and Concerns

Determining how much financial risk the client might retain and how much she might transfer occurs through the steps of understanding her objectives, her current financial position, and how both might be jeopardized by a disabling accident or illness. The table below lists basic questions that can help uncover her concerns and objectives related to disability. Beginning with open probe questions, and then appropriately transitioning to closed probes as one seeks to uncover fact-based information, makes it easier to move the process forward with her.

The Art of Discovery
Women and Disability Income
• If you were to become disabled tomorrow, how would you (and your family) manage?
• What changes would you need to make to your (and your family's) lifestyle?
• Would you be able to put your children through college if you (and/or your husband/partner) became disabled?
• How would the loss of your income (and that of your husband/partner) affect your ability to achieve financial security and your retirement goals?
• What kind of disability income protection do you currently have in place?
• Do you think it is adequate to meet your goals of (rephrase goals)? Would you like to know?
• So, if I hear you correctly, you are concerned about achieving (restate goal/s), and are unsure if you have the appropriate protection in place. Is that right?

Beyond discovering her feelings, goals and concerns, it is essential to know how the client spends her current income since disability insurance is designed to only partially replace earnings. One must also evaluate her assets and liabilities to better understand her ability to retain risk. Whenever possible, she should provide the consultant with both cash flow and net worth statements, the more accurate the better.

If she has either group or individual DI coverage, it is also necessary to obtain an employee benefit manual as well as any personal disability insurance contract(s). Women who are fortunate enough to have group disability coverage through their employer may be lulled into a false sense of security about their benefits. They may not fully appreciate the limitations of coverage, or realize that the amount provided may be insufficient to cover even the bare essential expenses plus additional medical costs often associated with long-term disability. For example:

- The majority of employer-provided long-term disability insurance covers 60 percent of basic salary, but excludes additional income (e.g., bonuses, or employer contributions to health insurance and retirement plans/pensions).

- Many group disability plans are integrated/offset by Social Security benefits (if paid) and do not have inflation indexing on the basic benefit amount.

- If the employer pays the premium or, if she pays the premium with pre-tax dollars, the benefit could be taxable.

These shortcomings must be taken into account when developing her plan. Examining her employee benefit manual may help to address some potential gaps in coverage. Very often, however, one will need to gain her authorization to speak with her employer's human resource department manager for more complete answers.

Disability Risk Analysis

Once cash flow, net worth and existing coverage information has been gathered, then the consultant is ready to analyze the client's disability risk exposure. Disability software and calculators easily support this task and are generally among the more simple planning tools available. Most tools simply estimate income shortfalls should she become disabled today, and do not project financial losses well into the future.

Some consultants take a zero-based (bottom-up), cash-flow driven approach, looking at committed and discretionary expense items and adjusting what might change in the event of a disabling accident or illness. Others use the top-down, goal-based method, simply applying a percentage reduction (e.g., 20 or 30 percent) to total current expenses. Whichever sort of software the consultant uses, it is best to walk the client through her current expense patterns, asking what might increase, decrease, or remain the same. Whether using a cash-flow driven or goal-based tool, this exercise informs planning assumptions. Perhaps more importantly, discussing the impact of a disability on her line item living expenses serves to build both awareness of the risks involved, as well as her engagement and support for the plan.

If one does not already have access to a good disability planning tool that allows for specificity in expense line items, several websites provide useful calculators. The calculator represented in the screen shot below is from the Life and Health Insurance Foundation for Education (www.lifehappens.org) and is relatively straightforward, and quick and easy to complete. Disability expense worksheets and brochures can also be downloaded from the lifehappens.org website.

Reprinted with permission from the Life and Health Insurance Foundation for Education, Arlington, VA. Reproduction prohibited without publisher's written permission.

Once the financial impact of the client's possible disability has been analyzed, then the consultant is in a position to run disability insurance illustrations to address shortages, whether all or in part. Since disability insurers will not cover 100 percent of earned income—generally limiting replacement to 60-70 percent—it may not be possible to insure the full measure of anticipated needs. In addition, the client may not have sufficient means to afford premiums associated with the greatest transference of risk possible. As such, financial consultants may want to show alternative risk analysis results, along with multiple product illustrations modifying waiting periods, benefit length and riders. Assuming the consultant has also reviewed the structures of her cash flow and net worth, he/she may also be in a position to play dollar detective by showing the client areas of opportunity to fund coverage and/or absorb risk.

Disability Plan Considerations

While each woman and her needs are unique, there are several common considerations by market segment that may be helpful to factor into the disability risk management plan. The following discussion highlights several key issues to evaluate when developing a plan with women at various stages of life and/or lifestyles.

Lifestyle and Life-Stage Considerations in Disability Planning

Single women are obviously at highest financial risk should they become disabled, since there is not another income earner in the household. Depending on her life-stage and style however, there are different factors to bear in mind.

Single Women, Starting Out. This group generally represents both high need and favorable underwriting conditions for disability income protection. She has an entire career ahead of her, along with what could well be millions of dollars in earned income potential. Yet, she faces relatively high odds of becoming disabled during her working years and the attendant risk of losing her number one asset—the ability to earn an income. Data from the Social Security Administration indicates that a 20 year old has about one in three chance of becoming disabled before reaching retirement age.[219] On a positive note, it is more likely she will be in relatively good health, and this, coupled with her youth, may make the premiums attractive and lessen the chance of an insurability challenge.

Women Who Become Single Again. If divorce has brought on this lifestyle, she may find herself totally on her own financially. Even if there is a small amount of alimony coming in, her earned income may be in real need of protection now. Protecting any asset settlement from the divorce and protecting her own income stream should be of foremost concern. Since many divorced women are older and become financially vulnerable as the result of losing shared income and expenses, it is essential for the financial consultant to help her quantify how the inability to work might impact her remaining assets and affect her retirement security.

A woman who has just become widowed, depending on the state of the marital finances, may be in good shape financially with a secure income stream from assets, annuities, pension benefits, and so on. More likely, she has suffered a major financial hit in the loss of her husband's earned income or some or all of his pension income. In either case, the analysis of her ability to manage should she become disabled is vital to both her financial security and peace of mind.

Single Mothers. Even though they contribute significantly to their family's finances and security, fewer than half of mothers who earn an income outside the home have any disability insurance.[220] Financial risks associated with disability are clearly magnified for single mothers. In 2004, more than seven million families with children under 18 were headed by a single mother—almost 30 percent of all working families. Further, the labor force participation rate of

---

219. Social Security Administration, Disability Benefits, August 2009.
220. National Underwriter Life & Health Online, "Survey: Moms Need More Income Protection," (accessed April 23, 2008).

single mothers surpassed 77 percent in 2004.[221] There is a great deal at stake here.

The single parent has an enormous amount of responsibility—not only financial, but also for her children's well-being and development. If she is the sole breadwinner, it is of paramount importance to analyze the economic effect of disability on her family's financial safety. She will need not only to get care for herself but also keep the household running, perhaps hiring someone to care for the children, cook, and clean.

If the client shares financial responsibilities with a noncustodial former spouse, it is necessary to determine whether or not he has disability coverage, as well. In fact, when meeting with a young mother going through a divorce, the financial consultant might suggest that disability insurance be required of the former spouse in order to protect child support and/or alimony arrangements. One might also recommend that the father maintain life insurance with the now single mother as policy owner, and that the premium is paid as part of the child support obligation.

Stay-At-Home Mothers. Financial professionals must consider the economic contributions of stay-at-home mothers as well. Salary.com, a market-leading compensation service, estimates that a full-time mother at home with two children, one in pre-school and one in grade school, contributes an annual economic value to her household ranging between $68,000 to $180,000 in 2009.[222] The estimates reflected in the table below are based on replacement costs (i.e., hourly wages) for the following services, delivered at an average weekly rate.

Service Provider	Stay-At-Home Mom Average Hrs Per Week	Service Provider	Stay-At-Home Mom Average Hrs Per Week
Housekeeper	16.5	Van Driver	7.3
Day Care Center Teacher	14.7	Psychologist	7.2
Cook	13.1	Laundry Machine Operator	7.2
Computer Operator	9.2	Janitor	7.1
Facilities Manager	8.6	Chief Executive Officer	5.5
Source: Salary.com, Mom Salary Wizard, http://swz.salary.com/momsalarywizard (accessed July 18, 2009)			

---

221. "America's Families and Living Arrangements: 2004," Table FG5, http://www.census.gov/population/socdemo/hh-fam/cps2004/tabFG5-all.csv: "Women in the Labor Force: A Databook," Table 6, op. cit.

222. Salary.com, Mom Salary Wizard, http://swz.salary.com/momsalarywizard (accessed July 18, 2009).

While some may view these assumptions as inflated or arguable, the point remains that the replacement value of women who work exclusively in the home while caring for children should not be ignored. In recognition of this, an increasing number of insurers offer coverage for stay-at-home spouses, regardless of gender.

Women in Dual Income Households. If she is part of a dual-income family, earnings from both partners need to be factored into the risk management plan. The family's lifestyle most likely has been both expanded and enhanced by the presence of two incomes. Therefore it may be difficult, if not impossible, to scale back to just one income. For example, both incomes were probably considered when the couple applied for a mortgage. (In fact, both incomes were probably necessary in order to afford the mortgage.)

Expenses may actually increase, not decrease, when the disabled person is both a spouse/partner and a mother. The disability income analysis should include expense needs associated with costs for household maintenance, additional childcare, and transportation. In addition, one should take into account funding for children's education and retirement savings in the overall risk assessment.

Women Business Owners. The self-employed and/or business owner needs to proactively plan for what might happen to her business should she, or a key person, become disabled. A disability buy-sell agreement funded by insurance provides the necessary funds for a co-owner to purchase her partner's share of the business if she becomes unable to work due to an accident or illness. Personal disability insurance can also be obtained to provide the family with replacement income. In addition, overhead insurance, covering 24 months or less of business expenses, can be purchased to maintain operations during a short-term disability.

A woman business owner may also want to offer her employees a voluntary group disability plan that allows them to purchase or increase their benefits. According to LIMRA, just 33 percent of small businesses (firms with fewer than 100 employees) offer group long-term disability plans.[223] These plans may provide group discounts and the ability to pay premiums through automatic payroll deduction.

---

223. LIMRA, U.S. Small Business Market, 2000

Addressing Her Personal Risks—Disability, Long-Term Care and Survivor Needs

Disability Product Considerations

When developing product proposals for female clients, the following partial list of design considerations by rider and coverage type may prove helpful:

waiting period
benefit period
future purchase option
inflation indexing
own occupation protection
social insurance offset
pregnancy complications

- *Waiting period.* If she has built up significant cash reserves and/or has employer benefits that provide sick pay and/or short-term disability coverage, then a longer waiting period (and therefore lower premium) may be appropriate.

- *Benefit period.* The younger she is, the longer the work career ahead of her and the higher the risk of financial loss. When affordable, maximum benefit periods should be considered, especially for younger clients. If she is older or married, she may be in a better position to retain more of the risk, and a shorter benefit period may make better sense.

- *Future purchase options (FPO).* These riders enable her to purchase additional insurance as her income rises. For younger women, FPO riders can be especially beneficial as they "lock-in" her insurability.

- *Inflation indexing.* Except for those clients within roughly 10 years from retirement age, inflation riders should almost always be considered, to ensure benefits keep pace with rising expenses.

- *Own occupation protection.* For the highly skilled, high-earning professional woman, adding a rider that more narrowly defines disability as the inability to perform the material and substantial duties of her own occupation can be essential to protecting her lifestyle and assets.

- *Stay-at-home spouse.* Disability coverage is often overlooked but can be important for spouses staying at home to care for children.

- *Social insurance offset.* These riders provide supplemental income if Social Security or other government insurance (e.g., workers compensation) denies coverage or pays a reduced benefit. From a planning perspective, attaching the social insurance offset rider helps her know what income benefits she can count on, regardless of their source.

- *Pregnancy complications.* Some pregnancy-related disability insurance is available for clients who are still in their child bearing years. Generally, coverage is available for relatively serious conditions that also require hospitalization (e.g., gestational diabetes, toxemia). Most policies do not include problems that may be related to a difficult pregnancy, but not classified as a pregnancy complication (e.g., morning sickness, false labor, bed rest).

Disability Summary

Since many women have low awareness of both their risks and disability insurance benefits, more time may be required to enable an informed decision. Their delay has nothing to do with an inability to understand key concepts. It has everything to do with the fact that women want to learn and get it right. Therefore, they will ask questions, research their options and take time to choose insurance elements carefully.

LONG TERM CARE—A CRISIS IN THE MAKING?

long-term care

The sheer magnitude of those giving and needing care in this country is tremendous and growing. Long-term care needs are wide ranging and complex, and statistics can vary widely from study to study. Even so, most estimate that there are roughly 13 million Americans in need of care services. As Baby Boomers age, it is expected that these numbers will double by 2050.[224] Keep in mind that it is not just senior adults who receive long-term care services. According the U.S. Department of Health and Human Services, nearly 40 percent of care recipients in 2004 were under the age of 64.[225]

In light of 77 million Baby Boomers entering their senior years, rapidly escalating costs of care and the vast number of uninsured, some view long-term care as an American crisis in the making. An estimated $230 billion-plus is spent in the United States annually on long-term care delivered by professionals in the patient's home or in facilities.[226] However, those expenditures represent just a fraction of the true costs, since more than 80 percent of services are rendered in the home by family members.[227]

Given the growing numbers who require long-term care, it may come as a shock that only seven million Americans have insurance to offset the financial, physical and emotional tolls that long-term care exacts from the giver and recipient alike.

---

224. K. Henderson, Long Term Care Planning: Women Take Note! *What Working Women Want: Crossing the Gender Gap to a Secure Retirement,* 2007, www. insurancenews.net (accessed January 15, 2009).

225. U.S. Department of Health and Human Services and U.S. Department of Labor, *The Future Supply of Long–Term Care Workers in Relation to the Aging Baby Boom Generation* (Washington, D.C: Offices of the Assistant Secretary for Planning and Evaluation, 2003), http://aspe.hhs.gov/daltcp/reports/ltcwork.htm (accessed March 28, 2009).

226. Howard Gleckman, "What About Long-Term Care?" *USA Today,* May 26, 2009.

227. AARP Public Policy Institute. "Analysis of data from the 2005 National Health Interview Survey."

Women and Long-Term Care: Double Jeopardy

double jeopardy

If there is any one single financial issue that is a "woman's issue," this is it, since women are in "double jeopardy" when in comes to long-term care. That is, they represent the substantial majority of both caregivers and care recipients. These twin risks present significant financial dangers to female clients, and accounting for both can be a crucial component of a well-developed financial plan. As significant as their risks are, many women face an equally concerning risk with regard to long-term care—the denial of its very real possibility in their lives. The section below explores the double risks of giving and receiving care, as well as issues associated with avoidance.

Risk One—Caregiving

caregivers

Every day at noon, a middle-aged woman leaves her office to feed her homebound mother a nutritious lunch. Every night, after tucking her own children into bed, a young mother pays bills for her aging parents. These are just some of the realities that many caregivers face.

The numbers and costs associated with those giving informal care in this country are astonishing. The National Alliance for Caregiving estimates that roughly one out of every five households is involved in providing care to individuals over age 18. Thirty-four million of those caregivers support someone aged 50 or older.[228]

For many women, their first exposure to long-term care occurs when they are providing services and/or financial support to a loved one. Women represent not only the vast majority of professional or formal caregivers, but also those serving as the primary deliverers of informal home care. Approximately 75 percent of those giving home care are female, most often the daughter.[229] Beyond the greater likelihood of being the primary or sole care provider, women also spend 50 percent more time giving care than men do.[230]

What are the costs of care and how do those costs affect those who give it? The following table shows the range of costs across the nation captured by the Long-Term Care Group in their 2008 survey of home health aides, assisted living and nursing homes.

---

228. National Alliance for Caregiving and AARP, "Caregiving in the U.S.," Washington, D.C., 2004.
229. "Where Will I Live, and Who Will Take Care of Me? Report by OWL, 2006.
230. K. Henderson, Long Term Care Planning: Women Take Note! *What Working Women Want: Crossing the Gender Gap to a Secure Retirement,* 2007. www. insurancenews.net (accessed January 15, 2009).

Cost in 2008	Home Health Aide (HHA)*					Assisted Living				Nursing Home			
	Per Hour	Per Day	Per Week	Per Month	Per Year	Per Day	Per Week	Per Month	Per Year	Per Day	Per Week	Per Month	Per Year
Highest	$88	$700	$3,500	$15,167	$182,000	$159	$1,092	$4,730	$56,760	$590	$4,130	$17,897	$214,760
Average	$26	$208	$1,040	$4,507	$54,080	$116	$792	$3,430	$41,160	$210	$1,470	$6,370	$76,440
Lowest	$13	$104	$520	$2,253	$27,040	$64	$438	$1,900	$22,800	$118	$826	$3,579	$42,952

Source: Long Term Care Group, Inc. Cost of Care Survey, November 2008, Commissioned by Northwestern Mutual Life. HHA refers to paid in-home caregivers.

While the high expense of facility care is generally well acknowledged, the costs and consequences associated with providing care in the home are far less well known. When factoring in contributions to medical expenses and other costs of care, the financial burden can be much greater than one might imagine. Brandeis University tracked 50 home caregivers in 2004 and estimated that the average total cost to the family of caregiving was well in excess of $500,000.[231]

Even if a family is fortunate enough to have the means to pay for a home health aide, there are still untold costs and consequences. According to the Long Term Care Group, the average nationwide cost of bringing in a home health aide to support the family in giving care is more than $54,000 per year, for just 40 hours per week. Consider the implications: $54,000 a year for 40 hours per week is pricey by anyone's standards. Even with help, however, the family, and especially women, are "on duty" every evening, every night and all weekend long for 52 weeks each year, without a break or vacation. One study shows that primary caregivers receive only an average of 11 hours of help a week from their own family and friends—a small fraction compared to the average of 87 hours of weekly care primary caregivers deliver.[232]

Beyond picking up the tab for care-related expenses and providing seemingly endless hours of care, there are other and often more troubling costs for caregivers. These costs potentially compromise their livelihoods, financial security and health. Consider these sobering facts:

Impact on Her Work. In 2006, more than 6.4 million working women were believed to be providing direct or indirect caregiving assistance. By 2010, it is projected that 10.1 million employed females will bear this emotional and financial burden.[233] In addition:

- More than four in ten female caregivers have full-time jobs.[234]

---

231. MetLife Mature Market Institute, "The MetLife Juggling Act Study," November 1999.
232. Ronald J. Iverson, "The Silent Crisis: Women and the Need for Long-Term Care Insurance Part 2," *CARING Magazine,* November 2003, 36.
233. "Where Will I Live, and Who Will Take Care of Me?" Report by OWL, 2006.
234. Graham Cox, "As Financial Obligations Grow, Women Should Rethink Life Insurance," *National Underwriter Life & Health* October 2008.

- Eighty four percent of working women who are also caregivers make formal arrangements with their employers to accommodate family responsibilities.[235] These changes include going to work late, leaving early, foregoing promotions and transfers, or switching to part-time work.

Impact on Her Finances. Beyond the potentially negative impact on her employment, caregiving also reduces pension accumulations, retirement plan contributions and financial well-being.

- In 2007, the National Center on Women and Aging estimated that family caregivers lose an average of $659,130 over a lifetime in reduced salary and retirement benefits.[236]
- According to research by Securian, 62 percent of women caregivers said they were concerned their money will not last through retirement, and 57 percent agreed that after meeting current financial obligations, there was little money to put away for retirement.[237]
- When women become caregivers, they are nearly three times more likely to end up impoverished and five times more likely to depend exclusively on Social Security.[238]

Impact on Her Health. In light of the financial and employment challenges that caregiving presents, it's not surprising that there are emotional and physical tolls as well:

- Forty four percent of female caregivers report high levels of physical strain or emotional stress,[239] while employed caregivers are more than twice as likely to develop depression.[240]
- Sixty six percent of family caregivers report significant health problems and 41 percent say their health is worse now than 5 years ago.[241]

---

235. "The MetLife Juggling Act Study," 1999.
236. National Center for Women and Aging, *Investment News*, October 29, 2007.
237. PRNewswire, "Women Expect to Care for Aging Parents But Seldom Prepare," April 23, 2007, http://www.redorbit.com/news/health/911975/women_expect_to_care_for_aging_parents_but_seldom_prepare/ 1
238. "Where Will I Live, and Who Will Take Care of Me?" Report by OWL, 2006
239. AARP Public Policy Institute, "Caregiving in the U.S.", 2005
240. Business and Professional Women's Foundation, "101 Facts on the Status of Working Women," October 2007, (compiled by the Family Caregiver Alliance, "Selected Caregiver Statistics," 2004).
241. Ronald J. Iverson, "The Silent Crisis: Women and the Need for Long-Term Care Insurance Part 2," *CARING Magazine,* November 2003, 36.

- Elderly people caring for their spouses were 63 percent more likely to die at an earlier age than non-caregivers.[242]
- Women who spend more than nine hours per week caring for a disabled spouse double their risk of coronary heart disease.[243]

As a result of great financial, physical and emotional burden, the experience of being a caregiver can compel much-needed action. Thirty seven percent of caregivers report taking specific steps to plan for their future as a result of their experience in caring for someone else. Among those individuals, 36 percent purchased additional life, health or long-term care insurance.[244] Despite the odds, however, most women remain alarmingly unprepared.

Risk Two—Care Receiving

care receiving

Significantly magnifying the client's risk is the significant probability that she will require care. As women live longer than men, many are without a spouse during the later years. She may find herself living alone with no one to assist her. The earlier death of the spouse may also affect her means to pay for her own care services due to reduced income and assets that may have been depleted for her husband's long-term care. These factors could translate into a tragic scenario: an older, quite possibly impaired woman, living alone with no ability to pay for needed care.

While the probability of needing long-term care is about 50 percent for the general population, it grows to 70 percent for women over 65.[245] Females are also more likely to be cared for in a facility, and for a longer period of time. Seventy percent of nursing home residents are female, with an average stay of 3.7 years versus 2.2 years for men. As a result of these factors, it is estimated that the average American female will incur more than twice the long-term care expense of the average male.[246] [247]

The greater longevity that many women enjoy also increases the likelihood that they will need assistance with the basic activities of life. These include activities of daily living (ADLs) which include continence, dressing,

---

242. Ronald J. Iverson, "The Silent Crisis: Women and the Need for Long-Term Care Insurance Part 2," *CARING Magazine,* November 2003, 36.
243. The American Association for Long-Term Care Insurance, Consumer Education Division, "A Women's Guide To Long-Term Care Insurance Protection," 2009.
244. Marcella De Simone, "Women Seen Often Driving the LTC Insurance Sale," *National Underwriter Life & Health,* May 12, 2003.
245. Genworth Financial, "Our Future, Ourselves. A Guide for Women and Their Advisors in Preparing for Long Term Care," 2007, (quoted from Jim Emerman, Senior Vice President of the American Society on Aging, Press Release, "Americans Fail to Act on Long Term Care Protection," May 2003)
246. American Health Care Association, "The Silent Crisis & The Need for Long Term Care," 2003.
247. U.S. Department of Health and Human Services.

transferring, eating, walking, hygiene and toileting, as well as instrumental activities of daily living (IADLs) such as driving, cooking, housework, and managing medications or finances. Longevity also increases the risk of Alzheimers disease, which is the number one reason for the largest long-term care claims and costs.[248] The chart below reflects how the need for help with these activities grows as individuals age, and the differences by age group between men and women.

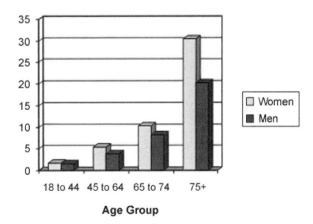

Source: LaPlante & Carlson, NHIS surveys

Her Third Risk—Denial and Avoidance

denial

In light of the double jeopardy that long-term care presents to a great many, one might think that most women would be clamoring to address their risks, right? Wrong.

There is a disturbing tendency to avoid the subject of long-term care until it is too late. While daughters and wives are often called upon to provide care for their parents or husband, few broach the subject with either, as these research findings reveal:

- A Securian Financial survey found that among women who were giving care to their parents, almost nine in ten (84 percent) said no plans were in place until care was actually needed.[249]

---

248. American Association for Long-Term Care Insurance Consumer Education Division, "A Woman's Guide to Long-Term care Insurance Protection," 2009.
249. Securian Financial Inc., Conducted by Gestalt, Inc., 2008

- Just 18 percent of women had talked to their spouse or partner about long-term care, according to Prudential Financial research.[250]

Social pressures about women and aging often lead to conflicted feelings and motivations related to planning for the second half of life. Health, energy and professional success can mislead women into believing that physical frailty or cognitive impairment are for someone else—for old women. The anti-aging movement, which includes a lucrative subspecialty of medicine, has risen in response to a growing demand for information, products, and services that will extend a healthy middle age well into or beyond traditional retirement age. Even if a woman avoids the physical, mental, and financial stress of being a hands-on caregiver, she faces rather sobering statistics on the probability of needing care herself. Yet, many women do not contemplate their risks:

- Only 35 percent of women in a 2009 survey by America's Health Insurance Plan (AHIP) said they had thought about or planned for how they will cover long-term care costs.[251]

- According to Genworth Financial, nearly 80 percent of workers have not given any thought to financing long-term care needs, and close to 90 percent of people ages 45 to 64 are uninsured for long-term care.[252]

Considering the frequently devastating impact of long-term care, denial and avoidance can be risks in their own right. As such, financial consultants may be challenged by the important task of helping women understand their magnified risks in a way that does not play on fear, but rather enhances their knowledge and understanding of the issues.

HER LONG-TERM CARE PLAN

Managing long-term care risks is similar to managing disability risks. Both address the probabilities of financial loss associated with an accident or illness that renders a woman incapable of performing key functions. However, disability risks deal with her inability to earn an income, while long-term care risks are associated with her inability to perform activities of daily living.

Identifying Her Long-Term Care Awareness and Concerns

According to Joan Bloom, senior vice president of Fidelity Life Insurance Group, a relatively small number of Americans—roughly five to seven

---

250. Prudential Financial "2006 Study on the Financial Experience and Behaviors Among Women."
251. "AHIP/Survey One," *Insurance Insider News,* January 28, 2009.
252. Genworth Financial, "Our Future, Ourselves: A Guide for Women and their Advisors in Preparing for Long Term Care," August 2007.

million—have long-term care insurance.[253] Since most of the American public, both men and women, are uninsured and unaware, financial professionals must first determine what clients understand about their risks and if any steps have been taken to reduce them. For a woman in particular, this means not only uncovering attitudes and awareness about her own need for care, but also the likelihood to be called upon to provide care for her parents, her spouse, or both. Asking female clients about their probabilities of being a caregiver can be an excellent way to open the dialogue. Many women either have been, will be or know someone who is, a caregiver. If indications are reasonably strong that the client will be a substantial participant in a network of care, the financial professional needs to help her develop realistic assumptions and incorporate those into her risk management plan.

Consider using questions like these when seeking to uncover the facts and feelings about long-term care, as well as her risks as a potential caregiver and/or receiver:

The Art of Discovery
Women and Long-Term Care

Caregiving

- How likely is it that you might become a caregiver for a loved one?
- Have you talked with your parents, in-laws or husband/partner about needing or giving long-term care?
- What plans do you currently have in place should a family member require care?
- If you cannot physically or financially manage to provide all the care that is needed, will your parents/spouse/partner agree to pay for outside help?

Care receiving

- What concerns you most about long term care?
- Where do you plan to retire? What are the costs of home care, assisted living and nursing homes in that area?
- How much retirement income and/or savings will you need to pay for care services in the future?
- How familiar are you with what funding the government does and does not provide when it comes to long term care?
- Does your employer offer long-term care insurance?
- Do you have a family history of Alzheimers or diabetes?
- Do you think you'll have enough to pay for both quality care and retirement income?
- Would you like to know?

---

253. Mark Jewel, Fidelity: $85k Needed for Long-Term Care Costs, Associated Press, June 26, 2008.

Women and Money

The majority of female clients are, in fact, worried about the damaging affect that long-term care might have on their financial security and future. Most have never had a trusted professional help them sort it out. Beyond facilitating a thoughtful discussion, one must look at retirement assets, income and expense needs. The diligent consultant can be tremendously valuable in helping her quantify the impact of long-term care (both receiving and giving, if appropriate) on her retirement plan. This means projecting retirement income needs and layering on the expense of a long-term care event or events.

Long-Term Care Risk Analysis

Helping her analyze the probabilities of care, costs and impact on retirement security can be an eye-opening exercise. A particularly useful resource is the long-term care planning tool found on the U.S. Government's Medicare website (www.medicare.gov). The calculator asks for inputs on age, gender, earnings, health, location of potential care services and family histories. Beyond providing a wealth of unbiased information, the calculator gives an individualized projection of care costs and probability based on gender, age and health history factors. Geographic differences in care costs are also incorporated in the estimates. Results reflect costs and probabilities for individuals with similar profiles based on a broadly representative databank. Here is a screen shot of partial results for a sample case:

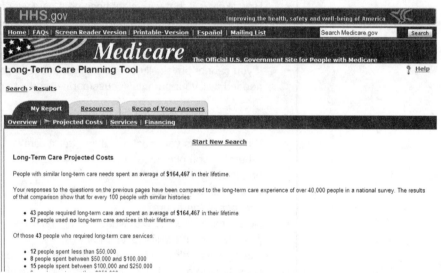

Once a reasonable approximation of her costs and probabilities is complete, the professional will need to analyze her ability to address them. There are two basic ways to approach the analysis: (1) a projection of sources and uses of cash in retirement, both with and without the assumed costs (based on geography and level) of long-term care; and (2) a simple projection of long-term care expenses and possible assets available to pay for them. Either method can incorporate cost assumptions derived from the client's own risks/cost estimates, as reflected in Medicare's online long-term care planning tool. Below are screen shots of an online calculator (at www.dinkytown.net) that reflects the second, more simplistic approach factoring in long-term care expenses and their impact on client assets.

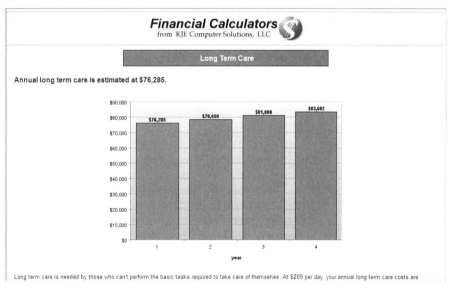

Whether using robust, cash-flow based financial planning software, or relatively simple planning calculators, the essential point is to plan. Planning crystallizes the enormity of risk that long-term care presents to her retirement resources and family. It brings a vaguely conceived or avoided notion into sharpened focus. In addition, planning can be very effective when working with spouses, especially when one is reluctant to purchase long-term care insurance, as is often the case. It is hard to argue with a well-developed and reasoned analysis. Planning removes the emotion from an often emotional subject.

Very few retirement portfolios and income streams (e.g., Social Security and pensions) will be able to withstand the financial impact that long-term care presents. Even those who may be able to self-insure may wish to transfer at least some of the risk. For those who wish to retain the risk, but are not in a financial position to do so, the financial consultant should determine what, if any, game plan is in place. Denial, or "I'll/we'll take my/our chances," is not a viable alternative given the enormity of risks involved. Some financial professionals draft a letter for clients to sign, in cases where risks have been determined to exceed the ability to self-insure, and the client still chooses to remain uninsured.

Long-Term Care Plan Considerations

Once both the costs of care are developed and acknowledged, along with their impact on the client's family and her retirement, then one can shift to how those risks can be managed, including insurance alternatives. This step may require education on both what the government, as well as private insurance, does and does not offer.

Research conducted by America's Health Insurance Plans (AHIP) in 2008 points out just how many Americans are misinformed about what might be available to pay for long-term care. Forty two percent of those without long-term care insurance say they will rely on government programs, such as Medicaid, and 23 percent incorrectly believe that other insurance would provide assistance for long-term care costs.[254] Private Medicare supplement (or Medigap) policies only fill in the deductibles and co-pays for what Medicare approves (hence, no custodial care coverage). Only 12 percent of nursing home costs were covered by Medicaid in 2004.[255]

The AHIP study also found that about one third of Americans believe that they will sell assets to pay for care costs. One of the biggest disconnects revealed in the research was that just 12 percent of individuals surveyed said they will rely on family members, despite the fact that nearly 80 percent of all care is now delivered by family in the home.[256] Financial professionals, insurers, the media and government entities will need to do far more in coming years to debunk long-term care myths, misinformation and misperceptions.

Product education is also vital, since industry studies show that both men and women have lower literacy rates with respect to long-term care insurance versus other financial products. Since females are at significantly higher risk, their lack of product knowledge puts them in even greater peril. According

---

254. AHIP/Survey One," Insurance Insider News, January 28, 2009.
255. Centers for Medicare and Medicaid Services (CMS) http://hhs.gov/statistics.nhe/default.asp.
256. AHIP/Survey One," *Insurance Insider News,* January 28, 2009.

to research by Prudential, only 14 percent—less than one in seven women surveyed—said they understood long-term care insurance "very well." Forty percent said they understood it "somewhat well," and almost half said they did not understand it well or at all.[257]

Long-Term Care, Life-Stage and Life Style Considerations

Beyond increasing awareness of risks and product alternatives, there are life-stage and lifestyle factors to consider when working on long-term care solutions for women clients.

Pre-Retired Women. The life-stage market for long-term care planning is relatively narrow, when compared to other financial areas. While close to 40 percent of those needing assistance with activities of daily living (ADL) are under age 65, the vast majority of concerns surface among pre-retired individuals. After a female client's children are grown, her thoughts likely turn—perhaps for the first time—to the remainder of her own life: how she is going to maximize her earnings and savings potential, spend her days both in business and in pleasure, stay or become more healthy, redefine her life, expand her social contacts, and prepare for her later years.

Women in or approaching their 50s have a very good chance of still being free from chronic conditions that may set in later, regardless of preventive measures taken. Assuming she is not able to retain or absorb all the risks that long-term care can present, insurability is generally less of a concern and relatively affordable at this point in her life, as this chart from The American Association for Long-Term Care Insurance illustrates.

Percentage of Long-Term Care Insurance Applicants Who Are "Health Declined"		Percentage of Long-Term Care Insurance Applicants Qualifying for "Good Health" Discounts	
Age of Applicant	Percent Declined	Age of Applicant	Percent Who Save
Under 50	7.3 percent	40 to 49	66.8 percent
50 to 59	13.9 percent	50 to 59	51.5 percent
60 to 69	22.9 percent	60 to 69	42.2 percent
70 to 79	44.8 percent	70 to 79	24.2 percent
80 and over	69.8 percent	80 and over	12.9 percent
Source: American Association for Long-Term Care Insurance, 2008 Industry Research Analysis			

---

257. Prudential Financial, "Financial Experience and Behaviors among Women," 2006

Since many women in this stage of life are, or will become, caregivers, they often appreciate help in planning and possibly placing insurance for their parents. Their mothers and/or fathers may still be relatively young, healthy and insurable. It is worth asking about, and investigating insurance feasibility along with coverage costs as part of both her and her parent's overall plan. If insurance coverage is not a viable option for her parents, then a thoughtful examination of care costs—both with her and ideally, with her parents as well—should be undertaken.

Retired Women. In the event that a long-term care plan was not already in place before this stage, there should be no more delaying! Women in this life-stage are concerned about protecting assets for the well spouse or survivors, and not wanting to burden the family with their care. It is common for retired individuals, even the affluent, to wish they had taken action sooner, before they became uninsurable or premiums became relatively out of reach. Since long-term care insurance pricing is determined by age at application, health status, and, in some states, marital status, it is important to investigate while all three factors are in the client's favor.

Married Women. Increasingly, couples who are mindful of the jeopardizing affect long-term care may have on their retirement security, are seeking insurance alternatives. Many insurers offer discounts for couples, ranging from 25 to 40 percent, when both spouses apply. Even if one spouse is declined, the approved spouse may still be eligible for at least a partial discount. Another important product development is the availability of shared policies or riders that connect two individual policies. These policies or riders enable spouses to draw from what amounts to a combined benefit pool. In 2005, approximately one-third of eligible long-term care policies issued included shared care provisions.[258] The relatively rapid rise of shared care contracts/riders is attributed to their easily understood benefit and the appeal (or the perception) of being able to distribute risk between both partners.

Domestic Partners. More insurers are providing couples' discounts to unmarried adults living together. In addition, shared care provisions are being made available to domestic partners by some insurers.[259]

Single Women. Whether single all of her life or as a result of death or divorce, a female client will likely feel vulnerable. She will want to know that she can afford care if that day comes, protect her income and assets for the remainder of her life and, most likely, will not want to burden remaining family members. In some cases, there may be no one else to depend on. Single

---

258. Published by: November 13, 2006 edition of the National Underwriter, Life and Health Edition, Towers Perrin, Tillinghast, The Rising Tide of Shared Care LTC Sales, December 2006, Claude Thau, Steven Plummer and Daniel B. Cathcart.

259. Ibid.

women, in particular, benefit more from having long-term care insurance protection than their male counterparts. Consider the percentage of claims paid by gender and marital status, according to the American Association of Long-Term Care Insurance and Genworth Financial:

Percentage of All Claims Paid		
	Women	Men
Single	41 percent	12 percent
Married	25 percent	22 percent
Source: Genworth Financial, 2008 Claimant Study, Reported in A Woman's Guide to Long-Term care Insurance Protection, Published by the American Association for Long-Term Care Insurance Consumer Education Division, 2009		

Long-term care premiums are the same for single women and men, despite a female's higher incidence of claim.[260] As such, their premiums represent a relative bargain for many female consumers.

In the case of divorce, newly single women do not always lose spousal coverage discounts. To protect their clients, especially female clients, savvy attorneys often include long-term care insurance as part of the divorce settlement. If the client is or will soon be going through the divorce process and she has been financially dependent on her husband, the consultant might ask about having her covered for long-term care with the husband being responsible for premiums. The husband could be directly billed or could fund an annuity with annual payments that would cover the premium, or alimony payments could take into consideration her need to fund long-term care insurance. Keep in mind that long-term care premiums are not guaranteed to stay the same, and an annuity or other alimony payments may not cover all future costs.

If she plans to remarry, she might be interested in ways to protect any children from the first marriage (in terms of preserving their inheritance). In many cases, a pre-nuptial agreement is wise. In addition to the "pre-nup," she would want to make sure that both she and her future spouse were insured for long-term care. In spite of any pre-nup agreement, the assets of one spouse are generally deemed available to the other spouse, as far as Medicaid eligibility goes. Should her future husband become impaired, need long-term care, and end up spending all his assets on the needed care, he might not be able to qualify for Medicaid assistance, until her assets were also depleted. This turn of events wipes out any dreams of leaving a financial legacy to the children of her first marriage.

---

260. American Association for Long-Term Care Insurance Consumer Education Division, "A Woman's Guide to Long-Term care Insurance Protection," 2009.

women business owners

Women Business Owners. Only nine percent of smaller women-owned companies and 19 percent of women-owned companies offered long-term care insurance to their employees in 2006.[261] Yet, there are also attractive tax advantages associated with securing individual and group policies for business owners and the self-employed. Offering voluntary long-term care insurance through the business can also provide employees with discounted coverage at no cost to the employer. According to the American Association of Long-Term Care Insurance, here are key considerations to take into account when working with business owners:

Long-Term Care Planning Advantages for Self-Employed and Business Owners
Long-term care insurance protection may be up to 100 percent tax deductible to a business, depending on its type. In addition to federal tax advantages, a growing number of states offer tax incentives for the purchase of long-term care insurance protection.
Business owners can generally choose who is covered, deducting the cost of qualified long-term care insurance protection for themselves, for their spouse and even for their eligible dependents (such as parents).
Corporations (C-Corps) can create an "Executive Carve-Out" plan, whereby the corporation pays the cost of insurance for designated individuals. Company-paid policies can cover spouses even though the corporation does not employ them. The premium paid by the business is excluded (not reported) from the employee's Adjusted Gross Income and benefits may be received tax-free. Self-employed individuals may deduct costs for tax-qualified, long-term care insurance up to the current year's age-based limit.
The availability of "10 pay" or "paid-up-at-65" policies enable individuals and business owners to maximize tax advantages and retirement income strategies. These products provide for fully paid-up protection prior to retirement and may eliminate exposure to future rate increases.
Source: A Woman's Guide to Long-Term Care Insurance Protection, Published by the American Association for Long-Term Care Insurance Consumer Education Division, 2009

Financial consultants should work with competent tax professionals to determine, if and how much, the female business owner might benefit from deducting long-term care insurance premiums.

Individuals who are eligible to receive group benefits through employers or associations should compare group premiums versus premiums for individual policies. Group coverage may have less stringent health underwriting, however, they generally do not provide discounts for spouses/partners or good-health rates.

---

261. Genworth Financial, "Our Future, Ourselves: A Guide for Women and Their Advisors in Preparing for Long Term Care," August 2007.

Other Long-Term Care Insurance Considerations

benefit length
inflation protection
tax qualified policies

Assuming the financial professional has evaluated the female client's costs and probability of care, as well as the impact on her financial future, an estimated benefit amount should be the first design component for long-term care insurance. Since there may be premium affordability issues to take into account as well, policy design considerations should also include:

- *Waiting period*—Evaluated dollars at risk and if the client has (and will likely continue to have in the future) adequate cash reserves to fund the elimination period. Assess premium differences between waiting periods and discuss pros/cons with the client.

- *Benefit length*—If she is not able to transfer all of the risk or fund an extended benefit period, it is important to more fully protect her assets as long as possible. Nancy Morith, CLU®, CASL®, Adjunct Professor of Insurance at The American College and long-term care expert, suggests that building a policy with a higher daily benefit and lower benefit period is the first line of retreat if resources are limited. Her rationale is that most claims last three to five years (longer for women) and preserving retirement assets as long as possible is critical. In other words, "fat and short" is better in most cases. However, one must also consider personal health history, genetic predisposition to certain diseases (e.g., Alzheimer's) and age differences between spouses when designing a policy. For example, in couples where the husband is more than five years older than the wife, it may be worthwhile considering a "fat and short" benefit for his contract and a longer period for hers.

- *Inflation protection*—Even if only some of the risk is covered, the great majority of policies should include compound inflation protection given the rapid increase of costs and high likelihood they will continue outpacing inflation in the future. In some instances however, especially with older clients, it makes more sense to beef up (e.g., double) the daily/monthly benefit versus purchasing the compound inflation rider. The consultant needs to work through the options, their possible impact on the plan and explore both pros and cons with clients.

- *"Tax qualified" policies*—Long-term care insurance premiums for contracts that are tax qualified can be treated as a personal medical expense for those who itemize their tax deductions and have total qualified medical expenses in excess of 7.5 percent of adjusted gross income. The amount that can be deducted each year depends on the person's age.

Long-Term Care Summary

Today, too many families are torn apart and women left destitute by leaving long-term care decisions to chance. Financial consultants can make a meaningful difference in the lives of their female clients and their families when they help them develop a long-term care plan. Building awareness of risks, analyzing risk exposure, showing three to four product design alternatives and educating her on their respective pros and cons demonstrates professionalism, compassion and knowledge. Whether it is long-term care or some other aspect of her financial life, this phrase bears repeating: "the plan's the thing."

HER SURVIVOR NEEDS AND LIFE INSURANCE

Only a generation or two ago, life insurance for women was an afterthought to the need for insuring men. At a time when fewer women worked outside the home, insurance was sold to them as part of a family rider in small units of coverage, combined with coverage on children. While much has changed in the last twenty to thirty years, mindsets and attitudes have not necessarily kept up. This is evidenced in disparities between men and women in their financial literacy, insurance coverage and preparedness for retirement. Planning for survivor needs is no exception.

Women and THEIR Survivors

survivors

Shifts in the demographic structure of the family in the United States, along with the changing role of women in the workforce, have created unprecedented needs to plan for survivors of the female client should she die prematurely. More than ever, families depend on two incomes to maintain the family's desired lifestyle. According to the U.S. Census Bureau, more than 60 percent of all married couples are dual-earner couples.[262] As previously noted, over half of all wives earn as much as their husbands, with at least a third earning more.[263] Further, the vast majority of single parents are women. The U.S. Census Bureau estimates that 19 percent of all households with children are headed by women and that women head 74 percent of all single-parent families.[264] As such, planning within the context of the family's financial needs and goals has become just as important for women today as it has historically been for men.

There is a broadly held misperception that women do not need life insurance, or at least not as much as men do. Perhaps that is why it is that today, women are less likely than men to own life insurance, both individual and group. LIMRA reports that only 40 percent of women own an individual life insurance policy, and just 36 percent have coverage through work. Almost one-third of American

---

262. U.S. Census Bureau, "Household and Family Units by Race and Origin," March 2006.
263. "Women and Life Insurance," LIMRA, 2005.
264. U.S. Census Bureau, "Household and Family Units by Race and Origin," March 2006.

adult females have no life insurance coverage at all, with about half of women aged 18 to 24 having none.[265] For women who have either group or individual coverage, the average death benefit ($129,400) is almost 40 percent lower than the average for men ($206,600).[266]

Despite gaps in coverage, studies have shown that women have a better understanding of life insurance as a product versus other financial vehicles. According to research by Prudential Financial, nearly 80 percent of women said they understood life insurance well or somewhat well (second only to their knowledge of savings accounts).[267] This suggests that even though the product may be well understood (or at least perceived as such), its utility perhaps is not. While women have made significant gains in their economic contributions in both the workplace and the home, their connection to the family's security is often overlooked, as these research findings indicate:

- Forty six percent of full-time working women have not taken any steps to determine their life insurance needs.[268]

- Fifty six percent of working women who have life insurance coverage do not believe or are unsure that the amount of coverage is adequate.[269]

- Sixty nine percent of Americans believe both parents in a household where one parent works and the other stays at home to care for children should have life insurance, but just seven percent report that to be the case in their home.[270]

Women as THE Survivor

Women are not the only ones who need a clearer picture of the value of their economic contributions to the family. Many men are also underinsured, assuming an average death benefit in the low $200,000 range. More than 75 percent of women are widowed at an average age of 56, and one in four of these women have exhausted their financial resources within two months of being widowed.[271] As a sad result, the U.S. General Accounting Office estimates that

---

265. LIMRA International, "Trends in Life Insurance Ownership Among U.S. Individuals," 2005.
266. Ibid.
267. Prudential Financial, "2008–2009 Study on the Financial Experience and Behaviors Among Women."
268. Annual MetLIfe Study of Employee Benefits, Press Release August 2008.
269. Ibid.
270. Country Insurance and Financial Services, PR Newswire, "Women Lag Behind Men on Life Insurance Coverage," May 2007.
271. Kathleen Williams, "Women and Investing: Be the Captain of Your Financial Life," http://www.womensmedia.com/new/Williams-Kathleen-Investing-for-Women.shtml.

four out of five widows living in poverty were not poor when their husbands were alive.[272] These are sobering statistics.

Perhaps women are not comfortable bringing this subject up with their husbands and may need the skilled assistance of a trusted financial consultant, as these findings suggest:

- Forty four percent of women have not discussed the issue of life insurance with their husbands.[273]

- Eighty one percent of women agree that it is important to be financially secure if they outlive their husband; however, just 25 percent feel very confident that they will be able to do so.[274]

It would not be an overstatement to say that *both* women and men seriously underestimate the monetary worth of their contributions to the household. Here is a great "litmus test" question to ask clients that dramatically illustrates the need to appreciate one's contribution to their family's financial security. This question comes from Associate Professor Ed Graves, CLU®, ChFC®, Zimmerman Chair in Life Insurance Education at The American College: "Is the amount of coverage that you currently have in force equal to the maximum amount you would seek in a wrongful death settlement?" Most Americans, male or female, would likely answer "no," which leads one to ponder why.

> "The striking power of death is tremendous, and why people with intelligence can't see the need for insuring the monetary worth of their life value, or, put another way, the continuance of their earning capacity and their savings effort, is beyond my comprehension."
>
> Solomon Heubner, PhD, Founder of The American College, 1927

PLANNING FOR SURVIVOR NEEDS

One of the most profound risks in life can be finding oneself unprepared as a survivor of an economic partnership, married or otherwise. However, few people have contemplated a game plan, and devised an appropriate risk management strategy. The trusted professional acts as a financial engineer in helping clients strengthen the bridges to their security, which span the chasms of financial risks. Diligent fact finding and well-thought-out analysis, along with researching and presenting alternative product options, fortifies the bridge for potential survivor(s) and sets one apart from the competition.

---

272. Kerry Hannon, "Suddenly Single," U.S. General Accounting Office, John Wiley and Sons, 1998.
273. Prudential Financial, "Financial Experience and Behaviors Among Women," 2006.
274. Ibid.

Identifying Survivor Needs

It is common for some producers to limit their fact finding exclusively to how much life insurance the insured can afford, or wishes to purchase. This approach ignores the client's ability to retain or the need to transfer risk, and most often excludes the very person life insurance is intended to benefit—the survivor. Without knowing what the survivor might do or need in the event of losing an economic partner, and building an analysis to reflect those needs, how accurate can any proposed amount or type of insurance be? This is why it is important to engage both spouses in discussions about survivor needs when determining the appropriate amount and design of life insurance coverage. Here are some questions that may be useful when uncovering survivor needs, goals and concerns:

The Art of Discovery
Women and Survivor Needs

• If you were to lose your husband/partner tomorrow, what would you do?
  – Would you change your lifestyle?
  – Would you return to work?
  – Would you go back to school?
  – Would you move?
 	
• How would you (and your family) manage if you were to die prematurely?
 	
• Would you (and/or) your survivors be financially secure?
 	
• Would your children be able to go to college if you (and/or your husband) were to die prematurely?
 	
• Will you (and/or you husband/partner) be able to retire with dignity?
 	
• What kind of life insurance do you (and husband/partner) have in place?
 	
• Do you think it is enough to meet your goals of (restate goals)?

Survivor Risk Analysis and Planning

survivor needs

When calculating risk and survivor needs, the financial consultant should incorporate these three basic factors:

1. *Final expenses*—funeral, probate costs and attorney fees

2. *Capital needs*—debt liquidation (e.g., mortgage, auto loans, credit cards), emergency cash reserves, goal funding (e.g., children's college education), estate taxes and charitable giving

3. ***Survivor income needs***—pre-retirement and post-retirement through life expectancy

There is a wide range of survivor needs analysis tools available, from basic calculators to more robust software. These help the consultant, client and spouse determine the appropriate amount of life insurance that is needed. Many insurance companies provide tools to derive a recommended amount of coverage based on the client's situation.

Cash-flow driven software enables one to vary the expenses and income streams throughout life expectancy that may provide a more accurate estimate of risk exposure especially for longer time horizons. For example, these tools can deal with Social Security benefits received by a widow (pre/post "blackout" period) and children under 18, along with varying assumptions by expense and income line items. Goal-based software typically takes a percentage of total income generated by the potential insured and calculates the present value of future earnings over his/her lifetime.

Some cash-flow driven and goal-based programs reflect insurance amounts for various life stages that are often useful to clients. Some clients, for instance, want to provide coverage just until the children are out of the house, others wish to ensure adequate protection throughout the surviving spouse's life expectancy. Since it is very common for younger clients to need large (if not huge) sums of money (and insurance) to transfer all of the survivor's risk, reflecting alternative amounts at respective life stages can be particularly helpful. This approach gives the client options in terms of how much risk she and her husband choose to retain or transfer. It also prepares an advance game plan for what is often unthinkable for many.

If one does not have access to a survivor needs tool, a useful calculator can be found on the Life and Health Insurance Foundation website (www.lifehappens.org). While it does not project alternate time intervals of insurance need, it does incorporate the three basic factors (final expenses, capital and survivor income needs) in its analysis. A "workaround" to reflect alternative amounts of need at different stages of life can be achieved by running iterations and changing the "number of years to provide income" field. The screen shot below illustrates partial results for a sample case.

Showing the survivor needs analysis, and presenting insurance design options with their respective costs/benefits, will set the stage for the client (and her spouse) to take action. The result of this process is usually not if she/they will do business with the consultant, rather, what kind of business will be done.

Life and Health Insurance Foundation for Education

Insurance needs calculator results

Lump Sum Needs at Death:

Final Expenses:	$ 15,000.00
Outstanding Debts:	+ $ 90,000.00
Mortgage:	+ $ 9,000.00
College Funding:	+ $ 118,648.59
Total lump sum needs:	= $ 232,648.59

Income needs:

Annual income to be provided:	$ 100.00
Number of years to provide income:	2
Estimated inflation rate:	3 %
After-tax net investment yield:	6 %

Calculation & Results:

Present Value of income needs*:	$ 197.17

> "We have been living altogether too much in an age of property economics, and it is high time that we adequately recognize the economic importance of human life values and extend to them, through life insurance, the same scientific treatment that we have for so many years applied to the organization, management and liquidation of property values."
>
> Solomon Heubner, PhD, Founder of The American College, 1927

Plan Considerations

As with other personal risks, there are common life styles and stages to keep in mind when planning for survivor needs. Since American women represent a broad set of group of consumers, their needs and motives for buying life insurance change, most often reflecting their stage in life and common life events.

Her Life Stages, Styles and Survivor Needs

Do single women need life insurance? Fifty one percent of females aged 15 and older—about 60 million women—were living without a spouse in 2005, according to the U.S. Census Bureau. This market segment—made up of women who are widowed, divorced, separated, never married, or living with a partner—is becoming a predominant force in our society. In 2005, for the first time ever, married couple families were a minority of all American households.[275]

---

275. Best Week, Issue 9, February 26, 2007, A.M. Best Company, Inc.

life insurance
insurability
tax-favored cash
 accumulation

Single Women, Starting Out. To the young single woman who is just starting her career or to the never-married older woman, a conversation about life insurance may seem pointless. However, there are several key factors to take into account:

- *Final Expenses*—These occur on or around the time of death and are inevitable. The costs of a funeral and burial expenses, estate administration expenses, outstanding debts, and the uncovered expenses of a final illness could become a financial burden to her survivors.

- *Debt Liquidation*—Some personal debts become due and payable upon the death of the borrower. These may include loans for automobiles, education, a business, credit cards and other retail debt. Generally, liabilities will be paid from her estate which may draw money away from funding her final wishes and the needs of her survivors and dependents.

- *Insurability*—To qualify for life insurance, a person must be in good health. Moreover, life insurance premiums increase with age, even with good health and other favorable underwriting factors (occupation, avocations, family history, and so on). As such, it can make sense for a woman to buy at least some life insurance, especially when she is young and healthy.

- *Tax-Favored Cash Accumulation*—Under current tax law, cash value life insurance policies have several tax advantages for accumulating money. The internal buildup of cash value is tax deferred and can be made available for the future (even prior to the death of the insured). Money taken from the policy in the form of loans or withdrawals may not be taxable and can provide tax-free income if the policy stays in force until the death of the insured. If the policy pays dividends, they can be withdrawn tax-free until the cost basis (the premiums paid) is recovered from the policy. It is important to note, however, that possible tax advantages of any financial product should not be the primary motivator for its placement.

The financial consultant may also want to determine what a young, single woman's needs might be in the future. A few areas to explore include:

- *Future Family*–Does she want to have a family? Will she work or stay at home with the children? If she works, how might her absence affect her family's financial situation? If she stays at home, who would do the work she does and how would her family pay for it if she were to die?

- *Parents or Other Older Relatives*—Are her parents still living? What is the plan if an elderly parent or older relative needs long-term care? Would they be able to afford it? Do they have long-term care insurance or other forms of financial support? The best option would be for them to buy long-term care insurance, but can they afford the premiums? If she were to subsidize the premiums, would it make sense to insure her share of the policy costs? Are there other relatives who depend on her for financial support, such as aunts, uncles, or siblings? Would life insurance be needed to continue that support if she died before them?

If, in discussions with her, the consultant uncovers a likely concern or responsibility that she can anticipate, what would the consequences be of needing life insurance and being rated or, worse, not being able to qualify because of a health condition that develops in the future?

Mothers. Mothers, of course, can be either married or single, stay-at-home or career-minded. These women should consider the following needs regarding the financial security of their family as a result of their death:

- ***Final Expenses***—The needs for final expenses are more pronounced for a woman in the mother and family stage than they are for the young, single, career woman. This need is heightened because the cost for her final expenses (without life insurance) will mean potentially fewer financial resources available to meet the needs of her surviving family.

- ***Income to Survivors, Especially in Readjustment and Dependency Periods***—The readjustment period is the interval of time immediately following the insured's death, during which, income is provided at or near the level the family enjoyed during the insured's lifetime. The purpose of the readjustment period is to permit the family to rebound and emotionally adjust to the loss of a loved one without feeling the economic pressures of daily life.

    The dependency period that follows extends from the date of the insured's death (or the end of the readjustment period, if needed) until the youngest child is self-sufficient, which today is assumed to occur at age 23 or when otherwise financially independent, unless a child is mentally or physically disabled. In the dependency period, the family's income needs may drop to a more realistic and sustainable level, or increase to provide for the additional expenses incurred to pay for the replacement of the services that were performed by the deceased spouse. A surviving spouse may need to be partially or fully subsidized during this dependency period as well, rather than being forced to reenter the workforce. Minor children from previous marriages or children with physical or mental disabilities may also need consideration and additional financial support. Life insurance proceeds can supplement other income sources that her survivors may receive.

Caregiving expenses should also be considered for both children and possibly, the deceased spouse's parents. Affording care is always a top concern. Average child care fees in a licensed child care center range from $3,803 to $13,480 a year for one child, and the costs vary widely based on regions of the country.[276]

- ***Mortgage/Debt Liquidation***. The average household may have at least one car loan or lease, credit card debt, a home equity loan, and a mortgage. With married women and mothers, the remaining debt typically will pass on to the surviving family by reducing the estate or requiring a surviving husband to continue making payments. The death of a wife and/or mother will undoubtedly affect the amount of income available to make debt payments, either because her income has ceased, the survivors experience higher expenses (in the form of any paid help to replace a woman's caregiving and domestic duties), or—worst of all—a combination of the two. For married women and mothers (whether married or single), debts are more likely to be passed on to their surviving family than for young, single, career women. Thus, life insurance earmarked for liquidating debts would reduce the financial stress on her family.

- ***Emergency Reserves***. The family should have an adequate source of emergency funds equal to about three to six months of typical expenses in liquid holdings to meet any need for immediate cash prior to or following the death of an income producer. If a family does not have sufficient cash reserves, it would be prudent to set them up at the death of a parent, because the odds of needing emergency funds are greater when a dual-income household becomes a single-income household.

- ***Education Funding***. Financial professionals need to ascertain their female clients' views on their children's education in general, not solely for college or technical school. Ask where they plan to send their children to preschool, grammar school, and high school. This may mean they plan to move to another school district at some point, or they may have strong feelings about private schools. What would they do if they lost an income earner? Would they still want to achieve these objectives? A surviving spouse may also need further education to increase future income potential to help support the family. The spouse may need a modest refresher course or training to return to a prior occupation. On the other hand, the spouse's need may be extensive, such as preparing to upgrade to a higher-paying career. These important educational objectives can be easily overlooked. Having both spouses involved in the discovery, fact-finding and

---

276. National Association of Child Care Resource and Referral Agencies, 2006

strategy discussions is critical to ensuring these types of needs are fully addressed.

Many of these same survivor needs apply, even if women are in a dual income family and/or without children.

Stay-at-Home Mothers. Nearly two out of every five married women with school-aged children do not work outside the home. The women who make this choice are often well educated and success oriented. As previously mentioned, their economic contributions to the family are often underappreciated, but could potentially be valued in the hundreds of thousands of dollars. It is important to discuss and analyze how the surviving family would adjust to the loss of the mother who chooses to stay at home with the children.

Retired Women. Once a woman has created, accumulated, or inherited a fair-sized estate, the emphasis moves to estate conservation. There is no clear point at which the transition from the accumulation phase to the conservation phase begins. Generally, estate conservation has three major capital objectives:

1. to minimize taxes and other transfer costs in order to maximize the estate that heirs will inherit

2. to provide adequate liquidity to avoid the forced sale of estate assets

3. to pass on to heirs income-producing property to replace, to the greatest extent possible, the breadwinner's earned income

The role of life insurance in this phase of estate planning shifts from income generation and creating capital to providing the funds to pay estate clearance costs and other practical considerations. Women who have accumulated sizable estates often need substantially more life insurance to preserve those assets than they had purchased during the creation phase. The beneficiary of a life insurance policy can be a trust for the benefit of dependents or other loved ones. One significant advantage of life insurance proceeds is that they generally are free of probate and are therefore not a matter of public record or subject to probate expenses. The donor of the gift can increase the value of the gift by using life insurance when transferring property to younger generations. Arrangements can be created to maximize gifts and transfer assets, often with tax advantages (e.g., irrevocable life insurance trusts, gifting premium amounts to beneficiaries with Crummey powers).

Women Business Owners. If she is a business owner, there are several other life insurance needs to consider. The first is that her death may mean the end of the business, unless planning steps are taken. Most businesses cannot run without the money, labor or leadership of the owner. The owner's death will result in a loss of creditworthiness, goodwill, customer service and income. Employees may leave in the face of uncertainty. Bills may go unpaid. Suppliers, creditors and lenders may freeze shipments and credit lines. Estate administration and taxes may deplete any remaining savings. Here are some questions that may be useful when working with female business owners:

The Art of Discovery
Her Business
• Tell me about your business…(pause for response)
• What do you do today?
• Where do you see yourself and your business in five years?
• How many people do you employ?
• How long have you been in business?
• What legal form of business do you have? (e.g., S or C Corp, LLC, sole proprietorship, partnership)
• What concerns you most about your business?
• How many employees do you have?
• How are you dealing with health insurance premiums?
• What are you doing to use tax deductions associated with employee benefits?
• How have you planned to pass the value of your business assets to your heirs?
• If your situation doesn't change, what do you think could happen?

To continue the business, the owner should consider instituting a buy-sell agreement and a key person policy for any employee critical to the business continuation. Some estate planning should be done to forecast potential estate expenses, along with methods to manage and minimize these expenses. Life insurance on the owner can create liquidity by providing cash to the estate, pay estate debts and expenses, equalize bequests to family members and provide income to survivors. Life insurance provides funding for buy-sell agreements designed to transfer ownership at the owner's death. Key person coverage funded with life insurance, provides cash to keep the business going during the difficult financial times following the death of a key employee.

Example Nancy owns a retail clothing store with the help of her grown son and daughter. She dies with a simple will that leaves her interest in the company to her children. Her estate is valued at $3 million, and after all exemptions, credits and deductions, her estate expenses and taxes total $350,000. Because neither the business nor Nancy has enough liquid assets to cover this, the estate expenses and tax liability will seriously impair her children's ability to keep the family business. Assets may have to be sold to pay the estate expenses.

Nancy could have purchased life insurance, using a trust or having one of the children own the policy, to keep the proceeds out of her estate. The life insurance proceeds would have provided the estate with the cash necessary for her children to continue the business and avoid business liquidation.

Last, the client may want to contemplate offering voluntary life insurance benefits to her employees. Just 39 percent of small businesses with less than 100 employees offer life insurance benefits.[277] Some plans enable costs to be shared between the employer and employees. Voluntary plans can be an attractive option for employers who want to provide employees with benefits, while keeping their costs down. When considering an employee benefits program, it is essential that the financial consultant work together with the client's accountant and attorney relative to plan structure and tax considerations.

Planning for Women Who Are Survivors

The largest percentage of women in this segment are widows. Financial consultants need to ensure that relationships with married couples are built with both the husband and wife, because it is likely that one of the two may wind up suddenly single. Many widows "fire" a producer because that individual dealt primarily with her husband. After her husband's death, the wife often feels abandoned and neglected.[278] Worse still, the surviving widow may not have adequate resources to sustain a reasonable standard of living as many find themselves in poverty, as previously discussed.

In addition to funding her retirement and well-being, the woman who becomes single again may also need life insurance for some or all of the following financial objectives.

- *Tax-Free Income to Help Fund Retirement.* One opportunity to address is the needs of a widow who is presented with a life insurance death claim check. A widow who is inexperienced in financial matters may allow the fund to remain in a low-yield savings account or CD, rather than in potentially more lucrative investment

---

277. LIMRA, "U.S. Small Business Market," 2000.
278. LIMRA, Women and Life Insurance, 2005.

vehicles. Reviewing her financial needs, assets, and income after the death of her spouse can be of great value. Since many widows experience grief, confusion and feel overwhelmed during this period, it is paramount that one is sensitive to her psychological and emotional state, and proceed with caution. Widows are often the most vulnerable prospects, and sadly, the most exploited by predatory sales people. A bereaved woman should focus on healing before making important financial decisions. If she has received lump-sum life insurance proceeds, she should consider placing money not required for immediate and foreseeable living expenses in a safe, relatively accessible place such as a money market account. She should not invest, spend, lend, or give away any of this money until she is prepared to execute a sound, long-term financial plan. Some financial professionals suggest waiting a year before any significant financial decisions are made.

- **Long-Term Care Expenses.** Most long-term care insurance is purchased as a stand-alone policy. However, some companies that market life insurance offer riders that provide long-term care benefits to cover some or all of the cost for home health care and nursing home care. Riders are not generally considered separate contracts, but additional terms or benefits incorporated into the policy, which remains a single, unified contract. There are essentially two kinds of long-term care riders that are added to cash value life insurance—acceleration and extension riders:

    1. ***The acceleration rider*** lets the insured take an advance on the death benefit, usually 1 or 2 percent of the face amount each month if long-term care becomes necessary. The rider makes it possible to accelerate payment of the death benefit in this situation.

    2. ***The extension rider,*** in certain situations, allows the insured to keep drawing money for long-term care expenses, even after the death benefit amount in the life insurance policy is exhausted.

- **Estate Planning.** Life insurance can play a critical role in estate planning. In Chapter 7, some opportunities to use life insurance for legacy purposes are developed further. Life insurance can fund charitable bequests, an education for grandchildren—even great grandchildren—and provide for payment of estate taxes.

acceleration rider

extension rider

Life Insurance Considerations

variable universal life

Beyond establishing the need for insurance through a well-conceived analysis, two basic questions come into play when designing life insurance proposals: (1) how long will insurance be needed, and (2) how much can the client afford? The benefit amount is determined by conducting analyses of income and capital needs, along with final expenses. At times, it may be necessary for the client to transfer some versus all of the risk.

For younger women and/or those with limited means, a term policy, preferably level for at least a 10-year period and convertible without evidence of insurability, may be considered. If insurance is likely to be required for decades, then it may be advisable to pair a term contract with a more permanent form of insurance (e.g., universal or whole life).

Variable universal life may be desirable for those clients with:

- long-term insurance needs

- capital accumulation goals more than 10 years in the future

- moderately aggressive to aggressive risk tolerances

- the ability to maximize premium contributions early in the contract

In light of usually high loads and expenses on most variable life products, unless these four conditions are all met, contracts may not perform as well as other forms of insurance.

One should run a range of illustrations, including various assumptions and analyzed cost structures, to develop sound proposals and rationale to present to clients. Regardless of product type, life insurance (or any type of insurance for that matter) should always be placed with a well rated, quality insurer.

Survivor Needs Summary

It is important for financial consultants to take the time to ensure that families depending on both a woman's income and caregiving are financially protected. When working with women, remember that they are often more receptive to both planning and life insurance than men. Women are more likely than men to consider life insurance as the best way to protect their family financially in the case of premature death, and more likely to say that someone in their household needs more life insurance.[279] Women are more prone to understand the risk and need for life insurance protection—and to do something about it.

---

279. Ibid

CHAPTER SUMMARY

Throughout this and the preceding chapter, we have reviewed the many facets of pure risk and the financial consequences that often accompany them. In most instances, women have greater risk exposure and less preparation than their male counterparts. This is especially the case with medical, disability, long term care and survivor risk exposures. In addition, women tend to have generally low rates of financial literacy about the products and strategies that can help them reduce or completely mitigate their risks. Through a thoughtful and deliberate planning process, financial professionals can help the female client create significantly more security for herself and her family, as well as reinforce the trust relationship.

Chapter 6 examines the other basic form of risk—speculative risk—along with proven techniques to minimize its impact on the client's financial goals. In addition, we will explore taxes and how they might affect her overall financial situation, both today and in the future. Our discussion covers:

- issues for women relative to taxes and investment planning

- understanding the basics of income taxation

- possible tax reduction strategies

- the major forms of investment risk and how they are managed

> "I learned to embrace risk, as long as it was well thought out and, in worst-case scenario, I'd still land on my feet."
>
> Eli Broad

CHAPTER 5 TOOLS AND RESOURCES

- Courses from The American College
    - FA 211 – Essentials of Disability Income Insurance
    - FA 255 – Essentials of Long-Term Care Insurance
    - FA 257 – Essentials of Life Insurance Products
    - HS 311 – Fundamentals of Insurance Planning
    - HS 323 – Individual Life Insurance
    - HS 324 – Life Insurance Law
    - HS 331 – Planning for Business Owners and Professionals
    - HS 351 – Health and Long-Term Care Financing for Seniors
    - GS 812 – Business Valuation
    - GS 836 – Business Succession Planning I
    - GS 838 – Business Succession Planning II
- Recommended reading

- *The Hard Questions for Adult Children to Ask Their Aging Parents*, Susan Piver, Penguin Group, 2004

- *How to Care for Aging Parents*, Virginia Morris, Thomas Allen & Son, 2004

• Websites
    - Medicare.gov (LTC probability and cost calculator)
    - Dinkytown.net (LTC needs calculator)
    - Lifehappens.org – Life and Health Insurance Foundation website (Disability and survivor needs calculators)

6

Managing Her Legislative and Speculative Risks—Taxes and Investments

Learning Objectives
An understanding of the material in this chapter should enable the student to
6-1. Define the terms: speculative and legislative risk.
6-2. Understand the basic mechanics and elements of income taxation.
6-3. Describe the concept of the "marriage penalty."
6-4. Explain basic tax reduction techniques.
6-5. Describe common attitudes and issues women share with regard to investing, including when caution is an advantage.
6-6. Define the major forms of speculative risk.
6-7. Explain techniques used to reduce forms of speculative risk.

INTRODUCTION

speculative risk

Women tend to be generally more risk averse than their male counterparts. As we have seen, their caution is often with good reason—as a group, they live longer, earn less, have lower financial literacy and face more challenges associated with health and caregiving than men do. These combined factors frequently put women at greater financial jeopardy throughout their lives, particularly as they age. Paradoxically, women also earn more and control more of the nation's wealth than ever before. Thus, it is important that financial consultants have at least a working familiarity of tax and investment management.

One of the most vital roles the financial professional plays is that of risk manager, helping client protect their assets and income, both now and into the future. In Chapter 4, we reviewed how financial risks can be broadly classified into two categories:

1. ***Pure risk***—involving only the possibility of financial loss

2. ***Speculative risk***— involving not only the possibility of financial loss, but also the possibility of financial gain

Insurance addresses exposure to pure risks such as financial losses associated with property, liability and personal risks. Developing risk management strategies to retain or transfer pure risks is critical to safeguarding her financial security, which is the foundation of the Financial Planning Pyramid. Our examination now turns to risks associated with the midsection of the pyramid, specifically those related to investment and taxes.

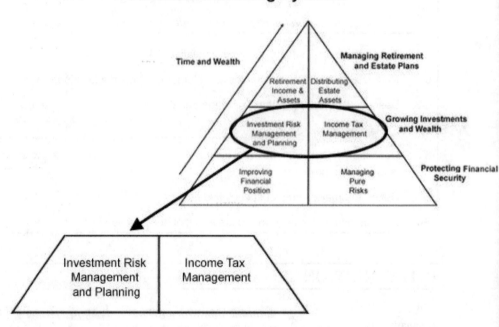

In this chapter, we identify forms of legislative risk related to changes and/or increases in tax laws, as well as the major forms of speculative risk relative to investments. We also look at specific tax and investment concerns for women, and general principles of how to manage risks associated with both.

> "Why does a slight tax increase cost you two hundred dollars and a substantial tax cut save you thirty cents?"
>
> Peg Bracken

INCOME TAXES AND LEGISLATIVE RISK

income taxes

legislative risk

For many Americans, regardless of gender, taxes represent a significant portion of the family budget. According to Eileen J. O'Connor, JD, CPA and board member of the Independent Women's Forum, "Many people are surprised to learn that one of their single largest expenses is taxes, and that taxes cost more than food, clothing, transportation, and shelter combined." She estimates that "taxes, including federal, state, local and payroll taxes, represent a whopping 37 percent of the average family's budget."[280]

Frequent tax legislation over past decades stands witness to the fact that government can drastically change the tax code. Regardless of personal viewpoints about taxes, tax liability or political persuasion; it is important for financial consultants to understand the basic mechanics and concepts associated with income taxes when advising clients, whether male or female. Incorporating this knowledge, enables financial professionals to serve more clients better.

While sophisticated tax planning is not the purpose of this discussion, we will outline some fundamental elements of income taxation. Since the recommendations that financial consultants make often affect both the client's current and future liabilities, it is important to be aware of key tax considerations and their associated implications. Recognizing tax reduction opportunities that the client may legitimately be entitled to can yield incremental dollars to put toward her asset accumulation and/or protection needs. Conversely, if there could be adverse tax consequences that may arise out of a financial professional's recommendations, it is essential that those are identified as well.

Note: Unless financial consultants have the necessary education, training and credentials, it is both illegal and unethical to hold oneself out as a tax or legal advisor. This does not mean, however, that one dismisses the responsibility of becoming familiar with the client's tax issues, challenges and opportunities. Consultants are advised to check with their compliance department or registered principal on what might be discussed with clients and what is out of scope.

> "In this world, nothing is certain but death and taxes."
>
> Benjamin Franklin

Income Tax Basics

This section deals with the basic principles of how income is taxed at the federal and (most) state levels. Even though planning techniques may be used

---

280. Independent Women's Forum, "Women & Taxes," October 1, 2000, www.iwf.org (written by IWF National Advisory Board member Eileen J. O'Connor, J.D., C.P.A.).

to minimize and/or avoid paying taxes, it is unlikely that tax relief is the only, or most important, goal of the client's financial plan. A financial strategy that focuses only on tax minimization or avoidance is a poor plan if it is inconsistent with the client's situation, goals and concerns. The best tax strategies are those that accurately reflect the full measure of the client's overall financial objectives.

Adjusted Gross Income and Exclusions

A thorough understanding of "gross income" is essential. Gross income includes every item of value, whether consisting of money or other property, that is either made available to, or comes into possession of, the taxpayer. In other words, anything of value is considered to be gross income for income tax purposes unless the Internal Revenue Code contains a specific provision that excludes a particular item from the client's gross income. An example of an item that may be excluded is income earned for military service in a war zone.

Adjusted gross income is an intermediate calculation that is made in the process of determining the client's or the taxpayer's income tax liability for a given year. An *exclusion* is an item of value received by the taxpayer that should be excluded from her gross income. For instance, interest earnings on most municipal bonds are excluded from adjusted gross income for federal tax purposes (however, certain municipal bond yields may be subject to the Alternative Minimum Tax, discussed below).

Deductions and Taxable Income

Taxable income, on the other hand, is the amount of income that will actually be subject to taxation in a given year. It is calculated by deducting certain items from the taxpayer's or client's adjusted gross income.

A *deduction* is an expense item that reduces the amount of income subject to taxation. When computing the client's tax liability, there are two basic types of deductions. The first consists of deductions that are subtracted from gross income to determine adjusted gross income. The second type consists of deductions that are subtracted from adjusted gross income to determine *taxable income*. The first type is known as *above-the-line* deductions, while the second is known as *below-the-line* deductions.

The standard deduction is a fixed amount that the individual may claim in lieu of claiming itemized deductions on Schedule A of the 1040. The amount of the standard deductions depends on the client's filing status—single taxpayer, unmarried head of household, married filing jointly, or married filing separately. If she is entitled to claim itemized deductions, that when added together are more than her standard deduction, then she should itemize. Either claim is considered a below-the-line deduction; that is, they are considered deductions taken in calculating taxable income.

The three basic categories of allowable deductions are business expenses, expenses for the production of income, and personal expenses. Whenever the client is determining whether a given item is deductible, there are certain factors to consider. The first is whether the Internal Revenue Code allows a deduction for the item. The second is under which basic category it falls. The third is whether the deduction is above-the-line or below-the-line. Finally, the fourth factor is whether there is a restriction on its deductibility, such as a floor, a ceiling, or a limitation.

paper deductions

Not all tax deductions are out-of-pocket expenses. Some deductions are allowable, even though they represent no corresponding cash outlay. These are referred to as *paper deductions,* because they represent, or are related to, some entry on the books of the taxpayer's business or investment activity, but they are not cash flow items. Depreciation of an asset is an example of a paper deduction.

Personal Exemption

personal exemption

Each individual taxpayer is allowed to claim a *personal exemption*. A married couple filing jointly may claim an exemption for each spouse. Individuals are also permitted to claim dependency exemptions for each dependent supported. The amount of these exemptions is subtracted from adjusted gross income. Exemptions are in addition to deductions, either standard or itemized.

Calculating Taxes Due

Once the taxpayer's gross income has been determined, then all above-the-line reductions allowable (e.g., contributions to self-employed retirement plans and IRAs, certain qualified educator, business, health savings, moving expenses, education expenses, alimony) are subtracted from it to determine adjusted gross income. Next, all deductions and exemptions allowable are subtracted from gross income. The net result is taxable income—the figure to which income tax rates are applied to determine the amount of tax payable for the year.

marginal tax rate

Currently, there are six income tax rates: 10, 15, 25, 28, 33, and 35 percent. The tax rate applicable to each income bracket is called the *marginal tax rate*. Once the tax rates have been applied to an individual's taxable income, the resulting figure is the individual's tentative tax. This tentative tax can be reduced if the individual is eligible to claim any income tax credits.

Tax Credits

tax credits

It is important to understand the difference between a tax credit and a tax deduction. A *tax credit* is a dollar-for-dollar reduction of the actual tax payable. A tax deduction, on the other hand, is an item of expense that only reduces the amount of the client or the taxpayer income that is subject to taxation. Therefore, although deductions are beneficial, an available tax credit is of more value to the client or the taxpayer than a deduction of equal amount.

Alternative Minimum Tax (AMT)

Alternative Minimum Tax (AMT)

The *Alternative Minimum Tax* (AMT) is a separate and parallel AMT system of income taxation to the regular system. It applies to any taxpayer whose tax liability under the parallel system is greater than the liability for that year, under the regular income tax system. The purpose of the AMT is to make certain that taxpayers who enjoy certain tax benefits are not permitted to reduce their tax liability below a minimum amount by claiming certain tax deductions.

Capital Gains and Losses

capital gains and losses

For tax purposes, *capital gains* are realized when an equity asset is sold for a profit, with the inverse being true for *capital losses*. Under current tax legislation, the highest marginal tax rate is 35 percent, while it is generally just 15 percent for long-term capital gains. Taxpayers can normally offset realized gains with realized losses, assuming that holding period requirements have been satisfied. In addition, a taxpayer can use $3,000 of capital losses in excess of capital gains against income. Unused capital losses can be carried forward to future tax years.

Filing Income Taxes—Individuals and Businesses

fiscal year

Individuals file tax returns on an annual basis. For the vast majority of individuals, income tax is calculated based on a calendar-year period. However, many business entities and some individuals report their tax liability based on a 12 month period other than the calendar year. Such a period is referred to as a *fiscal year*.

Taxable income must be computed not only on the basis of a fixed accounting period—that is, a taxable year—but also in accordance with a method of tax accounting that clearly reflects income. Most tax advisors and their clients use the cash-basis method, which means that they report income and pay taxes on the income only if it is received during the taxable year. The other popular method of accounting is the accrual method, which is typically used by C corporations. Under this method, income is accounted for when the right to receive it comes into being; that is, when all the events that determine the right have occurred. It is not the actual receipt, but the right to receive that governs.

> "People who complain about taxes can be divided into two classes: men and women."
>
> Author Unknown

MANAGING HER TAXES

The Internal Revenue Code is largely neutral with regard to gender, in that the Code applies the same rules equally to both males and females. But the impact of even gender neutral rules can have varying effects on men and women, depending on their earnings, occupation, and marital status.

Her Tax Facts

marriage penalty

Two of the most striking tax issues that affect women are the so-called *marriage penalty* and taxes for single heads of household. Consider the excerpt below on the marriage penalty from a fascinating white paper written for the National Center for Policy Analysis by Edward J. McCaffrey, Professor of Law at the University of Southern California:

> Taxes are central to all aspects of women's economic lives. Personal income taxes, payroll taxes, child care tax credits, earned income tax credits, and state and local taxes all have particular importance to women and all have aspects that adversely effect the majority of women. Largely for historical reasons, the American tax system is disconnected with the way women participate in the economy. The major elements of the tax system were put in place in the 1930s, 1940s and 1950s, when most women, certainly most mothers, were not in the workforce.
>
> - Today 70 percent of all married women work for wages.
> - Sixty percent of mothers with children under the age of 6 work for wages.
> - The tax laws are biased toward single-earner households in which only one spouse works and biased against two-earner households.
>
> The "marriage penalty" in the tax code is not really a tax on marriage. It is tax on two earner households. Combine a 28 percent federal income tax with an 8.5 percent state and local income tax, then add a 7.65 percent Social Security (FICA) payroll tax, and the marginal tax rate of the second earner in the average household is more than 44 percent. In addition, when both spouses work they must usually begin to purchase many services–child care, cooking, cleaning and so on. After these expenses, many women find that their actual net take-home pay is just a third of their wages. Some married working women actually lose money by entering the labor market.
>
> These marriage penalties hit at the top and the bottom of the income ladder. It hits those at the top particularly hard because

high-income earners are in the top tax brackets. Lower-income women also suffer a stiff marriage penalty because of the burden of accelerated phase-outs of the Earned Income Tax Credit (EITC), a federal program that gives low-wage workers extra cash through tax credits. Adding it all up, the tax system sends a curious message to American women:

- If you are middle- to upper-income and married, the incentive is not to work.
- If you are low-income and working, the incentive is not to marry.

The Social Security or federal payroll tax is particularly bad for working wives. This is because each spouse is already entitled to benefits based on the other spouse's earnings. For example, a wife who never works and never pays taxes is entitled to a retirement benefit equal to 50 percent of her husband's benefits. After he dies, she is entitled to 100 percent of his benefits. When women work and pay taxes, however, they will collect benefits based on their own contributions, or on their husband's contributions, but not both. As a result, many women discover they get little or nothing in return for years of paying taxes into the system because they claim a spousal share. In the case of two average income earners, for example, the wife's decision to work will double the couple's lifetime payroll taxes. But there will be very little increase in lifetime benefits.[281]

While Mr. McCaffery seems to assume that a woman's is the second earned income in the house, his hypothesis about possible disincentives relative to work or marriage, depending on her circumstances, is intriguing. His underlying point about the penalty is that a sometimes inequitable result can come about when a married couple files taxes jointly and ends up with a higher tax liability than if the two had filed as unmarried individuals. In addition, he reaches a compelling conclusion about a potentially uneven playing field when it comes to payment of Social Security benefits to couples where both spouses worked (and earned relatively comparable wages), compared to those where just one spouse worked outside the home for wages.

On the other end of the earnings spectrum, are single women who are heads of household. Many women in this category have both low earnings and dependents. Many also pay little or no federal income taxes. This is due in part to falling into low tax bracket(s), as well as eligibility for tax credits like the Earned Income Tax Credit (EITC) and Child/Dependent Care Credits.

Whether single or married, high or low income, understanding how taxes may affect her is an important aspect of "knowing your customer."

---

281. Edward J. McCaffery, "Women and Taxes," Executive Summary, 2/28/2002, National Center for Policy Analysis, www.ncpa.org.

Recommendations must be made with careful consideration of all possible tax benefits or consequences. For example, one would not advise a client who currently pays little or no federal income taxes, to invest in tax-exempt municipal debt instruments.

Reviewing Her Tax Situation

Discovering the unique aspects of the client's current and future tax liabilities requires interpersonal, analytical and technical skills. To begin with, a patient examination of her tax return(s) will yield insight and benefits for both client and consultant alike. There are often opportunities to identify incremental sources of cash or capital that could be made available to fund goals and/or finance needed protection. The table below provides general and select questions to ask about her tax situation and a line item review of her form 1040.

Note: For our purposes, these questions exclude reviewing support schedules and forms (e.g., Schedules A, B, C and C-EZ, D, E; Forms W2, 1099, 5498). These documents also provide revealing and important information. It is recommended that consultants learn these as well. The U.S. Internal Revenue Service website at www.irs.gov provides useful, detailed information by line item for all tax schedules and forms.

As the client responds to thoughtful questions about her situation, it is essential that the financial professional understand what the possible tax implications are. For example, key considerations might include:

- What is her current tax liability and what tax bracket does she and her joint filer, if applicable, fall into?

- Does she get a refund or owe federal taxes? If the former, are these dollars she can allocate to her financial goals and/or protection needs? If the latter, how will she come up with the shortfall?

- Where might there be opportunities to lower taxes, both current and anticipated?

- Is it reasonable to assume her tax liabilities will stay the same, increase or decrease in the foreseeable future?

- If she is a business owner, what strategies is she using to manage her taxes (e.g., deducting insurance premiums paid for business, health and retirement plans)? Are they aligned with her personal financial objectives?

The Art of Discovery		
Her Income Taxes		
<ul><li>How do you feel about the taxes you pay?</li><li>What concerns you most about your tax situation?</li><li>What have you done to reduce your taxes?</li><li>Do you usually owe income taxes or get a refund each year?</li><li>Do you think you're doing all you can to reduce your tax bite?</li><li>If I could show you a few ways to improve your tax situation, would that be worth an hour of your time?</li></ul>		
1040 Line(s)	**Category**	**Question**
7	W2 Salaries, Tips, Etc.	How has your earned income changed over the last five years? What do you see in the next five years?
8–9	Interests and Dividends	How are you using these taxable interest and dividends (e.g., needed for income, reinvested for growth, another purpose?) *(Related Schedule: B)*
11 and 31a	Alimony	Tell me about the terms of your divorce agreement (e.g., What is the amount and how long will you receive in alimony?)
12	Self-Employed Business Income (Loss)	How long have you been in business? Where do you see yourself and your business in five years? *(Related Schedule: C or C-EZ)*
13	Capital Gains/Losses	What are your thoughts about the capital gains taxes you're paying? Do you have unused capital losses? *(Related Schedule: D)*
15 – 16	IRAs and Pensions Received	How long have you been receiving distributions from your retirement plans?
17	Rental Real Estate	How long have you been a landlord? What are the plans for your property? *(Related Schedule: E)*
20	Social Security Benefits	What strategies are you using to reduce the impact of taxes on your Social Security benefit/s?
27–29	Self Employment Tax, Qualified Plans, Health Insurance	How have you thought about funding your retirement and health care through your business? *(Related Schedules: C, C-EZ, SE)*
32	IRA Deduction	What are your plans for the IRA?

40	Itemized Deductions	How have your itemized deductions changed in the last five years? *(Related Schedule: A)*
45	Alternative Minimum Tax	How do you feel about the AMT? *(Related Form: 6251)*
47–55, 64, 66, 68, 69, and 70	Credits: Foreign Tax, Dependent Care, Education, Child Tax, Earned Income, First-Time Homebuyer, Recovery Rebate	How long have you been able to claim (this_____) credit?
57–61	Self-Employment Taxes	*(Make sure she is seated before asking.)* How do you feel about the taxes you pay on your business?
72	Refund	How often do you receive a refund?
75	Amount Owed	How often do you end up owing?

Managing Her Taxes

Studying the client's situation, addressing tax issues, formulating recommendations that take these into account and coordinating with other professional advisors are all aspects of her well-thought-out financial plan. Where possible and sensible, combining tax considerations with other financial strategies can make both her current and future dollars work harder.

Basic Tax Reduction Techniques

tax reduction techniques

While complicated strategies to reduce or avoid taxes are out of the scope of this discussion, here are some basic techniques with which one should be familiar:

- income and deduction shifting, particularly deferral of income and acceleration of deductions for a given tax year; recognizing income when her tax bracket is low for the year; and accelerating deductions if her tax bracket is high

- avoiding income limitation thresholds on phased-out deductions

- participation in qualified retirement plans (e.g., SEPs, 401k, 403b, 457, deductible IRAs)

- participation in tax-exempt investments (e.g., municipal bonds)

- participation in investments that defer recognition of income (e.g., qualified retirement plans, annuities, inside build-up of life insurance cash value)

- transactions that result in a taxable loss or gain (e.g., selling assets with a capital loss to offset a capital gain)

- distinguishing ordinary income from qualified dividends and capital gains

> Did you ever notice that when you put the words "The" and "IRS" together, it spells "THEIRS"?
>
> Author unknown

Investment Earnings and Taxes

investment earnings and taxes

When it comes to investing and insurance products with an investment component, there are three basic strategies to contemplate when developing a tax management plan. These strategies deal with the timing of paying the taxes in question, as well as the possibilities to avoid (versus evade) them: (1) pay taxes today, (2) pay them later, and/or (3) (maybe) never pay taxes.

1. *Pay today*—If the client is now and will likely remain, in a low tax bracket, it may make sense for her to invest in securities that are fully taxable, especially those fixed income investments that generate taxable interest earnings (e.g., CDs and bonds). In addition, it may be prudent for higher income earners to take advantage of favorable tax rates on capital gains and qualified dividend income while they exist. Converting a traditional IRA into a Roth IRA, and paying the tax liability over one to two years is another strategy in this category.

2. *Pay later*—If she (and her joint filer) are currently in a high tax bracket, but will likely fall into a lower one later, investments that defer the realization of investment income and appreciation may have merit. Examples of these instruments are pre-tax contributions to retirement plans (e.g., SEPs, 401k, 403b, 457); deferred annuities, both fixed and variable; growth oriented equities and mutual funds; as well as the inside build-up of cash value that exceeds cost basis.

3. *(Maybe) Never pay*—(Maybe is the operative word, since tax legislation is fickle, as history shows.) As of this writing, current tax legislation allows for a limited set of financial vehicles and circumstances where investment earnings may never be fully taxed. Appropriately and judiciously used, these might include:

- tax credits for certain real estate investments (e.g., affordable housing)

- earnings on Roth IRAs and Roth 401ks

- education Coverdell accounts and 529 plans (when earnings are used for qualified educational expenses)

- interest on qualifying municipal debt obligations

- surrendering down cash value of a nonmodified endowment life insurance contract to owner's cost basis, then switching to loans (assuming policy is never allowed to lapse within the insured's lifetime)

For many clients, it is worth evaluating investment strategies that diversify their possible tax liabilities—some now, some later, and (quite possibly), some never. Investment analysis and decision making should always focus on the underlying economic facts and the client's best interest. In the past, investments made solely on the basis of their tax advantages at the time often created both tax problems and financial losses for their owners later on. Certainly, tax considerations can influence decisions and those effects must be analyzed. However, tax implications are just one element among many to consider when determining the fundamental worth of an investment.

The financial consultant's technical competencies in the more advanced concepts of taxation can provide significant value to clients, particularly among the more affluent. Since evolving tax legislation is a virtual certainty for years to come, one must establish and maintain a habit of continuous learning. In short, one can never know too much about the federal and state systems of taxation, and their planning implications for clients.

Building Relationships with Affiliated Professionals

affiliated professionals
attorneys
accountants

It is important to seek permission to contact her other professionals, especially when working with wealthy, sophisticated clients. Consultants should seek to build effective working relationships with the client's other financial advisors (e.g., attorneys, accountant, other agents and/or brokers). When making recommendations that have potentially large and lasting tax or legal implications it is essential to, at minimum, attempt communications on the consultant's rationale. Very rarely do CPAs and attorneys seek to coordinate aspects of the client's financial plan. By doing so, the financial consultant acts as her "gatekeeper," increasing both value-add and indispensability.

When one is able to display a firm grasp of tax and legal issues and incorporate them into recommendations made, other advisors will generally be supportive, or at least, not act as barriers to recommendations. While very few affiliated professionals will endorse the advice of others (after all, they have their own errors and omissions to worry about), the consultant can build a productive and rewarding relationship when mutually focused on the best interests of the shared female client and her family. Some of the very best client referrals come from attorneys and accountants. In addition, the consultant may want to create a marketing alliance with other professionals interested in targeting similar niche audiences.

WOMEN AND INVESTING

We now turn our examination to women, investments and speculative risk. "Speculative risk" is perhaps an unfortunate term because both investing and speculating involve speculative risk. However, there is a very clear difference between them. Investing is based on a reasoned consideration of expected return and the risk associated with that return. Speculating occurs when a person buys an asset in the hopes of receiving some form of return, without consideration or knowledge of the expected return or risk, or both. It is reasonably safe to say that, because women tend to be relatively conservative, they are more likely to be investors than speculators. Although women's needs for savings and investment strategies are similar to men's, women in general, tend to have relatively less investing experience and, therefore have a greater need for education and guidance.

Women and Investing—An Abundance of Caution

Pop-quiz:	The acronym F.E.A.R. stands for:
	1. False Evidence Appearing Real
	2. Finding Excuses And Reasons
	3. Forget Everything And Run
	4. All of the above
	Source: www.thefreedictionary.com/fear, March 2009

For women, there is a particular fear of losing everything. According to research by Allianz conducted in 2006, nearly 90 percent, the overwhelming majority of women, said they feared "losing it all."[282] This trepidation causes many women to be more cautious, sometimes too cautious, when it comes to investment risk. A study by Redbook magazine found that males are three times more likely to take a risk on investment decisions, versus females. Sixty two

---

282. "Allianz Women, Money & Power Study," 2006

percent of men in the survey said they were willing to take a risk on investment decisions versus only 19 percent of women.[283]

Acting out of fear when it comes to investing is almost always wrong. Yet, without question, the flames of investor fear continue to be fanned by some in the public eye, particularly in the wake of recent market meltdowns and institutional collapse. Emotionally driven investing is not unique to females, and is usually motivated by the vicious cycle of greed: the hope the markets will rise (buy high) and the fear they will fall (sell low.) Case in point: when a high-profile television personality exhorts the public to immediately liquidate stock positions if money is needed in 5 years, there is a huge sell-off in the market. Some liken this to being in a crowded theatre and yelling, "Fire!"

Cultural Imprinting?

cultural imprinting

Academics speculate that one underlying reason for female apprehension related to investing is rooted in gender stereotypes. As previously discussed, industry and academic studies reveal that boys are often more encouraged to earn and save earlier, as well as excel in math, than are girls.[284] Partly as a result of what some call *cultural imprinting*, many women approach investing with more than a little insecurity.

Women and Investment Literacy

investment literacy

When it comes to having a sufficient body of knowledge and to skillfully invest on one's own behalf, most women are lacking. Perhaps some never had the support to excel in math or learn even the basics of money management. Others may have been so involved with managing the home and family, that they had neither the time nor the inclination to learn more. Whatever the reason, women's financial literacy regarding investing concepts and products is frequently lower than men's. Here are several findings from recent Merrill Lynch studies that affirm these points:

- Forty one percent of women said they did not have enough expertise about money or investing to be involved in their savings/investing activities.[285]

---

283. Study by Redbook and Smart Money in 2004, published in "The Truth About Women and Money" (source: CFP Board Website, Women and Money–What's Biology Got to Do With It?).
284. Frozen in the Headlights: The Dynamics of Women and Money," FPA Journal, 2000, (citing findings on the 1997 Gender Investment Comparison Study, Dreyfus Corporation and The National Center for Women and Retirement Research).
285. "When It Comes to Investing, Gender A Strong Influence on Behavior," Merrill Lynch Investment Managers (MLIM), April 18, 2005.

- Forty seven percent of females in 2005 research said they did not feel they knew enough about investing, versus just 30 percent for men.[286]

- When comparing male/female familiarity with core investment concepts, women were less aware of dollar cost averaging than men (39 percent female versus 65 percent male) and less likely to correctly identify historical inflation rates (43 percent versus 67 percent).[287]

Perhaps most surprising of the investment knowledge gaps for women involves the essential concept of risk diversification. According to the Michigan Retirement Research Center, in 2005, less than half of women respondents (47 percent) said they knew about diversifying risks.[288]

In light of their generally low awareness of key economic, risk and investing concepts, perhaps it is not surprising that women lag in their understanding of investment products, as well. For example, research by Oppenheimer Funds in 2006, found that nearly two out of three women (62 percent) said they did not have a good understanding of how a mutual fund works.[289] One might reach the conclusion that a fundamental lack of investment know-how may contribute to lower ownership of some products. The data in the chart below seems to support this as a reasonable hypothesis. The chart reflects gender ownership disparities, based on a recent study by the Iowa State University Center for Survey Statistics and Methodology:[290]

Select Product Ownership—Female and Male		
Financial Product	Percent Women Owning	Percent Men Owning
Life insurance cash value	70.3%	63.6%
Annuities	33.9%	28.2%
Corporate bond/bond funds	25.3%	34.5%
Stock/stock mutual funds	75.9%	81.5%
Source: Gender Differences in Investment Behavior, Iowa State University, Milestone 3 Report, August 31, 2006		

Lower literacy rates, by either gender on virtually any topic, can contribute to one's fear or at least, apprehension, when confronted with them. As a byproduct of these and possibly other influences, women tend to have a lower tolerance for investment risks. According to the study, *Equity Ownership in*

---

286. Ibid.
287. Ibid.
288. Annamaria Lusardi, "Planning and Financial Literacy: How Do Women Fare?" Michigan Retirement Research Center, October 2006.
289. Morning Star Investment Research Center, "The Woman's Guide to Money Matters."
290. Iowa State University, "Gender Differences in Investment Behavior," Milestone 3 Report, August 31, 2006.

America 2005, women are less inclined to take high risks with their investments, as summarized in the following table:

Willingness to Take Investment Risks—Female and Male					
Decision Makers	Substantial Risk for Substantial Gain	Above Average Risk for Above Average Gain	Average Risk for Average Gain	Below Average Risk for Below Average Gain	Unwilling to Take Any Risk
Male	10%	35%	41%	8%	5%
Female	3%	23%	52%	10%	12%
Co-decision makers	5%	26%	52%	9%	7%
Source: Equity Ownership in America 2005, Securities Industry Association and the Investment Company Institute					

Where Caution and Skepticism May Work to Her Advantage

A little skepticism or fear can sometimes benefit investors when first contemplating an investment strategy—before the actual investing takes place. In a 2006 Harris Poll for Charles Schwab, 48 percent of women agreed with the statement "investing is scary for me." It is worth noting that this was twice the rate of men who shared the same sentiment;[291] not that a little "investophobia" is all that bad when it leads to looking before leaping and taking a long term view. In a recent survey by the FINRA Foundation, 79 percent of female respondents described themselves as wanting to know all the fine print when learning about investments.[292] In doing so, a female client may take her time to carefully evaluate the options. The Gender Comparison study by Iowa State University notes that women investors took up to 40 percent more time than men to evaluate stocks and were more skeptical about "tips."[293]

Women not only want to do their homework, but once they make an investment selection, most tend to stick with it longer than men do. Although men tend to be the more confident investors, they trade 45 percent more than women do, according to research done by The University of California at Davis.[294] The study goes on to suggest that, by trading more often and without enough research, men may increase their transaction and capital gains

---

291. N. Louth, "Why Women Make Better Investors," MSM Money, 2006.
292. H. Tahira, "Gender Differences in Investment Behavior," FINRA Foundation–Iowa State University/NASD, 2006.
293. Uma Shashikant, "Start Investing, Woman!" Outlook Money Online Magazine, June 30, 2003, http://money.outlookindia.com/article.aspx?88040
294. TheMotleyFool.com, "Warren Buffett Invests Like a Girl," March 20, 2008.

costs, along with reducing overall returns. It is noteworthy that the UC Davis research found that portfolios managed by men in the same survey significantly underperformed (–1.4 percent) investment returns generated by women.[295] Very often, female clients will take calculated risks, when informed of them and after weighing both their costs and benefits.

THE ROLE OF TRUSTED FINANCIAL CONSULTANTS AND INVESTMENT DECISIONS

A range of industry studies have shown that women are more receptive to professional advice when making investment decisions than men. According to research by the Investment Company Institute and Securities Industry Association, 64 percent of the female sole decision makers surveyed said they "always" or "sometimes" seek the counsel of financial consultants in making decisions.[296] Only 55 percent of the men said they solicited professional advice. In addition, 51 percent of sole decision-making women said they buy equities (stocks) through professionals, compared to 37 percent of men.[297] Industry research has also shown that approximately three in four women feel more comfortable with investing, and nearly two in three feel more confident about having money for the future, when working with a financial consultant.[298]

Providing Objectivity and Managing Emotions

emotions

Regardless of gender, confronting the possibility and/or reality of capital loss can trigger a range of emotions in clients that skillful financial consultants must help manage. Objectively refocusing clients, both female and male, away from the phobias of the moment and back to the investment purpose and strategy is both essential and valuable. If the female client's goals and/or situation have substantially changed since the plan was developed, then the consultant needs to review how those changes affect her investment strategies and adjust accordingly. In their useful and informative book, *Questions Great Financial Advisors Ask*, Alan Parisse and David Richman refer to this as "getting the emotion out" of investment decisions:[299]

---

295. Ibid.
296. Investment Company Institute and the Securities Industry Association, "Equity Ownership in America," 2005.
297. Ibid.
298. "Women & Investing: Make it Happen!" Oppenheimer Funds' Women & Investing Survey, 2007.
299. Ibid.

> **Get the Emotion Out**
>
> "A good investment advisor helps his or her clients get the emotion out of their investment decisions. Unfortunately, the information overload that bombards the public serves only to heighten rather than lessen emotions when it comes to investment decisions. Instead of calming fears of inflation or tempering hysteria about the next great bull market or devastating bear market, media reports often exacerbate or inflame such emotions."
>
> Source: Alan Parisse and David Richman, Questions Great Financial Advisors Ask, Kaplan Publishing, 2006

Through a disciplined approach to her investment analysis, planning, due diligence and disclosure, the consultant demonstrates traits that encourage client confidence. Among the most valuable benefits that the financial professional can deliver are: clear-eyed objectivity, a rational exploration of multiple alternatives, full and fair disclosure, as well as a sound rationale that supports recommendations made. This approach helps "get the emotion out" of important decisions that contribute to clients' present and future financial security.

HER INVESTMENT PLAN

Identifying Her Investment Risks

investment risks

Many in the popular press and even some financial services experts limit their discussions of investment risks to those exclusively associated with the U.S. stock market. Witness the near daily obsession with the Dow Jones Industrial Average and the S&P 500 Index as proxies for "investment risk and reward." This oversimplification can be damaging to clients to the extent that other risks, and their attendant management strategies, are often overlooked. While it is certainly important to consider when developing a prudent investment strategy, market risk is by no means the only risk the professional or client should take into account.

> "October: This is one of the particularly dangerous months to invest in stocks. Other dangerous months are July, January, September, April, November, May, March, June December, August and February."
>
> Mark Twain

Fixed Income and Equity Investment Risks

fixed income investments
equity investments

Degrees and forms of investment risk change dramatically, depending on the type of investment. In their simplest form, investments are limited to two types: those which one *owns* and those in which one *loans*.

When the client lends her money out, she is investing in *fixed income* instruments such as bonds, CDs and personal notes. Her anticipated reward is payment of interest, with the expectation that the capital she loaned out will be returned throughout the term of the loan or at its conclusion. Since she does not own part or all of the entity she lent her money to, she does not enjoy appreciation in value if the entity performs well. Conversely, she does not realize losses for its underperformance (assuming the enterprise remains viable).

By contrast, the client takes an ownership position when she invests in *equity investments* such as stocks, real estate, her business or precious metals. As such, she participates in the growth or capital appreciation of equity investments, as well as their potential for decline in value.

Pooled investments (such as mutual funds, variable universal life and variable annuity subaccounts, investment trusts, limited partnerships, fixed annuities, and life insurance cash values invested in the general account of an insurance company) are subject to the specific risks associated with their underlying assets. Underlying assets may consist of fixed income, equity investments, or some combination. While these investments can be significantly diversified, that does not mean they are without risk. Accordingly, it is imperative that one fully understands the inherent risks of each investment and its underlying assets.

Major Forms of Speculative Risk

An array of speculative risk factors contribute to an investment's potential for financial loss. When recommending investments to clients, it is extremely important to assess all risk factors in the investment analysis. Too often, investors look only at one or two of the more obvious risks and completely ignore other less obvious, yet very real risks. For purposes of investment analysis and planning, many of the risks to which an investor is exposed can be categorized into either *systematic risk* or *unsystematic risk* as the chart below illustrates.

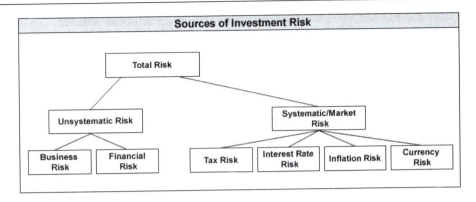

Systematic/Market Risks

systematic risks

Systematic Risks. Also known as market risks, *systematic risks* affect an entire economy, not just one business or industry. Systematic risks can be derived from political, economic, demographic, or social events and trends, as well. However, since not all investments are affected by the various kinds of systematic risk to the same degree, diversifying investments within a given economic system can lessen the effect, but not completely eliminate systematic risk. Types of systematic risks include inflation risk, interest rate risk, and exchange rate risk.

tax risk

Tax Risk. Most investments have some tax consequences. The extent to which an investment is exposed to changes in tax laws is its tax or legislative risk. As we have discussed, income and appreciation in value will, in most cases, be subject to income taxation. Investment assets may also be subject to estate and inheritance taxation and gift taxation when ownership is transferred. To cope with the effects of this type of systematic investment risk, one must monitor events occurring in the national tax arena and help clients make investment decisions accordingly.

interest rate risk

Interest Rate Risk. Interest rates fluctuate over time due to forces at work in the economy, such as actions by the Federal Reserve to control money supply, changes in the demand for borrowed funds, and movements of foreign exchange rates. The result of changing interest rates is that the value of securities, the income earned on securities, or both, will also be in flux. This effect is known as *interest rate risk*.

Interest rate risk occurs when a change in market interest rates triggers an opposite change in the value of investments. When interest rates rise (or fall), the value of an investment declines (or increases). This inverse relationship is most pronounced for debt instruments, such as bonds, mortgages, and U.S. Treasury bills that have a contractually specified rate of interest or return and a specified time to maturity. The longer the time until maturity, the greater the resulting change in market price. For other instruments, such as common stock or real estate, the relationship is not as pronounced, but it is nonetheless present. In fact, not only do changes in interest rates affect the valuation of securities, they also affect the profitability of many companies. When interest rates rise, some businesses, such as banks, tend to become more profitable.

Example

Suppose that Rachel's client, Laurie, purchased a bond when the market interest rate for the bond's risk was 8 percent. This $1,000 face-amount bond has a maturity date one year hence and pays interest of $80 annually. Next, assume that on the following day, the market interest rate for bonds of this same risk and grade maturity rises to 9 percent. Laurie now wants to sell her bond at $1,000. However, she will not be able to do so because a potential buyer can obtain $90 interest (instead of $80) by purchasing a newly issued, one year maturity bond. However, a price discount on Laurie's bond can be determined that would make the total return, both interest income and appreciation such that a potential buyer would be virtually indifferent to either the existing 8 percent or a newly issued 9 percent bond. The price of Laurie's bond would have to be discounted to less than $1,000 so that the buyer's total return would be in effect 9 percent. Alternatively, if the market interest rate had fallen to 7 percent, the value of her 8 percent bond would rise to a premium above its $1,000 face amount, so that the total return to the buyer would be equal to 7 percent.

It should be noted that inflation risk and interest rate risk are related because the rate of inflation is the major determinant of the level of interest rates. When inflation increases, interest rates rise, and vice versa when inflation rates decrease.

inflation or purchasing power risk

Inflation or Purchasing Power Risk. Another major source of systematic risk is *inflation risk* (sometimes called *purchasing power risk*). Inflation is the increase in the general level of prices. The rate of inflation is estimated by the Bureau of Labor Statistics, based on the concept of what it would take to buy a specified basket of goods and services, typically purchased by a family of four, living in an urban community. Published inflation rates are always, at best, an approximation because not everyone buys this same basket of goods and services or lives in an urban environment. In addition, changes in the quality of goods and services are difficult to incorporate into the calculation.

The impact of inflation on investments is often underestimated and misunderstood. An effective way to illustrate its impact is asking the client what she paid for movie tickets when she was a child, and/or how much she paid for her first car. Without a doubt, she will be able to relate to the fact that her dollars today will not buy as much as they did several years (or decades) ago. As many women seek to avoid or minimize market risk by keeping money in savings or investing in fixed income instruments that do not appreciate in value, they may be more exposed to inflation risk than men. In light of the fact that women, on average, live longer than men, they face even greater risk of losing purchasing power as a result of an overly conservative investment strategy.

Since inflation risk is most often only realized over a number of years and is far less dramatic than market or security risk, it can take on a more insidious form. Before the client realizes it, the value of her dollars invested in supposedly "safe" assets do not go as far as they used to. This situation is further exacerbated when the rate of inflation exceeds the nominal rate of return, because an investor will then realize a negative real rate of return. Such was the case for many investors during the late 1970s and early 1980s, when inflation rates in the United States neared and even exceeded 10 percent and the nominal return on some investments was 5 percent. The situation can be further aggravated for investors when after-tax returns are compared to inflation rates. Many women are surprised to learn they are actually losing money on their "safe" investments, especially if they have not invested in assets with the potential for capital appreciation, due to the double whammy of inflation and taxes.

> "A nickel ain't worth a dime anymore."
>
> Yogi Berra

currency or exchange rate risk

Currency or Exchange Rate Risk. Movements in currency exchange rates can also be a significant source of investment risk. Systematic *exchange rate risk* is relevant for individuals who invest in foreign companies because the value of their investments in dollars can decline, even if the foreign companies do well. This will occur if the value of the dollar rises relative to the value of the currency in the country where the investments are located. Even investments in U.S. companies are subject to exchange rate risk because virtually all large corporations (and even many medium and some smaller ones) generate considerable revenue overseas, manufacture overseas, or obtain raw materials from overseas. As with political risk, the primary tool for managing exchange rate risk is diversification.

> "Ask five economists and you'll get five different answers—six, if one went to Harvard."
>
> Edgar R. Fiedler

Unsystematic Risks

unsystematic risks

When a risk is unique to a single business or industry, it is known as an *unsystematic risk*. These are risks associated with a specific investment, not with the market as a whole. The distinction, however, between a systematic risk and an unsystematic risk is never really as exact as it is made out to be. Even the most narrow and peculiar bit of news about a company ripples through the economy. This is because every enterprise, no matter how small, is a part of the economy. Nonetheless, some risks are clearly more specific or unique to a single business or company than others. Types of unsystematic risks include business risk, default risk, and financial risk.

business risk

Business Risk. Enterprises can experience financial difficulties and fail for numerous reasons, including a change in consumer preference away from a particular good or service, ineffective management, changes in the law or foreign competition. The degree to which an enterprise's performance is subject to relatively unique events is its *business risk*. Since every enterprise has its own set of factors and degree of exposure, business risk is specific to each enterprise. Business risk is also a type of unsystematic risk that can be reduced through judicious diversification.

default risk

Default Risk. Closely related to business risk is *default risk*, which is the risk that contractual payments, primarily on debt securities, will not be honored. If principal or interest payments are not made on a timely basis, a borrower goes into default. This can occur with investments in both profit-seeking businesses and nonprofit institutions, such as municipalities. Because all debts must be paid in full before any remaining funds can flow to the stockholders, rarely is anything left to the owners of profit-seeking firms that have failed.

An investment strategy designed to minimize default risk is to purchase only investments issued by those companies with high credit ratings. Moody's, Standard & Poor's, Fitch, Duff & Phelps and others rate bonds, but obtaining the information on specific stocks can be difficult. One can look to the opinions and ratings (e.g., buy, hold, sell) of stock analysts relative to the strength of an enterprise and its anticipated prognosis. Financial consultants and their clients should use information from ratings agencies and analysts judiciously as there can be a broad range of opinion and fact-finding in respective analyses. Default risk, like business risk, can be reduced through thoughtful diversification across international economies, asset classes, sectors, and individual securities.

financial risk

Financial Risk. How much a firm relies on debt may cause an investment to be more or less risky. This is called *financial risk*. Although high debt may be problematic for a firm, no debt may mean that the firm is not taking advantage of appropriate opportunities.

DISCOVERING HER INVESTMENT OBJECTIVES

When building an investment strategy with a client, the financial consultant must first understand her specific objectives. According to research by the Iowa State University Center for Survey Statistics and Methodology, a substantial majority of women (90.3 percent versus 85.6 percent of men) said they preferred to set clear financial goals with timelines and dollar amounts.[300] Fortunately, these preferences are aligned with the consultant's responsibility to help female clients develop prudent investment plans to achieve their goals. Since few women are born wealthy, most will be able to realize their goals only through a disciplined, systematic approach to savings and investing.

Many in the public, the media, and even some investment producers become far too enamored with investments as "the end" rather than "the means." Investing with purpose shifts the focus from the product and the markets, to the client's goals. Increasing investment intentionality, along with developing a prudent investment strategy, helps remove significant emotion from the equation. The questions in the following table may be useful in discovering her goals and concerns when investing for a specified purpose.

The Art of Discovery
Determining Investment Goals and Funding Needs
• Tell me, why is this (name of investment goal) important? What does it mean to you and your family? • How much do you plan to set aside every month, or in a capital lump sum to achieve your goal? • What is your target rate of return on the investments for _____(goal)? How did you determine your targeted rate of return? • How will inflation affect your _____ goal? • What effect will taxes have on your goal of _____? • What have you done so far to achieve your _____ goal? • Do you think you have done enough? • Would you like to know? • If I can show you how to analyze your ____(investment goal) and investment options, along with their pros and cons, would that be worth an hour of your time?

In addition to discovering her investment objectives and attitudes, fact-finding should be thorough. One needs to surface both financial and nonfinancial information. Key financial factors that diligent fact-finding reveals are: cash flow issues, asset and liability ownership, insurances, investment

---

300. Iowa State University, "Gender Differences in Investment Behavior, Milestone 3 Report," August 31, 2006.

experience and risk tolerance. It can take considerable effort to assemble all of the pertinent facts about the client, but these steps are necessary in laying the groundwork for sound investment recommendations.

Determining Her Risk Tolerance

risk tolerance

One critical aspect of fact-finding is profiling the client's risk tolerance. Many companies use their own forms for this purpose, and financial consultants should check with their broker/dealer's compliance department regarding the availability of tools.

Most risk tolerance surveys place investors into one of four or five risk tolerance categories:

1. conservative investor
2. moderately conservative investor
3. moderate risk tolerance investor
4. moderately aggressive investor
5. aggressive investor

Determining her risk tolerance is a critical component in the creation of the client's investment strategy. Beyond the identification of her comfort or discomfort with investment volatility, the consultant also learns if there is a disconnect between a return requirement to reach a specific goal and her determined tolerance for investment risk.

Developing Investment Recommendations

Once fact-finding steps are complete, the financial professional can analyze the client's investment goals and funding strategies. Part of the analysis involves ascertaining whether and which strategies best fit her interests, attitudes, objectives, and needs. This has to do with the concept of suitability.

FINRA

Beyond building strong relationships and business practices, determining suitability is also a regulatory requirement. The Financial Regulatory Authority (FINRA) rules require registered representatives to make reasonable efforts to obtain information about the customer's financial status, tax status, investment objectives and other information to be used in making suitable recommendations. An example of these requirements is rule 2310, referred to by some as KYC, or "know your customer." It is reprinted here for reference.

Managing Her Legislative and Speculative Risks—Taxes and Investments

---

> **FINRA RULE 2310: Recommendations to Customers (Suitability)**
>
> (a) In recommending to a customer the purchase, sale or exchange of any security, a member shall have reasonable grounds for believing that the recommendation is suitable for such customer upon the basis of the facts, if any, disclosed by such customer as to his other security holdings and as to his financial situation and needs.
>
> (b) Prior to the execution of a transaction recommended to a noninstitutional customer, other than transactions with customers where investments are limited to money market mutual funds, a member shall make reasonable efforts to obtain information concerning:
>
> 1. the customer's financial status
> 2. the customer's tax status
> 3. the customer's investment objectives
> 4. other information used or considered to be reasonable by such member or registered representative in making recommendations to the customer
>
> Source: FINRA Manual: FINRA Website February 2009

How does one put together an investment plan that takes a potentially wide and diverse range of factors and risks into account? In some instances, a cash value life insurance product might be part of the option. In other cases, investment vehicles such as stocks, bonds, annuities or mutual funds may be best to meet the client's needs.

HER INVESTMENT PLAN—THE MATH AND THE HOMEWORK

Building a sound investment plan in partnership with female clients means doing the math and homework that is required. While this is true for all client situations at all times, it is especially the case when the financial professional hopes to grow his/her practice with more affluent, sophisticated and advice-receptive women clients.

Doing the Math

Dinkytown

A wide range of calculators can show the impacts of time, assumed investment returns, taxes, and inflation on the client's investment dollars. Most brokers/dealers provide their registered representatives with investment calculators. There are additional tools available online, including this useful calculator from dinkytown.net.[301] The screen shot below reflects output for the following assumptions:

---

301. http://www.dinkytown.net/java/InvestmentReturn.html

1. client investments of a $5,000 initial lump sum with $6,000 added annually for 20 years

2. "moderately conservative" before-tax annual rate of return at an average 6 percent, compounded yearly

3. 3 percent annual rate inflation

4. client is now, and will remain in a 28 percent tax bracket

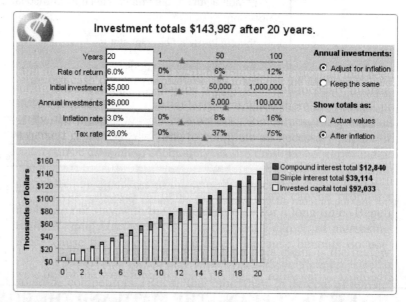

Fairly basic investment calculators can help the client develop a sense of how much needs to be saved, for how long and how her return is affected by time, taxes, and inflation. It is worth noting that the tool used in this instance does not provide random investment return modeling and/or statistical probabilities of achieving a specified goal (e.g., Monte Carlo probability testing). Nevertheless, it is better to approach quantifying her investment goals and support assumptions, even at a relatively high level of analysis, rather than no quantification at all. Some reasonably good calculators take only minutes from input to output and options.

As clients grow in wealth, they generally expect more sophisticated analysis and thorough examination of the issues. Developing a specific quantified funding approach that reflects capital and/or systematic contributions, alternative rates of return, and statistical success probabilities demonstrates competency and adds more value than the great majority of competitors. Both lead to increasing client confidence and capturing more assets under management.

When making investment recommendations, there are two additional benefits when one "does the math" for clients. The first is that it removes the client's focus from the investment product itself, and places it more appropriately on her needs (e.g., rates of return, lump sum and systematic capital contributions). The second benefit is to financial consultants when presenting defensible recommendations and rationale to clients, as regulatory authorities increasingly look for development and documentation of both.

Doing the Homework

due diligence

"Doing the homework" refers to conducting *due diligence* with regard to the client's situation and attitudes, as well as proposed strategies. A helpful definition of this concept can be found on Wikipedia: "Due diligence is a term used for a number of concepts involving either the performance of an investigation of a business or person, or the performance of an act with a certain standard of care" (http://en.wikipedia.org/wiki/Due_diligence). It means understanding, to the fullest extent possible, the client's financial situation, objectives and risk exposures. Due diligence also means a thorough examination of product options, along with a well-developed rationale for recommendations made.

Understanding the Options

It is important for the consultant to not only have a working familiarity of the products he/she offers and their potential impact on the client's situation, but also to grasp the range of alternatives that may be available to fund her goal. Likewise, it is essential to know the respective merits of each alternative. For example, she may be interested in funding her children's college education. What are some possible strategies and which might make the most sense for her situation? Based on current tax legislation, she might consider, a Coverdell Education Savings Account, a 529 College Savings Plan, a UTMA or UGMA, a family trust, tapping a traditional or Roth IRA, borrowing or surrendering life insurance cash value, along with savings, mutual funds, IRAs and/or retirement plans. What are the pros and cons of each alternative in terms of:

- How much can she contribute?

- Does she control the asset or does someone else?

- What are the tax benefits and/or consequences?

- How do accumulated assets affect the possible eligibility of financial aid?

Only one or two strategies may fit her situation. Demonstrating expertise in the alternatives and communicating their relative merits/disadvantages reinforces the perceptions of objectivity, professionalism, and that her best interests come first.

Managing Investment Risks

As discussed earlier, there are options for controlling when investment income is realized and taxed, depending on the vehicle used. Based on her present and future tax situation, evaluating which approach—pay now, later, or never—are important considerations to take into account. More than one approach may be warranted, in light of the unpredictably of legislative risk.

Many individuals new to the world of providing investment recommendations think that the planning process works in the reverse order. That is, they think that asset selection precedes asset allocation. They focus on the selection of specific assets by looking for something with high return, and little or no risk (as if there is such a thing), and end with seeing if the client is comfortable with the selection. However, investment research has consistently shown that correct allocation will do far more to benefit a client than selecting a specific investment.[302] It is of much greater priority for financial consultants to make sure that a client has an asset allocation that is consistent with her risk tolerance and ability to handle risk, than it is to pick occasional "winners." As with all forms of diversification, it makes sense to spread the risk around. This concept applies to strategically diversifying investment holdings as well. Most associate strategic investment diversification with asset allocation.

Asset Allocation

asset allocation

The term *asset allocation* is often casually tossed around. In its simplest form, it relates to the basic concept of "not putting all of your eggs in one basket." There is no simple formula, tool, or technique that allows a consultant to define the optimal portfolio, even if he/she has developed a perfect measure of the client's risk tolerance. To help deal with this ambiguity, many professionals construct recommended portfolios for different levels of risk tolerance.

Asset allocation portfolios are diversified, based on categories of assets, across the three major asset categories: equities, fixed income and cash equivalents. The emphasis is on what the percentage of each asset category should be in the portfolio based on the client's risk tolerance. Virtually every mutual fund provider, and many investment writers/experts as well, tout their latest asset allocation strategy for current market conditions. Very often, the allocations fall somewhere in the ranges reflected below:

---

302. Gary P. Brinson, Brian D. Singer, and Gilbert L. Beebower, "Determinants of Portfolio Performance," Financial Analysts Journal, July/August 1986. Updated in Financial Analysts Journal, May/June 1991, 40–48.

Sample Asset Allocations					
Asset Category	Conservative	Moderately Conservative	Moderate	Moderately Aggressive	Aggressive
Equities	20%	35%	50%	65%	80%
Fixed Income	70%	50%	40%	30%	15%
Cash	10%	15%	10%	5%	5%

Over the past five years, asset allocation "fund of funds" that align with these five basic risk tolerance categories have become increasingly popular. These investment companies provide diversified portfolios and are offered by most leading mutual funds and variable subaccount providers (i.e., variable annuity and life contract issuers). For most asset allocation funds, the proportion of fixed income to equity assets decreases as the investor moves up the risk tolerance continuum.

Diversifying Time Horizons

diversifying time horizons

Another frequently used risk management strategy is *diversifying time horizons* of investments according to their planned purpose and degree of short-term price variability (standard deviation).

The risk of equity investing (i.e., loss of capital invested) is generally thought to diminish over time. Investments in large, well capitalized common stocks that are owned individually or through investment companies should have a planned holding period of at least 5 years. For smaller, growth oriented company stocks, the horizon should extend further recognizing the high standard deviation in price movement. The problem of market timing, or when to buy or sell, and the transactions costs of the purchase and sale combine to make success quite difficult with shorter holding periods.

The historical behavior of the stock market favors at least a 5-year holding period, or better yet, 10 years. Combined with dividends earned on a portfolio of common stocks, the ups and downs are such that only a few 10 year periods fail to provide positive returns. However, many shorter periods, such as 3 to 5 years, have frequently produced negative total returns. Other equity investments, such as real estate, require even longer planned holding periods, due to their relatively higher transaction costs and their general lack of marketability. Indeed, for some limited partnerships that invest in real estate, investment professionals often recommend at least a 10 year holding period.

What inferences can be drawn from these diversification concepts?

- ***Diversify investment asset classes, tax treatment, and holding periods***, so that the portfolio matches the client's risk tolerance, return requirements, time horizons and anticipated tax bracket.

- **Set client expectations** for appropriate range(s) of volatility consistent with her suitability, risk tolerance, investment objectives, and timing.

It is important to allocate specific goals to time horizons and build portfolio(s), accordingly. Aligning portfolio objectives, asset allocation, and holding periods are essential elements of investment risk management. When managing significant assets for retired clients, for instance, it can be helpful to create multiple retirement portfolio "buckets," based on the time interval of each. Here is an example of a three-portfolio-bucket approach for an investment strategy that may span several decades:

1. ***Bucket One—One to Five Years—Objective:*** preservation of principal and security of income, investments subject to little or no market risk (often funded with low cost fixed debt investments and annuities)

2. ***Bucket Two—Six to Ten Years—Objective:*** balanced between income (high quality, intermediate debt instruments) and some growth (income oriented dividend paying equities, reinvested income earnings)

3. ***Bucket Three—More than Ten Years—Objective:*** longer term capital growth, minority percentage of portfolio in debt instruments, use of inflation hedging equities (e.g., "hard assets," such as real estate, precious metals, and so on)

Developing Her Investment Strategies

Once the consultant has completed both goal analysis and due diligence, the specific investment strategies can then be developed with the client. These strategies take into account where she is today, how much capital she can currently allocate to her goal, how much she will have to save systematically, her target rate of return and when assets will be needed. Together, the client and consultant should review investment alternatives and their merits/risks before agreeing upon an investment strategy to achieve her goals.

She may not be able to achieve her goals within her current means. For many clients, the prospect of falling short of an important financial goal can be discouraging and even debilitating. It is always helpful to encourage and remind those with funding challenges that they have options. Alternative strategies to address a goal funding shortfall include:

1. ***Reduce the goal***—For example, daughter Jessica can go to state college, versus private college.

2. ***Delay the goal***—Jessica can wait for two years to start with state college, working and going to community college in the meantime.

3. ***Add more capital or savings***—Allocate a grandparent's inheritance to Jessica's college fund, and/or step up contributions from current cash flow.

4. *Take more market risk*—Invest Jessica's college fund in more aggressive investment options, particularly if she has another 10–15 years until college age. As she nears her college career, equities will be strategically liquidated to grow a reserve pool with funds less exposed to market risk.

Life-Stage and Life Style Considerations

The same basic principles of prudent investing, diligence, and informed decision making apply to both women and men, regardless of life-stage or lifestyle. That said, there are a few attitudinal and generational differences to keep in mind. According to a survey by Charles Schwab in 2000, women are much more likely to be motivated to invest by life events than are men.[303] Specifically, men and women have different levels of concerns for the following:

- the daunting challenges of retirement—more often a serious concern for Boomer females (44 percent of women vs. 34 percent for male cohorts)

- marriage—a major factor especially for GenX women (35 percent of GenX women vs. 20 percent of GenX men)

- inheritance—a significant influence for senior women (26 percent for senior women versus 9 percent for senior men)[304]

Because there are few concrete "norms" when it comes to female (or any) investors, one should tailor recommendations to the client's specific goals, needs, and investor suitability. Major life-stage goals like education and retirement are now being redefined in terms of their meaning and reality. For many, the reexamination of life-stage goals and their financing has been compelled by the Great Recession and 2008/2009, and its eroding of asset values and economic opportunities. Encouraging the client to redefine her current situation and risks, while helping her imagine hopeful prospects.

Product Considerations

Selecting and managing some investments requires minimal expertise. For instance, one does not need to be an expert on short term debt securities to understand the relevant characteristics (degree of principal risk, expected return, liquidity, marketability and tax treatment) of Treasury Bills and similar securities. Similarly, some types of investments may be maintained with little or no effort (e.g., most bonds), while others require constant management (e.g.,

---

303. SmartPros, "Women Show Little Difference in Investing Confidence and Skills," October 5, 2000.
304. Ibid.

an apartment complex). However, individuals who invest in real estate, gold, soybean futures, options trading, and other forms of arbitrage presumably need special knowledge and talent. Both the consultant and the client need to carefully consider their individual and collective expertise, capabilities, and the time required to assemble and manage a particular type of investment portfolio. Financial consultants should never recommend an investment that neither they nor their clients fully understand.

Mutual Funds

Many women have limited investment resources and therefore limited ability to achieve broad diversification through holding individual stock and bond securities. Most can benefit from the extensive diversification that investment companies, also known as mutual funds, can offer. At the end of 2008, there were more than 10,000 mutual funds in existence. This overwhelming array of fund choices can create challenges when selecting the appropriate vehicle for a client. Carefully evaluating a mutual fund is not only an important part of due diligence, but it is also an essential aspect of risk management. This means that the financial consultant, and/or staff must develop subject matter expertise and research skills. Here are some key variables to consider when researching mutual funds:

- manager tenure (generally, the more years, the better)

- underlying asset risks (i.e., risks of the individual securities)

- portfolio diversification by asset category, class, sectors and securities

- top ten holdings by equity and/or fixed income security

- investment fees and commissions; surrender or withdrawal charges and penalties

- investor's risk tolerance, time horizon and suitability

- other considerations (e.g., tax exemption)

- portfolio turnover and capital gains exposure

Managing Her Legislative and Speculative Risks—Taxes and Investments

security selection
standard deviation
sharpe ratio
beta
alpha

Understanding and comparing the risk/return tradeoffs of a particular fund are also critical factors when analyzing alternatives. There are four commonly used metrics to evaluate a mutual fund based on its risk/return dynamics: *(1) standard deviation, (2) sharpe ratio, (3) beta,* and *(4) alpha.* The following table provides basic definitions of each, according to Morningstar Advisor Workstation.

Select Risk/Return Metrics Used to Evaluate Investments
• **Standard deviation** is a statistical measure of the volatility of a portfolio's returns around its mean. The mean generally is a market index (e.g., S&P 500) that consists of holdings in the same asset class.
• **Sharpe ratio** uses a portfolio's standard deviation and total return to determine reward per unit of risk. The higher the number in the ratio, the more return for unit of risk taken.
• **Beta** is a measure of the degree of change in value one can expect in a portfolio given a change in value in a benchmark index (e.g., S&P 500). A portfolio with a beta greater than one is generally more volatile than its benchmark index, and a portfolio with a beta of less than one is generally less volatile than its benchmark index.
• **Alpha** measures the difference between a fund portfolio's actual returns and its expected performance, given its beta and the actual returns of the benchmark index. Alpha is often seen as a measurement of the value added or subtracted by a portfolio's manager.
Source: Morningstar Advisor Workstation, explanation of portfolio risks, accessed online 7/31/2009.

Special Considerations about Women and Annuities

annuities

Annuities are financial products that women consistently choose in greater numbers than men do, in part because many women like the guarantees embedded in fixed annuities. At all ages, women are more likely than men to buy deferred annuities. Among all people who participate in deferred annuities through retirement plans at work, the majority—57 percent—are women, and 43 percent are men.[305] In addition, women are also more likely than men (53 percent compared to 47 percent) to buy nonqualified deferred annuities outside of their retirement plans.[306]

A recent academic study shows that more women should consider using appropriately structured annuities to address their risks associated with greater

---

305. LIMRA, "Deferred Annuity Owner Study: Characteristics and Attitudes," 2003.
306. Ibid.

longevity and frequently compromised retirement savings. The potential for guaranteed lifelong income combined with inflation indexing, can make select annuity products very attractive for certain women and their portfolios.

Annuities often play a vital role in helping women achieve financial security during retirement. As more American women enter retirement without employer-provided pensions and health insurance, and as the potential for a longer lifespan increases, women must personally fund an increasing share of their retirement costs. Due to women's greater longevity, the duration of their retirement is increasing. A woman who reaches age 65 today has an average remaining life expectancy of 22 years.[307] These factors to some degree predispose women to certain features inherent in annuity products.

Annuities do not represent one single financial option, but rather several products aimed at a variety of financial needs that can vary with her individual goals, situation, and risk tolerance. These contracts fall into four basic types:

Four Basic Types of Annuities			
Accumulation Phase			
Types of Annuities	Account Values	Risk Level	Income Distribution
Fixed-interest deferred annuities	Fixed	Low	Optional, later
Variable deferred annuities	Fluctuate	From low to high	Optional, later
Distribution Phase			
Types of Annuities	Account Values	Risk Level	Income Distribution
Immediate fixed annuities	Fixed	Low	Predictable
Immediate variable annuities	Fluctuate	From low to high	Not predictable

fixed annuities

Women and Fixed Annuities. Some women consider fixed-interest deferred annuities to be attractive alternatives to bank deposit products. Fixed-interest deferred annuities do not include FDIC insurance, but a guarantee to repay principal plus interest that is backed by the full claims-paying ability of the insurance company. For this reason, it is very important to select fixed-interest deferred annuities issued by financially strong companies. The best way to evaluate insurance company financial strength is to check its ratings leading ratings agencies (e.g., Moody's, Standard & Poor's, and A.M. Best). Ratings are published for virtually all major life insurance companies.

---

307. Women's Institute for a Secure Retirement in conjunction with MetLife Mature Market Institute, "What Today's Woman Needs to Know: A Retirement Journey," May 2007.

The higher ratings are, the greater the financial strength that stands behind a company's guarantee to pay annuity principal and interest.

If the interest rate on one fixed-interest deferred annuity contract becomes unattractive, some women take advantage of a feature called a "1035 exchange," to switch into either another deferred annuity fixed or variable. The 1035 exchange follows a "like-kind." This tax doctrine essentially means that gains realized on the sale of an asset can be deferred if the newly acquired asset is like-kind. Generally, it is best to make the exchange after the insurance company's annuity surrender charge has phased out, and without incurring additional cost or tax consequences.

Note: All costs and benefits of both an old contract/company versus a new contract/company/product must be carefully evaluated and fully disclosed to clients and prospects before any transaction occurs.

variable annuities
living benefits

Women and Variable Annuities. *Variable annuities* (VAs) are becoming increasingly popular, yet complicated due to significant product innovation, including:

- expanding subaccount fund options that enhance potential to customize portfolio(s) to the client's needs

- death benefit guarantees that preserve the net amount invested for her heirs, particularly valuable if she is otherwise uninsurable

- new options (usually riders) that are designed to increase contract owner's flexibility

Guaranteed Minimum Withdrawal Benefit (GMWB)
Guaranteed Minimum Income Benefit (GMIB)
Guaranteed Minimum Accumulation Benefit (GMAB)
Guaranteed Lifetime Withdrawal Benefit (GLWB)

New riders, referred to as living benefits, are growing substantially in both demand and distribution. Since these optional riders provide guarantees that may be appealing to women, it is important for financial consultants to have working familiarity with them. The four most common are reflected in the box below.

The annuity industry is also innovating contracts by adding new features for access and payment of long-term care services and facilities. Not surprisingly, these enhancements have costs. Even the tax deferral associated with investment gains can have a downside if the client is in a higher tax bracket when she withdraws funds than when she invested them. As with all investment and insurance product recommendations, one should fully disclose all VA costs—making her an informed consumer and reducing risks for both client and consultant.

> **What To Use When – A Living Benefit Refresher**
>
> 1. **Guaranteed minimum withdrawal benefit (GMWB).** No lifetime benefit is more popular among consumers than the GMWB. It guarantees that, regardless of how investments within a contract perform, the contract holder can withdraw a percentage (usually 5–7 percent) of total premium paid into a contract annually for a specified period of time, until the principal is exhausted. New GMWB wrinkles include step-up features that allow contract holders to lock in higher guaranteed withdrawals when subaccount investments perform well. GMWB riders typically cost between 35-75 basis points annually.
>
> 2. **Guaranteed minimum income benefit (GMIB).** Assures the contract holder a base amount from which to draw an annuitized lifetime income, regardless of how investments underlying the contract have performed, provided there have been no prior withdrawals or transfers from the account. Most riders in this class offer the assurance that when the contract holder annuitizes, payments from the contract will be derived from either (1) the principal amount plus additional funds credited to the account based on a pre-determined interest rate, or (2) the maximum anniversary value of the account prior to annuitization, whichever is greater. GMIB riders usually come with a 10 year holding period and cost in the range of 30–75 basis points.
>
> 3. **Guaranteed minimum accumulation benefit (GMAB).** Typically priced similar to—but significantly less popular than—a GMIB, this rider is all about principal protection. It guarantees that the contract value won't fall below the amount the contract holder had invested as of X years (usually 7–10), regardless of investment subaccount performance. Many GMABs require contract holders to meet certain asset allocation standards.
>
> 4. **Guaranteed lifetime withdrawal benefit (GLWB).** A subset of the GMWB class, this rider is designed to address investor concern about outliving their retirement savings. It guarantees the contract holder the ability to withdraw a certain percentage of principal each year for as long as she lives, even after money within the account has been exhausted. Some GLWBs now also come with a spousal continuation option. Typical cost for the rider ranges between 40–75 basis points annually.
>
> Source: The Boomer Market Advisor, What to Use When, A Living Benefit Refresher, with data from the National Association for Insured Retirement Solutions (NAVA), March 2008.

CHAPTER SUMMARY

This chapter has continued our discussion of financial risks to include legislative risks associated with changing tax legislation, and speculative risks associated with investments. Without a doubt, tax and investment planning represent two of the most challenging areas for financial consultants, in terms of their scope and complexities. Building expertise, competence and skill in both aspects of a female client's financial plan requires time and commitment. Furthermore, one needs to stay current on the latest developments in tax reform and investment markets. The learning process for these areas of financial competency never stops. That said, the more one can demonstrate expertise in the areas of taxation and investments, the greater the value-add. More added value leads to more business and referrals.

In Chapter 7, we examine the risks and planning issues associated with the female client's retirement and legacy, including:

- the need for a new retirement paradigm

- primary risk factors for women in retirement

- special challenges in Social Security planning for women (and men)

- investing for retirement income

- basic goals and techniques of estate planning

CHAPTER 6 TOOLS AND RESOURCES

- Courses from The American College
    - FA 264 Foundation of Investment Planning
    - HS 321 Income Taxation
    - HS 322 The Financial System and the Economy
    - HS 328 Investments
    - GS 817 Personal Tax Planning
    - GS 819 Mutual Funds: Analysis, Allocation and Performance Evaluation

- Tools
    - Risk Tolerance Questionnaire

- Websites
    - IRS.gov (Tax information)
    - Dinkytown.net (Funding analysis)
    - Morningstar.com (Investment analysis information)

7

Reinventing Retirement and Planning Her Legacy

Learning Objectives
An understanding of the material in this chapter should enable the student to

7-1. Describe the need for a new retirement paradigm.

7-2. Identify the five major risk factors women have when it comes to their retirement.

7-3. Define the difference between dreams and goals, and explain how SMART goals are established.

7-4. Identify special Social Security challenges women may have when planning for a secure retirement.

7-5. Explain key considerations to take into account with regard to employer sponsored qualified plans and IRAs.

7-6. Identify the goals of estate planning.

7-7. Define the basic concepts of durable powers of attorney, living wills, health care proxies, estate taxes, lifetime gifts and gift taxes, wills, revocable living trusts and irrevocable life insurance trusts.

INTRODUCTION

Chapters 4 and 5 examined how to strengthen the female client's financial position and ability to withstand pure losses associated with personal, property and liability exposures. The examination of the six areas of financial planning concludes with this chapter's look at her plans for retirement; specifically, how to help her manage retirement risks and create a lasting legacy. These two often complex areas of planning are depicted at the top of the Financial Planning pyramid.

Women and Money

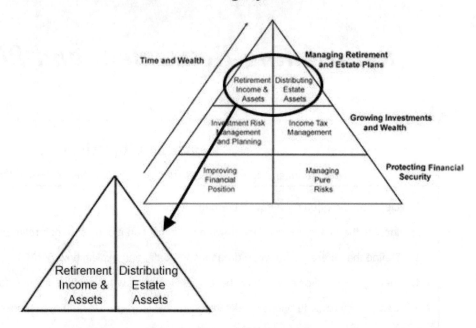

Retirement and estate planning needs are built from a lifetime of work and asset accumulation. The client's primary challenges in her later years are protecting financial well-being and dignity, along with preserving assets for her income needs and then for her beneficiaries. To help women understand their retirement risks, we explore the most common and most significant retirement challenges to account for when putting together an effective retirement plan for female clients. Perhaps nowhere is highly capable, trustworthy professional advice more needed than when encouraging her to envision and create a plan for her future as a thriving senior woman. Since significant challenges and complexity are also frequently involved, financial planning specialities in retirement and estate planning are often among the most lucrative for consultants.

THE NEW RETIREMENT REALITIES

Whether by goal or necessity, many of those approaching or already at traditional retirement age are now confronting new realities about their economic futures. It is important for financial professionals, many of whom grew up in the post-World War II era, to understand how the concept of retirement has changed and continues to evolve. Helping female clients articulate their dreams and goals for their later years and creating a sustainable, adjustable plan to meet these goals may require financial consultants to adopt a new mind-set as well.

The Need for a New Retirement Paradigm

Ken Dychtwald, Ph.D.

Even before the Great Recession of 2008/2009, Ken Dychtwald, Ph.D., psychologist, gerontologist and best-selling author, saw the opportunity and the need to break the conventional mold of what retirement had come to mean for so many. Dr. Dychtwald has spent most of his decades-long career studying retirement trends and the Baby Boom generation. In his groundbreaking book *Age Wave*, he describes how the perceptions of both aging and retirement will be transformed in the coming years. In effect, he predicts that a new paradigm of elder life will emerge.

The old paradigm of retirement meant that individuals were employed for three or four decades, then stopped work in their early/mid-sixties when pensions and Social Security old age income benefits became available. That mid-sixties age benchmark was set, of course, by the advent of Social Security in 1938. At that time, the average life expectancy for Americans was not-so-coincidentally, the early to middle part of their sixth decade. As longevity continued to extend well beyond the benchmark set in 1938, and as pensions, along with Social Security, provided the bulk of required income, the old retirement paradigm came into being. Retirement became a concept of relaxation, leisure and freedom from work. It is worth noting that before the genesis of these three combined factors—Social Security, pensions and longevity—the idea of retirement did not exist in concept or reality. Now, just decades later, the old paradigm of retirement is fast becoming an anachronism.

Today, many view the traditional concept of retirement enjoyed by previous generations not as the dream it was once considered to be. According to Dr. Dychtwald, the average retiree today watches 43 hours of television per week and 80 percent do not work. He further states that volunteer rates among these retirees are lowest among those with the most time on their hands. "Our long-lived men and women—the world's fastest growing natural resource—are profoundly underutilized."[308]

> "There's never enough time to do all the nothing you want."
>
> Bill Watterson, Calvin and Hobbes

For better or worse, retirement is changing, and perhaps rightly so. Close to half of Americans retire earlier than planned. Savings rates are at an historic low. Pensions have declined and the future of Social Security is questionable. If the concept of retirement does not change, the consequences could well be devastating to many (women in particular), and to the nation as a whole. A

---

308. Ken Dychtwald, Ph.D., Daniel J. Kadlec, *The Power Years* (John Wiley & Sons Publishing, 2005).

new vision of retirement, of living life to the fullest in one's later years, is emerging from a desire for a more useful and satisfying existence, along with the sometimes harsh economic realities associated with the need to generate income for a longer period of time.

Demographic shifts will have a profound influence on how the new paradigm of retirement plays out. From now until 2030, it is expected that the population of Americans over the age of 65 will more than double. Suffice it to say that the retirement vision of total leisure and freedom from work will be out of reach for most Baby Boomers (broadly defined as those born between 1946 and 1964).

There will be lasting financial challenges facing the Baby Boomers and possibly future generations for decades to come. Some of these challenges were reported in a study by the Employee Benefit Research Institute (EBRI) in 2008. They found that almost one in three Americans have no savings at all set aside for retirement.[309] EBRI also projected that, by 2020–2030, early Boomers (born between 1946 and 1956) will experience an income shortfall of over $400 billion in their ability to pay for even basic living expenses. It is worth noting that these basic expenses cover housing, food and health care and exclude "discretionary" (e.g., leisure activity) expenses so often associated with the old retirement paradigm. More disturbing yet, EBRI anticipates that for 80 percent of these early Boomers, Social Security will represent more than 50 percent of their income in retirement.[310]

Picturing a New Future–The Third Age

Third Age

Despite all the gloomy predictions, there is reason to be optimistic about shifting from the old retirement paradigm to a more vibrant, active and engaged stage of life. Ken Dychtwald refers to this stage as the *third age*—which extends from an individual's sixth decade to his or her ninth (and beyond).

Along with the risks and challenges facing older American women, the future also holds out the promise of not only living longer, but also better. Continued advances in science, medicine and nutrition give promise to even greater longevity and higher quality of life than women enjoy today. In addition, as they become more educated, own more businesses and advance in the workplace, women will be capable of generating more wealth, income and options for themselves in their later years.

> "To retire is to die."
>
> Pablo Cases

---

309. R. Helman, M. Greenwald, J. VanDerhei, C. Copeland, "Retirement Confidence Survey: Americans Much More Worried About Retirement, Health Costs a Big Concern," Employee Benefit Research Institute, 2008.

310. "Income of the Elderly Population Age 65 and Over, 2005," Employee Benefit Research Institute, 25, no. 5 May 2007, 2.

> **The Third Age**
>
> *A third age*, which spans the period from sixty to ninety (and longer), is unfolding ahead of us. This is a less-pressured period in which we can further develop our intellect, imagination, emotional maturity, and wisdom. This is also a period when we can give something back to society based on the lessons, resources and experiences we have accumulated over a lifetime. We need not be social outcasts, but instead can assume the role of a living bridge between yesterday and tomorrow, and in this way play a critical role that no other group is as well suited to perform.
>
> In recent decades a small but growing number of older adults have been rejecting the social pressure to "act their age." They have been rebelling against ageist stereotypes and seeking to remain productive, involved, and late blooming well into their mature years. They are everywhere—within our families, among our friends and in our communities: the executive who becomes a high school teacher; the grandmother who goes back to college or who writes her first book; the accountant who becomes an artist. Ask them when they think they'll start to feel elderly inside, and they'll probably say *"Never!"*
>
> Source: Ken Dychtwald, PhD, Daniel J. Kadlec, *The Power Years* (John Wiley & Sons Publishing, 2005).

In light of the profound complexities of planning for retirement, or third age, it should come as no surprise that professional help in this area is consistently ranked as the primary motivation for women to seek out a financial consultant. Two out of three women rate help with retirement planning as their number one reason to visit a financial professional.[311]

WOMEN AND RETIREMENT—HER FIVE BIG RISK FACTORS

Despite the bright prospects for some, the unfortunate truth is that many women face a nightmare of poverty in retirement. The U.S. Department of Labor states that women are twice as likely as men to live below the poverty line during retirement years and that almost three in four of all Americans over 65 living in poverty are women.[312] According to The Society of Actuaries in 2006, the median income for women over 65 is substantially lower—more than one third less—than their male peers.[313]

There are five major areas associated with this stage of life where a woman is likely to be at greater risk than her male counterparts. While

---

311. "Mainstay Investments Explores the 'Mars vs. Venus' Dynamic," New York Life Investment Management, April 3, 2007.
312. U.S. Census Bureau, "Current Population Survey, Annual Social and Economic Supplement, 2006," 2007.
313. Society of Actuaries, "Key Findings and Issues: The Impact of Retirement Risk on Women," 2005 Risks and Process of Retirement Survey.

these risk exposures are similar to those we have discussed previously, they are significantly exacerbated for older women and as such, merit deeper examination with regard to retirement planning. These exposures include:

1. greater longevity

2. lower levels of retirement resources, such as savings, Social Security and pension accumulations

3. singlehood, widowhood and divorce

4. health challenges

5. financial literacy about retirement planning

Her Longevity

longevity

According to the U.S. Census Bureau, in 2005, the average life expectancy at birth for an American female was 80.5 years versus 75.2 for men.[314] If she reaches age 50 both cancer and heart disease free, she may well make it to age 92.[315]

While a woman's greater longevity has been well documented, its planning implications are often not taken into account. On average, women will need to pay for roughly five more years of retirement than their male peers. A woman's greater longevity increases the need for reliable sources of long-term income and investment management. It is also critical to consider how her life expectancy might extend even further in the future.

As life expectancy continues to grow each decade, many of today's middle-aged American women may live over 100 years. However, few have a true appreciation of the possible ramifications associated with living beyond their parents' or grandparents' age of mortality. To help her recognize her own potential longevity and all that it means, financial consultants may suggest that she complete an online questionnaire at The Living to 100 website (www.livingto100.com). The site's calculator will estimate longevity based on her answers to questions about her family and personal health history, finances, lifestyle, nutrition and exercise habits. Quite often, the answers are surprising; she might live much longer than she thought. This exercise can be beneficial in compelling her to contemplate how she will productively fill and afford the next 30, 40, 50, 60 or more years of her life.

---

314. U.S. Census Bureau, Expectations of Life at Birth, 1970 to 2005, http://www.census.gov/compendia/statab/ tables/09s0100.pdf
315. Society of Actuaries.

Her Retirement Resources

Along with the prospects of greater longevity is the need to stretch retirement resources to fund the added years. This can be a particularly daunting change for women since many work in lower paying jobs and for employers who may not offer retirement benefits. In addition, they may interrupt their careers to take care of children or parents. As a result, their resources for retirement are often constrained. Consider these facts:

- About 50 percent of all women are or will be working in low-paying jobs without pension or other employer-sponsored retirement savings plans of any kind.[316]

- According to the Department of Labor, of the 60 million wage earning and salaried women working in the United States as of March 2005, just 47 percent participated in a retirement plan at work.[317]

- Of those women who were able to contribute to a 401k in 2006, just 41 percent did so.[318]

- A Scudder Kemper Investment Inc., survey of households with incomes of at least $30,000 found that 43 percent of the men had more than $100,000 in their 401(k) plans, while only 27 percent of the women had that much.[319]

- For women who do receive a pension from their employer, their average annual benefit is less than half of what men receive ($4,152 versus $8,400 per year).[320]

Singlehood, Widowhood and Divorce

singlehood
widowhood
divorce

Further compounding a female's retirement risks is the strong likelihood that she will be single in retirement. Women are more than twice as likely to be alone in their later years than men. This risk seriously jeopardizes an older woman's financial future. According to a recent study by the Social Security Administration, more than one in four (28 percent) single women aged 65 and older were classified as either "poor" or "near poor."[321] The Social Security

---

316. FINP/Distribution of Wealth 15, August 2006
317. Department of Labor pamphlet for Women and Retirement.
318. Employment Benefit Research Institute, Issue Brief No. 286, "Employment-Based Retirement Plan Participation: Geographic Differences and Trends," October 2005.
319. William Anthes, Ph.D., Bruce Most, FPA Journal- Frozen in the Headlights: The Dynamics of Women and Money, 2000, p3.
320. EBRI notes, 28. no 3, March 2007.
321. WISER report, "Unique Challenges Faced by Women in Preparing for and Managing Their Retirement Years."

Administration also reports that in 2005, 61 percent of women over 65 living alone had an annual income under $15,000.[322] Even adjusted for inflation, that average income still falls below $20,000 per year!

Married women are not immune to the risk of poverty brought on by becoming single later in life. Tragically, widowhood significantly increases the risk of an older woman becoming poor. In 2000, while only four percent of married elderly females lived in poverty, the number of widowed females 65 and older who lived in poverty was a whopping 17 percent—more than four times the number of married women.[323] In addition, more than 40 percent of widows of pensioners reported no pension income after their husband's deaths.[324] These sad statistics dispel the commonly held notion that life insurance is not needed in retirement.

qualified domestic relations orders

Taking into account her current and future marital status is also critical when planning for distributions from employer sponsored qualified plans (i.e., defined contribution plans and defined benefit plans) and Social Security benefits. If a woman is in the process of divorce, her consultant should ask if there is a *qualified domestic relations order (QDRO)* in place or pending, on either side. QDROs are judgments, decrees, or orders issued by state courts that allow a participant's retirement plan assets to be used for marital property rights, child support, or alimony payments to a former spouse or dependent.

Health Challenges and Older Women's Insurability

insurability

Maintaining and affording health care in retirement can present huge challenges for Americans, particularly for women. Since many women marry older men, they run the risk of losing benefits due to the early retirement of their spouse. For a woman in this situation, this means she may need to obtain private pay health insurance later in life when her *insurability* might be compromised. Her employment options and availability of employer paid health insurance may be limited due to care giving of parents, children, spouse or some combination.

Financial and Retirement Literacy

retirement literacy

Beyond these issues, there is a pervasive lack of understanding among both genders about basic retirement concepts. As we have seen, low financial literacy compounds risk exposure. A recent Prudential Financial study on the financial experiences of women underscores a broad lack of understanding of core financial products, especially those related to retirement. Specifically, the research showed that 58 percent of women said they did not understand annuities well or at all. Almost half (47 percent) did not have an adequate

---

322. Social Security Administration, "Income of the Population 55 or Older, 2002," March 2005.
323. Ibid.
324. Holden & Zick, 2000.

understanding of mutual funds, long-term care insurance (46 percent) estate planning (46 percent), or stocks and bonds (44 percent).[325] Since these financial tools are central to retirement planning and well-being, it is disturbing to see that nearly half (and sometimes more) of American women believe they do not have a sufficient grasp of them.

On a positive note, despite their challenges, most women, especially those who are single, are deeply interested in planning for their third age. Consider these statistics from a 2008 study by Allianz:

- 54 percent of all women wanted to learn more about retirement and maintaining their lifestyle in retirement.[326]

- 55 percent of single women without children said they want to learn more.[327]

- More than two-thirds (68 percent) of single women with children were interested in learning about retirement planning.[328]

HER RETIREMENT PLAN

Retirement planning is among the most multifaceted and most complicated disciplines for the financial consultant to master. In many ways, retirement planning is just as much of an art as it is a science. This description by C. Bruce Worsham, former faculty member at The American College and expert on taxation and insurance, is well stated:

> A successful financial advisor (consultant) must not only have a working knowledge of a large variety of financial planning and retirement-related topics but also know how to apply the knowledge to a client's particular situation.
>
> This requires understanding the client's goals, attitudes, and personal preferences. For example, an advisor [financial consultant] should be prepared to help a client meet the important goals of maintaining his or her preretirement standard of living during retirement, becoming economically self-sufficient, minimizing taxes on retirement distributions, adapting to the retirement lifestyle and taking care of a dependent parent or dealing with special health needs.
>
> In addition, the advisor should be prepared to deal with a variety of attitudes on how long the client wants to work, what the client's prospects are for health and longevity, whether the client can be

---

325. Prudential Financial, "Financial Experience & Behaviors Among Women," 2006.
326. "Allianz Women, Money and Power Study," 2006.
327. "Allianz: Women Keen on Finance," National Underwriter Life & Health Online, June 24, 2008.
328. Ibid.

disciplined enough to save for retirement, and to what extent the client accepts investment risk.

For the financial advisor [consultant], the primary responsibility in the "art of financial planning for retirement" is to make clients aware that they are making choices about their retirement every day.[329]

Dreams versus Goals

Many, if not most clients, have vague and nebulous ideas about how they will spend their later years. Discovering, crystallizing and quantifying her goals and, where necessary, distinguishing them from dreams are all important elements of the "art" of retirement planning. As the new paradigm of retirement or third age continues to evolve, financial professionals need to be at the forefront in helping their clients shape their goals accordingly.

According to a Prudential Financial study, almost nine in ten women (86 percent) said that maintaining their lifestyle in retirement was very important. However, just one in five (19 percent) felt confident they would be able to do so.[330] These figures beg the question: Are women setting goals and planning for their third age, or are they just dreaming?

There is a simple "acid test" to determine whether a desired financial outcome is a dream or a goal. It involves a two-part question to ask the client:

1. Are you *willing* to do whatever is necessary to accomplish your goal?

2. Are you *able* to do whatever is necessary to accomplish your goal?

In this context, *willing* means an unwavering commitment to realize the goal, no matter how difficult, how long it takes, or how much personal sacrifice is required. Being *able* means that the client has either current or potential capabilities, talents and resources to achieve her ambitions. Are her aspirations realistic relative to her abilities? For example, assume that Sally, a 69 year old client who cannot carry a tune or play a musical instrument, tells her financial consultant that she wants to be a rock star in her 70s. While Sally may be willing to do whatever is necessary to become a rock star; she does not currently possess the talent required to be successful.

If the client answers "no" to either of the acid test questions, then she is dreaming. Helping her adjust her dreams into goals that can be measured is part of the value that a skilled financial consultant can add. For a retirement (or any) plan to be effective, goals need to be crystal clear, defined and measurable.

---

329. *Foundations of Financial Planning: An Overview*, Chapter 6—Retirement Planning, Worsham, Bruce C., Editor, Copyright © 2009, The American College Press.

330. Prudential Financial, "Financial Experience & Behaviors Among Women," 2006.

SMART Goals

There is a time honored and familiar acronym often used to help people establish goals that can be planned for. It bears recounting here since many, if not most, clients and the public at large, fail to accomplish even this very basic and absolutely essential planning step. SMART goals are:

1. *Specific*—They are clear and unambiguous.

2. *Measurable*—They can be quantified in terms of both their achievement and ongoing progress.

3. *Actionable*—They are goals that can be acted upon.

4. *Realistic*—They are achievable (one is able to do what it takes).

5. *Time-Bound*—There is a specific timeframe set for goal achievement.

With the SMART framework in mind, consultants need to ask the right questions about their client's goals in order to build an effective plan to achieve them.

> "Aging is not 'lost youth' but a new stage of opportunity and strength."
> Source Unknown

Art of Discovery

discovery

For some, retirement is the point in time when work is entirely optional. That is, there are sufficient resources to sustain the client in her chosen lifestyle for the rest of her days—essentially the old retirement paradigm. Others may choose or need to work full or part-time later in life. In his book, *The Power Years*, Dr. Dychtwald predicts that this will be the course chosen or imposed upon most Baby Boomers. Many will "cycle in and out" of the workforce, seeking new careers and new ways to be productive, contributing members of society well into their advanced age. Here are several questions that may be helpful for financial professionals to use when helping the client envision and clarify third age goals:

The Art of Discovery
Her Retirement Goals and Concerns
• What does retirement mean to you?
• What do you see yourself doing in retirement?
• Will you work?
• When would you like to be financially independent—when work is completely optional?
• Will you travel? What should we budget for in your plan?
• What concerns you most about retirement?
• How concerned are you about outliving your assets?
• What might get in the way?
• How could the costs of health care and taxes affect your retirement security?
• Who might you need to take care of—your spouse, parents, children—later in life?
• What have you done so far to secure your retirement? Do you think it will be enough? Would you like to know?

Analyzing Her Retirement Goals

The next important task is determining how much she needs to save in order to achieve her retirement goals. Estimating her financial needs during retirement is like trying to predict the future; such estimates are fraught with complicating factors and clouded by frequently unknown variables. For example, the consultant and client must establish what standard of living is desired during retirement, when retirement will begin, what inflation assumptions should be, and what rates of return can be earned on invested funds. Building sound assumptions are essential at this stage of the process. This means taking an in-depth look at her current financial situation and together determining what will change. Whether or not one envisions a new or old retirement paradigm, there are some common variables to consider and assumptions to develop when analyzing her retirement goals:

- What expenses will increase, decrease, or stay the same?

- When will these expense changes happen?

- What expense items might outpace the general rate of inflation (e.g., health care, taxes)? How will the growth of those line items impact her overall retirement picture?

- How and when will part-time, full time and/or self-employment affect her income?

- When should she claim Social Security benefits?

- How will her assets and liabilities change? Will she pay off a mortgage and/or other debt? If so, how will cash flow be affected and when?

- Will she move and/or downsize, using excess equity in her former residence as a retirement asset?

- How will a long-term care event affect her assets, income and expense streams?

In light of the range of planning complexities, simply plugging in a certain percent of today's income or expenses into a financial calculator will fall far short for the great majority of clients. While many in the media and do-it-yourself websites advocate this method, there are significant dangers in oversimplifying, since formidable risks are often understated, or worse yet, ignored altogether.

To analyze a female client's retirement risks, goals and needs, consultants turn to a range of financial planning software tools to assist in the process. Tools range in complexity and sophistication from basic calculators, to goal-based financial planning software, to cash-flow driven software. More advanced tools include statistical probability testing (most often Monte Carlo modeling) that project the probability of success (i.e., retirement goal achievement) based on multiple trials with a range of select, randomized variables (e.g., rates of investment return and inflation).

Whatever tool the financial professional selects, it is critical that the root assumptions are sound. Otherwise, even with the most sophisticated software, the old adage applies: "garbage in, garbage out." As such, it is important for consultants to spend enough time with clients early in the process to ensure assumptions are realistic and in sufficient detail to incorporate at least those anticipated lifestyle changes that have major economic impact (e.g., sale of a home, long-term care event, stopping/restarting work, and so on). While the tools a consultant uses may be simple and basic, the assumptions should not be. They should realistically and objectively project her current expense and lifestyle realities versus future goals.

SPECIAL PLANNING CONSIDERATIONS FOR WOMEN

Social Security and Women

Social Security

Social Security is especially important to women as they tend to rely on its benefits more, and for a longer period of time, than men do. In light of the complexity of the *Social Security* benefit system, this section highlights only those points that affect women most. It is particularly important that the financial consultant concentrates on the issues surrounding how she becomes eligible for benefits (i.e., worker or survivor, her own earnings or her husband's) and when retirement benefits are taken. If one has not studied Social Security rules and benefits recently, it is well worth a visit to the Social Security website for a refresher (www.ssa.gov).

Lower wages result in smaller Social Security checks for women. In 2007, the monthly retired worker benefit that women received from Social Security averaged $935.20 while men, on average, receive $1,215.70.[331] This is all the more troubling since retired women are more reliant on Social Security than are retired men. Forty four percent of older unmarried women depend on Social Security for at least 90 percent of their income compared to 35 percent of older unmarried men.[332]

Almost two thirds of Social Security beneficiaries over the age of 70 are women. For those 85 and older, almost three out of four beneficiaries are women. Social Security currently replaces 41 percent of income for both male and female retirees. However, dependence on Social Security benefits is much greater for single women—on average replacing 50 percent of income. Further, for 25 percent—one in four—of unmarried women, Social Security is their only source of income.[333]

Despite the importance of Social Security, Americans continue to be relatively unaware of the value of their benefits and the impact that individual choices have on them. For example, in the EBRI 2007 Retirement Confidence survey, only 18 percent of workers were aware of the age at which they can receive full retirement benefits from Social Security without a reduction for early retirement.[334]

---

331. Annual Statistical Supplement 2008, http://www.socialsecurity.gov/policy/docs/statcomps/supplement/2008/5c.pdf
332. National Council of Women's Organizations http://www.now.org/issues/economic/social/012705ncwo.html
333. National Economic Council Interagency Working Group on Social Security, "Women and Retirement Security," www.ssa.gov. October, 1998.
334. Employee Benefit Research Institute, "Retirement Confidence Survey," 2007.

How Are Retirement Benefits Calculated?

Social Security benefits are based on earnings averaged over most of a worker's lifetime. Actual earnings (limited to the taxable wage base) are indexed to account for changes in average wages since the year the earnings were received. Then, average indexed monthly earnings (AIME) are calculated, counting the 35 years in which the woman earned the most. It is important to note that women with fewer than 35 years of wages are penalized as those years with no earnings are credited in the calculation as $0 (zero dollars). Social Security applies a formula to these earnings and arrives at the primary insurance amount (PIA), which is the amount payable at her full retirement age.

Eligibility for Retirement Benefits

A woman can be eligible for retirement benefits from Social Security in a number of ways. The nature and timing of the Social Security benefits she is entitled to depend on her earnings, timing and marital status.

workers benefits

Workers Benefits. She may be eligible based on her own wages. A woman who is fully insured is entitled to receive monthly retirement benefits as early as age 62. Fully insured means that a covered worker has earned 40 credits (formerly referred to as quarters of coverage). A worker earns up to four credits a year if she earns at least $4,360 (in 2009) of wages subject to Social Security taxes. This means that a woman who has years absent from the work force will still be eligible if she works, even part-time, for 10 years or more.

spousal benefits

Spousal Benefits. Today, many retired women are recipients of Social Security benefits through their husbands. This is due to the fact that most of these women were born before 1932 and came of age during the 50s and 60s, prior to many of the advances realized in women's earnings during the second half of the 20th century. As more higher earning women approach retirement age, it is expected that many will shift from collecting a spousal benefit to their own workers benefit.

A married spouse is entitled to a spousal retirement benefit beginning as early as age 62, based on the worker's earnings. The marriage must have lasted one year. A woman's spousal benefit may be paid at any age if she is caring for at least one child of the retired worker, and the child is: (1) under age 16, or (2) disabled and entitled to a child's benefit. Assuming she wishes to make a spousal benefit claim, a woman must wait until the covered worker (for our purposes, the husband) starts receiving benefits.

It is important to note the spousal benefit amount is primarily tied to the spouse's (in this case, wife's) age. At her full retirement age, as a spouse, she can receive 50 percent of her husband's full worker's benefit or primary insurance amount (PIA). Note there is no reduction in her benefit if her husband retired early. As long as she waits until her full retirement age, she will still receive 50 percent of the full benefit that her husband would have received had he waited until his full retirement age. Assuming she is also eligible for her own worker's Social Security benefit, she would get the higher amount of the two.

A divorced woman aged 62 or older may be eligible for spousal benefits as long as she was married 10 years or more (and has not remarried when she submits the claim), and her ex-spouse is eligible for retirement benefits.

Note that while spouses can receive a spousal benefit as early as age 62 or past full retirement age, there is a reduction for collecting early but there is no increase for claiming spousal benefits later than the full retirement age.

survivor benefits

Survivor Benefits. A number of *survivor benefits* can help support women and families if the worker was insured at the time of death (with at least six quarters of coverage). The first is a lump-sum death benefit of $255, payable to a surviving spouse who was living with a deceased worker at the time of his death or, if there is no spouse, to children eligible for monthly benefits. In addition, these two categories of persons become eligible for income benefits as survivors:

- dependent, unmarried children under the same conditions as previously described for retirement benefits

- a spouse (including a divorced spouse) caring for a child or children under the same conditions as previously described for retirement benefits

If the deceased worker was fully insured, the following categories of persons are also eligible for benefits:

- a widow or widower at age 60

- a divorced spouse at age 60, if the marriage lasted at least 10 years

- a parent aged 62 or over who was dependent on the deceased worker at the time of death

It is important to understand that a widow's benefit is based on when her husband began receiving Social Security benefits. There are three basic scenarios that are essential for consultants to be familiar with:

1. The worker waited until his full retirement age to collect benefits; in which case, the widow can receive full benefits.

2. The worker claimed early retirement benefits (at 62, for example), in which case the widow would generally receive a reduced benefit. However, the reduction of the Primary Insurance Amount (PIA) will not fall below 17.5 percent, even if the worker's benefit was reduced more than that.

3. The worker had not taken or deferred his benefits. This alternative allows the widow to take advantage of a higher PIA, either through her

husband's deferral (if he had taken benefits later than full retirement age), or through her own deferral (if he had not yet claimed benefits).

The point here is that the worker's decision regarding the timing of retirement benefits has a significant impact on what is paid to survivors. If the husband takes an earlier retirement benefit, she might well be penalized for a long time if she survives him, particularly in light of her greater life expectancy. Remarriage can also have an effect on benefits. The benefit to a surviving spouse terminates upon remarriage unless she remarries after age 60.

dual benefits

Eligibility for Dual Benefits. In many cases, a woman is eligible for more than one type of Social Security benefit. According to the Social Security Administration in 2008, 28 percent of American women over 62 were eligible for dual benefits, and that percentage is steadily increasing.[335] The most common situation occurs when a woman is eligible for both her husband's benefit and a retirement benefit based on her own Social Security record. In this case and in any other case when a woman is eligible for dual benefits, only an amount equal to the higher benefit is paid. Another common situation is if a woman's husband dies and she became eligible for a survivor benefit, and was also eligible for a retirement benefit based on her own wages.

Early and Late Retirement. Full retirement benefits (for the worker, 100 percent of the PIA) are payable at the participant's full retirement age. Full retirement age (FRA) depends on the individual's year of birth. For women born between 1943 and 1954, it is age 66. FRA gradually increases from 66 in a series of two month increments to age 67 for workers born after 1960. Persons can retire as early as age 62, but the monthly benefit is permanently reduced. (The spousal benefit is subject to a different reduction.)

Workers who delay applying for retirement benefits until after attaining full retirement age are eligible for an increased benefit. For persons born in 1943 or later, the increase is 8 percent for each year of delay up to age 70. There is no advantage to deferring retirement benefits until after age 70. Considering their longer life expectancies, this is an important planning consideration for women; not only because of the increase due to deferral, but also the potential to increase Primary Insurance Amount (PIA) as a result of possibly higher income in later years and adding more quarters worked. Since women frequently take time out of work for care giving, this can be particularly important if there were less than 35 years of wages. Deferral potentially provides her with an opportunity to catch up.

The chart below illustrates the impact of timing on benefit amounts for a worker reaching full retirement age at 66.

---

335. Social Security Administration, Fast Facts & Figures About Social Security, 2009

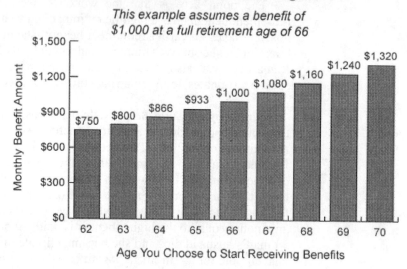

Source: Social Security Website, www.ssa.gov

Electing when to begin retirement benefits is a difficult and crucial decision that can have a major impact on a woman's retirement security. While there has been an industry guideline breakeven age for longevity—usually age 77 and 78—using this figure can be deceptive, even dangerous, for women. Benefit and breakeven ages are based on unisex tables, which do not account for women's greater life expectancy. Consider this example:

Example

Edna, is single aged 60 and in good health. She has accumulated $200,000 in her 401(k) plan. Edna has been thinking about taking her Social Security retirement benefits at age 62, even though her full retirement age is 66. She has a home with a small mortgage, which she plans to stay in after retirement. Her Social Security statement shows her full retirement benefit to be $1,200 a month. If Edna takes the benefit at 62, she will receive $900 a month. If she waits until age 67 to receive benefits based on this estimate, she will receive almost $1,300 a month (probably a bit more, assuming her compensation continues to increase). This is a $400 a month difference—almost $5,000 a year. Remember, too, that Social Security benefits increase with cost-of-living increases each year.

Edna has an important decision to make.

The bottom line: simply relying on the Social Security benefit statement of projected benefits (as many in the public do) is inadequate when planning for a decision that will have decades of ramifications associated with it. Deciding when and how to take Social Security benefits is the single most important retirement planning decision many women make. To assist consultants and their clients in this task, the Social Security website has a wealth of information, as well as calculator tools to analyze different timing and benefit scenarios.

Employer-Sponsored Qualified Plans and Women

employer-sponsored qualified plans

In addition to understanding the mechanics of Social Security benefits, financial professionals must also be well grounded in *employer-sponsored qualified plans*, and how they relate to women. As mentioned earlier, women have generally lower participation and less accumulated in workplace retirement plans than men do.

What can be done about these gaps? First and foremost, women need to be educated about employer-sponsored retirement plans and take advantage of opportunities to participate when they are available. They must also evaluate retirement plan benefits when making decisions about which job to accept, whether to change jobs, or whether to leave the workforce for a period of time. Married women need to know about their own plans, as well as their spouse's benefits. Women who are not covered by an employer plan must be familiar with individual retirement plan options, or how to establish their own retirement plan if they are self-employed.

Defined-Contribution Plans

defined-contribution plans

All plans classified as *defined-contribution plans*, as well as SEPs, SIMPLEs, and 403(b) plans, pay out a benefit based on an accumulated account balance, which makes for a very simple accumulation vehicle. Defined-contribution benefits are portable; thus, if a woman changes jobs, she does not have to interrupt retirement savings. As long as the participant is vested when she terminates employment, benefits can remain in the old plan, or rolled into an IRA or a new employer's plan.

The downside is that the long-term value of the retirement benefit is unpredictable because the account depends on the amount of contributions and investment return. Participation over a long period of time (starting early), good investment return, and avoidance of preretirement loans and distributions will all have a positive impact on the overall value. Even so, they are still somewhat unpredictable, and the fluctuation in value as the market changes can be unnerving.

While each woman's situation and needs are different, here are basic considerations to take into account with regard to defined-contributions plans:

- participate early—especially for women who are often in and out of the workforce

- "snatch the match"—meaning contribute at least up to the employer's matching amount, all the more important for women who need to stretch resources further

- understand the impact of termination on the participant's benefits

- select the right investments for the situation and risk tolerance

- do not cash out of plan dollars when leaving an employer

Defined Benefit Plans

defined benefit plans

From a planning perspective, defined-benefit plans generally provide a predictable retirement income benefit that replaces a specified percentage of employment compensation. It can be the foundation of a woman's retirement planning strategy. However, defined-benefit plans can be problematic for women who do not stay with the same employer for a long time. Benefits tend to grow more rapidly at the end of a participant's career, as increasing salary and service cause the benefits to increase. Because benefits do not accrue evenly over time, they can provide inadequate benefits for women who change jobs, cycle out of the workforce for care giving, or retire early. To illustrate this discrepancy, consider that among current retired workers, just about half of men over 65 receive some sort of pension, while less than one-third of women do.[336]

Terminating Employment

Too often, employees, especially women, quit work, transfer to another job, or interrupt their work lives just short of the time required to become vested in a plan. With defined-benefit plans, it is common to require 5 years of service before an individual is entitled to benefits. Under the Pension Protection Act, defined-contribution plans, which cover the bulk of employees, must fully vest employees with 3 years of service unless the plan uses graded vesting; in which case, the participant must be gradually vested over 6 years of service. All types of employee contributions (including 401(k) salary deferrals) must be fully vested at all times. In 401(k) plans, both profit sharing and matching contributions can be subject to a vesting schedule (unless they are 401(k)

---

336. "Workforce Management," www.wachovia.com, January 2005, (data cited from Social Security Administration, August 2004).

safe harbor contributions). This can have an impact on whether a short-term participant elects to make salary deferral contributions.

Death Benefits

Death benefits from an employer-sponsored qualified plan can be an important part of the retirement picture for a married couple. It is imperative that a married woman understand her own plan's provisions, as well as the provisions of her husband's plan. Retirement plans may offer pre-retirement or post-retirement death benefits. ERISA has a required minimum pre-retirement death benefit for married participants that must be paid to the spouse, unless both the participant and spouse agree otherwise. Defined-benefit plans often provide a minimum required benefit. Defined-contribution plans often pay out the entire account balance to the participant's beneficiaries.

Whether there are any post-retirement death benefits depends on the form of payment the participant elects. With a life annuity, payments cease at the death of the participant. With a 50 percent joint and survivor annuity, 50 percent of the benefit is payable to the surviving beneficiary.

If a married woman either has no pension (or the smaller pension in the family), having her spouse choose an annuity that does not provide a survivor benefit can be devastating to her long-term financial well-being. ERISA requires that the normal form of payment from many retirement plan pensions is a joint and survivor annuity, and both the participant and the spouse have to give up these rights to receive an alternate form of payment. Unfortunately, many spouses waive their rights to the joint annuity without fully understanding the impact of that decision. If their husbands receive a single life annuity, the payments will be slightly higher, but payments stop when the husband dies—often leaving the wife without any pension.

Rollovers

Assuming she will be in a tax bracket at retirement that is equal to or lower than her current bracket, the best way for many women to maximize the value of tax-advantaged plans is to defer taxes as long as possible (until benefits are consumed). The law accommodates this strategy by allowing a rollover of most distributions from a qualified retirement plan into an IRA or other tax-advantaged plan.

A married woman can generally roll a benefit from any tax-advantaged plan she inherits from her husband to her own IRA. She can leave it in her husband's name or retitle the account. Retitling the account is often one of the best choices because of the required minimum distribution rules, but it may not be the right choice for a woman who has not yet attained age 59½. In this case, she should generally leave the IRA in her husband's name so that any distributions are considered death benefits and not subject to the 10 percent early withdrawal penalty tax.

When the benefit is inherited from anyone other than a spouse, the rules are different. If an IRA is inherited, it must stay in the name of the decedent and is generally referred to as an inherited IRA. Under the minimum distribution rules, inherited IRAs must generally be withdrawn more quickly than an IRA in the individual's own name. For example, if a 50 year old woman inherits an IRA from one of her parents, required distributions must begin in the year following death. Nonspouse death beneficiaries are allowed to roll distributions from a qualified plan, 403(b) plan, or government-sponsored 457 plan into an inherited IRA.

Tax Treatment

If a participant does not roll benefits into another plan, the distributions will be subject to tax. In most cases, the full value of benefits distributed to a participant is taxed as ordinary income. Distributions to participants under age 59½ may also be subject to an early withdrawal penalty.

Note that the tax treatment for Roth IRAs and Roth 401(k) and 403(b) accounts (discussed below) is quite different from the treatment for pre-tax plans. As long as certain eligibility requirements are satisfied, distributions from Roth IRAs and Roth 401(k) and 403(b) accounts are tax free.

Individual Retirement Plans

Traditional IRAs

traditional IRAs

Workers under age 70½ who do not participate in an employer-sponsored retirement plan are allowed to make deductible contributions to a traditional IRA. Contributions are usually deductible if the individual does not participate in an employer-sponsored retirement plan. Even if a deduction is not allowed, nondeductible contributions can be made with employment income for any person under age 70½. IRAs also act as a rollover vehicle. As women change jobs or retire, benefits can be rolled over into an IRA without limits. An IRA can be established with a custodial account or trust or with an annuity contract.

Roth IRAs and Designated Roth Contributions (DRCs)

Roth IRAs

Roth IRA contributions are not deductible, but qualified distributions are tax free. Eligibility for Roth IRA contributions depends only on income. This means that many women who participate in an employer-sponsored retirement plan can also take advantage of the Roth IRA, as long as their adjusted gross income (AGI) is below a specified limit.

A Roth IRA can also be created through a conversion from a traditional IRA. Converting a traditional IRA to a Roth IRA results in taxable income, but future growth can be eligible for tax-free treatment. As of this writing, to be eligible, a taxpayer (single or married) must have an adjusted gross income of $100,000 or less. This income cap is scheduled to disappear in 2010, allowing all taxpayers the option to convert. If it is likely she will be in a higher tax bracket during retirement, converting a traditional IRA to a Roth IRA (and paying associated income taxes) is a strategy worth considering.

A third way a woman can take advantage of the Roth IRA tax-free payout is with the designated Roth contribution election in a 401(k) or 403(b) plan. The employer may (but does not have to) offer participants the option to have some or all of their pretax salary deferral contributions treated as Designated Roth Contributions (DRCs). As long as certain requirements are satisfied, DRCs will be eligible for tax-free treatment. DRCs have no income phaseout rules, meaning that taxpayers of all income levels can take advantage of this opportunity. In most cases, DRCs may also be rolled into Roth IRAs after termination of employment.

Self-Employed Women

SEP

The self-employed (or incorporated) woman has many different options for saving on a tax-deferred basis. This is important, considering that one out of every 11 working women owns her own business. For those with a limited ability to save, the traditional IRA or Roth IRA may be sufficient. However, there are many other options for saving more. Self-employed women can establish the same retirement plans as a corporation, including an SEP, profit-sharing plan, and a 401(k) plan. These plans can be an important consideration for the woman who is looking to save aggressively as she nears retirement. They may also work well for a married woman who is employed part-time and has limited income in relation to the family's overall income, as well as for the couple who is looking to save all or part of the woman's income.

For the older professional woman who hasn't saved enough for retirement, a defined-benefit plan may be a way for her to save significant money over a short period of time.

Investing In Retirement

Essentially, there are two phases of investing for retirement: accumulation and distribution. Most clients and many financial consultants are familiar with investing for deferred goals, or accumulation. Far fewer are well-versed in putting together sound investment strategies for the distribution phase.

Investing in retirement presents a new risk/return paradigm. The female client is no longer investing for growth, but for lifelong income—balancing the need for immediate, secure income with growth and inflation offset for later years. Increasingly, her risk becomes longevity and along with it, running out of assets.

Recently there has been growing popularity of products and tools related to retirement income distribution, as well as an emergence of significant research on retirement income and withdrawal rates. Many experts agree that annuities should play at least some role in a woman's retirement plan by providing a minimum "floor" of guaranteed income. Laddering annuities and/or creating multiple portfolios (or "buckets") for different retirement phases are increasingly common strategies.

Financial consultants need to analyze how much income is needed and when. In addition, one must project how these income needs may change over decades, including the impact of inflation, changing lifestyles and her longevity. Considering the wide range of factors to consider with retirement income distribution, the best financial consultants are indeed both artists and scientists in this regard.

Financial Planner:	"It doesn't look like you're saving anything for the future!"
Cop:	"Well, you know how it is with cops. I'll be shot three days before retirement. In the business, we call it "retirony"."
Financial Planner:	"But, what if you don't get shot?"
Cop:	"What a terrible thing to say! Oh, look! You made my wife cry!"

The Simpsons, Matt Groenig, Creator

ESTATE PLANNING AND WOMEN

Regardless of their life-stage or status, women should be proactive in planning and protecting their estates. Although every situation is unique, there are some common estate planning concerns that affect a woman and her family.

Estate planning is a discipline that protects the resources and values she has spent a lifetime accumulating. As with other areas in the financial planning pyramid, estate planning involves reducing the risks of unnecessary financial loss as a result of life events. Planning her estate is primarily focused on helping her live confidently and well.

"Living benefits" associated with what is commonly called estate planning are the joy and satisfaction the client experiences when able to pass on her possessions or values, as well as the dignity she preserves when her wishes are carried out. To encourage a woman to develop her own estate plan, financial consultants should highlight some of the living benefits of estate planning:

- She can name the beneficiaries she wants to receive her assets.

- She can rely on the fact that her wishes will be carried out under law.

Women and Their Health—Durable Powers of Attorney and Living Wills

Because women tend to live longer than men, an important part of a woman's estate plan can be the instructions that she provides for managing her affairs, including health care, if she becomes incapacitated. Two important tools that women can consider are the durable power of attorney and living will.

Durable Powers of Attorney

durable powers of attorney

According to a recent AARP study, *durable powers of attorney* had been executed by 45 percent of AARP members over age 50 and by 70 percent of those of age 70.[337] However, only 27 percent of all adult Americans have created powers of attorney for health care, and 69 percent of Americans have no living will or medical directive.[338]

Any adult can give a power of attorney to another person as legal permission to conduct business. However, a regular power of attorney is invalid if the giver becomes incapacitated. A durable power includes instructions stating that it will remain in effect during a period of incapacity. Since a power of attorney (including durable) cannot be executed by an incapacitated person, it is essential to draft the power before the incapacity.

In some cases, the power can be written to take effect ("spring") in the event of incapacity. A power of attorney may be defined narrowly (e.g., permission to sign checks on one bank account) or broadly (e.g., permission to manage all of her financial affairs). In either case, it is important to make sure that the financial institutions involved will honor it. Banks and brokerage firms are not required to accept powers that do not conform to their standards.

Living Wills

living wills

In recent years, many people have become aware of the need to plan for the end of life. A *living will* is a legal document that addresses a woman's desires for medical treatment if she is unable to provide instructions. It typically describes the types of medical treatment she wishes to receive and chooses not to receive. Most often, living wills are used to reject extraordinary measures to extend life, such as intravenous feeding and mechanical respirators, in cases when death appears imminent.

The purpose of a living will is to let others know of a woman's medical wishes if she becomes terminally ill or goes into a vegetative state and is unable to communicate. It authorizes a doctor to withhold or withdraw life support under certain conditions. Because it is a legal document, it must meet the requirements of the jurisdiction in which it is applicable.

The living will indicates informed consent to withhold food, water, or medications if they are used only to prolong terminal illness of an incapacitated individual. Each state has different laws and regulations that determine the application of these wills. Even so, most people feel that it is better to have a living will in place than to have no instructions at all.

---

337. AARP Research Group Study: Where There Is a Will, 2000.
338. Omnibus Study conducted by Harris Interactive for LexisNexis Martindale-Hubbell, April 2004.

> **Living Wills—Five Wishes**
>
> *Five Wishes* advance directive gives you a way to control something very important-how you are treated if you become seriously ill. It was written with the help of the American Bar Association's Commission on Law and Aging.
>
> *Five Wishes* lets your family and doctors know:
>
> - Who you want to make health care decisions for you when you can't make them.
> - The kind of medical treatment you want or don't want.
> - How comfortable you want to be.
> - How you want people to treat you.
> - What you want your loved ones to know.
>
> *Five Wishes* is changing the way America talks about and plans for care at the end of life. More than 12 million copies of *Five Wishes* are in circulation across the nation, distributed by more than 15,000 organizations. *Five Wishes* meets the legal requirements in 40 states and is useful in all 50.
>
> *Five Wishes* has become America's most popular living will because it is written in everyday language and helps start and structure important conversations about care in times of serious illness.
>
> *Five Wishes* was introduced in 1997 and originally distributed with support from a grant by The Robert Wood Johnson Foundation, the nation's largest philanthropy devoted exclusively to health and health care. With assistance from the United Health Foundation, *Five Wishes* is now available in 23 languages.

Health Care Proxy or Medical Power of Attorney

health care proxy
medical power of attorney

Although a living will makes a person's medical treatment wishes known, it does not guarantee that these wishes will be followed. Someone still has to make the necessary decisions about whether or not to continue treatment—a difficult, emotional decision. Sometimes close relatives are reluctant to let their loved one die. A *health care proxy* or *medical power of attorney* form is a signed (declared) and witnessed legal document. This document legally grants an agent, usually a close family member, the authority to act for the declarant and in the declarant's best interests in a medical context. The health care proxy goes into effect when the person is no longer able to make health care decisions. Sometimes the proxy is incorporated in a medical power of attorney.

Whatever type of health care directive she chooses, the chances of her wishes being followed are increased by also naming a health care agent to advocate on her behalf. The financial consultant should advise her that must choose health care agents carefully, naming a person whom she can completely trust. Executing these documents and naming a health care agent can spare loved ones the anguish of having to make difficult decisions in the absence of personal directives.

Financial consultants should encourage their female clients, regardless of their age, to work with a qualified estate attorney to execute documents required for durable powers of attorney, a living will, and a health care proxy. The benefits of having these important legal documents in place prior to incapacitation provide tremendous peace of mind for the client and for her family.

Women and Their Wealth—Transfers of Her Property

It is well acknowledged that in the coming years, there will be a significant transfer of inherited wealth in this country. Two Cornell University professors, Robert Avery and Michael Rendall, conducted a comprehensive study of the U.S. wealth transfer market. They concluded that the Baby Boom generation will receive total inheritances worth $10.4 trillion over a 55-year period.[339] In a similar study, two researchers at Boston College, John J. Havens and Paul G. Schervish, sought to determine the value of all wealth transfers projected over a 55-year period, including transfers to Boomers and younger generations. They arrived at total projected wealth transfers of $41 trillion. While the gap between $10.4 trillion and $41 trillion is fairly large, either number indicates the greatest generational transfer of wealth in history.[340]

Since women control significant wealth, it is important to answer these two key questions: (1) What do the terms estate planning and philanthropy mean? and, (2) Why do women need professional help with both? As context, consider these facts:

- The average millionaire woman's estate is worth $2.5 million.[341]

- Of all estates over $5 million, 48 percent are controlled by women.[342]

- In a review of estates at death, the IRS revealed that one in five women millionaires were educators. In general, educators tend to be steady savers and prudent investors with frugal lifestyles.[343]

- Affluent women are generous; 7 percent of their income is donated to charity versus 2 percent for the U.S. population as a whole.[344]

---

339. Robert B. Avery, and Michael S. Rendell, Estimating the Size and Distribution of the Baby Boomers' Prospective Inheritances, Cornell University, 1993.
340. Paul G. Schervish and John J. Havens, "Millionaires and the Millennium: New Estimates of the Forthcoming Wealth Transfer and the Prospects for a Golden Age of Philanthropy," Boston College Social Welfare Research Institute, February 2000.
341. Stanley, Thomas J., *The Millionaire Women Next Door: The Many Journeys of Successful American Businesswomen*, Andrew McMeel Publishing, 2004.
342. Ibid.
343. Ibid.
344. Ibid.

- Sixty-three percent of dollars bequeathed to charity were given by women, and 22.1 percent of women made donations compared with 12.6 percent of men.[345]

Brief Definitions of Estate Planning and Philanthropy

estate planning

Estate planning is a process that focuses mainly on two areas: (1) settlement of the estate, and (2) an orderly transfer of assets during an individual's life or after death.

A probate estate is created at the moment of death for the purpose of settling affairs, paying debts, distributing assets, and meeting income and estate tax obligations. The individual charged with managing the affairs of a probate estate is either an executor or administrator. An executor is usually designated in a person's will; an estate administrator is appointed by the probate court to perform the same duties.

The second part of the process involves the orderly transfer of assets. Estate planning can address effective ways to transfer assets during an individual's life. This can help to accomplish personal goals while reducing both income taxes and estate taxes.

philanthropy

Philanthropy is a desire to benefit others by giving of the individual's time, effort, or assets. Giving property or money to charity is a common form of philanthropy. Many women traditionally have donated time and talents to support worthwhile charitable causes, and such "gifts of oneself" represent meaningful philanthropic activities. While we will briefly touch on points related to philanthropy and charitable giving, due to their scope and complexity, a more detailed discussion is out of range for our purposes.

Why Women Need Professional Help with Estate Planning and Philanthropy

Women of all ages participate in casual activities of estate planning and philanthropy. Examples include:

- joining local civic or charitable groups and donating time or money

- completing beneficiary designations on bank accounts, life insurance or brokerage accounts

- writing a simple will

These activities are not very complex or time consuming, and they may not require extensive professional help. For example, in many communities, people can write simple wills inexpensively, using template documents or software. Two motivators cause women (and men) to move from these casual

---

345. McGranahan, Leslie, The Widow's Offering: Inheritance, Family Structure, and the Charitable Gifts of Women (November 2007). FRB of Chicago Working Paper No. 2007-18.

activities to estate planning/philanthropy services that require more extensive professional help. When financial consultants identify these motivators, there are opportunities to develop comprehensive estate planning cases:

- *Motivator #1:* A woman recognizes that she has assets that she may not need to support herself during her own lifetime.

- *Motivator #2:* A woman has a strong desire to use excess personal assets in self-directed ways to help others.

Goals of Estate Planning

Education about estate planning can be a lifelong process. Women generally become candidates for a professionally assisted estate planning process as they approach retirement and believe they may have adequate financial resources to support themselves for the rest of their lives. What goals can the estate planning process help a woman achieve?

- It can help her to organize and plan her personal affairs so that her loved ones won't have to spend months trying to track down assets, debts, and important documents.

- For a married woman, the process can reassure her that her spouse or any dependent child who survives her will be cared for.

- It can reduce the estate settlement costs and taxes that might otherwise erode assets that would be available for her heirs.

- It can provide liquidity to her estate so that her heirs will not have to sell property at potentially reduced values to pay estate settlement costs.

- By avoiding or reducing the public probate process, estate planning can protect the privacy of bequests and transactions.

- Property is efficiently distributed according to the wishes of the decedent, preventing delays and family friction.

- It can reward her favorite charity or help her maintain continuity in managing her business or other assets.

To help uncover the client's goals for her legacy, consider these questions:

The Art of Discovery
Her Legacy
• What do you know about how federal laws and those of the state of ____ affect your estate? • What values would you like to make sure that you pass on to your family? • What are your plans to pass assets to your family, charity, or both? • What have you done so far to ensure your legacy plans are carried out? • How do you feel about income and estate taxes associated with passing on assets to your heirs? • Do you have a will or trust? When were your documents drawn up? • Do you own property in another state? • There are only three beneficiary options for your estate: your loved ones, charity and the government. Who would receive your assets if you were to meet your maker today? • What plans have you made should you become incapacitated? • Who is your attorney? Would it be alright for me to contact him/her to discuss your financial plan? (You may suggest that the client call the attorney first.)

As the financial consultant seeks to understand the client's objectives during the discovery step of the process, it is also important to review how assets are titled and asset ownership implications on her overall estate plan.

Estate Planning and Property Ownership

property transfers at death
One of the most essential concepts in estate planning deals with the major forms of property ownership and how they pass differently when one dies. Knowledge of how *property transfers at death* under the laws of the jurisdictional state is necessary to plan an estate. A common misconception is that the client's will determines the distribution of the estate at her death. Under most circumstances, the will usually affects the distribution of only a small portion of a client's property. This fact does not minimize the importance of a carefully drafted will, but merely emphasizes the importance of coordinating all of the client's testamentary transfers, including those affected by her will, in the estate and financial planning process. Here is a list of forms of property

ownership and whether they pass through the probate process (as determined at the state level).

Property Transfers at Death

Probate estate:
 	
 • Fee simple ownership
 • Nonterminating ownership interests (certain life estates, term interests, future interests, beneficial interests, and powers that do not terminate at the client's death)
 • Tenancy in common
 	
 Nonprobate estate:
 	
 • Transfers by operation of law
   – Joint tenancy with right of survivorship
   – Tenancy by the entirety
   – Community property (in community property states)
   – Living trusts
   – Totten trusts
 • Transfers by operation of contract
   – Life insurance proceeds payable to a named beneficiary (rather than to the client's estate or executor)
   – Retirement plan death benefits payable to a named beneficiary
   – Payable at death investment accounts

Source: *Foundations of Financial Planning: An Overview*, Chapter 6: Estate Planning, Worsham, Bruce C., Editor, Copyright © 2009, The American College Press

What Is Included In Her Estate?

Each woman's probate estate includes property that she owned outright in her name, plus half of all property she owned jointly with her spouse or some proportion of property she owned jointly with another person. Estates commonly include bank accounts, brokerage accounts, and the fair market value of real estate and tangible property, such as cars and collectibles. Also, the death benefits of any life insurance policies that the deceased owned are included in the estate, as is the full value of IRAs and retirement plans.

The values of all these properties are totaled, and this defines the amount of the gross estate that potentially can be distributed to heirs. However, significant costs can reduce the size of the estate before assets pass to heirs. These costs include:

- debts and mortgages
- funeral bills
- medical bills

- probate expenses
- state death and inheritance taxes
- federal estate taxes
- income taxes on some assets that beneficiaries receive (e.g., Income in Respect of the Decedent [IRD] assets)

Heirs stand in line behind all of the above to receive their share of the estate. In effect, they get whatever is left, and unless a woman plans her estate well, they may receive much less than anyone imagined. Estate planning helps to anticipate these costs and reduce or fund them. When assets are removed from the estate prior to death, taxes and other costs can be significantly reduced. When life insurance is included in the estate plan, taxes and other costs can be paid directly from proceeds, allowing more of the gross estate to pass to heirs.

Some types of property are included in the gross estate, even if they pass outside of the will and probate. They include: (1) property owned jointly with right of survivorship, which passes automatically to the remaining joint owner(s); (2) life insurance proceeds, which are paid directly to the named beneficiary outside of probate; (3) retirement plan accounts with named beneficiaries; and (4) accounts with a payable-on-death provision, which pass directly to the individual named.

Taxes Assessed on Transfers of Her Wealth

The most significant costs of transferring wealth are the various transfer taxes imposed at the federal and state levels. The tax rates applicable to affected transfers can be quite high. The relatively large impact of these transfer taxes makes tax reduction a primary focus in the estate and financial plan with respect to the conservation of her wealth. By optimizing solutions to "who," "how" and "when" questions, the client may be able to implement a plan that will achieve her stated goals and keep erosion of her estate to a minimum.

Federal Transfer Taxes

The federal transfer tax system consists of three components—gift taxation, estate taxation and generation-skipping taxation. Two of these components, the gift tax and the estate tax, are unified in that they share one progressive set of tax rates.

federal estate taxes

Estate Taxes. In the past, Congress has created laws that are a compromise between some lawmakers who wanted to eliminate the federal estate tax altogether and others who wanted to retain it. This compromise provided temporary relief from the estate tax without repealing the tax. Most believe the best way to plan for the future is to assume that there will be some form of federal estate tax, but that the tax rates and unified exemption amounts will be uncertain and subject to change. One should encourage female clients to plan conservatively, which often means assuming that at least part of their estate may be subject to some tax. In addition, it is extremely important to review and/or remind clients to review and update their estate plans regularly.

For federal estate tax purposes, in 2009, the schedule below reflects how the decedents total estate is calculated.

			CHART FOR COMPUTING FEDERAL ESTATE TAX		
	STEP 1	(1)	Gross estate		$_____
minus		(2)	Funeral and administration expenses (estimated as _____ % of _____	$_____	
		(3)	Debts and taxes	_____	
		(4)	Losses	_____	(−)_____
equals	STEP 2	(5)	Adjusted gross estate		$_____
minus		(6)	Marital deduction	$_____	
		(7)	Charitable deduction	_____	
		(8)	State death tax deduction[1]	_____	(−)_____
equals	STEP 3	(9)	Taxable estate		$_____
plus		(10)	Adjusted taxable gifts (taxable portion of post-1976 lifetime taxable transfers not included in gross estate)		+_____
equals		(11)	Tentative tax base (total of taxable estate and adjusted taxable gifts)		$_____
compute		(12)	Tentative tax		$_____
minus		(13)	Gift taxes payable on post-1976 gifts[2]		(−)_____
equals	STEP 4	(14)	Estate tax payable before credits		$_____
minus		(15)	Tax credits		
		(a)	Applicable credit amount	$_____	
		(b)	Allowable state death tax credit[3]	_____	
		(c)	Credit for foreign death taxes[4]	_____	
		(d)	Credit for gift tax for pre-1977 gifts[5]	_____	
		(e)	Credit for tax on prior transfers	_____	(−)_____
equals	STEP 5	(16)	Net federal estate tax payable		$_____

1. 2005 through 2009 (replaces Step 4(15)(b)).
2. Once the tentative tax is determined, gift taxes generated by taxable gifts made after 1976 in excess of the applicable credit amount are subtracted from it.
3. Reduced by 25 percent in 2002, 50 percent in 2003, and 75 percent in 2004; repealed in 2005 and replaced with a deduction in 2005 through 2009 as shown in Step 2(8).
4. Irrelevant credit for calculation purposes in this course.
5. Credit still exists for gift taxes paid by a deceased on taxable gifts made before 1977 if the property is included in the gross estate. Irrelevant credit for calculation purposes in this course.

Source: *Foundations of Financial Planning: An Overview*, Chapter 6-Estate Planning, Worsham, Bruce C., Editor, Copyright © 2009, The American College Press

federal gift taxes

Gift Taxes. The federal gift tax applies only if the following two elements are present:

- There is a completed transfer and acceptance of the property.

- The transfer of the property is for less than full and adequate consideration.

These two essential elements of a taxable gift are based on several facts. First, only property transfers are subject to gift taxation. A transfer of services by a client is not a taxable gift. Second, all completed transfers, including direct and indirect gifts of property are taxable. Finally, for transfer tax purposes, the less than full and adequate consideration requirement generally does not contain an element of intent. Therefore it is not necessary that the grantor intends to make a gift. It is merely required that the transfer be for less than full and adequate consideration.

Much of the design and complexity involved in gift tax planning relates to the gift tax annual exclusion. In 2009, qualifying gifts of up to $13,000 (indexed for inflation beginning in 1999) may be made by a donor to each of any number of donees without gift tax. The annual exclusion was instituted to eliminate the need for a taxpayer donor to keep an account of or report numerous small gifts. Moreover, the $13,000 exempt amount can be increased to $26,000 (also indexed) if the donor is married and the donor's spouse elects to split the gift with the donor. In other words, $13,000 can be given per donor, per donee, per year.

Federal Gift and Estate Tax Credit and Exclusion Amounts Schedule		
Year	Applicable Credit Amount	Applicable Exclusion Amount (Size of Estate Sheltered)
1982	$ 62,800	$ 225,000
1983	79,300	275,000
1984	96,300	325,000
1985	121,800	400,000
1986	155,800	500,000
1987 to 1998	192,800	600,000
1998	202,050	625,000
1999	211,300	650,000
2000 and 2001	220,550	675,000
2002 and 2003	345,800	1,000,000
2004 and 2005	555,800	1,500,000
2006, 2007, and 2008	780,800	2,000,000
2009	1,455,800	3,500,000

Source: *Foundations of Financial Planning: An Overview*, Chapter 6-Estate Planning, Worsham, Bruce C., Editor, Copyright © 2009, The American College Press

Amounts exceeding the annual gift tax exclusion are deducted from the cumulative credit available in the year of the donor's death. The table above reflects the applicable credit for estate and gift tax imposed on transfers of property, and how it has changed from 1982 to 2009.

Intergenerational Wealth Transfer Strategies

intergenerational wealth transfer

By 2010, there will be approximately 80 million grandparents in the U.S. and they will spend $30 billion per year to support their grandchildren.[346] The term *intergenerational wealth transfer* encompasses several techniques for passing financial resources to younger generations such as the following:

- lifetime gifts
- college funding programs (e.g., UGMA, UTMA, 529 accounts)
- revocable living trusts
- irrevocable life insurance trusts

Here are possible family wealth transfer strategies that can address a woman's needs during her lifetime and beyond.

Lifetime Gifts

lifetime gifts

A gift made while the donor is alive (that is, a lifetime gift) is a way to help a child or grandchild now, when the donor is needed and appreciated. Moreover, the giver can receive the reward of supporting a worthwhile cause. A lifetime gift removes assets (and the potential future growth in the value of those assets) from the giver's taxable estate. Under U.S. tax law, if the gift is of appreciated property—such as low-cost-basis stocks—the donor is not responsible for paying the capital gains tax on the increase in value. The donee generally will pay this tax when the assets are sold, using the tax basis of the donor.

Beyond the annual gift tax exclusion mentioned above, each person may make lifetime taxable gifts worth $1 million before any federal gift tax is due.

Example

Helen and Dan own $115,000 in investments—mostly stock that they bought many years ago. If they sell those stocks and give their grandchildren money, they will owe a substantial capital gains tax. By giving the grandchildren the stocks, however, they can avoid paying this tax. The children will pay the capital gains when the stocks are sold, perhaps at a lower tax rate. Each of the spouses could give each of their nine grandchildren up to $13,000 in stocks per year without any federal gift

---

346. AARP Special Study, 2002.

tax consequences. In addition, Dan and Helen can both give a total of $1 million in his or her lifetime without any federal gift tax consequences.

There are other options for Helen. She can give cash to her grandchildren and capable financial consultants can advise her how to structure her gifts (e.g., creating a trust or trusts) so that each grandchild does not have access to the money while he or she is still too immature to manage it wisely. She could also set up UTMA/UGMA (Unified Transfer to Minors Act or Unified Gift to Minors Act) accounts, depending on her state of residence and the family situation.

Since grandparents frequently wish to support their grandchildren's higher education, here are some popular strategies that financial consultants could explain to them:

Savings Plans for College and Educational Gifts. Only 28 percent of women claim they are "very confident" that they will have the resources to send their children to college, and only 35 percent are "somewhat confident."[347] The average student's average debt load upon graduation has increased to just under $20,000, from roughly half that amount a decade ago.[348] As such, grandparents with sufficient financial means can greatly benefit both their children and grandchildren by making contributions to offset educational expenses.

The three most common forms of educational funding vehicles are:

- Coverdell Savings Accounts (CESAs)
- 529 Savings Plans
- direct tuition gifts

Coverdell Education Savings Accounts

Coverdell Education Savings Accounts. CESAs are trust or custodial accounts set up to pay education expenses of the child-beneficiary of the account. Currently, annual contributions are subject to contributor adjusted gross income limitations, made with after-tax dollars, and limited to $2,000. Earnings grow tax deferred, and withdrawals made for qualified education expenses are income tax free.

529 Savings Plans

529 Savings Plans. Annual exclusion gifts may be made to these accounts. Under federal tax law, donors may contribute up to 5 years' worth of annual exclusions (at $13,000 per year, this equals $65,000 in total) to a 529 Savings Plan for a beneficiary in one year.

Example   In 2009, Katherine can contribute $65,000 to a 529 savings plan for each of her grandchildren. If her

---

347. Marti Barletta, Marketing to Women (2nd ed.).
348. American Council on Education, as quoted in The Wall Street Journal, March 29, 2007.

husband, Jim, does the same, the couple can contribute $130,000 per grandchild. Funds grow tax deferred, and distributions used for qualified higher education expenses are federal income tax free. If Katherine and Jim start contributing to a 529 plan today while their grandchildren are very young, they will be getting a significant head start toward college funding.

These education savings plans have now been established by all states, and some states allow limited tax deductions or credits for contributions to 529 plans. (Some states allow such deductions for both their own and out-of-state plans.) Contributions are removed from the giver's potential taxable estate. The owner of the plan retains control over when distributions are made, and even has the ability to change the beneficiary (within limits). It is important to note that some states offer two types of 529 plans: (1) savings plans (described above) and (2) prepaid tuition plans. The main advantage of the prepaid tuition plans is the opportunity to lock in future college tuition costs at in-state universities.

Some grandparents erroneously believe that setting up 529 plans for their grandchildren can affect a student's ability to qualify for financial aid. This myth is simply false. A 529 plan owned by a grandparent is not even reported on the financial aid application. The application does take into account 529 plans that parents own, as well as UTMA accounts that students own. The impact of 529 plans on the student's ability to qualify for financial aid is generally lower than that of UTMA accounts.

Direct Tuition Gifts. One way to make a gift of tuition without paying gift taxes is to pay the tuition bill directly to the college or university. This tuition gift is separate from any annual exclusion gift the contributor makes during the year to the same student.

Transferring Property at Her Death

At the time of a woman's death, there are several techniques often used to preserve and transfer assets for family members. In light of the changing nature of families, it is important that professionals consider her marital status as federal and estate legislation provides some preferential treatment to married individuals. In addition, it is essential that one have at least a working familiarity with the most commonly used estate planning strategies, among these are wills, revocable living trusts (RLTs) and irrevocable life insurance trusts (ILITs).

Married or Single?

Many married couples mistakenly believe they do not need a will if they plan to leave everything to their spouse. However, without a valid will when a person dies, property distribution is made according to the state laws of intestacy. In some states, a surviving spouse may not receive all of a deceased spouse's property. According to one study, 18 percent of Americans say they have personally experienced problems after a loved one's death or incapacitation, due in part to the lack of a comprehensive estate plan. [349]

There are two advantages that married women have over single women when it comes to estate planning purposes. They have access to the marital deduction and certain benefits when retirement plan assets are passed to a surviving spouse. Single women (including widowed, divorced and those living in domestic partnerships) face more obstacles in estate planning than married women for two main reasons that deal with the unlimited marital deduction and passing retirement plan benefits to a surviving spouse.

1. Single women cannot take advantage of the unlimited marital deduction, which shelters from federal estate tax any amount of assets passed between spouses after death, provided the surviving spouse is a U.S. citizen. The marital deduction provides that certain transfers at death from a deceased spouse to a surviving spouse are fully deductible from the gross estate for federal estate tax purposes. The deduction is unlimited as long as property is included in the gross estate of the deceased spouse and is transferred to the surviving spouse in a qualifying manner. Through maximum use of the marital deduction, a married couple can, at their option, eliminate all federal estate taxes due at the first death of the two spouses.

2. Single women cannot take advantage of special tax breaks in passing a retirement plan and IRA benefits to a surviving spouse. A surviving spouse may be able to "step into the shoes" of the decedent or (alternatively) roll the account balance over into the surviving spouse's IRA. If the surviving spouse steps into the shoes of the decedent, she must begin minimum withdrawals when the decedent reached (or would have reached) age 70½. If a surviving spouse rolls over the decedent's IRA into her own IRA, she must begin minimum withdrawals when she reaches age 70½.

Wills

wills

Although wills are the cornerstone of estate planning, it has been estimated that fewer than 30 percent of Americans have a valid will.[350] Since simple wills are not expensive to create, this seems to be a serious planning omission, especially for women.

A will is a personal and legal declaration in which a person specifies how probate property is to be distributed at death. Its terms do not become operative

---

349. Omnibus Study conducted by Harris Interactive® for LexisNexis Martindale-Hubbell, April 2004.
350. Vickie Bajtelsmit, *Estate Planning*, Chapter 17, "Personal Finance," 2005.

or legally enforceable until death. If she moves to another state, her will should be reviewed for compliance with her new state of residence.

Prior to her death, a woman can amend, revoke, or destroy all copies of her will at any time. By making sure that women understand this, financial professionals can help some women overcome their fears of making mistakes or being locked into ironclad contracts.

Revocable Living Trusts

revocable living trusts

A living trust is a planning device that many consider as important as a will. A properly drafted living trust can provide instructions for property management during a woman's old age, and it can avoid probate expenses. A revocable living trust (RLT) allows its creator to maintain control of the property contained in it and to alter its provisions or revoke its existence as its creator sees fit.

The individual who creates the trust by having the trust agreement drawn up and placing property into the trust is called the grantor. This individual is also usually named as the trustee. The trustee is responsible for safekeeping the trust assets and acts in a fiduciary capacity. This effectively allows the grantor-trustee to exercise control over the property placed in the trust. In addition to being named as trustee, the individual creating the trust is typically named as beneficiary of the trust. The trust document also names other beneficiaries to receive the property following the death of the individual who created the trust.

The practical difference between an RLT and other types of trusts is that the RLT is established primarily for the benefit of the person setting it up. A well-drafted RLT can ensure that a woman's specifically designated instructions are carried out according to her wishes, for her benefit, and for the benefit of the named trust beneficiaries. This can help safeguard her assets during her life. If she becomes unhappy with the trust terms or disillusioned with its operation, she can alter or revoke the trust.

Irrevocable Life Insurance Trusts

irrevocable life insurance trusts

Unlike a revocable trust, an irrevocable trust does not allow the grantor to retain any powers or control over trust terms. Any property the grantor transfers during her lifetime is permanently transferred and considered a completed gift.

One type of irrevocable trust is an irrevocable life insurance trust (ILIT). ILITs are one of the most efficient ways for women to achieve multiple estate planning goals: (1) reduction of federal income and estate taxes, (2) privacy, and (3) professional supervision of assets for future generations. They address the fears that some women have about whether heirs have enough knowledge or sophistication to manage money well. The following example illustrates the benefits of ILITs.

Example

Helen and Dan have assets that they would like to divide equitably among their children and grandchildren after Helen and Dan are gone. But they worry about how to do this without creating family friction. As Helen observes, if they leave these assets in a will, "Everybody will know what everybody else is getting." There are some other nagging problems. For example, they would like to pass down their $115,000 investment portfolio, but they don't think any of their children know how to manage investments.

Helen has another dream: "What if we could leave behind a fixed pool of money, such as half a million dollars, and give instructions that this money will be paid out to the children or grandchildren who truly need it most? And what if it would all be income tax free?"

This goal can be more than a dream, thanks to a wealth transfer vehicle called an irrevocable life insurance trust. In the simplest structure, a grantor sets up an ILIT, donates cash or property to it, and is also the insured person. The trust is governed by a document prepared by a qualified estate planning attorney, and a professional trustee is named to manage the trust.

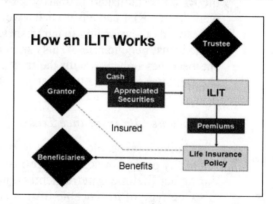

As the illustration shows, the trust uses the donated cash or property to pay annual premiums on a life insurance policy. At the death of the insured, the life insurance death benefit is received by the trust free of federal income tax. When an ILIT purchases the life insurance policy on the life of the grantor, the death benefit will also be free of federal estate taxes.

The ILIT trustee can be a family member, family attorney, or a close trusted friend. A professional trustee is often recommended since that trustee is a fiduciary and must act for the sole benefit of the trust's beneficiaries. In addition, the trustee is also responsible for property valuations, tax filings, distributions, and beneficiary notifications. The trustee earns a fee for providing the service, usually paid for from the trust's assets, which reduces the amount of assets available to pay premiums. The life insurance death benefit will be paid to the trust or other beneficiary named in the policy income tax free.

One benefit of this structure is the grantor's ability to write instructions that direct the trustee's actions. Once these instructions are written, they may not be changed—thus, the categorization of an ILIT as an irrevocable trust. Since property is permanently donated to the trust, it is removed from the donor's taxable estate. Any property that passes through an ILIT can be private, which can be an advantage, compared to the public disclosures involved in the probate process. An ILIT should always be established with the help of a qualified estate planning attorney.

CHAPTER SUMMARY

This chapter demonstrates that a women's mature years, or third age, can be a time of reinvention, renewal and excitement. Many women become free of caregiving responsibilities during this phase of life and as such, can shift their focus to fulfilling their lifelong goals. Financial consultants who understand how to help women envision their future and shape financial plans around goals and risk management will be both indispensible and worthy of their clients' trust.

Financial professionals should be aware of and build competency in the complex issues involved in planning for a female client's retirement and later stages of life. Developing the technical expertise and skills to effectively address the full range of challenges that older clients often face can require years of training and study. Consultants benefit significantly when they are proficient in retirement, estate and elder-care issues in terms of multigenerational planning opportunities, assets under management and protection needs met. Last, the ability to work joint cases with qualified estate and tax professionals on wealth management and estate planning cases yields significant long-term benefits in terms of strengthened client relationships and referrals.

In our next and concluding chapter, we wrap up our discussion on marketing financial services to women with a focus on client service. Specifically, we examine:

- why outstanding service is critical to success in the women's market
- the differences between customer and client service
- how to generate repeat business and referrals

CHAPTER 7 TOOLS AND RESOURCES

- Courses from The American College
  - FA 261 Foundations of Retirement Planning

- FA 262 Foundations of Financial Planning: An Overview
- FA 271 Foundations of Estate Planning
- HS 326 Planning for Retirement Needs
- HS 330 Fundamentals of Estate Planning
- HS 334 Estate Planning Applications
- HS 350 Understanding the Older Client
- HS 352 Financial Decisions at Retirement
- GS 814 Qualified Retirement Plans
- GS 815 Advanced Estate Planning I
- GS 816 Advanced Estate Planning II
- GS 836 Business Succession Planning I
- GS 838 Business Succession Planning II
- GS 839 Charitable Giving
- GS 849 Charitable Giving Applications

- Recommended Reading

    - *The Age Wave: How The Most Important Trend Of Our Time Can Change Your Future*, Ken Dychtwald, Bantam Books, 1990

    - *The Power Years: A User's Guide to the Rest of Your Life*, Ken Dychtwald and Daniel J. Kadlec, John Wiley & Sons Publishing, 2005

    - *The Millionaire Woman Next Door: The Many Journeys of Successful American Businesswomen*, Thomas Stanley, Andrews McMeel Publishing, 2004

- Websites

    - Social Security Administration Website (www.ssa.gov)
    - Living to 100 Website (www.livingto100.com)

8

Exceeding Her Expectations Through Client Service

Learning Objectives
An understanding of the material in this chapter should enable the student to
8-1. Describe why client service is so important to both clients and financial consultants.
8-2. Identify the objectives of client service.
8-3. Explain the differences between customer and client service.
8-4. Define key elements of an exceptional client service plan.
8-5. Outline the reasons why a financial consultant might want to conduct client satisfaction surveys and how they are usually fielded.
8-6. Explain techniques for generating repeat business.
8-7. Describe the barriers and builders of referrals.

INTRODUCTION

Throughout this book, we have discussed how the consultative planning process is important to achieving trust and competitive advantage in the women's market. We also examined how attaining high degrees of effectiveness requires a great deal of deliberate thought, energy and skill development. As a result of the substantial effort and expense necessary to succeed in these initial phases, the last phase—servicing the plan—all too often becomes an afterthought. This is a serious mistake.

If one hopes to achieve and sustain success in the women's market, men's market, or in any of their respective segments, subsegments and niches, excelling at client service is critical. Through the adoption and implementation of strong client service systems; financial consultants maximize return on time and resources spent acquiring clients, while also sharpening their competitive edge.

Since client service becomes a "make or break" proposition for long-term viability in any market, this chapter focuses exclusively on this last vital phase of the marketing/consultative planning process. In our examination of client service, we review the same best practices that successful financial professionals apply to create loyal female (and male) clients for the remainder of their careers. Our discussion also includes how to reap and maximize the rewards of excellent, trustworthy client service: repeat business and referrals.

As context, we are at both the end, and the beginning, of the marketing/planning process reflected in the table below.

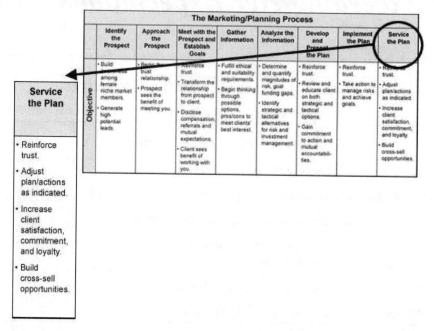

The service phase represents how clients are retained and relationships are enriched. However, as referrals are generated from existing clients, the cycle repeats itself by working the referred prospect through the beginning of the consultative planning process. In addition, as existing client plans are regularly monitored, steps 3 and 4 (establish goals, gather information) are repeated, as are the analysis, recommendation and implementation steps.

WHY IS CLIENT SERVICE SO IMPORTANT?

client service

Industry research and client service experts point to big disconnects between what both male and female consumers expect, and what they receive. Relative to women and financial services professionals, most consumers are disappointed and underwhelmed. While the attitudes and experiences of female clients have not been extensively studied, findings from existing research reveal these telling gaps in both the level and frequency of service:

- In the 2008 Allianz study, "Women, Money & Power," most respondents reported infrequent service interaction. Just 24 percent have actually met with their advisor in the last 24 months. (Put another way, three out of four women had not met with their advisor in two years.)[351]

- According to recent research by State Farm, only about one in ten women surveyed said that lawyers (11 percent) and financial advisors (12 percent) go above and beyond their normal service level to keep them happy.[352]

Even affluent women, arguably the most profitable of female clients, can feel snubbed. Industry experts Russ Prince and Hannah Grove researched the experiences and attitudes among wealthy women and found that almost all (98.8 percent) had switched away from a former financial advisor. The top two reasons for leaving? More than 70 percent said their advisor did not understand them, and 31 percent felt they did not get the attention they required. As perspective, just over 20 percent cited poor investment performance.[353] These findings suggest that relationship and service trump product and performance.

Whether or not one places investments for clients, and whether or not one works with wealthy women, these findings are universally relevant to financial consultants. What can be learned from them? First, respect for the female client and understanding of her goals are ongoing requirements, extending well beyond the initial phases of the consultative planning process. (Recall the Prince/Grove research found that clients, not prospects, terminated an existing relationship with a financial advisor.) Next, it is not sufficient to give service that fits the consultant's own business model, but it must also at least meet the client's expectations.

Of course, women are not alone in their disappointments with client service, nor are other industries immune. Similar sentiments are echoed in broader research by experts and consultants who study client service trends and perceptions as shown in these compelling findings:

- Across virtually all industries, an average of two thirds (or 66 percent) of American consumers do not feel valued by those serving them.[354]

- On average, happy customers tell four others about their positive experience while those that are dissatisfied tell 12 how bad it was.[355]

---

351. Allianz, "Women, Money & Power Study," 2008.
352. State Farm "The Musts of Trust" Women Consumer Survey, Kelton Research, Golan-Harris, Newsworthy Analysis published May 2008.
353. Russ Alan Prince, and Hannah Shaw Grove, Women of Wealth: Understanding Today's Affluent Female Investor, National Underwriter, 2004.
354. Focus Plus Service Auditors, 2006.
355. Ibid.

- 70 percent of customers leave a provider of products or services because of a perceived lack of attention.[356]

These telling facts about client service (or its absence) underscore significant risks and opportunities for financial consultants and point to this important fact: Service is the key to client building, which is the key to long-term success.

The Objectives of Client Service

Success at client building will accomplish the following objectives for the financial consultant's business:

- lower expenses and increase profitability

- build repeat sales and referrals

- retain clients and defend against competitive threats

- increase client loyalty

Lower Expenses and Increase Profitability

Delivering extraordinary client service is an essential element to improving profitability. A range of studies have consistently shown that it is far more expensive, by some accounts costing six to seven times more, to gain a new customer than it is to retain an existing customer.[357] As perspective, think for a moment about all the steps and resources involved to generate a new client.

- research target markets

- align one's practice and value proposition to meet target market needs

- build awareness through communications networks, media and events

- call prospects for appointments

- meet with prospects

- convert prospects to clients

In light of the substantial effort and costs to acquire clients, along with the consequences associated with those who become dissatisfied and leave, even a small increase in retention can boost profits. Bain & Company, a global

---

356. Ibid.
357. Ibid.

consulting firm with expertise in customer satisfaction, found in its research that improving retention by just five percent improved profits by 25–95 percent.[358]

Build Repeat Sales and Referrals

Successful, seasoned financial professionals will share that as much as 75 percent or more of their new business comes from existing clients, or the referrals that these clients provide. If one is relatively new to the business, preoccupied with generating production and struggling to find a market, imagine the difference it would make if most business came from clients who had already done business, or from the new clients they referred. Since women are twice as likely to recommend their financial professional as are men, serving female clients may well take on even greater importance.[359] Remember that people have a tendency to refer those like themselves. As such, this natural inclination can complement the consultant's niche marketing efforts and can help stretch limited resources even further.

Retain Clients and Defend Against Competitive Threats

A strong client relationship can prevent competitors from replacing hard-won business. In this intensely competitive climate, service is clearly a necessary defensive strategy. Maintaining a high profile with clients through service activities and contacts builds both client loyalty and commitment. A client who feels no such loyalty or commitment will not think twice about accepting a compelling product recommendation that comes along. As a result, the consultant's persistency and income will suffer unless one takes the steps necessary to keep client satisfaction high.

Increase Client Loyalty

client loyalty

As financial consultants create service systems and processes, the goal should ultimately be to develop *client loyalty*, not just satisfaction. In his best-selling book, *Customer Satisfaction is Worthless, Customer Loyalty is Priceless*, author Jeffrey Gitomer defines the key differences between satisfied customers and those who are loyal.

In essence, client satisfaction is too low a standard upon which to measure effectiveness in customer service, according to Gitomer. After all, it is far more cost effective to keep a client than to find a new one. Yet this concept still has not penetrated the core of American business. If customers are satisfied, many believe, that is good enough. They are wrong. The goal should be to go beyond mere satisfaction. The goal should be client loyalty.

Below is a summary of Gitomer's levels of client satisfaction. Note how much of an advocate a loyal client can be for the financial consultant's practice.

---

358. Ibid.
359. Susan Sweetser, "Real Opportunity," MDRT, May/June 2007.

Levels of Client Satisfaction			
When Your Client Is	**Tells Others**	**Refers Others**	**Buys Again**
Loyal	Everyone, all the time	At every opportunity	Always, for ever and ever
Satisfied	If asked	If asked	If convenient
Apathetic	No	If asked	Maybe, maybe not
Unhappy	10 people	No	Maybe, after several years
Wronged	25 people	No	Never
Angry	Everyone, all the time	Never	Never

Source: Gitomer, Jeffrey, *Customer Satisfaction is Worthless, Customer Loyalty is Priceless* (Austin, TX: Bard Press, 1998), p. 50.

In his book, Gitomer adds a lower level of client dissatisfaction, which he calls *lawsuit*. Guess how many people are told at this level? *The whole city!*

Many of us have experienced dissatisfaction with a business in such a way that it is almost irresistible to spread the word about substandard experience. This is called giving "reverse referrals," and the same dynamics that can do wonders for spreading the good news about one's value and service proposition can also work against him or her. Beware!

> "To keep a lamp burning, we have to keep putting oil in it."
>
> Mother Teresa

HOW DO FINANCIAL CONSULTANTS DEVELOP LOYAL FEMALE CLIENTS?

Recognizing that there is in fact, a distinction between satisfied and loyal clients is an important step in its own right. Here are several key service characteristics that differentiate client satisfaction from loyalty:

Differentiation	Satisfied Client	Loyal Client
Expectations and Promises	Meets expectations and delivers on promises	Exceeds promises and over-delivers on promises
Service Delivery	Reactive and responsive	Proactive and responsive
Service Focus	Product focused	Goal and plan focused
Service Systems	Support efficient timely response	Support goal achievement

An operating assumption is that both satisfied and loyal clients receive excellent service. However, the focus and level of service differ depending on how one segments his/her client base. The following section discusses various approaches to service and stratify of clients. How does the consultant move clients from satisfaction to loyalty? What are the practices to adopt and implement? How can client service systems be made so efficient that the consultant (and/or team) controls them versus the other way around?

Promises Kept and Expectations Set

expectations

It goes without saying that keeping the promises one makes to others is a fundamental aspect of trust. At the very minimum, the financial consultant needs to deliver on promises made and meet his/her client's expectations. By making a promise, one places his/her word, integrity and reputation on the line. When a service provider fails to keep a promise made, no matter how large or small, there is a breach in trust. Even seemingly small infractions, like promising the client a follow-up call at a specific time and failing to do so until the next day, unravels the trust relationship. If she cannot trust her financial consultant in the small things, how can she be expected to trust him or her with matters of greater importance?

While violations of trust usually signal the "beginning of the end," they are for the most part, avoidable. To a significant extent, the consultant sets and controls many of the expectations that clients have. One of the first rules of exceeding expectations is to consistently *under-promise* and *over-deliver*. Never make a promise, that cannot be kept or better yet, improved upon. Always strive to respond sooner than promised.

Marketing guru John Moore, who helped create the exceptional customer experience for Starbucks and Whole Foods, shares these thoughts on expectations and promises in his book, *Tribal Knowledge*:

> **Over-Deliver on All Promises**
>
> When businesses follow through on the promises they've made to their customers, they're displaying an integrity that's necessary to building trust between customers and the brand; they're also showing a pride in what they do—the products they make and the services they deliver. Ultimately, how a company follows through on its promises is more a reflection of who that company is and its reason for existing than anything else. A [company] that delivers what it claims it will is simply treating its [customers] exactly the way it would like to be treated.
>
> But delivering on promises is not enough today. Businesses, big or small, must find ways to over-deliver on their promises, implied and expressly stated. That means exceeding the usual expectations and going beyond the minimum [company] standard.
>
> Leading questions:
>
> 1. In what ways, if any, does your [company] over-deliver on its promises to customers on a regular basis?
>
> 2. What obstacles stand in the way of creating a [company] culture that over-delivers on promises, not as the exception, but the norm?
>
> 3. What programs could you [your company] implement to over-deliver on promises?
>
> Source: Excerpts from *Tribal Knowledge, Business Wisdom Brewed from the Grounds of Starbucks Corporate Culture*, John Moore, Kaplan Publishing, 2006.

With the ultimate goal of exceeding client expectations, it is first helpful to establish what the minimum standards might be. There are, of course, different expectations based on the extent of business and relationships one has developed. In other words, what *customers* expect is different than what *clients* require.

Service Focus: Customers and Products versus Clients and Plans

While all clients are customers, not all customers are clients. Both may buy products and/or services from a provider, but their expectations and needs are different. What are the minimum levels of expectations that the financial consultant should set and for his/her clients to require? How are they different if she is a customer or if she is a client? Simply put: when working with a customer, the objective is to service the *product*. Working with a client, however, requires monitoring her *plan* and *progress* towards goals.

The Consumer and Her Product

Customers expect to be provided product service when the need arises. For example, customers often buy an insurance policy from a salesperson, throw the contract in a drawer and never review it. Most consumers in these types of situations never develop a personal relationship with the salesperson from whom they buy a product. Service in this context is *reactive versus proactive*. Examples of reactive service include responding to customer requests for assistance in changing beneficiaries, addresses, billing, ownership and servicing claims.

Customers assume that service on their product(s) will be done in a friendly, efficient and responsive manner. Just as they expect high quality, competitive products and services from their providers, excellent product service is a cost of entry or minimum standard. Product service rarely sets one apart from the competition. It may contribute to satisfaction, but not to loyalty. On the other hand, product service that is uneven, slow and unresponsive opens the door to competitors and virtually guarantees lost business.

The Client and Her Plan

By contrast, monitoring progress on a plan is a critical service component that separates the financial consultant from a product focused salesperson. While seeking to deliver excellent service to a client, a planning relationship requires more of the consultant. When a plan is appropriately monitored, the focus shifts from servicing a product to proactively working to achieve the client's goals. Monitoring her progress is the very backbone of client service activity for financial consultants. Servicing the plan is future oriented and as such, it is *proactive versus reactive*.

From the very start of the consultative planning relationship, it is critical to set client expectations about the value of proactive service. Lay the groundwork early in the process, as early as the initial interview when explaining the planning process and support services offered. The consultant should position him- or herself as a knowledgeable professional who helps clients crystallize their goals, analyze what is required to achieve them, and monitors their plan to ensure they stay on track. By describing the planning process, consultants reveal a genuine interest in their client's objectives, financial success and security. Very often, setting these expectations alone will lead a prospective client to hire a prospective financial consultant.

Servicing the Plan

When working with a client through a planning relationship, the consultant's overarching responsibility is to help her achieve financial goals and security. Managing financial risks and achieving/maintaining financial security are perpetual works in progress. Even when initial goals are achieved, situations change and new objectives emerge. Beyond changing personal dynamics, the environment in which we live and work is constantly in flux. Tax laws change on average every two years. Markets go up and down. Businesses succeed and fail. Forces of nature wreak havoc on personal property and finances. Family demands are often significant and ongoing. In light of the fluid nature of our financial lives, the client's plan—no matter how well conceived— frequently becomes obsolete soon after its completion.

Since realizing most goals is often a decades long process that requires continual monitoring and adjustment, one is likely to have many meetings with planning clients over the coming months and years. Here are some of the basic service exchanges and actions required in servicing a plan.

Holding Action Meetings

The more comprehensive the plan and recommendations, the less likely the client (and her financial consultant) will be able to implement all that needs to be done during one meeting. She may be unable to simultaneously finance all the steps recommended. This is particularly true when there are several products and/or steps that need to be put into action. Sometimes, the consultant finds him- or herself running out of time to complete all necessary paperwork. For the client, it can be difficult to adequately absorb multiple concepts and products simultaneously. A series of meeting is often required to get everything done, especially early in the process of implementing a comprehensive plan.

Conducting Review Meetings

review meetings

One of the most important services offered to a client is the review of her plan. This is a key service aspect that truly differentiates the financial consultant from would-be competitors. (Recall that more than 76 percent of female clients had not seen their financial advisor in two years.)[360] Set the expectation that her progress will be reviewed once a year, at the very least. For certain clients and types of accounts, annual reviews alone are not sufficient. The more the client has implemented, the more service she is likely to expect. As one grows his/her practice with high net worth female clients, many will merit or expect at least a semi-annual meeting. For those with wealth management advisory accounts or retainers in place, many broker/dealers require (at least the attempt of) quarterly meetings for compliance purposes. Whether meeting quarterly, semiannually or annually, the consultant should explain to the client what the review process entails so that she understands the value of these meetings, their benefit to her, and the consultant's commitment to her financial future.

Whenever possible, schedule the next review at the conclusion of each action meeting. Doing so reinforces that one is personally and professionally committed to the achievement of her financial goals/security. It also eliminates the necessity for the consultant or his/her staff to track a follow-up item, and saves time in calling (and recalling if unavailable) to schedule the next meeting. Be aware, however, that one should not force every client to agree to a review

---

360. Alliance, "Women, Money, and Power Study," 2008.

date; different clients have different needs and expectations. Rather, the client and consultant should determine together a mutually agreeable schedule for reviews.

Key points to cover when conducting a planning review include:

- Evaluate the client's progress towards achieving goals and reducing risks.

- Ensure that initial action steps are taken.

- Identify changes in conditions that would affect the current plan.

- Obtain information from the client to determine changes in her personal circumstances.

- Review work that was done for the client by other financial professionals.

- Adjust the original plan as needed.

> "It is a bad plan that admits no modification."
>
> Publilius Syrus

Keeping Good Records

Record keeping is extremely important to both the client and the consultant. An up-to-date client file and/or computer records will help one prepare for the review and keep everyone on track. Maintaining complete records shortens preparation time, projects a professional image, and ensures that one has the relevant information to review. Chapter 3 discussed how to capture recommendations, rationale, timing and responsibilities in a simple letter and action table. This tool can be very useful during the review process to help the consultant document progress as the plan is implemented. Here is an example of an outstanding item in an action table:

Recommendation	Rationale	Timing	Responsibility
Increase contributions to Jason's college fund by $100 per month when Janice gets her raise.	Increase to full funding when cash flow becomes available.	October 1st	(Client's name) and (Consultant's name)

Make sure that client files also include information about her family (for example, children's names and ages, and the names and ages of grandchildren), personal interests and product performance. Of course, one needs to follow the broker/dealer's or insurance principal's compliance requirements for record keeping.

Confirming the Review

Call to confirm the appointment. Let the client know in advance what documents she might need to bring to the review. For example, if the consultant is following up on a disability income plan, she will need her to bring a W-2 form and Social Security and/or employee benefits statements to the meeting. If the appointment was not set in advance, send a letter along with a checklist to remind her of the review, and then follow up with a phone call to set the date for the appointment.

(Note: A sample prereview [financial checkup] meeting letter and review checklist are in the Appendix.)

Preparing for the Review

Some consultants use a formal agenda for these meetings. If the consultant has kept good records, preparing for the review appointment will be much easier. Take 15 minutes in advance to review the needs analysis and the financial information the client provided. Reexamine information previously gathered on her attitudes, values, and goals. Review plan recommendations, and pay attention to which recommendations were implemented and which were not. Put together a quick summary of areas where needs still exist.

Recapping the Review

Once the review is complete, draft a brief letter documenting action steps, timing and responsibilities. Just as with the summary of plan recommendations, putting together a concise letter and action table can be helpful and is generally all that is required. The same action table described above can be used for recapping items from the review meeting.

DELIVERING EXCEPTIONAL SERVICE – THE SERVICE PLAN

The best financial consultants deliver exceptional, not just excellent, service. Delivering exceptional service that generates female client loyalty is not something that one can leave to chance or do on an ad hoc basis. Truly proactive client service requires careful planning, which then enables the consultant to "get out in front" of the business. In other words, it is important to drive client service activity versus just the opposite. To accomplish this, the consultant and her/his team need to design and implement a service plan. Without it, one ends up in perpetual react mode, putting out fires and missing opportunities.

There are three key elements to building an effective service plan: (1) segmenting the client base, (2) identifying service intervals and deliverables that will increase client loyalty by each segment, and (3) developing an operational system for making service as turnkey and automated as possible.

> "You can't build a reputation on what you are going to do."
>
> Henry Ford

Segmenting the Client/Customer Base

segmenting the client/customer base

Unless the financial consultant has made a conscious and strategic decision to work with only a small number of clients; it is usually impractical, if not impossible, to deliver the same level of service to all clients as the book of business grows. Just as it is necessary to subdivide the women's market into manageable niche markets, so it is with segmenting the client base. There is a range of demographic and qualitative criteria one can use to segment clients.

Typical demographic criteria are as follows:

- gender
- net worth
- household income
- age range
- occupation or industry
- niche market membership

Qualitative criteria include the following:

- revenue generated
- current and potential (movable) assets
- long-term goals
- service requirements
- history or probability of following the consultant's advice
- loyalty potential, including additional business and source of referrals
- likability

A combination of demographic and qualitative characteristics may move the client up or down in the groupings. This is largely a subjective call, based on the consultant's ideal client profile. A traditional way to classify clients is the A-B-C method, in which one segments clients into three categories or classes:

"A" = Ideal Clients

ideal clients

The ideal client is an individual who trusts and believes in her financial consultant, along with the services and products he/she provides. The client herself is trustworthy and a source of repeat business and referrals. The long-range goal for many consultants is to work only with their "A" or ideal clients. These individuals warrant the very best service. A useful exercise can be to create a list the characteristics of the 20 best female clients in the consultant's practice, as well as those of the female niche market he or she is targeting. What consistent characteristics do they have? What products and services do they need? How well does the client service experience match their expectations?

"B" = Clients and Customers with Potential to Become Ideal

This individual is a customer who could become an ideal client. Perhaps she purchased a product but has yet to commit to a more in-depth planning relationship. Customers/potential clients like these are "B" clients. In addition, any customer/client who is also member of the consultant's niche market should automatically fall into this category, at minimum. For most financial professionals, except those in the advanced stages of their careers, "B" customers/clients represent the majority. These individuals are typically offered a smaller range of services than the "A" group, but more than those in the "C" group. Ultimately, the goal is either to lower them to the "C" group or raise them to "A" client status.

"C" = Customers

This is someone who has bought a product and that is all she wants. Customers have demonstrated that they do not wish to enter into an ongoing client-advisor relationship. These are "C" clients to whom only basic product services are offered in order to maintain product persistency and acceptable levels of customer satisfaction (for example, basic annual reviews and follow-ups on information and service requests).

Why Segment The Client/Customer Base?

In the same way one would generally not put all of a client's money in low-yielding investments, the financial consultant should not expend time, energy, and money in a low-profit segment of the book of business. Segmenting the customer/client base requires making a conscious business decision about where to focus service resources. Exercise some caution here. Do not focus solely on her income or assets. Recall the total profitability of the client, as discussed earlier in this chapter. Look at her potential to positively impact the business. This can measured in three ways:

1. Is she a source (or potential source) for repeat business?

Example	Jessica is a young woman who does not have a lot of business with her financial consultant right now. However, she has demonstrated an appreciation for the planning process and recommendations. She also has the motivation and ability to increase her income over the years. It is likely, therefore, that Jessica will be a source of repeat business.

2. Is she a source (or potential source) for referrals?

Example

Laura is nurse who is a part of a nurse's union, a niche market that her consultant, Kelly is interested in targeting. The union meets regularly for programs on interesting topics. This could be an opportunity for Kelly to present a seminar to union members at one of their meetings.

3. Is she a good client easy to get along with and not high maintenance? (Stay away from high maintenance, low value clients. One can spend a great deal of time and energy with them and receive a low, or negative net return.)

Example

Selena has been Joe's client for two years. She has many personality traits that match Joe's ideal client profile. She also does not call him repeatedly with irrelevant and time-consuming questions. Although her net worth is lower than others in Joe's "A" group, Selena has the potential to be a high-value client.

How Segmenting Works

One way to increase the effective, or better yet, exceptional delivery of client service is to think of it as a marketing process in its own right. Just as one needs to break markets down into segments, subsegments and ultimately niches, similar procedures are followed with the customer/client base. However, rather than focusing on an external audience, marketing efforts are directed towards an internal audience—those who have a business relationship with the consultant.

In Chapter 2, we discussed how to identify and evaluate niche market opportunities, conduct research with influential members of a targeted community, build a strong value proposition to appeal to an intended audience, and develop/implement a media plan using a shared communications network. The same steps are put to work in the client service process; however, the business objectives are to deepen client relationships and increase loyalty, as well as generate repeat business and an ongoing stream of referrals.

Identifying "A" clients, "B" clients/customers, and "C" customers allows the consultant to treat each category according to its profitability, demographic and qualitative criteria. One can distinguish between basic and discretionary services and select which services to offer each category of client. It is prudent for consultants to be selective in how to invest resources in discretionary services, such as greeting cards, lunches, receptions, and other gifts. One is not obligated to include all customers and clients on a newsletter mailing list or to send everyone special clippings from the local newspaper with personal notes. These can be expensive and time-consuming gestures that would simply be wasted on some.

service package

Discretionary service activities are important because of the impact they can have on the client. Both the consultant and client should see services provided as timely, professional, and top quality. In addition, the astute consultants view exceptional service as an opportunity to add more value and distinguish themselves from the competition. Here are three possible service packages for the three categories of clients:

- Standard package—"C" customers

- Premium package—"B" customers/clients

- Superior package—"A" clients

Beyond standard product service levels, it is an industry best practice to enhance the experience of those who are, or have the potential to become, ideal clients. The extra services delivered should accomplish at least one of the following objectives:

- *Create visibility*. The goal is for clients to think of their financial consultant first when there are any financial needs or concerns.

- *Reinforce the perception of value delivered*. Clients both know and appreciate the scope of resources available to them through their financial consultant.

- *Create a sense of high touch*. Clients know their consultant is someone who personally cares about them. They view him/her as a trusted, indispensible advisor, or their financial "gatekeeper."

After segmenting the client base, one then creates a plan for service delivery to the respective groups. This is done by selecting services that one wants to establish as standard, as well as those identified as extra or discretionary services for the A, B and C client groups. Here are some examples of how to go about defining, describing and delivering different levels of service:

Standard Service Package—"C" Customers

Excellent customer service is the price of admission; it is the expectation, not the exception. This means that the standard package must provide high-quality product service to all customers and clients, regardless of their value to the business. These three steps can help consultants determine what his/her standard service level might be.

1. **Define It**. Define the standard service package. What services will be provided to everyone and at what level? Standard services may include the following basics:

    - annual reviews of her product(s) and their performance
    - birthday cards
    - holiday cards

    Also define standard product response parameters that the customer can expect. For example:

    - prompt handling of plan changes and inquiries
    - claims assistance
    - accessibility (When can she reach the consultant and/or staff? What after-hours services are available, if any?)
    - response time (How quickly will she receive a response to calls, e-mails, or letters? A general guideline is 24 hours or less.)

2. **Describe It**. Once the standard service package has been defined, communicate it to customers. Tell them what they should expect. The best time to do this is when establishing a new account. Many consultants include a flyer that explains servicing information.

3. **Deliver It**. The next step is to follow through and hold oneself and staff accountable to what has been committed. Some basic tips for delivering service:

    - When receiving a request, let the customer know how long it will take to satisfy it. When will the consultant or someone in the team get back to her?
    - Telephone the client after her service request to confirm that the information or action taken was what she requested. Make sure that the service was prompt, courteous and efficient. Take the opportunity to discuss any issues that were left unresolved.

Premium Service Package "B" Customers/Clients

The same three steps are followed for the premium and superior service packages: define, describe and deliver. For "B" customers/clients, strong service and relationship building put the trusted consultant in a favorable position to inquire about her other financial needs. When she is a client with a plan, this is relatively easy. However, there are customers who may not have done any planning, but have the potential to become ideal clients. Remember that these are clients/customers who have been identified as having potential to become "ideal." As such, care for them in a manner that goes above and beyond what is expected. Here are examples of premium package extras that can be superimposed over the standard level of service:

- semiannual reviews
- invitation to one client appreciation event per year
- quarterly newsletters
- quarterly telephone call

Superior Service Package—"A" Clients

Superior service and the most personal attention is saved for the very best clients. This means one must identify what services will be delivered as extras and which clients will receive them. The purpose of superior service is to turn every contact with best clients into an opportunity for strengthening client loyalty, new business and/or referrals. The superior package might layer on these types of services over the standard and premium offerings:

- quarterly reviews
- invitation to two or three client appreciation events per year
- monthly telephone calls
- anniversary cards
- articles of interest
- contributions to her favorite charity

Systematizing the Service Plan

service plan

Once service packages have been determined and the customer/client base segmented, it is desirable to automate the process as much as possible. The more the financial consultant plans ahead and systematizes services provided, the more likely it is they will actually be performed. This, in turn, leads to a higher efficiency and the probability of generating a return on resources invested to develop a client relationship.

While the financial consultant must personally complete the tasks of segmenting the client/customer base or determining levels of service, most of the service system can be automated and delegated. Computer software for customer relationship management (CRM) like EZ Data, ACT!, Goldmine, or Advisor's Assistant can help staff manage these activities with precision. If one is fortunate enough to already have an assistant, he or she can enter in birthdays, anniversaries, plan implementation and review dates and code all clients by segment level. Once those data points are entered into the system, it is relatively easy to print out lists of key monthly activities for all customers/clients two weeks before the month begins. A best practice is to review all upcoming customer/client activities in weekly or bi-weekly staff meetings. In addition, assistants can manage many of the tasks that do not require personal interaction (e.g., sending out cards, newsletters, appointment reminder calls, and so on). Should the consultant not yet have an administrative assistant, it may be worth considering one, even if only on a temporary basis to enter in client segment codes, and key dates (e.g., birthdays, anniversaries, review appointments).

Sample Service Plan and Investment

Remember that when it comes to service, what works for one advisor may not work for another. What one client finds interesting, may annoy another. Seek to add value, increase visibility and build relationships, but do not take on more than can be handled well. It is better to do a few things consistently and well than to do many things inconsistently and poorly.

The table below illustrates a sample service plan and roles/responsibilities for those tasks the consultant must do him- or herself and those that can be delegated and/or automated. The plan assumes 75 "A" clients, 150 "B" clients/customers and 75 "C" customers. As perspective, service items along with rough cost assumptions have also been provided. Let us further assume that the 300 existing clients generate approximately $15,000 per year in trailers and repeat business prior to implementation of the service plan. The example reflects a service investment of $4,511.25 (excluding the consultant's time and fixed administrative costs). In this instance, the investment works out to $15.04 per client and a total of 5,400 potential impressions (recall from Chapter 2 that reach x frequency = impressions) against the client base.

The more of these services one wishes to pursue, the more important a competent staff becomes. View good staff not as an expense, but as an investment in developing the business that frees the consultant to do what he/she does best—building relationships, planning and implementing. Take the time to clearly explain to staff members what extras will be offered and to whom. Make sure that these can be delivered, and that they are cost effective from both a monetary and time standpoint.

The financial consultant needs to consider the services to include, what the investment is for each activity, and if the plan that can be realistically implemented. Integrate the service plan into an overall business strategy. It can be helpful to compare anticipated investment, revenues and return from existing clients versus those for newly acquired clients. Evaluate the return on investment from both. Both are forms of marketing, both should have clearly defined audiences, and both are necessary. To get started, here are several best practice ideas for extra or discretionary services.

Sample Client Service Delivery Plan				
"A" Clients (75)	"B" Clients and Customers (150)	"C" Customers (75)	Who Does?	Estimated Extra Cost
Monthly call	Quarterly call	Semi-annual call	Financial Consultant (FC)	—
Annual review plus three quarterly performance reviews	Annual review plus one semi-annual performance review	Annual formal review	FC	—
Quarterly newsletter	Quarterly newsletter	Quarterly newsletter	Assistant (Asst)	$0.75 x 300 x 4 = $900
Article of interest 2x/year	—	—	FC	300 x $0.50 = $150
Birthday cards and phone call	Birthday cards and phone call	Birthday cards	FC and Asst	300 x $1.50 = $450
Holiday cards	Holiday cards	Holiday cards	Asst	300 x $1.50 = $450
Anniversary cards	Anniversary cards	—	Asst	225 (x 70% married) x $1.50 = $236.25
Invitation to three client appreciation events	Invitation to one client appreciation event	—	FC and Asst	Invitations (3 x 75 x $1.00) + (1 x 150 x $1.00) = $375 Attendance 30/event 3 events @ $15/head = $1350
Client satisfaction survey	Client satisfaction survey	Client satisfaction survey	Asst	300 x $2.00 = $600 (Includes return postage)
Contacts /year = 30	**Contacts /year = 16**	**Contacts /year = 10**		**Total Investment = $4,511.25**

Service Activities and Ideas

service activities and ideas   Study the "A" and "B" client lists, along with the budgeted service investment, and determine what should be done to provide exceptional service for ideal and high potential clients. Which of the following might work best?

Send Financial and Market Update Information to Increase Literacy

Regularly providing information on markets, the economy and personal finance is not only an excellent way to keep in touch, but can also lead to higher referral rates as well. According to a recent study by the Financial Planning Association and *USA Today*, clients who are likely to refer their consultant are twice as likely to agree that their consultant frequently provides them with information to improve their financial literacy. The research also determined that financial literacy information is a key driver of client satisfaction.[361]

Magazine or Newspaper Subscriptions

If her interests are known, give annual subscriptions to a favorite magazine or book-of-the-month club. Clubs that send their members a different item every month (food, books, music, wine, fruit, and so on) are a great way to remind clients regularly of their ongoing relationship and its importance—without having to call them.

Client Appreciation and Educational Events

Conducting informative client appreciation events can be an excellent opportunity to keep in front of clients, seek referrals and demonstrate competence. One can also use educational seminars conducted by or with others (e.g., CPAs and attorneys) as a way to offer extraordinary service.

Example   A client appreciation approach that one financial consultant has found successful with women clients is co-hosting a Saturday morning education event with a local CPA and attorney. While it is virtually impossible to get busy women to come to an event during the week, Saturday mornings are a time when many can break away from family and other commitments. The consultant, accountant and attorney each invite their respective female clients and share the cost of the event.

---

361. Research Spotlight, Third Quarter 2009, Planner-Client Communication: Driving Satisfaction, Longevity and Referrals Through Your Communications, The FPA Research Group and USA Today Study, March 2009.

They bill the event as a "Financial Planning for Women" workshop. Client response and referrals have been so strong, the event is now an annual affair.

Tickets to Special Events

Many women enjoy attending concerts, art openings, plays and movies—there is virtually no limit to the activities that can be offered to ideal clients. Purchase tickets and ask if clients would like to attend individually or as a group. With the appropriate fact-finding process, one can learn about their interests and be able to provide suitable tickets.

Offer a Complimentary Service

Providing a complimentary service can be an unexpected bonus to the client that enhances the client-consultant relationship. Think of one that the client will value and talk about to others. Because women today are so pressed for time, one might consider a time-saving gift for the most valuable female clients such as a car wash, dry cleaning, house cleaning services, or home-delivered meals, for example. All it takes is a little imagination.

Example	One consultant offers to drive her clients to the airport—especially for early morning flights. According to the consultant, "You can't really trust that a cab will always show up on time." The advisor says that she receives more referrals from this group of clients than she does from any other group.

Birthday, Holiday, and Special Occasion Cards

Send birthday and holiday cards to clients and their families. Cards can be custom printed with one's name and address. In addition, the selection of messages is generally wide enough to fit one's own personal style. The costs of cards, mailing and associated labor are usually deductible as business expenses, so keep track of these for tax purposes.

There are also internet sites that allow the consultant (or his/her staff) to personalize and customize greetings. Some like to send out letters that detail all the notable historic events that happened on the client's day of birth. Software for this application can be downloaded from the web. One site that features multiple software options is http://clientbirthday.com/birthday.htm.

This approach is fun, likely to get read, and can be perceived as more personal since it is customized to the client. In addition, these letters can often be more cost effective than sending out a card. If one wants to take it up a notch, personally delivering balloons, or a birthday cake to her place of work are often appreciated gestures.

Contact clients at other significant dates such as weddings, christenings, bar/bat mitzvahs, births, home purchases, new jobs, or promotions. Do not limit contacts only to happy occasions. Show genuine sympathy and support when there are deaths in client families or if the client or client's spouse loses a job. Clients appreciate concern, and just as important, may need the financial consultant's advice and assistance during a difficult time.

Handwritten Notes

In this era of high technology and fast-paced living, a handwritten note is an especially thoughtful gesture and adds a genuine personal touch. Be sure to hand address the envelope and use a commemorative postage stamp, if possible. A note like this will certainly stand out from the onslaught of mass-produced, computer-generated envelopes, flyers, magazines, and newspapers. Consider having note cards custom imprinted for a more personal touch. As with marketing to prospects, work on projecting the desired message. For example, when writing a note to a new client, one can communicate much more than a simple "thank you."

Example	"Thank you for your trust and the business you have placed with me. I look forward to serving you in the coming months and years as we work together on your financial goals and plan."

Newspaper Articles

Scan the local newspaper every day, and copy articles that might be of interest to one or more ideal clients. Mail the article with a personal note that simply says, "I was thinking of you when I came across this article," or "Here's an idea I thought you'd enjoy."

Similarly, when seeing an announcement about her family or business, send a copy of it with a brief personal note. Be sure to include the publication name and date. The announcement may also indicate a new sales or service opportunity. For example, the consultant may learn that the client has been named a member of a community club or professional organization that may be a great niche market to target.

Care Packages to Family Members in the Armed Services

If clients have sons or daughters serving in the military, send care packages to them. Cookies, cakes, or anything else from home is a great morale builder. Clients are sure to appreciate these thoughtful and meaningful actions.

Regular Phone Contacts

Stay in touch with clients through regular phone calls. The appropriate interval between calls is typically based on the A, B and C customer/client categories. These calls are often intentionally unrelated to business. Some consultants actually refuse to discuss business during such calls. This goes to the old saying that "People don't care about how much you know, until they know how much you care." Regular phone contacts are a key part of strengthening relationships with clients.

Newsletters

Sending a newsletter is an excellent way to maintain visibility on a regular basis and build the consultant's credibility in the process. Newsletters can often be purchased through the consultant's company or third party marketing outlet. If the consultant and/or team has sufficient resources, then there is the possibility to create an original newsletter series. Be careful to avoid explicit promotion of the products and services one offers as industry research has found that clients often perceive this information as overselling and off putting. On the other hand, providing interesting and informative articles about tax laws and planning, insurance and other financial matters is favorably viewed and appreciated.

Customized Letters and Gifts

To keep their names prominent in the minds of their clients, many financial professionals give imprinted calendars and other customized items. Shop around. Look for package offers and quantity discounts on larger purchases. Clients enjoy receiving pens, refrigerator magnets, and other items customized with your information, if they are attractive and useful.

Food and Beverage Baskets

Whether a food basket, pizza, or bagels for an office or family, food gets noticed—not only by clients, but also by their colleagues and/or families. "Who sent this?" they are likely to ask. The consultant's name and relationship is then likely to become the topic of favorable conversation.

Here is a compelling testimony about working on the extras of client service:

> **Commitment to Service**
>
> One highly successful financial consultant who has made a commitment to his service plan reports that approximately 90 percent of new business now comes directly from clients and 10 percent from people referred by clients.
>
> This advisor works exclusively with young professionals, meets with most clients in his office, and employs a full-time staff of three to handle the service work. He also states that he has not had to prospect for new business in more than two years.
>
> This consultant is convinced that if you want to build a continuing business among people who look to you as their advisor, good service is key to helping you accomplish that objective.

MEASURING CLIENT SATISFACTION

While the financial consultant has significant control over services provided and expectations set, one cannot control the expectations clients and prospects have or what they might say. Out of politeness or desire to preserve the relationship or avoid conflict, few will ever say if there is a problem. In fact, client service experts estimate that only one out of 25 dissatisfied customers will express dissatisfaction. Put another way, more than 90 percent will not let it be known that there is something wrong.[362]

How and when does the consultant know what clients would say about his/her integrity, expertise and service delivery? Is one falling short, meeting or exceeding expectations? What do clients perceive as specific strengths or opportunities for improvement? Are they willing to refer others? Unless one asks them outright, the answers to these questions are mere guesswork.

Achieving high levels of client satisfaction and, better yet, client loyalty should not be a guessing game. While customer surveys are standard in many other industries, they are less common in financial services. Some financial companies will field client satisfaction surveys that include aspects of how well their producers are fulfilling their responsibilities. However, these surveys frequently fall short of providing detailed and actionable information on how the consultant is measuring up relative to client expectations.

Asking for an honest appraisal of performance takes courage. In the quest for improvement and loyal clients, one has to be willing to take both the good and bad together. Whether or not the sponsoring company conducts some sort of client satisfaction survey, the consultant can benefit significantly by fielding his/her own. By doing so, one not only gains insight on client perceptions, but also the ability to pinpoint what needs to be addressed in strengthening the value proposition, reputation, repeat business opportunities and referrals. Equally, if not more valuable, conducting a client satisfaction survey sends a meaningful

---

362. Focus Plus Service Auditors, 2006.

message to clients: "I value your business. Your opinions are important to me. I am interested in improvement."

Client Satisfaction Survey—What to Learn?

client satisfaction survey

What are the key drivers of satisfaction? What are those elements that the client is looking for? Based on industry studies about women, trust and client satisfaction, asking for feedback on how she perceives the following attributes can yield important insights:

- trustworthiness and integrity

- value proposition

- knowledge, expertise and professionalism

- ability to deliver solutions that meet her needs

- responsiveness to requests

- accessibility to address questions and concerns

It is also helpful to provide space for written suggestions about how the value of advice and services can be enhanced, along with specific compliments or complaints.

A sample client satisfaction survey and cover letter are included in the Appendix.

How to Implement a Client Satisfaction Survey

Best practices include not only conducting annual surveys, but also communicating results to clients. The first survey acts as a "benchmark," establishing a point of reference for the current situation and providing a basis of comparison for future surveys. The goal of course, is to see gradual improvement across the key drivers of satisfaction.

Consider sending out surveys or posting a link on the consultant's and/or team's web site during late August through mid-September. This gives time to incorporate findings into the strategic planning process for the fall. Send out a cover letter or e-mail (if soliciting feedback electronically) stating the purpose of the survey and its benefits to her through improved service. When mailing surveys, be sure to include a postage paid, self-addressed envelope for their return. Reassure clients that responses are confidential and they can remain anonymous, if they so desire.

To increase both the response rate and information quality of surveys, industry veteran and expert Deena Katz, CFP®, suggests having a third party administer them. In her book, *Deena Katz on Practice Management*, she describes her experience in sending out surveys directly to clients and how responses were at first, less than completely forthcoming: "Clients are not going to jeopardize a good relationship with you by telling you that your reports are ugly and your response time for phone calls could be improved. The next time we contracted with a local secretarial service that conducted our survey. The results were much more helpful, because clients were not responding directly to us. It does make a difference."[363]

It may be useful to send surveys out in waves with different intervals based on the segmentation of clients (i.e., A, B and C clients). This enables one to honor anonymity, while at the same time providing insight on how the best clients perceive their service delivery versus other client groups.

Another method to consider using is online survey services such as Survey Monkey (www.surveymonkey.com). These services allow financial professionals to create basic online surveys for free or very little cost. Clients are invited to participate through a link in an e-mail sent to clients or through a popup invitation on the financial consultant's web page. Results are tabulated instantaneously and can be illustrated in graph and table forms, which can shared with clients.

Once answers have been tabulated, extract three to five common themes about what is being done well and what could be improved. Describe specific actions that will be taken and communicate these to both team members and clients.

THE REWARDS OF EXCELLENT SERVICE—REPEAT BUSINESS AND REFERRALS

Throughout this book, we have discussed the critical and multifaceted elements of trust. When acting as a trustworthy financial consultant, the overriding objective is to put her interests first. Of course, this does not mean that one does not stand to gain from working with her, but rather that the benefits are mutual. Through an equitable exchange of value, she receives the advice and services she needs, and the consultant is fairly compensated in return. This value exchange leads to a lasting relationship and repeat business.

Repeat Business

repeat business

For our purposes, repeat business has to do with implementation phases after all the initial steps are taken and/or products/services purchased. Since achievement of financial security takes years, if not decades, there will always be outstanding issues to address and business to write. Frequently, there are service issues (and opportunities) that arise throughout the year that cannot, and should not wait until the annual review. Here are just a few examples of these ongoing service requirements:

---

363. Deena Katz, Deena Katz on Practice Management (Princeton: Bloomberg Press, 1999).

- goals achieved or changed

- CDs coming due or loans paid off, freeing up cash flow to fund other goals/needs

- anticipated capital windfalls (e.g., inheritance, bonus)

- pay raises that need to be captured and saved

- expiration of a level term period on a term life insurance contract

- insurance policies with future purchase options to exercise

Most often, the longer term elements of monitoring and servicing the plan are not well tracked or managed. Many financial professionals, especially those relatively new to the business, do not have a routine method in place to track unimplemented action items and business. Without even a simple system, outstanding issues all too frequently fall between the cracks or are left to chance. Since it is only through action that a plan of has any value, neglecting aspects of service activity may seriously compromise the achievement of the client's financial goals and security. Furthermore, one runs the risk of leaving repeat business on the table, or worse yet, seeing it snapped up by the competition.

Beyond the annual review, here are two ways that many successful financial consultants make sure needed action continues over the long term:

1. Record outstanding items from the plan, service and annual review meetings in a summary letter. This was discussed in Chapter 3. *(A sample of the annual review meeting letter is in the Appendix.)*

2. Keep and continually update a log of unimplemented business/action and rough timing of potential implementation (e.g., rollover Mary's 401k in June, 2011). Some call this log a "money list." The list includes not only action items captured in summary letters, but also business identified outside of the scope of her plan. Anticipated capital windfalls, retirement plan rollovers, assets with a competitor that one hopes to capture over time are examples of items that can be added to a money list. The consultant may also want to add a probability column that provides a best guess as to how likely it is that this business will come in.

A best practice is to create an Excel spreadsheet that enables one to sort by timing, client name, investment and/or premium amount and probability. Here is a sample money list:

Action Month*	Client	Action Item	Fee Amount	Investment Amount	Premium Amount	Probability
200901	Bob Styles	Add to Jason's 529 plan ($100/mo)	—	$1,200/yr	—	High
200901	Bob/Janice Styles	See estate attorney for wills and trusts	—	—	—	High
200902	Sarah Morgan	Plan Fee	$1,500	—	—	Medium
200903	Liz Martinez	Invest CD into mutual fund	—	$10,000	—	High
200906	Jenna Chandler	Exercise disability future purchase option ($50/mo)	—	—	$600	Medium
999999	Ann Newby	Rollover 401k to IRA	—	$387,000	—	Medium

Note: For date sorting purposes, put year first and then month without spaces or characters between them. For example, January 2009 reads as 200901; February 2010 as 201002, October 2011 as 201110 and so on. If a specific date has not been identified, then simply put a code in as 999999. This will drop unallocated time frames to the bottom of the sorted list. In addition, annualize both systematic investments and premium payments.

Recording, communicating and tracking unimplemented action not only demonstrates professionalism and long-term commitment to the client, but also helps one proactively plan for writing more business. As the list grows, so does the potential for reaping the rewards of competent advice and excellent client service.

Referrals

In today's business environment, where roughly two out of three women do not trust financial advisors[364] and three out of four are skeptical when first

---

364. State Farm, "Musts of Trust Survey," 2008.

meeting a financial consultant,[365] being referred by a female client to a female prospect is a significant competitive advantage. When combined with the fact that most women prefer receiving financial information from friends and family, leveraging referral potential needs to be a critical element of the business model and plan if one wishes to succeed in the women's market.[366]

Referrals are the client's way of endorsing the consultant as a trustworthy and competent provider of financial advice. Industry studies consistently reveal that referrals are important builders of trust. Dan Richards, author of *Getting Clients, Keeping Clients*, says that "Referrals = Implied Endorsement = Trust." His spectrum of trust puts a visual representation to the relative merits of referrals versus other client acquisition techniques.

The Trust Spectrum
Nobel Peace Prize
Client Referral
Guest Speaker
Community Involvement
Seminar
Direct Mail
Advertisement, Web site
Cold Call

Source: *Getting Clients, Keeping Clients*, Richards, Dan, Wiley Publishing, 2000

It goes without saying that referrals are desirable. Referrals save the time, effort and money spent marketing to prospects. Industry studies consistently show that referrals are the primary client acquisition technique, far outnumbering all others. Further, individuals who are referred have considerably higher rates of conversion to clients than other methods (e.g., company-provided leads, seminars, cold calling from approved lists, and so on). Last, meeting and working with an individual who has been recommended by another is, more often than not, both enjoyable and fulfilling.

Referrals not only benefit the financial consultant, but also benefit clients. How? The less time, money and effort one needs to expend on marketing frees those resources up to improve one's technical competencies and value proposition. The quest for continuous improvement should be one the client recognizes and supports.

In the financial services industry, asking for referrals has often been taught as a process that is frequently perceived as manipulative. The old methods of asking: "who do you know…," or "who are the five people you know that might benefit from working with me?" and sitting silent with pen poised, waiting for a response is viewed as both calculated and controlling. Some trainers teach that the first person who says something "loses." Others suggest running

---

365. Ibid.
366. "2008–2009 Prudential Study, Financial Experience & Behaviors Among Women."

promotions that in effect bribe clients to give referrals. This approach builds neither relationships nor trust.

While it is not necessary to wait until she has been a client for years to ask her for referrals, most clients are not ready until they have experienced both the value and integrity that the financial consultant offers. Some women may appreciate these qualities as early as the initial interview. Others need to see consistent demonstration of trustworthy behavior through the quality of products and services placed, delivery on promises, and exceeding, or at least meeting, her expectations. In the end, referrals become the client's way of validating the esteem she places in the consultant. However, unless she is asked, it is unlikely she will give referrals on her own.

Many financial professionals, even those with many years in the business, admit they are not very effective at asking for referrals. Perhaps that is why the majority of referrals for even the most seasoned financial advisors are passive (given without invitation) versus proactive (asked for). According to a recent study of independent financial advisors, almost two out of three referrals (57 percent) were passive, as this chart reveals:[367]

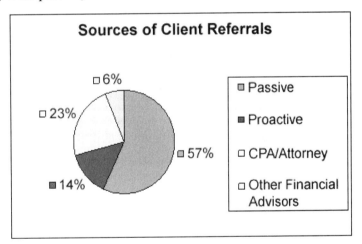

Note: While we will not be covering professional referrals (i.e., recommendations from CPAs, attorneys and other financial advisors), many of the same principles discussed below apply to these relationships as well.

Barriers to Referrals

barriers to referrals

So then, in light of their importance, why are so many financial professionals reluctant to ask for referrals? Furthermore, why don't clients, even those who have demonstrated complete trust and confidence refer more people, more often?

There are barriers on both sides—client and consultant—to be aware of before they can effectively be broken down. Recognizing these obstacles is

---

367. Advisorbenchmarking.com, "2001 Study of Independent Financial Advisors."

the first step in dealing with them. The table below illustrates some of the most commonly held sticking points:

Referral Obstacles	
Financial Consultants	**Clients**
Fears: rejection, appearance of weakness by asking for help	Fears: she will be embarrassed and her relationships damaged
Do not want to pressure her	She does not want to be pressured
Think it is unprofessional	She is concerned about confidentiality–hers and others'
Forget to ask and/or "run out of time"	She is unclear about how the consultant contacts referrals
Do not have clearly defined ideal/niche prospects	She is not sure about who to refer to the consultant

Do any of these sound familiar? Because of these barriers, the outdated approaches recommended by some trainers in the industry result in outcomes that are either ineffective (i.e., she will not refer) or less than optimal (i.e., she refers only a few prospects and/or they are not well qualified).

Overcoming these obstacles is a process versus an event. When one "just asks" for referrals in a haphazard way, that exchange is an event. Alternatively, when referrals are intertwined with everything the consultant does, they become a natural extension of the process. Weaving a systematic approach to asking for referrals throughout the process, and especially during the service and monitoring phase can help maximize referral success.

Asking for Referrals

asking for referrals

Effectively asking for and receiving quality referrals begins with sharing goals for working with female clients just like her. That vision centers around the value proposition, discussed in Chapter 2. The value proposition describes how the financial consultant will help her reach her goals and provide outstanding service, while doing so better than anyone else will. As mentioned in Chapter 2, an important benefit of niche marketing efforts is sharpening one's position statement and value to appeal to niche members. Another benefit is the enhanced ability to gain referrals through the niche. That said, she clearly does not need to be part of the financial consultant's niche market for her to give quality referrals.

Integrating the referral process into the consultative planning approach consists of the following steps:

1. ***Describe the goals for the practice.*** Set the expectation early on that referrals will be sought throughout the working relationship and describe how they will benefit her. Stating the goals for the practice goes something like this...

"One thing I would like to accomplish today is to share the goals I have for my business. These goals are quite simple: First, I seek to honor the trust you place in me. Second, I hope to serve you exceptionally well and add value every time we meet. And, third, I am looking to take on new clients exclusively through referrals.

These goals enable me to focus my energies on what is most important: growing and protecting your financial security, improving how I serve you and, on a personal note, spending more time with my family.

Through our working relationship in the coming weeks (months, years), my hope is you will feel that I deliver the kind of value to you that is worthy of referring me to others.

Are you comfortable with this approach to our relationship?"

The answer to this last question is a "no lose" proposition for the consultant. If she is not comfortable giving referrals, that discomfort is revealed early in the process. If this is the case, the consultant can follow-up with clarifying her reasons for resistance (e.g., *"Help me understand your concerns"*). More likely, she will be open to this approach, which sets the stage for the next step.

2. **Ask her if she has experienced benefit and value.** The consultant does not have to wait for client satisfaction survey results to get feedback from clients. Asking questions about the value and benefits delivered throughout the process demonstrates genuine concern and gives one real-time dynamic opinions. In most instances, assuming the consultant has consistently proven his/her trustworthiness and competence, asking about how she feels about the value provided thus far will generate a positive response. At the end of a conversation, meeting, or anytime value is delivered, one might say:

    "I'd like to take a moment to check in with you and see how our working relationship is going for you. (Select one or more of the following open-ended questions):

    - *How has this process helped you so far?*

    - *What do you think has been most beneficial part of our working together?*

    - *What do you like the most about working with me?*

    - *How am I doing?*

    Just as with the first step, one can only gain by her providing feedback to these sorts of questions. Whether or not she is satisfied, delighted or disappointed, the consultant wants to know. Hearing her positive feedback not only boosts one's confidence, but also sets an encouraging stage to ask for referrals.

If the financial consultant learns that there is room for improvement, then seek to clarify what areas need improvement. Ask for her concerns in a nonthreatening and genuine way (e.g., *"What should I/we be working on?", "What could we be doing better?"*) Answering gives her the opportunity to share her expectations. Once those are more clearly defined, the consultant is in a better position to meet and ideally exceed them. To make sure the door remains open for the prospect of asking for and receiving referrals, one might close the discussion with a statement like: *"To be sure that I am/we are serving you the way you would like to be served, is it okay for me to check in with you from time to time?"*

3. **Respect her wishes by giving her a choice to refer (or not).** This next step assumes she has responded positively to questions about how she views the value of provided services and the relationship. At this point, the consultant will want to not only acknowledge her appreciation, but also continue to demonstrate that her wishes will be respected.

    "Terrific! It is very gratifying for me to know that our working relationship has been both productive and rewarding for you. It has been for me, too.

    As you know by now, it is always important for me to respect your wishes about how we work together.

    At this point, I'd like to ask if you are open to discussing others (one may insert the name of the targeted niche market if she is a member) who might also benefit from working with me."

    Should she give a negative response, then the consultant needs to go back to clarifying her concerns, using questions similar to those noted above. In most cases, however, if one has progressed this far in the referral process, the answer will be positive. This affirmative response enables the consultant to proceed to the next step.

4. **Describe how referred individuals will be contacted.** One of the key referral barriers that clients have is they are either consciously or unconsciously concerned about jeopardizing relationships they have with others. While research could not be found that supports this hypothesis, it is not unreasonable to assume this may be especially true for women, in light of the greater importance they frequently place on their rapport with others. As such, it is important for the consultant to completely remove any questions she might have.

    "Thank you, (name). I am honored by your trust.

    Since clients are sometimes curious and maybe even concerned about how I contact those you refer to me, I want to tell you up front how I follow-up.

Some clients prefer to contact those they recommend first. If you want to do that too, that's completely fine by me.

In either case, here's what I will do. First, I'll send an introductory letter explaining who I am, what my services are, and how I know you. After that, I'll wait for a week before calling them so that you have a chance to contact them if you want to. If you find that they do not want me to call them, that's perfectly fine. Please just let me know.

Otherwise, I will call them to schedule an initial consultation where we will together determine just two things: (1) if I can help them, and (2) if they want my help. My promise to you is that they will not feel in any way pressured to meet with me. If they choose to meet, that's great. If they don't, that's okay too.

Last, I want to assure you that everything we discuss is completely confidential. You and your friends, family and colleagues can talk about me as much as you'd like to. But, I will never talk about you.

Is this approach acceptable to you?"

5. ***Describe the types of individuals you can help the most.*** At times, even the most willing clients will have a "deer in the headlights" moment when it comes to identifying those who would be a good fit for a working relationship with the consultant. That is, they simply blank out. Other times, they may refer prospects who are not well qualified or able to pay for even minimal levels of products and services (e.g., budget cases). Prompting her by describing the types of clients that one specializes in can be enormously helpful to both the consultant and client.

   "Please know that I will work with anyone you refer to me who also wants my help. That said, here are the types of people (women) that I specialize in and can help the most:

   - *women and their spouses who are both working professionals and parents, juggling the demands of family and finances*

   - *single women who want to make sure they're doing all they can to build and protect their financial security*

   - *widows who are not sure whom to trust and need help in managing their assets and estate plans*

   The consultant should customize prospect descriptions based on his/her particular value proposition and targeted niche members.

6. ***Ask!*** Through this approach, the barriers to referrals are broken down. The consultant has not manipulated or pressured her, demonstrated respect and provided necessary assurances. Now the consultant is in a position to pose the question:

"As you think about the value I deliver, and the types of people (women) I specialize in working with, who do you believe would benefit most by working with me?"

7. ***Follow-up.*** Once she has recommended a number of prospective clients, it is important to follow-up promptly and as promised. The next steps are to:

- **Within 24 hours**
    - Send an introductory letter to referred individual/s along with a biography and brochure or summary of services.
    - Send the client a thank you note or small gift if she provided multiple names (e.g., a potted plant, gift certificate to a book store or coffee shop).

- **After one week**
    - Wait for a week to see if the client calls with any objections to the consultant contacting referred individuals. If not, then call referred individuals to set up the initial consultation.

- **After one month**
    - Call the client back and let her know that everyone referred has been contacted. There is no need to divulge any sensitive information about what one learned from those individuals, only that one has had contacted all of them. This reaffirms that the consultant's word is good and that the client's confidence in the consultant is valued.

Integrating referrals into the planning and service processes is a natural part of what one does as a trusted and trustworthy financial consultant. By doing so in a respectful and methodical manner, a "win win" situation is created for both the client and the consultant. As one seeks to build his/her practice through more effective relationships with female prospects and clients, referrals will ultimately be a key ingredient to success.

CHAPTER AND BOOK SUMMARY

In this chapter, we have examined the relationship between client service and prospecting. Providing her with extraordinary service is essential to building client loyalty, and client loyalty is critical to repeat business and referrals to new prospects. This is where service and prospecting intersect. The diagram below reflects the marketing/planning process as a circle—a seamless integration of eight steps. When thoughtfully and skillfully implemented, exceptional client service generates both new business and new clients.

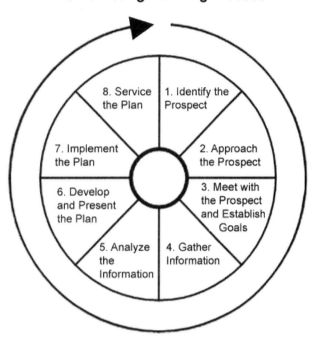

The Marketing/Planning Process

As discussed in Chapters 1 and 3, developing client relationships through the consultative planning process is mutually beneficial for the consultant and the client. She knows she will receive promised services and ongoing advice as her needs change. The consultant benefits by higher rates of implementation, client loyalty and increased rate of return on resources. For indispensible financial consultants, the sale is not the end; it is the beginning. One must fulfill all the promises of service made during the consultative planning process, seek to exceed client expectations. This entails more work than merely servicing a product, but it is also more rewarding. As the client-consultant relationship grows, one is able to meet more of the client's financial needs; and more doors open through referrals.

What can be done to cement client relationships and protect business from competitive threats? Here are some ideas:

- Broaden the product and services portfolio offered to clients, and develop strategic alliances (discussed in Chapter 2) with other producers and professionals who offer needed solutions that you do not.

- Expand areas of expertise. Pursue professional designations, add licenses, and generally augment the knowledge and skills that make you more valuable to clients.

- Be sure to tell prospects and clients frequently, through mail and personal contact, about all the services and products you offer as solutions to their financial goals and concerns. Highlight those you may not have previously addressed.

Clients are the financial consultant's most valuable business asset by far. Success in the women's market can be best achieved when female clients provide enough referrals and repeat business to enable one to attain personal and professional goals.

Throughout this book, we have examined a vast range of concepts about growing the trusted and indispensible financial consultant's "share" of the women's market while acting with integrity, competence and compassion. The process (six steps) and the skills associated with consultative planning help solidify trust and mutually beneficial relationships. The scope (six areas) of consultative planning require the technical competencies that add value and worth to the advice given. Without a doubt, there is a significant amount of both skills and competencies to be mastered to be effective in the women's market. The rewards, however, can be immeasurable when one makes excellence a habit.

Make Excellence a Habit
"Integrity is defined as "a firm adherence to a code or standard of values; soundness."
What would an integrity check reveal about you? It's something to think about.
People of integrity are committed to a life of excellence—seeking to be better or go beyond what is normally expected of them. Having integrity means you do the right thing even when no one is looking…and you keep your word even if it costs you something."
Joyce Meyer, *Ending Your Day Right*, Time Warner Book Group, 2004

CHAPTER 8 TOOLS AND RESOURCES

- Courses from The American College
    - FA 200 Techniques for Prospecting: Prospect or Perish
    - FA 290 Ethics for the Financial Services Professional
    - FA 202 Techniques for Meeting Client Needs

- Recommended Reading

- *The E-Myth Revisited: Why Most Small Businesses Don't Work and What to Do About It*, Michael Gerber, Harper Collins, 2001

- *Deena Katz On Practice Management*, Deena Katz, Bloomberg Press, 1999

• Tools

- Client satisfaction survey and Sample client satisfaction survey cover letter
- Review appointment checklist and cover letter

• Websites

- "Your birthday in history" greetings: Clientbirthday.com
- Client surveys: SurveyMonkey.com

Appendix A
Informational Interview

Name of Group:	Member Name:	Date:

Introduction:
Thank you for setting aside time today to meet and talk about _____ group. As I mentioned during our phone conversation, I enjoy working with you and value your opinion. My professional goals are to deliver exceptional financial solutions and service to people just like you – those who value our relationship and are enjoyable to work with. (Desired, but optional: In addition, I have a deep commitment to helping others [name of group's interest, cause.]) Today, I'd like to ask you a few questions about _____ group to gain more insights about your special interests, financial needs, and means of communicating. I'd also like to get your advice on how I might be thinking about this and next steps. Does this agenda work for you?

1. **How long have you been a member of this group? Why did you join?**

2. **What are other related organizations that you and your members might belong to?**

3. **What special publications, print or on-line, might you and your members read related to _____ (interest?)**

4. **How is your group organized—national, regional, chapters, small groups? (Circle those that apply.) What are the regional and local affiliates?**

5. **Does your group have national and/or regional conferences, chapter and/or small group meetings? (Circle those that apply.) When and where are these usually held?**

6. **How do you as a group regularly communicate? Do you have a newsletter, website, webcasts/webinars, blog, on-line social network? (Circle those that apply.) How frequently are these updated?**

7. **What personal priorities and concerns are commonly shared in your group? Why are those important?**

8. Do you and other members talk about personal finances? If yes, what sorts of topics and issues do you discuss? If no, why not? How would you characterize the commonly held financial goals or concerns of your group?

9. What other professional financial advisors specialize in working with your group (e.g., attorney, CPA, stockbroker, insurance agent, financial planner, other)? Are there any other professionals (e.g., medical, architects, engineers, consultants, etc.) that your group might work with?

10. What is the best way to approach your group? Why?

11. What is the worst way to approach your group? Why?

12. In addition to our discussion today, what other research should I do?

13. If you were in my shoes, who else would you be talking to?

14. Are there local leaders for your group I might talk with? Who are they?

15. Is it OK for me to use your name when I contact others in your group?

16. If others in your group have questions about me or our discussion today, is it OK for me to have them call or e-mail you?

17. As I do more research about your group, would you be open to reconnecting so that I might gain additional insights? At minimum, I'll circle back to you in a month to let you know about progress I made. Is that OK?

18. Other questions, topics, ideas

Conclusion:
Thank you for your time today, _____. The perspectives and insights you have shared are very helpful. I appreciate your taking time out of your busy schedule and your willingness to help me grow my practice.

Send thank you note and/or gift immediately when you return to your office.

Appendix B

Initial Interview Cover Letter

Date

Your Name, Designations, Title
Your Company Name
Street Address, Suite Letter/Number
City Address and Zip

Dear (Valued Client's Name),

The purpose of this letter is to confirm our meeting at *(time)* on *(day, date)* at *(location.)*

During our appointment, we will discuss *(the specific financial goals and concerns you shared with me during our introductory call.)*

There is no charge or obligation for this initial consultation. At the conclusion of our time together, we will determine: 1) whether or not I can help you, and 2) whether or not you want my help.

I have enclosed a financial position "check-up" worksheet and document checklist. Please spend just 30 minutes or so pulling together information for the meeting. That said, the more you are able to bring with you, the more productive our time together will be for you. This information establishes a better understanding of your current situation and how it relates to *(the financial goals and concerns you shared with me during our introductory call.)*

I look forward to a thoughtful discussion about how you might address your *(financial goals/concerns)*. Until then, should you have any questions about our appointment, the enclosed materials or my background, or company, please just call me at *(phone number.)*

Best Regards,

Your Name, Designations, Title

(cc: Correspondence File)

Appendix C

30-Minute Financial Position Checkup Worksheet

Net Worth	Cash Flow	
Net Worth	**Monthly Committed Expenses**	**Monthly Discretionary Expenses (C)**
Personal Property	*Household*	*Savings*
Primary Residence	Rent	Retirement
Car 1	Rent/Homeowner Insurance	Other
Car 2	Property Taxes	**Total Savings** *(K)*:
Furnishings	Association Fees	*Personal Recreation and Interests*
Other	Electricity	Health Club/Gym
Total Personal Assets *(A)*:	Internet	Home Improvements/Decor
Savings and Investments	Water and Sewer (Included)	Dining Out
Investment Real Estate	Heating (Gas and Oil)	Babysitter
Retirement Accounts	Telephone (Land and Cell	Children's Allowance/s
Stocks/Bonds	Groceries	Children's Extra Curricular
Mutual Funds	Daycare While at Work	Hobbies
Savings, CDs	Other	Cable TV, Movies
Life Insurance Cash Value	**Total Household Expenses** *(F)*:	Monthly Subscriptions
Annuities	*Debt Payments*	Vacations
Business	Mortgage(s)	Clothing
Other	Credit Card(s)	Personal Care
Total Savings/Investments *(B)*:	Student Loans	Family Gifts
Total All Assets *(C)*:	Auto Loans	Charitable Donations
(A+B):	Other Loans	Pet Food, Groom, Board
Liabilities	**Total Debt Payments** *(G)*:	Other Miscellaneous
1st Mortgage	*Transportation*	**Total Personal Interests** *(L)*:
2nd Mortage	Fuel (Gas, Diesel)	**Total Savings and Personal** *(M)*:
Auto Loans	Registration	*(K+L)*
Student Loans	Auto Insurance	**Monthly After Tax Income**

C.1

30-Minute Financial Position Checkup Worksheet

Credit Cards	Repairs, Maintenance	Wage and Bonus
Investment Real Estate	Other (Tolls, Transit, Taxi)	Wage and Bonus
Other Liabilities	**Total Transportation** *(H)*:	Investment Income
Total Liabilities *(D)*:	*Personal Insurances*	Social Security
	Medical	Pension
Net Worth	Disability	Miscellaneous Income
Asset minus Liabilities *(E)*:	Long Term Care	**Total After Tax Income** *(N)*:
(C-D):	Life	**Monthly Net Cash Flow**
Notes:	**Total Personal Insurances** *(I)*:	**Income minus Expenses** *(O)*:
	Total Committed Expenses *(J):(F+G+H+I)*:	*(N-J-L)*:

Appendix D

Document Checklist

Documents to Bring to Our Initial Interview
Bring the following of these items that you can easily access:
☐ 30-minute financial position checkup ☐ Tax returns for last two years ☐ Two months of paystubs ☐ Wills, trusts ☐ Life, disability, long-term care insurance contracts ☐ Property and casualty outline of coverage ☐ Employer retirement benefit statement (pension, 401k, 403b, 457 plans) ☐ Employee benefit manual ☐ Investment statements

Appendix E

Prospect Phone Approach Model and Script

Model Step	Script
Introduce Self, Extend Courtesy.	Hello. Is (prospect name) available? This is (your name) with company in (your town/city.) I hope I'm catching you at a convenient time. Do you have just a moment? *(If not, ask for a good time to call back, get off the phone and follow-up as promised.)*
State Purpose of Call.	Thank you. The reason for the call is to follow-up on the letter I sent you and see if what I do might be of benefit to you.
Use Positioning Statement.	In a nutshell, I help clients increase their financial security through a planning approach that identifies goals, risks and the best alternatives to address them.
Probe to Identify Needs.	Many of my clients these days are especially concerned about making money work as hard as it can for them. Their concerns usually include *(select two or three)*: building cash reserves, putting kids through college, reducing their tax bite, re-evaluating retirement plans, generating enough income in retirement, managing their survivor and health risks. Which of these are most important to you?
Use Probe "Funnel" Sequence.	What concerns you most about (specify goal/concern)? What have you done so far to address (specify goal/concern)? How did you determine that/those strategy/ies? Do you think you will have enough? Would you like to know? So, if I hear you correctly, you are concerned about (specify goal/concern) by (timeframe) and additional goal/concern.) You are not quite sure that what you've done so far will meet your (specify goal/concern) needs. Is that right? *(pause)....* I think I might be able to help you. May I ask a few more questions to make sure I understand your situation? (Pause, assume consent.) Thank you. Are you married? What is your husband's name? What kind of work do you/does he do? How's your/his health? Do you have children? What are their names? How old are they? Nice family! *(Determine if prospect is right or wrong fit in your practice. If so, proceed, if not, close call.)*

State the Benefit of Meeting with You.	(Name), it sounds to me like you (and spouse's name) might benefit from putting together a well-thought-out plan to address your goal/concern of (specify) goals/concerns.
Explain How You Work. *(Continue to either A or B.)*	Let me explain how I work. The first time we meet, there will be no charge, costs or surprises and I won't try to sell you anything. What we will accomplish is a review of your goals and where you are now. At the end of our time together, we'll determine one of two things: (1) if I can help you, and (2) if you want my help. If we agree to work together, then we will discuss a course of action and right up front, the possible costs. Then you (and spouse's name) can decide if you'd like to go on from there. (slow down) Does that sound reasonable? (pause, wait for response)
(A) Prospect Cannot Meet Now. Extend Empathy. Agree on Recontact.	I understand. It sounds to me like you are serious about your (specify) goal/concern, but this is not a good time for you to meet. How about if I contact you in (3 – 6 months) to see if that is a better time to us to meet to plan for (specify). Will that work? In the meantime, we offer educational seminars and newsletters on a range of financial issues. Would you like to be included on our mailing list?
(B) Prospect Can Meet Now.	Great! Our office is conveniently located at (intersection/location). Are we able to meet here? (Preferred.) If not, where would you like to meet?
Set Up Appointment.	I have (day/date) at (time) or ____ at ____ available. Which works for you? OK. I have you down for (date) at (time) in (location).
Discuss Homework.	In the meantime, I will send you a simple worksheet and checklist that summarizes your income, expenses, assets and liabilities. Please do not spend more than 30 minutes on this. Just do what you can in a half hour. Whatever you are able to bring to the appointment will make the time more productive for you. This will give me the opportunity to better understand your situation and add value right away. Do you think you can do that? Great! I look forward to seeing you (and spouse's name) and starting our conversation about (specify goal/concern).
Confirm Prospect Sees Benefit.	Can you see the benefit of our meeting? *(Confirming the prospect understands the benefit increases the likelihood the meeting will happen.)*

Appendix F

Solution Presentation Summary Letter

Date

Your Name, Designations, Title
Your Company Name
Street Address, Suite Letter/Number
City Address and Zip

Dear (Valued Client's Name),

The purpose of this letter is to summarize recommendations and next steps discussed during our meeting on day/date. Here are the action items, timing and responsibilities we agreed upon: (sample table below)

Recommendation	Rationale	Timing	Responsible
Purchase $378,000 of 20-year level term life insurance on Janice.	The analysis reveals a $378,000 gap in Bob's survivor income until his retirement when he is then eligible for his pension.	Today (March 1st)	Janice and (insert financial consultant name)
For Jason's college education, start contributing to a 529 plan with Bob as custodian in a growth oriented mutual fund.	The analysis shows a monthly funding shortfall of $450 invested @ 8% for Jason's college fund. You are only able to commit $350/mo at the present time.	Today (March 1st)	Bob and (insert financial consultant name)
Increase contributions to Jason's college fund by $100 per month when Janice gets her raise.	Increase to full funding when cash flow becomes available.	October 1st	Bob and (insert financial consultant name)

Your next appointment is scheduled for *day, date, time*. At that time, we will accomplish these items *(list)*; as well as review progress made and any changes to your plan or situation. Until then, should you have any questions or concerns please just call.

Thank you for the opportunity to serve you. I look forward to helping you reach your financial goals in the months and years to come.

F.2 Solution Presentation Summary Letter

Best Regards,

Your Name, Designations, Title

(cc: Correspondence File)

Appendix G

Review/Financial Check-Up Cover Letter

Date

Your Name, Designations, Title
Your Company Name
Street Address, Suite Letter/Number
City Address and Zip

Dear (Valued Client's Name),

Thank you for your business and continued trust. As your financial consultant *(team, if appropriate)* I am *(we are)* committed to helping you improve and maintain financial wellness throughout your life

The ingredients for building and sustaining financial health are similar to those we need for our physical health. We need a plan, the right behaviors to follow, the best tools available and regular monitoring to ensure that systems are functioning properly. Conducting routine "check-ups" is an important aspect of financial wellness. With that in mind, I would like to meet to review your financial goals, situation and plans to make sure you remain on track.
To help make our time together more productive for you, I have enclosed the following item(s):
- Financial Check-Up Checklist
- 30 Minute Financial Position Worksheet (*Optional)
- Document Checklist (*Optional)

Please spend no more than 30 minutes to complete these. That said, the more you are able to bring, the more value I am able to add during our meeting. *(*Optional)*

In the next two weeks, I (or my assistant) will call you to schedule a time for your financial check-up. Should you questions or concerns in the meantime, please just call.

I *(we)* look forward to seeing you soon.

Best Regards,

Your Name, Designations, Title

Encl.
(cc: Correspondence File)

*Note: While it is a best practice to send all three documents, the worksheet and document checklist are optional, depending on the financial consultant's practice and client relationship at time of sending the letter.

Appendix H
Financial Check-Up Checklist

Please spend a few moments reviewing and checking those items needing an update.

Changes to Financial Situation and/or Goals

Since our last meeting, the following changes have taken place:

☐ Changed jobs	☐ Had a baby	☐ Retired or will soon retired
☐ Received bonus, raise, promotion	☐ Expecting a baby	☐ Changed marital status
☐ Started a new business	☐ Child/ren need/s day care	☐ Change in health
☐ Paid off or increased debt/s	☐ Child starting/completing college	☐ Received inheritance
☐ Moved	☐ Giving care to parents/loved one	☐ Changed my will and/or trust

Financial Planning Areas to Review

I would like to discuss the following:

Financial Position
- ☐ Creating/sustaining cash reserves for emergencies
- ☐ Improving yield on cash reserve assets
- ☐ Understanding where money is going
- ☐ Reducing debt
- ☐ Other_____

Investment Planning
- ☐ Discussing my investment goals
- ☐ Reviewing my progress towards achieving _____ goal
- ☐ Assessing and adjusting my risk tolerance
- ☐ Reviewing investment asset allocation and diversification
- ☐ Other_____

Protection Planning
- ☐ Reviewing property/casualty coverage
- ☐ Reviewing liability risks and coverage alternatives
- ☐ Managing risks associated with disability, surviving a spouse, long term care and medical care
- ☐ Other_____

Retirement Planning
- ☐ Developing or adjusting a clearer picture of retirement goals
- ☐ Understanding Social Security, pensions and when to take benefits
- ☐ Evaluating retirement savings alternatives
- ☐ Other_____

Financial Check-Up Checklist

Tax Planning	Estate and Legacy Planning
☐ Evaluating how changes in tax laws might affect me	☐ Reviewing current wills, trusts and beneficiary designations
☐ Understanding possible options to reduce my tax liability	☐ Reducing estate taxes
☐ Working with my accountant to coordinate tax planning with my overall financial plan	☐ Evaluating charitable gifting strategies including those that may provide tax advantages during my lifetime
☐ Other_____	☐ Other_____

Business Owners	Notes
☐ Reviewing employee benefits and costs	I would also like to discuss the following issue/s:
☐ Understanding how to integrate my personal financial plan with my business plan	
☐ Developing or monitoring business succession plans	
☐ Other_____	

Appendix I

Client Satisfaction Survey Cover E-Mail or Letter

Date

Your Name, Designations, Title
Your Company Name
Street Address, Suite Letter/Number
City Address and Zip

Dear (Valued Client's Name),

The purpose of this note is twofold: (1) to thank you for your business and the trust you have placed in me (us if team,) and (2) to ask for your help in serving you better.

Among the core principles I (we) have for my practice is to deliver exceptional advice and service to our clients. With that in mind, my (our) hope is that you might take a few moments to complete a brief survey that will help me (us) know how I am (we are) doing. Your answers will remain completely confidential unless you choose otherwise.

If using an on-line survey tool (e.g,. Survey Monkey): By clicking on the link below, you will be redirected to the survey site.

If using a direct mail approach: Please complete the enclosed survey and return to our office in the self-addressed-stamped-envelope enclosed.

The survey should take only five to ten minutes to complete. If you wish to be contacted, please indicate this with your name at the conclusion of the survey. Otherwise, your responses are anonymous.

Thank you for the privilege of working with you and your help in making my (our) support more valuable. I (we) look forward to serving you in the coming months and years.

Best Regards,

Your Name, Designations, Title

(cc: Correspondence File)

Appendix J

Client Satisfaction Survey

Your Name, Designations, Title (& Associates if Applicable)

Note: This survey should take only five to ten minutes to complete. Please respond to the statements and questions below. If you have specific remarks and/or would like to be contacted, please place comments in the box at the end of the survey questions and/or responses. Your responses will remain anonymous unless you indicate otherwise. Thank you for your help in enabling me (us) to serve you better.

My financial consultant (insert or substitute name) is highly knowledgeable. ○ Strongly agree ○ Agree ○ Neutral ○ Somewhat agree ○ Strongly disagree	**My financial consultant (insert or substitute name) takes the time to educate me on financial issues, options and products.** ○ Strongly agree ○ Agree ○ Neutral ○ Somewhat agree ○ Strongly disagree
My financial consultant (insert or substitute name) listens and understands my financial goals and concerns. ○ Strongly agree ○ Agree ○ Neutral ○ Somewhat agree ○ Strongly disagree	**The quality of service I receive from my financial consultant (insert or substitute name and team name/s) is:** ○ Exceptional ○ Better than average ○ Average ○ Worse than average ○ Taking my business elsewhere and telling the whole town
My financial consultant (insert or substitute name) helps me understand my financial risks. ○ Strongly agree ○ Agree ○ Neutral ○ Somewhat agree ○ Strongly disagree	**I plan to refer others who might also benefit from working with my financial consultant (insert or substitute name):** ○ Strongly agree ○ Agree ○ Neutral ○ Somewhat agree ○ Strongly disagree

My financial consultant (insert or substitute name) helps me develop and follow a plan to achieve my financial objectives. ○ Strongly agree ○ Agree ○ Neutral ○ Somewhat agree ○ Strongly disagree	**I rate my overall satisfaction with my financial consultant (insert or substitute name and team name/s) as:** ○ Very satisfied ○ Satisfied ○ Neutral ○ Dissatisfied ○ Very dissatisfied
My financial consultant (insert or substitute name) helps me develop and follow a plan to reduce my financial risks. ○ Strongly agree ○ Agree ○ Neutral ○ Somewhat agree ○ Strongly disagree	**Comments, suggestions, praise, concerns:**

INDEX

Index

529 Savings Plans, 7.36

Acceleration Rider, 5.42
Accountants, 6.14
Active listening, 3.13
Activity Management Systems, 2.34
Adjusted Gross Income, 6.4
Affiliated Professionals, 6.14
Alpha, 6.35
Alternative Minimum Tax (AMT), 6.6
Amiables, 3.11
Analytics, 3.10
Annuities, 6.35
    Fixed Annuities, 6.36
    Variable Annuities, 6.37
Asian Women, 1.14
Asset Allocation, 6.30
Attorneys, 6.14
Auto Insurance, 4.26

Bankruptcy, 4.21
Behavior, 1.26
Benefit Length, 5.29
Benefit Period, 5.13
Benefits, 2.27
Beta, 6.35
Black Women, 1.14
Bodily Injury, 4.32
Builders, 2.8
Business Owners, 1.8, 5.39
Business Risk, 6.24

Capital Gains and Losses, 6.6
Care giving, 5.16
Care Receiving, 5.18
Caregivers, 5.15
Cash Flow, 4.9
Cash Flow Driven, 3.30

Cash Reserve Pyramid, 4.16
Cash Reserves, 4.12
Cash Value, 5.42
CD Laddering, 4.17
CDs, 4.15
Client Loyalty, 8.5
Client Satisfaction Survey, 8.26
Client Service, 8.2
Clients, 2.13
Communications, 3.2
Compensatory Damages, 4.32
Competency, 1.28
Compliance, 1.25
Confidentiality, 1.27
Consultative Planning, 3.19
Consultative Planning Process, 1.29
Consultative Planning Scope, 3.23
Consultative Selling, 3.19
Contractual liability, 4.32
Conversion, 2.35
Coverdell Education Savings Accounts, 7.36
Covey, Stephen, 3.2
Credit, 4.19
Cultural Imprinting, 6.15
Currency or Exchange Rate Risk, 6.23
Customers, 2.13

Debt, 4.20
Deductions, 6.4
Default Risk, 6.24
Defined Contribution Plans, 7.19
Defined-Benefit Plans, 7.20
Denial, 5.19
Dinkytown, 6.27
Disability, 5.2
Disclosure, 1.27
Discovery, 7.11
Diversifying, 6.31
Divorce, 1.16, 7.8
Double Jeopardy, 5.15
Drivers, 3.10
Dual benefits, 7.17
Due diligence, 6.29
Durable Powers of Attorney, 7.25
Dychtwald, Ken, 7.3

Earnings, 1.10
Education, 1.4
Elders, 2.10
Emotions, 6.18
Employer Sponsored Qualified Plans, 7.19
Employment, 1.5
Equity Investments, 6.20
Estate Planning, 7.28
Ethics, 1.25
Ethnicity, 1.13
Exclusions, 6.4
Expectations, 8.7
Expressives, 3.11
Extension Rider, 5.42

FDIC Insurance, 4.15
Features, 2.26
Federal Estate Taxes, 7.32
Federal Gift Taxes, 7.33
Female Brain, 3.5
Financial Literacy, 1.18
Financial Planning Pyramid, 3.25
Financial Position, 4.7
Financial Risk, 6.24
FINRA, 6.26
Fiscal Year, 6.6
Fixed Investments, 6.20
Future Purchase Option, 5.13

Gatekeepers, 2.13
Goal Based, 3.29
Guaranteed Lifetime Withdrawal Benefit (GLWB), 6.38
Guaranteed Minimum Accumulation Benefit (GMAB), 6.38
Guaranteed Minimum Income Benefit (GMIB), 6.38
Guaranteed Minimum Withdrawal Benefit (GMWB), 6.38

Health Care Proxy, 7.26
Hispanic Women, 1.13
Homeowner Insurance, 4.30
Homes, 4.28

Ideal Clients, 8.13
Inaction, 3.8
Income Taxes, 6.3
Individual Retirement Plans
    Roth IRAs, 7.22
    SEP, 7.23
    Traditional IRAs, 7.22
Inflation Indexing, 5.13

Inflation or Purchasing Power Risk, 6.22
Inflation Protection, 5.29
Informational Interviews, 2.23
Insurability, 5.36, 7.8
Interest Rate Risk, 6.21
Intergenerational Wealth Transfer, 7.35
Investment Earnings and Taxes, 6.12
Investment Literacy, 6.15
Investment Risks, 6.19
Irrevocable Life Insurance Trusts, 7.39

Leads, 2.33
Liability Limits, 4.27
Liability Losses, 4.32
Life Insurance, 5.36
Lifetime Gifts, 7.35
Listening, 3.13
Living Benefits, 6.37
Living Wills, 7.25
Long-Term Care, 5.14
Longevity, 7.6
Loss control, 4.4
Loss financing, 4.4

Marginal Tax Rate, 6.5
Marketing, 2.2
Marketing Activity Plan, 2.31
Marketing Plan, 2.25
Marriage penalty, 6.7
Maximizers, 2.8
Media, 2.29
Media Plan, 2.30
Medical Insurance, 4.35
Medical Payments, 4.27
Medical Power of Attorney, 7.26
Medical Risks, 4.33
Municipal Bonds, 4.18

Nature or Nuture, 3.5
Niche Marketing, 2.15

Objections, 3.18
Own Occupation Protection, 5.13

Paper Deductions, 6.5
People Generalists, 2.5
People Specialists, 2.5
Personal Exemption, 6.5

Personal Injury, 4.32
Philanthropy, 7.28
Physical Damage, 4.27
Planning Processes, 3.26
Planning Software, 3.29
Positioning, 2.27
Poverty, 1.20
Pregnancy Complications, 5.13
Preservers, 2.9
Product Generalists, 2.5
Product Literacy, 1.20
Product Specialists, 2.5
Professionalism, 1.25
Professions, 1.7
Property Damage, 4.32
Property Transfers at Death, 7.31
Punitive Damages, 4.32

Qualified Domestic Relations Orders, 7.8
Questions, 3.14

Referrals
    Asking for Referrals, 8.32
    Barriers to Referrals, 8.31
Repeat Business, 8.27
Review Meetings, 8.10
Revocable Living Trusts, 7.39
Risk, 4.3
    Managing Risks, 4.3
Risk Tolerance, 6.26
Risks
    Liability risks, 4.3
    Personal risks, 4.3
    Property risks, 4.3
    Pure risk, 4.3
    Risk avoidance, 4.4
    Risk prevention, 4.5
    Risk reduction, 4.5
    Risk retention, 4.5
    Risk transference, 4.6
    Speculative risk, 4.3

S.W.O.T. Analysis, 2.19
Savings, 4.13
Segmenting the Client/Customer Base, 8.13
Segments, 2.6
Service Activities and Ideas, 8.21

Service Package, 8.16
Service Plan, 8.18
Sharpe Ratio, 6.35
Singlehood, 7.7
Six Areas, 3.23
Social Insurance Offset, 5.13
Social Networking, 2.17
Social Security, 7.14
    Spousal benefit, 7.15
    Survivor benefits, 7.16
    Workers benefits, 7.15
Social Styles, 3.9
Speculative Risk, 6.2
Standard Deviation, 6.35
Starters, 2.7
Strategy call, 3.30
Survivor Needs, 5.33
Survivors, 5.30
Systematic risks, 6.21

Tax Credits, 6.5
Tax Qualified Policies, 5.29
Tax Reduction Techniques, 6.11
Tax Risk, 6.21
Tax-favored Cash Accumulation, 5.36
Taxable Income, 6.4
Third Age, 7.4
Transfer all, some or none, 4.6

Unsystematic risks, 6.24

Value Proposition, 2.28
Variable Universal Life, 5.43
Vendors, 2.12

Waiting Period, 5.13
Wealth Drivers, 1.12
Widowhood, 1.17
Wills, 7.38
Women Business Owners, 5.28
Women's Market Paradox, 1.1
Women's Organizations, 2.21
Work, 1.6
Worry, 3.7
Wrongful acts, 4.32